Microeconomics

Microeconomics
Optimization, Experiments, and Behavior

John P. Burkett

OXFORD
UNIVERSITY PRESS
2006

OXFORD

UNIVERSITY PRESS

Oxford University Press, Inc., publishes works that further
Oxford University's objective of excellence
in research, scholarship, and education.

Oxford   New York
Auckland   Cape Town   Dar es Salaam   Hong Kong   Karachi
Kuala Lumpur   Madrid   Melbourne   Mexico City   Nairobi
New Delhi   Shanghai   Taipei   Toronto

With offices in
Argentina   Austria   Brazil   Chile   Czech Republic   France   Greece
Guatemala   Hungary   Italy   Japan   Poland   Portugal   Singapore
South Korea   Switzerland   Thailand   Turkey   Ukraine   Vietnam

Published by Oxford University Press, Inc.
198 Madison Avenue, New York, New York 10016

www.oup.com

Library of Congress Cataloging-in-Publication Data
Burkett, John P.
Microeconomics : optimization, experiments, and behavior / John P. Burkett
p.   cm.
ISBN-13 978-0-19-518962-9
ISBN 0-19-518962-0
1. Microeconomics.   I. Title.
HB172.B875   2006
338.5—dc22   2005051286

9 8 7 6 5 4 3 2 1

Printed in the United States of America
on acid-free paper

For Bojana, Keith, and Nicholas.

Preface

A modern introduction to microeconomics should, in my opinion, (1) convey a sense of how microeconomics has developed in response to a changing array of practical problems and anomalies; (2) maintain a clear distinction between normative and positive theories; (3) integrate findings of behavioral and experimental economics; (4) cover recent, as well as classic, works; (5) feature clear and concise exposition; (6) move from simple, concrete applications to more difficult and abstract ones; (7) offer enough quantitative examples and exercises to show how microeconomic theory is applied and to help students to begin developing the mathematical skills required for success in advanced economics; and (8) provide—through footnotes and citations—links to more advanced treatments. With those goals in mind, I wrote the present text.

The most innovative feature of the book is its extensive coverage of recent research in behavioral and experimental economics. This research not only documents behavior inconsistent with some elements of traditional theory but also advances positive theories with superior predictive power. The research I cover includes studies of loss aversion, reference-dependent preferences, the context and framing of choice, hyperbolic discounting and inconsistent intertemporal choice, predictable errors in updating probabilities, nonlinear weighting of probabilities, and prospect theory. The importance of this material was highlighted by the Swedish Academy of Sciences when it awarded the 2002 Prize in Economic Sciences to Daniel Kahneman (a psychologist who helped lay the foundations of behavioral economics) and Vernon Smith (an experimental economist). Although the topics are "advanced" in the sense that they are near the frontier of economic research and seldom covered in textbooks, they are readily comprehended because they center on simple controlled experiments and relate to everyday concerns.

Covering results from behavioral and experimental economics along with traditional microeconomic doctrine involves rebalancing three key components of economics: issues, theory, and data. Traditional introductions emphasize issues, sketch theory, and use data only to illustrate theory. More advanced texts traditionally focus on theory, relegating issues and data to asides. Any data in traditional texts are usually from observational (nonexperimental) studies. The relationship between theory and observational data is likely to be ambiguous until probed by advanced econometric methods and may remain so even then. Recognizing that few students have the econometric skills needed for serious analysis of observational data, some authors focus their texts almost exclusively on theory and issues. Although widely used, such texts arouse misgivings in students and professors to whom data-free exposition smells of indoctrination (Leamer 1997). In comparison to traditional texts, this book places more emphasis on experimental data, both when they support received theory and when they reveal anomalies. Thus the book covers both feedlot experiments that generate conventionally shaped isoquants and choice experiments that cast doubt on the predictive value of expected utility theory.

The book presupposes nothing beyond high-school algebra and intellectual curiosity. It is intended for undergraduate classes and independent reading.

Anyone writing for an audience that includes undergraduates must decide how to handle the growing gap between the rudimentary mathematical skills acquired in secondary schools, particularly in the United States, and the growing mathematical prerequisites for reading economists' professional journals. This gap must somehow be bridged if undergraduates are to be prepared for employment or graduate study in economics and related fields. To be fully prepared, students need not only classes in mathematics but also practice in formulating and solving quantitative economic problems. Too many texts either omit such problems or assume that students come fully equipped to handle them. In contrast, this text offers many opportunities to apply high-school algebra in an economic context and to develop basic skills in linear programming and risk modeling. Through footnotes and parenthetical remarks, it also encourages readers to make good use of any calculus they know. Exercises appear where appropriate in the text; solutions and supplemental problems are collected at the ends of chapters. When teaching from the book, I usually start each class by asking students if they had trouble solving any problems in the previous chapter and end class by helping students tackle the problems in the current chapter. By solving the problems, students can make appreciable progress toward becoming competent economists.

Acknowledgments

Carole Miller carefully read the entire manuscript, providing scores of helpful suggestions. Others who contributed useful comments include Christopher Anderson, Calvin Blackwell, Wentworth Boynton, Keith Burkett, Bruce Cater, Joel Dirlam, Glenn Erickson, Phillip Fanchon, John Gates, Ernesto Lucas, Charles Plott, Yngve Ramstad, Bojana Ristich, Mohammed Sharif, Jon Sutinen, Kathryn Zeiler, and many former students.

While a graduate student at the University of California (Berkeley), I benefited from contact with many excellent professors, among whom six are particularly relevant to this work: From George Akerlof and Roy Radner I learned to appreciate rigorous theoretical analysis of both optimizing and nonoptimizing behavior. From Daniel McFadden and Thomas Rothenberg I learned how much economics can benefit from careful linkage of theory and data. From Laura D'Andrea Tyson and Benjamin Ward I learned the value of close attention to interactions between economic institutions and behavior.

Like most textbook authors, I am indebted to my predecessors. Microeconomic texts and treatises that I have used with pleasure as a student or a teacher include A. Asimakopulos's *An Introduction to Economic Theory: Microeconomics*, Theodore C. Bergstrom and John H. Miller's *Experiments with Economic Principles*, William J. Baumol's *Economic Theory and Operations Analysis*, Samuel Bowles and David Kendrick's *Notes and Problems in Microeconomic Theory*, Jae Wan Chung's *Utility and Production Functions*, Richard M. Cyert and James G. March's *A Behavioral Theory of the Firm*, Gerard Debreu's *Theory of Value*, A. K. Dixit's *Optimization in Economic Theory*, Robert H. Frank's *Microeconomics and Behavior*, C. E. Ferguson's *Microeconomic Theory*, James M. Henderson and Richard E. Quandt's *Microeconomic Theory: A Mathematical Approach*, Michael D. Intriligator's *Mathematical Optimization and Economic Theory*, Geoffrey A. Jehle and Philip J. Reny's *Advanced Microeconomic Theory*, David M. Kreps's *Notes on the Theory of Choice*, Heinz D. Kurz and Neri Salvadori's *Theory of Production*, Edmond Malinvaud's *Lectures on Microeconomic Theory*, Andreu Mas-Colell, Michael D. Whinston, and Jerry R. Green's *Microeconomic Theory*, Richard R. Nelson and Sidney G. Winter's *An Evolutionary Theory of Economic Change*, Walter Nicholson's *Microeconomic Theory: Basic Principles and Extensions*, Edmund S. Phelps's *Political Economy*, Robert S. Pindyck and Daniel L. Rubinfeld's *Microeconomics*, Dominick Salvatore's *Microeconomics: Theory and Applications*, Paul A. Samuelson's *Foundations of Economic Analysis*, Andrew Schotter's *Microeconomics: A Modern Approach*, Oz Shy's *Industrial Organization*, Joseph E. Stiglitz's *Principles of Microeconomics*, Henri Theil's *Optimal Decision Rules for Government and Industry* and *The System-Wide Approach to Microeconomics*, Hal R. Varian's *Microeconomic Analysis*, and W. Kip Viscusi, John M Vernon, and Joseph E. Harrington Jr.'s *Economics of Regulation and Antitrust*.

The staff of Oxford University Press has been very helpful. Special thanks for thoughtful and expeditious work are due to the acquiring editor, Terry Vaughn; the editorial assistant, Catherine Rae; the production editor, Keith Faivre; and the copyeditor, Barbara Conner.

Production of the book was greatly facilitated by Donald Knuth's TeX and Leslie Lamport's LaTeX.

Contents

 **Microeconomics**

1

The Origins and Scope of Microeconomics

1.1 Definitions of Economics

A student consulting several modern texts or reference volumes may easily collect a disconcerting variety of definitions of economics. Here are two representative examples:

> The art of regulating income and expenditure [or] the science relating to the production and distribution of material wealth. (*Oxford English Dictionary*, second edition, 1989)

> The study of the allocation of scarce resources among unlimited and competing uses. (*International Encyclopedia of the Social Sciences*, 1968)

The diversity of definitions arises at least in part because studies with some claim to being called "economics" have a long and varied history. The various definitions cover overlapping but not coextensive subsets of these studies. Rather than search for a (possibly nonexistent) common thread connecting all such studies, we shall briefly trace their evolution.

1.2 Ancient Origins

Like many sciences, economics has roots in Greek antiquity. Indeed, the term "economist" is derived from two Greek words, *oikos* (house) and *nomos* (managing). Thus the original meaning of "economist" was household manager. However, the well-to-do households with which ancient Greek writers concerned themselves often included farms or workshops. Hence economy or household management subsumed farm and business management. In *Oikonomikos* (translated as "the skilled economist"), Xenophon (circa 430–355 B.C.) recollected discussions between Socrates and other Athenians about management of farms and households. Here, household management is described as knowledge of how to increase a household's possessions, construed as all those things it can use for its benefit.

Four issues raised in *Oikonomikos* lie near the core of economics even today.

1. How are limited resources best allocated to competing needs? One of Xenophon's characters, Ischomachos (a gentleman-farmer), discusses this issue in the context of designating uses for rooms in a house. He recommends storing grain in dry rooms, storing wine in cool rooms, and working in well-lit rooms. He does not explain what to do with a house in which the dry rooms also are cool and well lit whereas the humid rooms are warm and dark. Should the dry, cool, and well-lit rooms be used for grain, wine, or work? Such problems remained perplexing until they were clarified some 2200 years later by David Ricardo's principle of comparative advantage, which we will study in Chapter 7.

2. What can a manager do to motivate a subordinate to work hard? Ischomachos notes that those managers "who can make the workers eager, energetic, and persevering in the work are the ones who accomplish the most good and produce a large surplus" (p. 79). He adds that the art of motivating workers is not one that can be learned simply "by seeing it or by hearing of it once" (p. 80). Some modern views of motivation are discussed in Chapter 13.

3. What does it take to be a good manager? Understanding economic principles is a necessary but not sufficient condition. Ischomachos suggests that although application of economic principles to planning farm operations is simple, consistently implementing the plans is difficult. It is one thing to resolve to save some grain for seed; it is another to actually refrain from eating it when hungry. It is one thing to resolve to get an early start on farm chores; it is another to get out of bed on a cold, dark morning. Two managers with identical plans can produce different outcomes if one has the strength of character to implement the plans but the other does not.[1] Modern economists and psychologists have made some fascinating discoveries about the problems many people have in carrying out their plans. You will get an introduction to these discoveries in Chapter 18.

4. How should we choose our actions when the consequences of alternative actions are uncertain? How, for example, should a farmer choose a time for sowing seed when the weather is unpredictable? Noting that "one year is finest for the early sowing, another for the middle, another for the latest," Ischomachos asks Socrates whether it is better "to choose one of these sowings . . . or rather to begin with the earliest sowing and continue right through the latest" (p. 64). Socrates replies that the sowing should be spread out over all the possible times because "it is much better always to have enough grain than to have very much at one time and not enough at another" (p. 64). Here Socrates provides an intriguing hint about risk-averse choice. We will study modern ideas about risk in Chapters 19–22.

Over time, the interests of economists widened considerably. Some ancient Greek writers, including Aristotle and Xenophon, discussed city government by analogy to household management. The management of empires and kingdoms was brought within the scope of economy by Roman and early French and English scholars.[2]

The analogy between management of an ancient Greek household and that of a city or kingdom is imperfect in one crucial respect: The manager of an ancient Greek household was largely concerned with crops, livestock, and slaves, whereas a public administrator is concerned above all with citizens. A household manager did not have to worry much about what crops, livestock, or slaves might think of his conduct. In contrast, a public administrator must recognize that citizens may adjust their behavior to their expectations of his policies. Unlike crops and livestock, citizens form expectations; unlike slaves, they have enough autonomy to act strategically on the basis of those expectations. This fact was duly noted by medieval writers on political economy. For example, Abu Said Ibn Khaldun (A.D. 1332–1406) observed that when citizens expect tax rates to be high, they avoid engaging

---

[1] Similarly, "in traveling it sometimes happens that two human beings, though both are young and healthy, differ from each other in speed by as much as a hundred stadia in two hundred when one does what he set out to do and keeps walking, while the other, idle and easy in his soul, lingers at fountains and shady places, looks at the sights, and hunts soft breezes" (p. 76).

[2] Latin writers used the word *oeconomia* to mean not only household management but also management in general. In French, *oeconomie* took over this wider meaning. Seventeenth-century French writers introduced the expression *oeconomie politique*, meaning public administration or management of the affairs of state. In the late seventeenth century, English writers like William Petty began to use the term "political economy" in a sense similar to that of its French counterpart.

in activities subject to taxation. Their behavior makes tax revenues a nonlinear function of tax rates. Income tax rates of 0% or 100% generate no revenue, but intermediate ones may yield positive revenue. Plotting tax revenue against tax rates produces a hill-shaped curve.[3] Recognizing that outcomes (e.g., tax revenue) are the joint result of policies (e.g., tax rates) and citizen's choices (e.g., work hours), economists and policymakers became interested in predicting those choices.

1.3   Classical Concepts

1.3.1 Predictable and Rational Behavior

Interest in predicting individual economic behavior grew in eighteenth-century Europe as agriculture, commerce, and manufacturing slipped from the grasp of kings and their vassals and fell increasingly into the hands of private farmers, merchants, and industrialists, all interacting in markets. Up to this time economic writings had a predominantly prescriptive tone: If you want to maximize your wealth, you should do this, that, and the other. As David Hume (1711–76) had recognized, there is a logical gulf between normative and prescriptive assertions, on the one hand, and positive (descriptive or predictive) assertions, on the other.[4] A "should" does not necessarily imply an "is" or a "will." However, economists could convert their prescriptions into predictions by postulating that people act as economists would advise them to do. This postulate—known as the **rationality assumption**—seemed plausible as long as economists' prescriptions were little more than codified common sense and provided people had enough time to implement them.

Perhaps the first important prescription to be thus converted into a prediction was "buy low, sell high." If people buy goods and services where they are cheap and sell them where they are dear—an activity economists call **arbitrage**—they thereby bid up prices where they are low and bid down prices where they are high. Absent transportation costs, economists predict that arbitrage will eventually equalize the price of a homogeneous good or service in all markets. When transportation costs matter, the price for a homogeneous good or service in town A will eventually differ from that in town B by no more than the cost of moving it from one town to the other. In other words, prices for a homogeneous good or service in various markets converge until there is no incentive for further arbitrage. Application of this "no-arbitrage" principle to markets for labor and capital led "classical" economists—most notably Adam Smith (1723–90), David Ricardo (1778–1823), and John Stuart Mill (1806–73)—to base their analyses on the assumption that wages and profit rates tend to equality across localities and industries. This assumption remained basic to economic theory down to the 1920s (Kurz and Salvadori 1995). Even today, the no-arbitrage principle is extensively used in some branches of economics, most notably finance (Ross 2005).

---

[3] Ibn Khaldun's observation was resurrected in the 1980s by "supply-side economists," who suggested—erroneously—that tax rates in the United States were then so high that cutting them would raise tax revenue. This episode is discussed by Becsi (2000) and Pescatrice (2004).

[4] Prescriptions derive at least in part from norms. Indeed, many economists use the terms "prescriptive" and "normative" interchangeably. However, some economists and many decision analysts draw the following distinction: A normative statement establishes an ideal, which may or may not be attainable, whereas a prescriptive statement recommends or requires practical steps to approximate an ideal as closely as possible. An influential delineation of normative, prescriptive, and positive statements in economics appears in John Neville Keynes (1955).

1.3.2 Cost-Benefit Analysis and Utility Maximization

Generalizing from the "buy low, sell high" adage, economists arrived at a widely applicable principle: *An activity is worth undertaking if and only if its cost is less than its benefit.* For this principle to be meaningful, cost and benefits must be measured in comparable units. Money is a useful unit of account for this purpose even when none is received or spent in the course of the activity. The benefit of an activity, expressed in money, is the maximum the decision maker would willingly pay, if need be, to engage in the activity. The cost in question is the **opportunity cost** of the activity—that is, the forgone benefit of the best alternative activity, using the same resources.[5] When choosing among alternative activities that use the same resources, a decision maker using the cost-benefit criterion chooses the activity with the greatest benefit. Decision makers who consistently apply the cost-benefit criterion are termed **utility maximizers**.[6]

Giving monetary expression to benefits and costs is not always a simple task. On the benefit side, a decision maker tries to estimate a payment that would leave him or her indifferent between engaging in the activity and making the payment, on the one hand, and abstaining from the activity and keeping the money, on the other. Estimating this payment may be relatively easy for a person who has previously engaged in the activity at various prices.[7] However, a person contemplating a novel activity may have greater difficulty making such an estimate. Whether the initial estimation process is better described as discovering one's preferences or constructing them is an open question (Cubitt et al. 2001; Hoeffler and Ariely 1999; Payne et al. 1999; Plott 1996; Slovic 1991). In either case, decision makers may have to be unusually vigilant to avoid being swayed by irrelevant features of the decision context, as we shall see in Chapters 11 and 12.

On the cost side, decision makers try with varying degrees of success to distinguish relevant and irrelevant expenses, summing the former and ignoring the latter. Common mistakes are to ignore costs that are not readily expressible in terms of money and to count past monetary costs that are no longer relevant.[8]

Overlooking costs not readily expressed in money is an easily committed error. For example, if you were calculating the costs of taking a course, you would surely include the registration fee but might forget to include the value of other activities that you have to forgo to take this course. If this course occupies 150 hours of your time and if you could get a job at $8 an hour, then taking this course involves forgoing earnings of $1200. Or if another course for which you would have paid up to $1500 meets at the same time as this course, then by taking this course you are forgoing an opportunity worth $1500. Opportunity cost is subjective and can vary from individual to individual. In our example the opportunity cost of taking this class is at least $1500 to a student who would have paid that much to take another class that meets at this hour.

Counting irrelevant costs among the costs of an activity is another easily made mistake. Beginners are particularly likely to erroneously include **sunk costs**—that is, past outlays that can no longer be recovered. Suppose for example you go with a friend to a crafts fair.

---

[5] The concept of opportunity cost was formulated in the nineteenth century by John Stuart Mill, Friedrich von Wieser, and David I. Green (Blaug 1996; Niehans 1990).

[6] Utility maximization, as a guide to individual and political action, was forcibly advocated by Jeremy Bentham (1748–1832).

[7] Even in this relatively easy case, problems arise if the decision maker has imperfect recall of previous experiences, as often is the case (Kahneman et al. 1997).

[8] A clear introduction to cost-benefit analysis is provided by Brent (1996). Several interesting examples are discussed by Frank (2003).

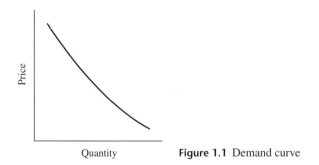

Quantity   **Figure 1.1** Demand curve

You each pay a $5 admission fee. Seeing nothing worth buying, you propose to leave. Your friend replies that he wants to buy something, so as not to waste the admission fee. Your friend is making the mistake of worrying about sunk costs. The fee is now irrelevant because it cannot be recovered.

EXERCISE 1.1

Consider a consultant who has purchased a nonrefundable airline ticket for $300 in order to meet a remote client who will pay him $700 for the meeting. After paying for the ticket the consultant is offered $800 to meet a local client at the same time as the consultant had planned to meet with the remote client. Neither client is willing to reschedule a meeting. The consultant cannot sell the airline ticket. Meeting the local client would entail spending $30 on cabs. Should the consultant meet with the remote client or the local one? (Answers to exercises can be found at the end of the chapters in which they appear.)

1.3.3 Demand and Supply

Economists have found that cost-benefit considerations can often be conveniently summarized in terms of demand and supply curves. Such curves were constructed as early as the seventeenth century and became ubiquitous in the economic literature of the twentieth century.[9]

A demand curve for a good shows the relationship between the price of the good and quantity of the good demanded—that is, the quantity people are willing to buy. It summarizes the cost-benefit assessments made by potential buyers. Potential buyers consider how many units, if any, to purchase. The cost of purchasing one unit of the good is, of course, the price of the good. The benefit of the purchase is the product's contribution to the buyer's welfare. Demand curves are usually negatively sloped, as illustrated in Figure 1.1, because cost-benefit comparison generally justifies buying more units of a good as its price falls.[10]

For any given price, a demand curve indicates the quantity buyers want to purchase. Of course, buyers would be happier to purchase a given quantity at a lower price. But given the market price, buyers would rather purchase the quantity indicated by the demand schedule than any other quantity.

---

[9] Gregory King (1648–1712) developed a empirically based demand curve for grain around 1696 (Niehans 1990).

[10] The empirical observation that almost all demand curves are negatively sloped is sometimes called "the law of demand." However, a different proposition, with an analytical rather than an empirical basis, sometimes goes by the same name. It is discussed in Chapter 9.

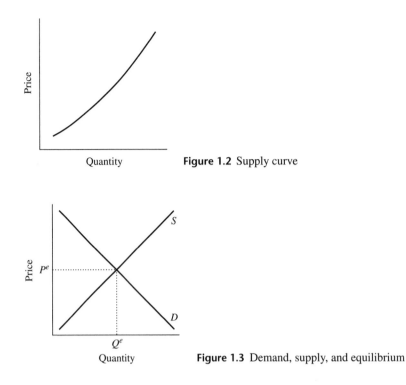

Figure 1.2 Supply curve

Figure 1.3 Demand, supply, and equilibrium

Now let us examine the supply side of the market. As the price of a good rises, the quantity supplied normally increases, as in Figure 1.2. The reason the supply curve usually slopes up is that a higher price commonly makes it profitable to produce more of the good. For example, grain can be grown on land of varying fertility. It is more work to grow a bushel of grain on poor land than on fertile land. A higher price for grain makes it worthwhile to bring more land into cultivation.

For any given price, a supply curve shows the quantity that suppliers want to sell. Selling any other quantity at the given price would leave the suppliers worse off.

1.3.4 Equilibrium Price

The price at which the demand and supply curves intersect is the **market-clearing price**. At this price the quantities demanded and supplied are equal. In that sense, both buyers and suppliers are satisfied with the quantity traded, and neither is motivated to behave differently. Since buyers and sellers have no reason to change their behavior, the market clearing price is an **equilibrium price**—that is, a price that can persist. When product's price is at its market-clearing level and the product's demanders and suppliers buy and sell the quantities they prefer at that price, economists say the market for that good is in equilibrium. **Economic equilibrium** may be defined as a situation that can persist because no one involved in the situation has an incentive to change his or her behavior. A market in equilibrium is often represented by a diagram in which price and quantity are the coordinates of the intersection point of a demand curve and a supply curve,[11] as in Figure 1.3.

---

[11] Such an intersection is often called a Marshallian cross, in honor of Alfred Marshall, who originated it (Niehans 1990).

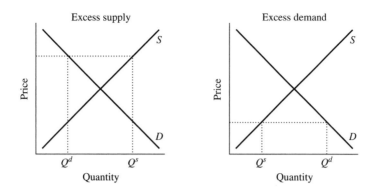

Figure 1.4 Excess supply occurs when a price is above its equilibrium value; excess demand occurs when a price is below its equilibrium value

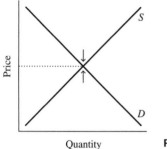

Figure 1.5 Convergence to equilibrium

When a product's price is not at its equilibrium level, buyers or sellers are dissatisfied and motivated to change the price. When the price is above equilibrium, sellers cannot sell as much as they want. Economists say there is **excess supply**, measured as the horizontal distance between the demand and supply curves, as in the left panel of Figure 1.4. When there is excess supply, sellers tend to bid prices down. Similarly, when the price is below equilibrium, buyers are frustrated, unable to buy as much as they want. In this case we say that there is **excess demand**, again measured as the horizontal distance between supply and demand curves, as in the right panel of Figure 1.4. In this case buyers tend to bid the price up. In general, market prices tend to move toward equilibrium, as in Figure 1.5.[12]

1.3.5 Determinants of Demand and Supply

It is important to distinguish a shift of the demand curve from a movement along a stationary demand curve. Similarly, it is important to distinguish a shift in the supply curve from a movement along it. To make this distinction succinctly, economists use the following terminology. When we mean a shift of the demand or supply curve, we speak about a change in *demand* or *supply*. In contrast, when we mean a movement along a demand or supply curve, we speak about a change in the *quantity demanded* or the *quantity supplied* (see Figure 1.6). For example, we may say that an increase in supply brings about a fall in price

---

[12] The tendency for market prices to move toward equilibrium is sometimes called the law of supply and demand.

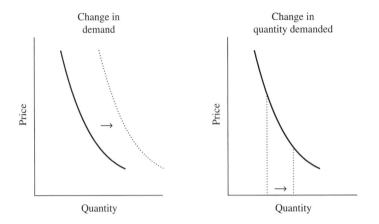

Figure 1.6 Changes in demand and quantity demanded

and an increase in the quantity demanded. Similarly, we may say that an increase in demand brings about a rise in price and an increase in the quantity supplied.

The remainder of this section outlines a few important and easily understood forces affecting demand and supply. Further analysis and examples of these forces can be found in later chapters of this book and in lengthier texts.[13]

Demand

1. Demand varies with *tastes* or *preferences*. Variations in tastes occur over space and time. The British traditionally like tea, whereas Turks go for coffee. In the United States, tastes have been moving from whiskey toward wine.
2. An increase in a person's *income* raises his or her demand for most but not all goods and services. We say a good is **normal** if demand for it increases with per capita income. We say that a good is **inferior** if demand for it falls as per capita income rises. Whether a particular good is normal or inferior may depend on time and location. Examples of inferior goods found in recent studies include corn tortillas in Mexico (Mckenzie 2002) and public transportation in France (Bresson et al. 2004). As their incomes rose, the individuals covered by these studies diversified their diets and bought automobiles.

    Aggregate income is increased by population growth, as well as growth of per capita incomes. Increases in aggregate income due to population growth tend to increase aggregate demand for most goods and services.
3. Demand for durable and nonperishable goods is affected by buyers' inventories or stocks. For example, demand for new cars was high in the United States in the late 1940s because the Great Depression and World War II had depleted consumers' stock of cars.
4. Demand for a good or service can be influenced by the *prices of its complements and substitutes*. Baseballs and baseball bats are **complements** in the sense that an increase in the price of one tends to reduce demand for the other. Gasoline and sport utility vehicles are another example of complements. Artificial and natural Christmas trees are **substitutes** in the sense that a decrease in the price of artificial trees lowers demand for

---

[13] Good expositions, listed in order from elementary to advanced, include Stiglitz (1997), Frank (2003), Nicholson (1995), and Mas-Colell et al. (1995).

natural ones (Davis and Wohlgenant 1993). Similarly, heroin and cocaine are substitutes in the sense that an increase in the price of heroin increases demand for cocaine (Petry and Bickel 1998).

5. *Expectations* about future income and prices can influence demand. The larger our expected future income, the greater our present demand for most goods and services. Similarly, we may demand more of a nonperishable good now if we expect its price to rise in the future. For example, if you expect gasoline prices to rise tomorrow, you may try to fill your tank today. The magnitude of the effects of expectations on demand may increase with opportunities to borrow and lend.

Supply

The aggregate supply of a product increases either when existing producers become willing to sell more at any given price or when new producers enter the market. Similarly, aggregate supply diminishes either when existing producers reduce the quantities they are willing to sell at given prices or when some producers exit the industry. Influences affecting firms' supply curves, entry and exit decisions, and aggregate supply include the following:

1. *Factor productivity*—that is, the quantity of output obtained from given amounts of land, labor, and capital—is an important influence on supply because it conditions the cost of production, which in turn determines the quantity supplied at any given price.

   Factor productivity varies over time for various reasons. From year to year, weather changes can strongly influence productivity in agriculture, construction, and transportation. For example, in the winters of 1990–91 and 1998–99, cold weather ruined a large part of the California orange crop and pushed the supply curve for oranges well to the left. Over longer periods, technological progress raises factor productivity. For example, technological progress in the computer industry has vastly increased its productivity and expanded the supply of computers. Productivity is also affected by a variety of circumstances, including workers' health, industrial disputes, and government regulations.

2. *Factor prices*—that is, the prices of land, labor, and capital—are also important determinants of suppliers' costs and hence the position of supply curves. If rents, wages, and interest rates go up, we can expect supply curves for products of land, labor, and capital to shift upward.

3. *Price expectations* influence supply, as well as demand. For example, when grain prices are expected to rise sharply, farmers tend to store their grain harvest rather than sell it immediately. Similarly, owners of petroleum reserves are likely to defer extraction when they anticipate markedly higher oil prices.

1.3.6   Effects of Demand and Supply on Prices and Quantities

If we can predict shifts in demand and supply curves, we can predict the resulting changes in equilibrium quantities and prices. Assuming that demand curves are negatively sloped and supply curves are positively sloped, we can make the following assertions: An increase in demand causes the equilibrium price and quantity to increase, whereas a fall in demand has the opposite effects, as in Figure 1.7.

An increase in supply causes the equilibrium price to fall and the equilibrium quantity to rise, whereas a fall in supply has the opposite effects, as in Figure 1.8. For example, a few years ago the arrest of leaders of the Cali drug cartel raised the price of cocaine in New York City from $50 to $80 a gram.

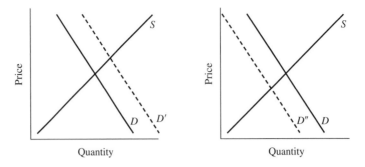

Figure 1.7 An increase in demand from D to D' in the left panel raises the equilibrium price and quantity; a decrease in demand from D to D'' in the right panel has the opposite effect

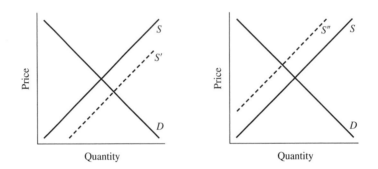

Figure 1.8 An increase in supply from S to S' in the left panel lowers the equilibrium price and raises the equilibrium quantity; a decrease in supply from S to S'' in the right panel has the opposite effects

Thus if price and quantity movements move in the same direction, we may suspect that changes in demand are responsible, whereas if price and quantity movements move in opposite directions, we can suspect that supply changes are the cause.

EXERCISE 1.2

Consider a country in which some cattle herds are destroyed to contain an outbreak of foot-and-mouth disease. In what direction does the supply curve for beef shift? What happens to the price of beef? If beef and pork are substitutes, what happens to demand for pork? What happens to the price of pork? If beef and cabbage are complements, what happens to demand for cabbage? What happens to the price of cabbage?

1.4   Mathematical Methods

To advance beyond commonsense advice like "buy low, sell high," economists had to overcome four technical problems. First, many economic decisions involve variables that are continuous or at least take more values than can easily be tabulated. For example, an agricultural economist might be asked how much fertilizer should be applied to a field or how much time should be spent weeding a field. Because time is continuous and fertilizer is minutely divisible, we should not be content with considering a few discrete alternatives. Many problems involving an optimal choice of values for continuous variables

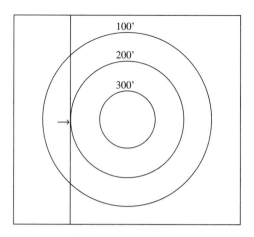

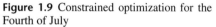

Figure 1.9 Constrained optimization for the Fourth of July

were intractable until Isaac Newton (1642–1727) and Gottfried Wilhelm von Leibnitz (1646–1726) developed calculus. Early applications of calculus to economic problems included analysis of gambling (Bernoulli 1954 [1738]), farm management (Buquoy 1815, cited in Theocharis 1983), profit-maximizing firms (Cournot 1927 [1838]), and wage determination (Thünen [1860]).[14] Today, calculus has become one of the basic tools of economics. Anyone contemplating a career in economics should study calculus at his or her earliest opportunity. Familiarity with calculus helped economists recognize in the 1930s and 1940s that many economic problems faced by individuals and organizations have a common formal structure: They are, in mathematical terms, problems of constrained optimization. In plain English, they are problems of choosing how to use scarce resources as effectively as possible in pursuit of an objective. For example, suppose that on the Fourth of July, you want to climb a hill to get a good view of the fireworks. You get out a topographic map and find that a fence prevents you from reaching the top. (That's a constraint.) The constrained optimum is the tangency between the fence and a contour line in Figure 1.9. Economists are interested in solutions to problems of this form, both ideal solutions and the cruder attempted solutions sometimes found in practice.

Second, pursuit of an objective (e.g., maximizing farm income) often involves deciding on the scale of various activities (e.g., growing corn, raising hogs) subject to constraints on the usage of various resources (e.g., land, labor). As the number of activities and constraints increases, the optimal solution becomes increasingly difficult to detect by informal methods. Complicated problems, such as maximizing the output of a publicly owned industry or minimizing the military shipping costs associated with winning a war, cry out for systematic methods for finding an optimal solution. Just such problems inspired the development of linear programming by Leonid Kantorovich, a Soviet mathematician, and Tjalling Koopmans, an economist employed during World War II by the Combined Shipping Adjustment Board. Today, linear programming is a standard tool of business managers and is easily

---

[14] To get a feel for these early applications, consider an example based on work by Georg von Buquoy. Letting p denote plowing depth in centimeters, suppose the revenue derived from a field is $R = 256\sqrt{p}$, and the cost of cultivating it is $C = p^2$. The profit derived from the field is $\pi = R - C = 256\sqrt{p} - p^2$. If you have studied calculus, you can see that the first and second derivatives are $d\pi/dp = 128/\sqrt{p} - 2p$ and $d^2\pi/dp^2 = -64p^{-3/2} - 2$. Setting the first derivative equal to zero and solving for p, we find that π attains an extreme value when $p = 16$. Noting that the second derivative is negative, we conclude that this extreme value is a maximum. Thus a farmer who wants to maximize profit from this field should plow to a depth of 16 cm.

implemented in readily available computer software. For their contributions to developing and applying this and related techniques, Kantorovich and Koopmans were awarded the 1975 Nobel Prize in Economics.[15] A short introduction to linear programming as applied to cost minimization problems is offered in Chapter 3.

Third, economic outcomes are often influenced by random (uncertain) variables, as well as by decision variables. For example, a crop yield may depend on the weather, as well as on how much fertilizer is applied and how much weeding is done. Such uncertainty poses special challenges for both decision makers and social scientists. If the weather cannot be predicted with certainty, how can a decision maker determine the optimal amounts of fertilizer and weeding? A clear answer to such questions could only be given after the concepts of randomness and uncertainty were clarified by early probability theorists such as Jakob Bernoulli (1654–1705) and Thomas Bayes (1702–61). Modern applications and extensions of their ideas are discussed in Chapters 19–22.

Probability theory has proved no less important for social scientists, economists included, than for decision makers. Efforts to measure the effect of a policy instrument (e.g., welfare regulations) on an outcome (e.g., welfare dependence) are often frustrated by confounding factors (e.g., the age structure of the population) and limited opportunities for controlled experiments. To disentangle the effects of policy instruments from those of confounding variables when using nonexperimental data, it was necessary to develop special techniques rooted in probability theory. The most important of these techniques, multiple regression analysis, was developed by George Udny Yule (1871–1951). His technique involves fitting an equation to data by using calculus to minimize a sum of squared differences between the observed and fitted values of the dependent variable. Applying this technique to British data, he found evidence that after controlling for the effects of changes in the size and age structure of the population, changes in "pauperism" (the share of the population receiving public relief) were positively related to changes in the share of paupers who were allowed to find their own housing rather than being confined to workhouses (Yule 1899). Yule's results lent empirical support to a hypothesis (entertained by several nineteenth-century economists) that shifting from a system of workhouses to "out-relief" tended to encourage welfare dependence. Extending Yule's work, twentieth-century economists like Ragnar Frisch, Jan Tinbergen, Tryve Haavelmo, Lawrence Klein, and Richard Stone laid the foundations for econometrics, a field that applies mathematical and statistical methods to economic problems. Frisch, Tinbergen, Haavelmo, Klein, and Stone have all received Nobel Prizes in Economics for their work. Anyone who wants to become a professional economist should plan on studying econometrics after mastering calculus.

Fourth, an individual's well-being is often influenced by not only her own decisions but also decisions of other individuals pursuing their own objectives. To analyze such situations of strategic interaction, economists and mathematicians collaborated in the development of game theory, a subject surveyed in Chapter 21.

1.5 Interdisciplinary Inquiries

Economists have found that one of the benefits of mathematical literacy is that it gives specialists in many topics, from international trade to public finance, a common vocabulary, the vocabulary of mathematics. Indeed, economists share this mathematical vocabulary with re-

---

[15] The Prize in Economic Sciences in Memory of Alfred Nobel has been awarded annually since 1969 by the Royal Swedish Academy of Science, using funds provided by the Central Bank of Sweden.

searchers in many other fields: physics, chemistry, biology, psychology, and engineering.[16] Sharing a mathematical vocabulary has helped economists and other scientists working on seemingly diverse problems to recognize deep formal similarities. Breakthroughs in one field are now rapidly followed by parallel breakthroughs in other fields. Economists are now part of a scientific community that is more unified and dynamic than ever. It is an exciting time to begin studying the sciences in general and economics in particular.

Modern economics, conceived as a study of choice in the face of scarcity, aspires to illuminate more than just the production and distribution of material wealth. Problems of choice in the face of scarcity arise in virtually all human pursuits, including politics and family life. It is indicative of the breadth of modern economics that in recent years economists have received Nobel prizes for research on politics (James Buchanan), family life (Gary Becker), and psychology and computer science (Herbert Simon). I would not be surprised to see a Nobel prize soon going to an economist for studies of legal problems. At the same time, economists have been borrowing many ideas related to scarcity and choice from biologists and psychologists. Indicative of the importance of these borrowings is the fact that a psychologist, Daniel Kahneman, shared the 2002 Nobel Prize in Economics.

1.6 Predictive Problems

Economists' ability to predict the behavior of other decision makers has not progressed so dramatically as their ability to solve constrained optimization problems. The old trick of turning economists' prescriptions into predictions by assuming that people follow the prescriptions looks increasingly dubious as the economists' prescriptions become ever more sophisticated. Although it is plausible to assume that people tend to buy low and sell high, it is not credible that everyone routinely uses calculus, linear programming, probability theory, and game theory to optimize in complex situations. Indeed, no serious economist asserts that everyone literally optimizes an objective function subject to mathematically formulated constraints. At most, economists claim that decision makers (or at least those who survive in the market long enough to exert significant influence on resource allocation) discover, by trial and error, near optimal solutions to their problems and thus behave *as if* they had mathematically solved their constrained optimization problems. This *as if* assumption is controversial, being supported by Milton Friedman (1953) but disputed by Richard R. Nelson and Sidney G. Winter (1982).

Some economists believe that although people make errors, their errors are random. If people make random errors, attempts to predict their behavior by using optimization methods and the *as if* assumption will be flawed but hard to beat. Random errors are by definition unpredictable. Furthermore, individuals' random errors may largely offset each other, yielding aggregate outcomes in conformity with predictions based on models of optimal behavior. Other economists, appealing to evolutionary theory, argue that people display behavior patterns that had survival value in earlier periods but now induce predictable departures from optimal decisions. When most people err in the same direction, their errors cumulate rather than cancel out, yielding aggregate outcomes that may differ in predictable ways from those

---

[16] Starting in the late nineteenth century, economists, to emphasize the parallels between their subject and other sciences—with physics taken as a leading example—tended increasingly to replace the term "political economy" with "economics." The analogy between economics and physics is imperfect, in part because economics is more concerned with solving problems and less concerned with discovering laws and symmetries than is physics. Indeed, in its focus on problem solving, economics is more like engineering or medicine. This resemblance is evident in economists' usage of terms like circuit breakers, pump priming, shock therapy, and institutional sclerosis.

implied by models of optimal behavior. Herbert A. Simon (1976), a Nobel prize–winning pioneer in developing predictive models of nonoptimal behavior, stresses the importance of **bounded rationality** (the limited cognitive and computational abilities of human decision makers) and **satisficing** (behavior that satisfies limited aspirations without optimizing).

Given the current theoretical uncertainties, a prudent forecaster would do well to compare the predictive accuracy of models of optimizing and satisficing behavior. If no one model yields consistently superior forecasts, it may be reasonable to construct a weighted average of forecasts from several models, with weights based on the models' past accuracy.

Despite their problems, economists can often forecast economic variables appreciably better than laypersons. Recognizing this fact, some firms are willing to pay high salaries to skilled economists. For example, a New York investment and securities firm in the 1980s offered a starting salary of $300,000 to a young economist with a specialty in multivariate forecasting.

Accurate predictions can be costly in time, databases, software, and hardware. Thus forecasters usually face a tradeoff between accuracy and cost. Different forecasting methods may be appropriate for different circumstances. An individual who has to prepare weekly forecasts on a laptop computer will typically use simpler and less accurate methods than a team that prepares annual forecasts on a super-computer. The individual's forecasts may nonetheless be optimal for his or her circumstances. Forecasting may also involve other tradeoffs. For example, a method that minimizes absolute deviations between predictions and outcomes may yield different forecasts than one that minimizes squared deviations. Which forecasting method is appropriate may depend on what problem needs to be solved. Two equally competent forecasters may come up with conflicting forecasts if their budgets or problems are different.

1.7   Empirical Endeavors

Whether an economist aims at finding an optimal allocation of scarce resources or at predicting the behavior of other decision makers, he or she must frequently begin with two empirical endeavors: collecting and summarizing pertinent data.

Economists have traditionally gotten more of their data from observation of individuals and organizations going about their daily business than from controlled experiments. Most of these data are collected by government surveys and presented in aggregate form to preserve individuals' privacy and firms' trade secrets. However, partly because of difficulties in distinguishing optimal behavior from random errors on the basis of aggregate data, economists are increasingly using experimental methods to generate data on individual behavior. The modern experimental economics literature begins with Chamberlin (1948) and is ably surveyed by Davis and Holt (1993) and Friedman and Sunder (1994). Important contributions to experimental methods have been made by Vernon L. Smith, a recipient of the 2002 Nobel Prize in Economics.[17] Three classroom experiments are described in appendices to later chapters in this text.

Economists are today swamped with data. The *Statistical Abstract of the United States* alone annually publishes about a 1000 pages of tables of data. Add to that the statistical handbooks of 50 states and hundreds of foreign countries, not to mention specialized data sets on computer tapes and disks, and you have more data than anyone can hold in memory.

---

[17] Several of his papers on experimental methods are reprinted in V. Smith (1991).

A necessary first step in scientific reasoning about masses of data is to summarize them. Data summaries usually take the form of **statistics**—that is, mathematical functions of data. Univariate statistics summarize several observations on a single variable. Two such statistics—the mean and standard deviation—are used in this book. Multivariate statistics, which summarize the relationship between two variables or among several variables, are beyond the scope of this book but central to econometrics.

1.8   Micro and Macro

Economics is divided into two large branches: microeconomics and macroeconomics. **Microeconomics**—the subject of this book—is concerned with how individuals and organizations make decisions about allocation of scarce resources and how these individuals and organizations, interacting in markets, determine relative prices, wages, and rents. It overlaps with management science in its examination of optimal business decisions but extends beyond that field into normative and positive analysis of households, unions, government agencies, and international trade.

Macroeconomics is concerned with aggregative results of individual decisions. Thus the relationships among employment, income, and inflation at the national level are characteristic concerns of macroeconomists.

In recent decades, economists have been trying to more closely integrate microeconomic and macroeconomic analysis. Microeconomics is now often viewed as the foundation on which macroeconomics builds.

1.9   Summary

1. Economics has a long and varied history, giving rise to several different definitions of the subject. The original meaning of "economist" is household manager. Today many economists conceive of their subject as a study of the allocation of scarce resources among competing uses.
2. A central principle of normative economics is to engage in an activity if and only if its benefit exceeds its cost. The cost in question is opportunity cost—that is, the benefit of the best alternative activity, using the same resources.
3. Economists sometimes try to convert their prescriptions for rational conduct into predictions by assuming that decision makers follow their advice. For example, the prescription to "buy low, sell high," together with a rationality assumption, yields a prediction that all opportunities for profitable arbitrage will be fully exploited. Similarly, the prescription to choose activities whose benefits exceed their costs, together with the rationality assumption, yields a prediction that people act to maximize their utility.
4. Cost-benefit calculations can often be summarized with demand and supply curves. For any good or service, the relationship between the quantity demanded and the price can be represented by a demand curve, which is usually negatively sloped. The relationship between the quantity supplied and the price in a competitive market can be represented by a supply curve, which is usually positively sloped, at least in the short run.
5. A market-clearing price is a price at which the quantities demanded and supplied are the same. At this price, both buyers and sellers are satisfied with the quantity transacted. Consequently, a market-clearing price is usually an equilibrium price. In contrast, prices tend to fall when there is excess supply and rise when there is excess demand.

6. The position and shape of a demand curve are influenced by buyers' preferences, incomes, and stocks; the prices of complements and substitutes; and expectations about future income and prices. The position and shape of a supply curve are influenced by factor productivity, factor prices, and price expectations.

7. Economists' ability to optimally allocate resources has been greatly increased by the application of mathematical methods such as calculus, linear programming, probability theory, and game theory.

8. Economists' ability to predict the behavior of decision makers has not kept pace with their ability to solve constrained optimization problems. There is controversy about whether forecasters should impute full rationality to decision makers. Nonetheless, skilled economists make better-than-average forecasters.

9. Economic inquiries often involve collecting and summarizing relevant data. Data can be collected by observing economic activity or by experimentation. Data summaries usually take the form of statistics such as means and standard deviations.

10. Economics is divided into two large branches. Microeconomics is concerned with how individuals and organizations make decisions about allocation of scarce resources and how these decisions affect relative prices, wages, and rents. Macroeconomics is concerned with the aggregate results of individual decisions.

1.10 Solutions to Exercises

1.1. The consultant should meet with the local client. To see why, we can tabulate the benefits and costs of meeting with one of the clients. The benefits and costs of meeting with the local client are shown Table 1.1.

The $300 airline ticket does not appear in the table because it is a sunk cost. The $700 fee offered by the remote client appears in the cost column because it is part of the opportunity cost of meeting the local client. The total benefits of meeting the local client exceed the total costs; hence the consultant should meet the local client instead of the remote one.

If you drew up a table for the benefits and costs of meeting the remote client, you would find that the total benefits are $730 and the total costs are $800. Because the benefits of meeting the remote client fall short of the costs, the consultant should cancel the meeting with the remote client and meet the local one instead.

The costs and benefits in this problem all occur within a short span of time and all are known with certainty. In more complicated problems, costs and benefits may be distributed over long time periods and some may be risky or involve strategic interaction. For example, a consultant might believe that keeping an appointment with a client now will improve chances of doing business with the same client in

Table 1.1 Benefits and costs of meeting with local client

Benefits		Costs	
$800	fee	$700	forgone
		30	cab fare
$800	total	$730	total

future years. To deal with such problems, we will need concepts of discounting, expectations, and games, which are developed in Chapters 16, 19, 20, and 21.

1.2. The supply curve for beef shifts to the left; the price of beef rises; demand for pork rises; the price of pork rises; demand for cabbage falls; the price of cabbage falls.

1.11   Problems

Part I: What economists think about in the theater

1. In *City of Angels*, Stone, a private detective, is asked to find a missing girl. Suppose that he is offered $200 a day to take the case. Assume that his overhead expenses (which he must pay in any event) are $100 a day. If he rejects this case he can take another case paying $150 a day. Should Stone look for the missing girl?

2. Sidney Stratton can spend the next month putting the finishing touches on his new synthetic fabric or working as a lab assistant. By finishing the fabric project, Sidney would obtain a new suit worth £200 and personal satisfaction worth £1700. He has already spent six months on the fabric project. To finish it, he would have to spend £600 on materials and equipment. As a lab assistant he could earn £1000. What should Sidney do?

3. Will Hunting could spend the afternoon at a baseball game or a mathematics lecture. Will has paid $20 for a ticket to the game and would have been willing to pay up to $30. It is too late to return or sell the ticket. The lecture is free, although Will would have been willing to pay up to $40 to attend. Round-trip transportation would cost $6 for the game and $10 for the lecture. Which should Will attend?

4. The tyrannosaurs in Jurassic Park will eat either goats or hogs. The raptors will eat either goats or chickens. The gamekeeper has paid $1000 (nonrefundable) for goats, enough to feed either the tyrannosaurs or the raptors for a week. The prices of hogs and chickens have now fallen, so that he can buy enough hogs to feed the tyrannosaurs for a week for $900 and enough chickens to feed the raptors for a week for $800. What should he do with the goats?

5. Inspired by *The Crying Game*, a young man in London develops passions for terror and transvestites. He buys a nonrefundable £40 ticket to an opera where he expects to see and shoot the head of the British military intelligence agency, MI5. Then he learns that his favorite transvestite singer is performing at the same time in another theater. Attending the latter event is worth £12 more to him than the former. Going to the theater where the transvestite is singing involves a £6 cab fare and a £5 cover charge. Where should he go? Can the head of MI5 use cost-benefit reasoning to predict the young man's choice and thus decide whether it is safe to go to the opera?

Part II: What economists think about elsewhere

6. Suppose Sri Lanka, a leading tea-producing country, drifts toward civil war. Worldwide, both tea producers and tea drinkers expect the price of tea to rise when war finally breaks out.
    a. What happens to the price of tea?
    b. What happens to the demand for coffee?
    c. What happens to the price of coffee?
    d. What happens to the demand for lemons? (You may assume that lemons are a complement of tea.)

7. Suppose that taste changes reduce demand for meat.
   a. What happens to the quantity of livestock raised?
   b. What happens to the supply of leather?
   c. What happens to the prices of baseballs and baseball gloves?
   d. What happens to the demand for baseball bats?

8. Suppose some raptors escape from Jurassic Park, multiply in the wild, and eat a large number of goats and chickens on nearby farms.
   a. What happens to the prices of goats and chickens?
   b. What happens to the demand for hogs? (Recall from a previous problem that tyrannosaurs can be fed either goats or hogs.)
   c. What happens to the price of bacon?
   d. What happens to demand for eggs? (You may assume eggs and bacon are complements.)

9. Suppose that in the wheat market we observe simultaneous increases in price and quantity. Did demand or supply shift? In which direction?

10. Suppose that in the soy bean market we observe a rise in price concurrent with a fall in quantity. Did demand or supply shift? In which direction?

11. Suppose that in the corn market we observe prices and quantities rising and falling together. Is this positive correlation due to fluctuations in demand or supply?

2

Inputs, Outputs, and Costs

2.1 Basic Concepts

Resources used in production are called **inputs**. The products are called **outputs**. For example, farmers turn inputs such as labor, land, seed, water, fertilizer, pesticide, and plows into outputs such as corn and soybeans. In this chapter we will examine simple production processes with only two inputs and one output. Our focus will be on methods for solving a **cost minimization problem**—that is, finding the cheapest combination of inputs yielding a given output.

2.2 Input Substitution

If one input is increased, another may be decreased while holding either output or costs constant. We shall examine first substitution with constant output and then substitution with constant cost. Understanding these two forms of substitution will provide a foundation for thinking about cost minimization.

2.2.1 Constant Output

Farmers have long experimented with alternative input combinations. Some of the first recorded agricultural experiments were performed and analyzed by a German farmer and economist, Johann Heinrich von Thünen (1783–1850; Figure 2.1). Thünen found that, for crops raised on his farm, the output per worker was roughly proportional to a fractional power of capital[1] per worker; that is,

$$\frac{Q}{L} = A \left(\frac{K}{L} \right)^{\alpha},$$

(2.1)

where Q denotes the quantity of output, L labor input, K capital input, A a positive constant, and α a constant in the interval $(0, 1)$. Equation 2.1 implies that

$$\log L = \frac{1}{1-\alpha} \log(Q/A) - \frac{\alpha}{1-\alpha} \log K.$$

(2.2)

---

[1] By "capital," Thünen probably meant the value of nonlabor inputs consumed in the production process, most notably seed. In modern usage, the term usually refers to the value of structures and equipment.

Figure 2.1 Johann Heinrich von Thünen. (The image comes from The Warren J. Samuels Portrait Collection at Duke University.)

Taking Q as given, we can interpret Equation 2.2 as describing a negative relationship between capital and labor inputs. It indicates that a farm manager who increases capital input can reduce labor input, while holding output constant. The set of points in (K, L) space that satisfy this equation is an example of an **isoquant**, defined as a set of input combinations all of which produce the same amount of output. (Isoquants are sometimes called isoproduct curves or production contours.)

EXERCISE 2.1

Verify that Equation 2.1 implies Equation 2.2, referring to the appendix on logarithms if necessary.

Log-linear equations such as 2.2 provide good fits to data generated in many production experiments with a wide variety of inputs and outputs. As an example, consider an experiment in which 528 pigs were fed various combinations of corn and soybean meal until each pig's weight increased from 60 to 100 lbs.[2] The experimenters found that their data could be summarized by the equation

$$\log C = 5.66 - 0.48 \log S, \tag{2.3}$$

where C and S denote pounds of corn and soybean meal and the logarithms are natural (Boggess et al. 1984). This equation is plotted in Figure 2.2.

Although log-linear equations often provide a good fit to experimental data, other equations may be better in some cases. An example where an alternative functional form was preferred is provided by Heady et al. (1980), who report experiments with feeding hens various combinations of corn and soybean meal. The experimenters kept track of how many

---

[2] In complexity and nuance, the vocabulary of farmers for swine rivals that of Eskimos for snow. Whereas all immature swine may be called "pigs," those in the 60- to 100-lb range fall within a subgroup traditionally called "shoats" (weaned pigs). Most 60- to 100-lb swine also fall in a narrower and more modern category, "grow-finish pigs" (swine between nursery and market ages).

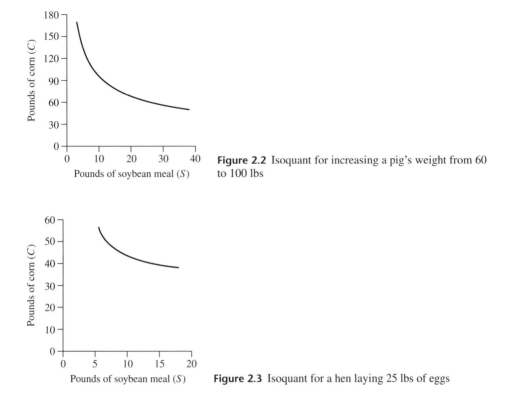

Figure 2.2 Isoquant for increasing a pig's weight from 60 to 100 lbs

Figure 2.3 Isoquant for a hen laying 25 lbs of eggs

pounds of eggs were laid over a 280-day period by hens on various diets. Their data allowed them to construct isoquants for several levels of egg production. They found, for example, that hens would lay about 25 lbs of eggs when fed any combination of corn and soybean meal satisfying the following equation:

$$C = 56.865 - [19.231(-0.843 + 0.173S - 0.004S^2)^{0.5}],$$

where C and S denote pounds of corn and soybean meal. This equation is plotted in Figure 2.3.

Although isoquants can take a wide variety of shapes, almost all have two features in common. First, they are negatively sloped, meaning that an increase in one input allows a reduction in another with no change in output.[3] Points on a negatively sloped isoquant yield more output than points below it but less output than points above it. The absolute value of the slope of an isoquant at a point is called the **marginal rate of substitution** (*MRS*) between the inputs at that point.[4] When we need to explicitly distinguish a *MRS* from its reciprocal, we follow the convention of listing the good on the horizontal axis first. For

---

[3] If one of two inputs consistently tends to reduce output, resulting in a positively sloped isoquant, that input should be eliminated! (An example might be straw as cattle feed: Cattle may use more energy digesting the straw than they can extract from it.) Thus all economically interesting isoquants are negatively sloped over at least part of their range. In some cases isoquants may have both positively and negatively sloped regions. But again, no reasonable manager would ever choose a combination of two costly inputs such that both could be reduced with no loss in output. Hence, in the economically interesting region of input space, isoquants are always negatively sloped.

[4] Some authors call it the marginal rate of *technical* substitution or the *technical* rate of substitution to distinguish it from a similar concept pertaining to substitution in consumption.

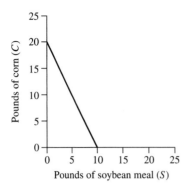

Pounds of soybean meal (S)   **Figure 2.4** Isocost line for $1 worth of feed-stocks

example, the absolute value of the slope of the isoquant in Figure 2.3 could be called the marginal rate of substitution between soybean meal and corn, denoted by MRS_{SC}. However, we can safely omit reference to the inputs when they are clear from context.

Second, isoquants are bowed toward the origin. More precisely, they are **convex** in the sense that their chords lie on or above their arcs.[5] Along a convex isoquant, the MRS declines from left to right.

Isoquants pertaining to the same technology are nonintersecting. (Intersecting isoquants would indicate that both inputs could be cut without reducing output, which is impossible with given technology.)

2.2.2 Constant Cost

Combinations of corn and soybean meal that cost $1.00 satisfy an equation of the form $P_cC + P_sS = 1$, where P_c and P_s are the prices of corn and soybean meal and C and S are the quantities. Provided that the prices are given, independent of the quantities, equations of this form establish a linear relationship between inputs, $C = 1/P_c - (P_s/P_c)S$. For example, if corn costs $P_c = \$0.05$/lb and soybean meal costs $P_s = \$0.10$/lb, the relationship is $C = 20 - 2S$. The set of points with nonnegative coordinates satisfying this equation, shown in Figure 2.4, is an example of an **isocost line**, defined as a set of input combinations that cost the same amount.

Provided that both inputs have positive prices, an isocost line must have a negative slope. The absolute value of the slope is the relative price of the input on the horizontal axis. An isocost line divides input space into two regions. Input combinations on the line cost more than combinations below it but less than combinations above it.

2.3   Cost Minimization Problem

The problem of choosing inputs to minimize the cost of producing a given quantity of output can be easily solved by using isoquants and isocost lines. With the output quantity given, our

---

[5] A possible exception may be found in feeding beef cattle. Some feeding experiments suggest that the relevant isoquants have a concave region. A cow may gain weight faster on a diet that is either all corn silage or predominately a concentrate of corn grain and alfalfa pellets than on a diet that is half silage and half concentrate (Bhide et al. 1984). However, any concavity in an isoquant for a cow can be removed from the corresponding isoquant for a herd by simply feeding silage to some herd members and feeding mainly concentrate to others. Thus the isoquant for the herd will have a linear segment whereas the isoquant for a cow had a concave segment.

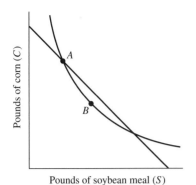

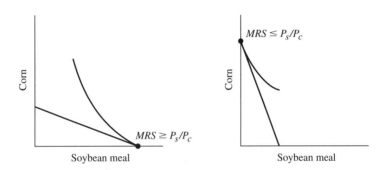

Figure 2.5 The input bundle *A* is not optimal because bundle *B* yields as much output at lower cost

Figure 2.6 Two corner solutions to a problem of optimal input choice

choice of input combinations is limited to the corresponding isoquant. Finding the minimum cost bundle of inputs on this isoquant is equivalent to finding the point on the isoquant that lies on the isocost line closest to the origin. We can immediately rule out any point at which the isoquant is crossed by an isocost line. For example, consider point *A* in Figure 2.5. The quantity of output is the same at *B* as at *A* (because the points are on the same isoquant), but *B* costs less than *A* (because *B* falls below the isocost line running through *A*).

Because a least-cost input combination yielding a specified output cannot be at a point where an isoquant and an isocost line cross and yet must be on the given isoquant and on some isocost line, we conclude that it must be at a point where the given isoquant and some isocost line touch without crossing. Such a point could be found in one of two places.

2.3.1 Corner Solutions

First, if the relevant isoquant intersects an axis (meaning that the specified output can be produced with only the input measured on that axis), the intersection point minimizes costs provided that the isocost line through this point lies below the isoquant, as in Figure 2.6. This point, or indeed any optimal point where only a proper subset of possible inputs is used, is called a **corner solution** to the cost minimization problem.[6] At a corner solution on the horizontal axis, the *MRS* (the absolute value of the slope of the isoquant) is greater than or equal to the relative price of the input on the horizontal axis (the absolute value of the slope of the isocost line). In contrast, at a corner solution on the vertical axis, the *MRS*

---

[6] Some authors call it a boundary solution.

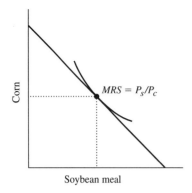

Corn

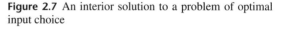

$MRS = P_S/P_C$

Soybean meal

Figure 2.7 An interior solution to a problem of optimal input choice

is less than or equal to the relative price of the good on the horizontal axis. Corner solutions are rare when only two inputs are considered (because few goods can be produced with a single input) but become more common as the number of possible inputs increases.

2.3.2 Interior Solutions

Second, if the cost-minimizing input bundle includes positive quantities of all inputs, it is called an **interior solution** because it corresponds to a point in the interior of the first quadrant of input space. At an interior solution, an isoquant and an isocost line are tangent. If—as we will usually assume—the isoquants and isocost lines are smooth (not kinked) at the tangency, they share the same slope at this point, as in Figure 2.7. In such cases the *MRS* is equal to the relative price of the input on the horizontal axis.

To calculate the cost-minimizing pair of input quantities for a given output, we can start with the equation for the isoquant and a formula equating the slopes of the isoquant and isocost lines. Solving these two equations simultaneously, we obtain quantities for the two inputs. If both quantities are positive, they form an interior solution. If one is negative, no interior solution exists. In that case, a corner solution can be found by replacing the negative quantity by zero and using the isoquant equation to determine the other quantity.

EXERCISE 2.2

The isoquant for increasing a pig's weight from 60 to 100 pounds (Equation 2.3) implies that the *MRS* is $0.48C/S$. (If you know calculus, verify that implication.) Suppose that the prices of corn and soybean meal are \$0.05/lb and \$0.10/lb. Find the least-cost diet for the indicated weight gain.

EXERCISE 2.3

Suppose the price of soybean meal rose but the price of corn remained constant. What would happen to the slope of the isocost lines? What would happen to the amounts of soybean meal and corn in the least-cost diet?

EXERCISE 2.4

Given the pig-feeding isoquant (Equation 2.3), is there any relative price for soybean meal that would induce a corner solution? Do you believe that the implication of this equation for the existence of a corner solution tells us something about pigs, or is it just an artifact of the functional form?

2.4 Summary

1. A given output can usually be produced with more than one combination of inputs. Finding the cheapest such combination of inputs is the cost minimization problem.
2. An isoquant is a set of input combinations that yield the same output. Two-dimensional isoquants are generally negatively sloped and convex. Points on an isoquant yield more output than points beneath it but less output than points above it. The absolute value of the slope of an isoquant is called the marginal rate of substitution (*MRS*).
3. An isocost line is a set of input combinations that all cost the same. The absolute value of the slope of an isocost line is the ratio of the price of the input on the horizontal axis to the price of the input on the vertical axis.
4. If there is a corner solution to a cost minimization problem, it is found on an axis where the given isoquant converges from above to an isocost line.
5. If there is an interior solution to a cost minimization problem, it is found at a point in the first quadrant where the given isoquant touches an isocost line. Provided that the isoquant and the isocost line are smooth at this tangency, their slopes at this point are equal.
6. To calculate the cost-minimizing combination of inputs, we use the isoquant's equation together with a formula equating the *MRS* and the relative price of the input on the horizontal axis. Solving these equations simultaneously, we obtain two input quantities. If both are positive, they constitute an interior solution. If one is negative, we find a corner solution by replacing the negative value by zero and using the isoquant equation to determine the other input quantity.

2.5 Solutions to Exercises

2.1. Solving Equation 2.1 for L, we get $L = (Q/A)^{[1/(1-\alpha)]} K^{-[\alpha/(1-\alpha)]}$. Taking logs of both sides of the last equation (using the first and third rules in the appendix on logarithms), we get Equation 2.2.

2.2. The relative price of soybean meal is $P_s/P_c = 0.10/0.05 = 2$. The tangency condition ($MRS = P_s/P_c$) is $0.48C/S = 2$. Solving that condition for C, we get $C = (25/6)S$. Taking exponential functions of both sides of the isoquant formula (Equation 2.3), we get $C = 287.1S^{-0.48}$. Substituting $(25/6)S$ for C in the last equation, we get $(25/6)S = 287.1S^{-0.48}$. Solving for S, we get $S = 17.46$. Substituting 17.46 for S in either equation for C, we get $C = 72.75$. Thus the least-cost diet for raising a pig's weight from 60 to 100 lbs consists of 17.46 lbs soybean meal and 72.75 lbs corn, as shown in Figure 2.8.

2.3. An increase in the relative price of soybean meal would make the isocost lines steeper, that is, increase the absolute value of their slopes. The tangency point would move along the isoquant, reducing the amount of soybean meal and increasing the amount of corn in the least-cost diet.

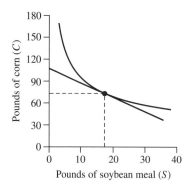

Figure 2.8 Use of an isoquant and isocost line to determine the least-cost diet for increasing a pig's weight from 60 to 100 lbs

2.4. The isoquant's form implies that there cannot be a corner solution. To see why, note that whereas making S arbitrarily large can make log C arbitrarily small, it can never drive C to zero because the logarithm function maps *positive* numbers onto real numbers and is undefined at zero. Similarly, making C large makes log S small but never makes S equal zero. The same point can be made by taking the exponential function of each side of Equation 2.3 and getting $C = 287.1S^{-0.048}$. As S gets arbitrarily large, C approaches zero but never equals zero. Solving the last equation for S, we get $S = (C/287.1)^{-1/0.48}$. Thus, as C gets large, S tends toward zero but never quite gets there. In other words, the isoquant is asymptotic to the S and C axes, never intersecting them.

The absence of a corner solution probably says less about pigs than about the approximate nature of the functional form chosen for the isoquant. No physical meaning can be attached to increasing C or S without limit. After all, even a pig has a limited gut capacity. If fed enough corn or enough soybean meal, a 60-lb pig will eventually grow to 100 lbs or die. The isoquant's form was probably chosen as a simple but reasonably accurate approximation to the experimental data in the central region of input space. It may become much less accurate near the axes.

2.6 Problems

1. Mary Jane grows herbs in her attic. The relationship between her inputs and outputs is given by the production function is $Q = 3K^{0.5}L^{0.5}$, where Q is value added (value of gross output less cost of electricity, fertilizer, seed, and food for a guard dog), K is the value of capital goods (lamps, sprinklers, pots, and security systems), and L is Mary's hours of labor. The isoquants corresponding to this production function have slope $-\frac{L}{K}$. The rental cost of capital (interest rate plus depreciation rate) is 0.20. The opportunity cost of Mary's labor is $7.20 per hour. Mary's goal is to obtain a value added of $18,000 as cheaply as possible.
   a. Find the optimal values of K and L.
   b. Can Mary make a profit?

2. To defend her stash, Mary keeps a pit bull terrier. An animal nutritionist tells Mary that a pit bull can stay in fighting trim on any combination of shark meat and chitterlings satisfying the equation

$$C = \frac{12}{S+2} - 2,$$

where C is chitterlings and S is shark meat, both measured in terms of pounds per day.

a. Calculate the values of C corresponding to each of the following values of S: 0, 1, 2, 4. Sketch the isoquant for feeding a pit bull, putting S on the horizontal axis and C on the vertical axis.

b. The slope of the isoquant is

$$-\frac{12}{(S+2)^2}.$$

(If you know calculus, you can verify the slope by taking the derivative of C with respect to S.) Suppose the prices of shark meat and chitterlings are \$4/lb and \$1/lb. What is the least-cost diet for the pit bull? Is this a corner solution or an interior solution?

c. On your isoquant diagram, sketch the isocost line passing through the point representing the least-cost diet.

2.7 Appendix: Review of Exponents and Logarithms

An exponent of a number or variable indicates the power to which that number or variable is to be raised—that is, how many such numbers or variables are to be multiplied together. For example, $5^2 = 5 \times 5$ and $b^3 = b \times b \times b$, for any b. From this definition, we can easily derive the following three rules:

- $b^x \times b^y = b^{x+y}$.
- $\frac{b^x}{b^y} = b^{x-y}$ for $b \neq 0$.
- $(b^x)^y = b^{xy}$.

The logarithm to the base b, denoted $\log_b(\cdot)$, is the inverse function for the corresponding exponential. Thus if $x = b^u$, where b is a positive constant other than 1, then $\log_b(x) = u$. For example, if $b = 10$ and $x = 1000$, then $\log_{10}(1000) = 3$. The function $\log_b(x)$ is defined and continuous for all positive values x.

Logarithms with base 10 are called common (or Briggs'), and those with base $e = 2.71828\ldots$ are called natural (or Napierian). The notations $\log_e(\cdot)$ and $\ln(\cdot)$ are used interchangeably. For most applications in this text, any base can be used. When we do not need to specify the base, we may write $\log(\cdot)$.

The following three rules, which can be deduced from the corresponding rules for exponents and the definition of a logarithm, are valid for logarithms to any base and for all positive values of x and y.

- $\log(xy) = \log x + \log y$.
- $\log(x/y) = \log x - \log y$.
- $\log(x^n) = n \log x$ for any number n.

3
Cost Minimization Using Linear Programming

3.1 Limitations of Production Experiments

From the early 1800s to the present, production experiments, such as those examined in the last chapter, have yielded much information about the shape of isoquants and have been of great practical value to managers seeking to cut costs. Yet production experiments have three serious limitations.

First, production experiments merely describe input-substitution possibilities without explaining them. For example, experimenters may summarize their findings with an isoquant but be unable to explain its shape or position. Documented production experiments and isoquants are now so numerous that anyone trying to survey them soon feels the need for a deeper and simpler structure to organize the information.

Second, production experiments are usually limited to two or at most three inputs. Experiments with more inputs are likely to require very large sample sizes and correspondingly large budgets.[1]

Third, past production experiments are uninformative about substitution possibilities involving new inputs. For example, production experiments with established varieties of corn and soybeans are uninformative about substitution possibilities involving new genetically modified varieties.

These limitations of production experiments motivated researchers to seek alternative methods that would provide deeper and simpler models, facilitate consideration of many inputs, and support predictions about substitution possibilities involving new inputs.

3.2 Reformulation of the Least-cost Diet Problem in Terms of Nutrients

One of the first cost minimization problems reformulated to overcome the limitations of traditional production experiments was the least-cost diet. Its reformulation involved contributions from nutritionists, food scientists, and mathematicians.

3.2.1 Nutrients

In the twentieth century, nutritionists made great progress in quantifying various animals' needs for specific nutrients, such as carbohydrates, proteins, minerals, and vitamins. Si-

---

[1] If we experiment with k levels for each of n inputs, we have k^n input combinations. For example, 5 levels of 2 inputs lead to 25 combinations, and 5 levels of 3 inputs lead to 125 combinations. In a hog-feeding experiment with 10 hogs on each feed combination, the first experimental design requires 250 hogs and the second requires 1250. Few researchers have budgets adequate to purchase and feed 1250 hogs.

multaneously, food scientists made great strides in determining what quantities of these nutrients are contained in a pound of each animal feed. By the 1940s, enough was known about the nutritional requirements of some animals (including humans) and the nutritional composition of foods that researchers could start looking for low-cost diets that would satisfy the newly established nutritional standards. At first, researchers used trial-and-error methods. During World War II, researchers in several countries sought diets that would cheaply keep soldiers and civilian workers healthy. Elsie Widdowson (1906–2000), an English nutritionist, found that bread, cabbage, and potatoes cheaply supply all the nutrients humans need (*The Economist*, July 1, 2000). George Stigler (1911–91), an American economist and winner of the 1982 Nobel Prize in Economics, found that a human could live for a year on wheat flour, milk, cabbage, spinach, and navy beans costing just $39.93 (G. Stigler 1945).

Although trial and error methods can identify low-cost diets, they are tedious to apply and cannot be relied on to find a *least*-cost diet. More mathematically sophisticated methods are required to reduce the tedium and assure cost minimization.

3.2.2 Linear Programming

As noted in Chapter 1, linear programming was developed by American and Soviet researchers concerned with such problems as minimizing military shipping costs or maximizing the output of a publicly owned industry. It soon spawned a theoretical and applied literature too vast to summarize here. In the remainder of this chapter we merely examine how elementary linear programming helps understand and solve cost minimization problems.

Linear programming was used in 1947 by George Dantzig and Jack Laderman to obtain a general solution to the least-cost diet problem and many related problems (Dorfman et al. 1987[1958]). To express their ideas, we will need the following notation:

$$m = \text{number of nutrients}$$
$$n = \text{number of foods}$$
$$a_{ij} = \text{amount of nutrient } i \text{ in a unit of food } j$$
$$b_i = \text{minimum amount of nutrient } i \text{ required}$$
$$c_j = \text{cost per unit of food } j$$
$$x_j = \text{number of units of food } j \text{ to be used}$$

The task known in the linear programming literature as the **diet problem** is the following:
Choose $x_1, x_2, \ldots, x_n$ so as to minimize the cost function

$$c_1 x_1 + c_2 x_2 + \cdots + c_n x_n$$

subject to the nutritional constraints

$$a_{11} x_1 + a_{12} x_2 + \cdots + a_{1n} x_n \geq b_1$$
$$a_{21} x_1 + a_{22} x_2 + \cdots + a_{2n} x_n \geq b_2$$
$$\vdots \qquad\qquad\qquad \vdots \quad\ \vdots$$
$$a_{m1} x_1 + a_{m2} x_2 + \cdots + a_{mn} x_n \geq b_m$$

and the nonnegativity constraints $x_j \geq 0$, $j = 1, 2, \ldots, n$.

The set of points in n dimensional space that satisfy all the constraints is called the **feasible set**. This set is **convex** in the sense that it contains the line segment connecting any pair of its points. If a particular constraint holds as an equality at a point in the feasible set,

Table 3.1 Nutritional values of foods and requirements for a 154-lb man

Nutrient	Nutritional values		Minimum daily requirement[a]
	Cabbage	Potatoes	
Calories	96	325	3000
Protein (grams)	4.63	7.63	70
Vitamin A (iu[b])	266	152	5000

[a] Nutritional requirements are taken from G. Stigler (1945).

[b] Vitamins are expressed in international units.

this constraint is said to be **binding** at that point. Otherwise, the constraint is said to be **slack** at that point. For example, if the problem's constraints are $2x_1 + x_2 \geq 4$ and $x_1 + 2x_2 \geq 4$, then at the point (1, 2) the former constraint is binding and the latter is slack.[2]

3.2.3 The Geometry of the Diet Problem

When the number of foods (n) is just two, the diet problem has an interesting geometric interpretation in terms of isoquants and isocost lines.

Isoquants

Let us suppose that the only available foods are cabbages and potatoes and that their nutritional values per pound (a_{ij}) are as shown in the first two columns of Table 3.1. Further, suppose that the only nutritional requirements (b_i) are three established in the 1940s by the U.S. National Research Council for a moderately active 154-lb man, as shown in the last column of Table 3.1.

Finally, suppose that cabbages and potatoes cost \$0.30 and \$0.20 per pound. Letting x_1 and x_2 denote pounds of cabbage and potatoes per day, we can express our diet problem as follows:

Choose x_1 and x_2 to minimize $0.30x_1 + 0.20x_2$ subject to

$$96x_1 + 325x_2 \geq 3000$$
$$4.63x_1 + 7.63x_2 \geq 70$$
$$266x_1 + 152x_2 \geq 5000$$
$$x_1 \geq 0$$
$$x_2 \geq 0$$

In a figure with x_1 and x_2 on the horizontal and vertical axes, the last two constraints (nonnegativity) limit feasible solutions to the first quadrant. The geometric implications of the first three constraints can be seen more easily if we convert them to equalities and find their horizontal and vertical intercepts. For example, $96x_1 + 325x_2 = 3000$ is a line whose horizontal and vertical intercepts are $3000/96 = 31.25$ and $3000/325 = 9.23$. These

---

[2] If a diet places *upper* limits on consumption of some substances, such as mercury or pesticides, these limits can be converted to *lower* bounds by multiplying the inequality by -1. For example, the constraint $a_{j1}x_1 + \ldots + a_{jn}x_n \leq b_j$ could be rewritten as $-a_{j1}x_1 - \ldots - a_{jn}x_n \geq -b_j$. If no point satisfies all constraints, the feasible set is said to be empty or void. For example, the feasible set is empty if the constraints include $x_1 + x_2 \geq 2$ and $-x_1 - x_2 \geq -1$.

intercepts indicate that 3000 calories could be obtained from either 31.25 lbs of cabbage or 9.23 lbs of potatoes. The calorie constraint limits the feasible solutions to points above a line whose horizontal and vertical intercepts are 31.25 and 9.23. Similarly, the protein constraint limits solutions to points above a line whose intercepts are 15.12 and 9.174, and the vitamin A constraint limits solutions to the region above a line whose intercepts are 18.80 and 32.89. These lines are shown in Figure 3.1.

From Figure 3.1, we can see immediately that the protein constraint is satisfied wherever the calorie and vitamin A constraints are satisfied. In other words, the protein requirement will never be a binding constraint on the solution to this diet problem. Because the protein constraint is redundant, it can be henceforth ignored. The calorie and vitamin A constraints intersect at the point (16.27, 4.425). The calorie constraint is binding below this point; the vitamin A constraint is binding above it.

The piecewise linear curve formed from the calorie constraint below (16.27, 4.425) and the vitamin A constraint above this point is shown in Figure 3.2. Any point on or above this curve satisfies all the nutrient requirements. This curve is an isoquant for feeding one man for one day.

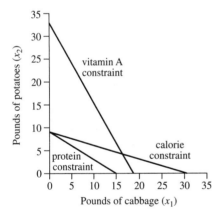

Figure 3.1 Nutrient constraints

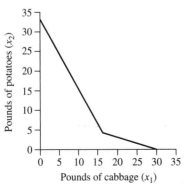

Figure 3.2 The upper contour formed by the intersection of the calorie and vitamin A constraints

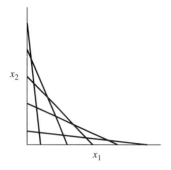

Figure 3.3 A piecewise linear isoquant, formed as the outer envelope of many constraint lines, can closely approximate a smooth curve

EXERCISE 3.1

Suppose that nutritionists revise the minimum daily requirement for protein, raising it from 70 to 130 grams. Assuming no change in the minimum daily requirements for calories and vitamin A, draw the new isoquant for feeding one man for one day.

Like the isoquants obtained from production experiments, such as discussed in Chapter 2, those derived by linear programming are convex—that is, their chords lie on or above their arcs. Unlike production experiments, linear programming provides an explanation for the convexity. In the case of feeding animals, including humans, the explanation is that animals have minimum daily requirements for several nutrients, which are found in various quantities in various foods. Each nutrient constraint is linear; the upper contour or outer envelope of the constraints is convex. More generally, production of a given output usually requires constituent parts or elements found in varying proportions in various possible inputs. Each of the constraints is linear, and their outer envelope is convex. An isoquant in a linear programming problem is convex because it is the lower boundary of a set of points satisfying *each* of several intersecting linear constraints. In contrast, the lower boundary of a set of points satisfying *any* of several such constraints would be concave.

Although the isoquants derived from production experiments are usually smooth, those derived by linear programming are kinked. The discrepancy is due to different approximations used in the two approaches. Production experiments generate large amounts of messy data—for example, the feed consumption and weight gain of hundreds of hogs—that are conveniently summarized by smooth curves.[3] Any kinks that may exist are obscured by random variation, for example, because of genetic variation, one hog may gain more weight than another on the same diet. Linear programming, in contrast, takes as given the minimum daily requirements reported by nutritionists. These requirements are conventionally tabulated nutrient by nutrient, as though interactions among nutrients were unimportant. Allowing for interactions might smooth otherwise kinked isoquants.

The isoquant in Figure 3.2 has a single kink because, for simplicity, we considered only two potentially binding nutritional constraints. In a more realistic example, more numerous nutritional constraints would be considered, producing a diagram resembling that in Figure 3.3, where the outer envelope, composed of many short line segments, closely approximates a smooth curve. Thus, in practice, the isoquants derived from production experiments and from linear programming are similar in shape.

---

[3] "Smooth" means, in calculus terms, differentiable.

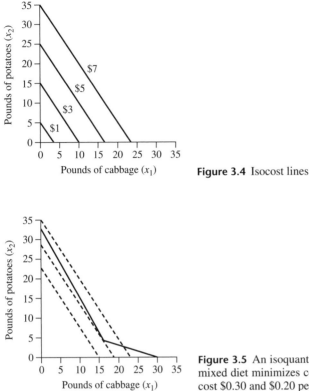

Figure 3.4 Isocost lines

Figure 3.5 An isoquant superimposed on isocost lines; a mixed diet minimizes costs when cabbages and potatoes cost $0.30 and $0.20 per pound

Isocost Lines

To determine which of the diets that satisfy all nutrient requirements is cheapest, we need to supplement the isoquant with isocost lines. The absolute value of the slope of the isocost lines is the relative price of cabbage, $0.30/0.20 = 1.5$. Four such isocost lines are shown in Figure 3.4. Costs are higher along isoquants further from the origin.

In Figure 3.5, the upper contour formed by the calorie and vitamin A constraints (solid line) is superimposed on three isocost lines (dashes). From this figure we can see that neither an all-cabbage nor an all-potato diet will minimize cost, given the assumed prices. The minimum-cost diet is found at the kink in the nutrient requirement curve—that is, at the point $(16.27, 4.425)$. Thus an expenditure of $0.30(16.27) + 0.20(4.425) = 5.77$ per day suffices to purchase the minimum-cost cabbage and potato diet.[4] Monotonous in the extreme, the diet was nonetheless deemed nutritionally adequate and might have seemed luxurious to people caught in the Irish potato famine of the 1840s.

The minimum-cost combination of cabbage and potatoes depends on the price of potatoes relative to that of cabbage. In the example above, we assumed that the relative price of cabbage was $0.30/0.20 = 1.5$. Thus the isocost lines had a slope of -1.5. The calorie

---

[4] The diet satisfies G. Stigler's (1945) full list of nine nutritional requirements, not just the three discussed above. However, one may doubt whether a typical man's stomach could daily accommodate 20.7 lbs of cabbage and potatoes. If the stomach can process at most $\bar{b}$ lbs of food per day, we should include in our linear programming problem the constraint $x_1 + x_2 \leq \bar{b}$. If $\bar{b}$ were less than 20.7, the cabbage and potato diet would be infeasible and we would have to consider other foods.

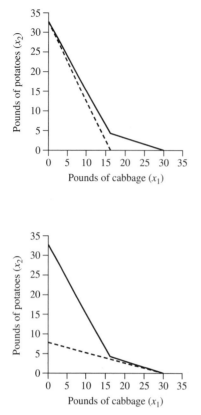

Figure 3.6 An all-potato diet minimizes cost when the prices of cabbages and potatoes are $0.40 and $0.20 per pound, respectively

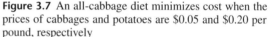

Figure 3.7 An all-cabbage diet minimizes cost when the prices of cabbages and potatoes are $0.05 and $0.20 per pound, respectively

constraint has a slope of $-96/325 = -0.2954$, and the vitamin A constraint has a slope of $-266/152 = -1.75$. If the relative price of cabbage were to rise above 1.75, the minimum-cost diet would consist entirely of potatoes. For example, if the price of cabbage rose to $0.40 while that of potatoes remained at $0.20, an all-potato diet would cost $0.20(32.89) = 6.58$, compared to $0.40(16.27) + 0.20(4.425) = 7.38$ for the mixed diet selected earlier. In this case, illustrated in Figure 3.6, the point (0, 32.89) is a corner solution to the diet problem.

If the relative price of cabbage were to fall below 0.2954, the minimum-cost diet would consist exclusively of cabbage. For example, if the price of cabbage fell to $0.05 while that of potatoes remained at $0.20, an all-cabbage diet would cost $0.05(31.25) = 1.56$, compared to $0.05(16.27) + 0.20(4.425) = 1.70$ for the mixed diet. This case is illustrated in Figure 3.7.

Whereas the relative price of cabbage could take any value from zero to infinity, a minimum-cost diet can always be found by checking just three possibilities: the all-cabbage diet, the all-potato diet, and the mixed diet consisting of 16.27 lbs of cabbage and 4.425 lbs of potatoes.

In general, minimum-cost diets are to be found at intersection points between constraints or between a constraint and an axis. Each such intersection is an **extreme point** of the feasible set in the sense that it is not on any line segment terminating at two other points of the set. The feasible set has a finite number of extreme points.

If two extreme points both qualify as minimum-cost diets, then so do all points on the line segment joining these extreme points. For example, if the relative price of cabbage were exactly 1.75, then all points on the line segment from (0, 32.89) to (16.27, 4.425) would be minimum-cost diets. Similarly, if the relative price of cabbage were exactly 0.2954, all points on the line segment from (16.27, 4.425) to (31.25, 0) would be minimum-cost diets.

EXERCISE 3.2

As in the previous exercise, suppose that nutritionists raise the minimum daily requirement for protein to 130 grams while keeping the old requirements for calories and vitamin A. Continue to suppose that cabbage and potatoes cost $0.30 and $0.20 per pound. Using the isoquant you constructed in the last exercise and an isocost line based on the prices of cabbage and potatoes, find the least-cost diet and calculate its cost.

The minimum-cost diet when only cabbage and potatoes are available is not necessarily the minimum-cost diet when there is a wider variety of foods from which to choose. Seventy-seven foods were included in the pioneering studies of the diet problem. Of these foods, nine were selected by linear programming to form a minimum-cost diet, given the prices of 1939. This nine-food diet costs only 15% as much as the diet that consists exclusively of cabbage and potatoes.[5]

If three foods are available, we can visualize the linear programming problem in the following terms: Each nutritional requirement corresponds to a plane in a three-dimensional space of foods. The set of nutritionally adequate diets is bounded away from the origin by one or more polygons lying in such planes. In other words, the set of nutritionally adequate diets consists of points in the positive orthant that lie on or above all the planes representing nutritional requirements.[6] A set of diets that all cost the same is an isocost triangle with vertices on the axes of the positive orthant. An isocost triangle that touches an extreme point of the set of adequate diets without crossing into its interior defines the minimum expenditure necessary to purchase an adequate diet. Any point that is in both this plane and the set of adequate diets is a minimum-cost diet. To find a cost-minimizing diet, we only have to calculate the costs at the extreme points and choose the least of these, just as in the two-dimensional case.

3.2.4 Primal and Dual Problems

Linear programming problems come in pairs, whose elements are called primal and dual. If the diet problem is regarded as primal, its dual involves calculating the **imputed value** of each nutrient—i.e., the most we should be willing to pay for a dietary supplement containing one unit of the nutrient. Each imputed value (also known as an accounting, fictitious, or shadow price) represents the amount by which expenditure on food could be reduced when such a dietary supplement is used. A straightforward way of calculating the value of a nutrient is to reduce the nutrient requirement and recalculate the solution to the primal problem. The change in the minimum expenditure represents the value of the nutrient. For example, if we reduce the calorie requirement from 3000 to 2900, the intercepts on the calorie constraint shift inward to $2900/96 = 30.21$ and $2900/325 = 8.923$. The intersection point of the calorie and vitamin A constraints shifts right and down to (16.48, 4.055). The

---

[5] The nine-foods were whole wheat flour, corn meal, evaporated milk, peanut butter, lard, beef liver, cabbage, potatoes, and spinach (Gass 1970). Assuming that the nine food diet still costs about 15% of the cabbage and potato diet, we can conclude that it costs only about $0.15(5.77) = 0.87$ per day, a result worth pondering before sticking a dollar into a soda machine.

[6] In this context, saying that a point lies above a plane means that it and the origin lie on opposite sides of the plane.

cost of the least-expensive diet falls roughly from $5.77 to $5.76. Thus a dietary supplement that provided 100 calories would have a value of approximately 1 cent.

EXERCISE 3.3

Starting from the diet problem on page 30, determine the imputed value of 1 gram of protein.

EXERCISE 3.4

Starting again from the same diet problem on page 30, determine the imputed value of 10 i.u.'s of vitamin A.

If a diet problem involves many nutrient constraints, deriving the corresponding imputed values by solving many variants of the primal problem could be vexing. (Primal scream, anyone?) Fortunately, an ingenious mathematical shortcut, proposed by John von Neumann, enables us to calculate all of the imputed values in one operation. If the primal problem involves choosing quantities of n foods to minimize cost subject to m nutritional constraints and n nonnegativity constraints, von Neumann's formulation of the dual involves choosing m imputed values to maximize the total value of required nutrients subject to n constraints on food values and m nonnegativity constraints. More specifically, the dual problem corresponding to the general primal diet problem on page 29 is the following:

Choose $v_1, v_2, \ldots, v_m$ to maximize $b_1 v_1 + b_2 v_2 + \cdots + b_m v_m$ subject to the valuation constraints

$$
\begin{aligned}
a_{11} v_1 + a_{21} v_2 + \cdots + a_{m1} v_m &\leq c_1 \\
a_{12} v_1 + a_{22} v_2 + \cdots + a_{m2} v_m &\leq c_2 \\
&\vdots \\
a_{1n} v_1 + a_{2n} v_2 + \cdots + a_{mn} v_m &\leq c_n
\end{aligned}
$$

and the nonnegativity constraints $v_i \geq 0$, $i = 1, 2, \ldots, m$.

For example, letting v_1, v_2, and v_3 denote the imputed values of 1 calorie, 1 gram of protein, and 1 i.u. of vitamin A, we may express the dual of the specific primal diet problem on page 30 as follows:

Choose v_1, v_2, and v_3 to maximize $3000 v_1 + 70 v_2 + 5000 v_3$ subject to

$$96 v_1 + 4.63 v_2 + 266 v_3 \leq .30$$

$$325 v_1 + 7.63 v_2 + 152 v_3 \leq .20$$

$$v_1 \geq 0$$

$$v_2 \geq 0$$

$$v_3 \geq 0.$$

Although this dual does not lend itself to two-dimensional graphical solution, it can be easily solved by techniques discussed in Section 3.3

3.2.5 Applications and Extensions

Linear programming has not been widely applied to human diets because concerns with taste and variety have prevailed over frugality. However, it is now commonly used to minimize the cost of feeding livestock. The diet problem has analogs in many industries. Whether a firm produces an alloy, chemical, drug, fabric, fertilizer, fiber, fuel, or paint, it has an interest in finding the least-expensive mix of inputs capable of yielding a product with specified attributes.

The diet problem is comparatively simple because it involves only one product. As such, the diet problem is a special case of a **blending problem**, which may involve any number of products. In a typical blending problem, a manager seeks to minimize cost subject to constraints on raw material availability and the quality and quantity of each of several products. Such problems are common in the chemical, metallurgical, pharmaceutical, and textile industries. More information about blending problems and techniques for solving them is provided by El Mogahzy (1992a, 1992b) and the SAS Institute (1999).

Linear programming has become an attractive alternative to production experiments because it can be applied to any number of inputs of known composition, including inputs not yet available in quantities sufficient for large-scale experiments. Applications of linear programming to problems of economic data analysis, space allocation, and probability assessment will be noted in Chapters 4, 7, and 19. For more information about applications, consult Beneke and Winterboer (1973), Charnes et al. (1994), Dorfman et al. (1987 [1958]), Farrell (1957), and Gass (1970).

3.3   Linear Programming Techniques

In the diet problem, as we have seen, a cost-minimizing diet lies at an extreme point of the set of nutritionally adequate diets. In general, an optimal solution to a linear programming problem lies at an extreme point of the feasible set. The challenge in linear programming problems is to locate the optimal point in an efficient manner. When a problem is too complicated to solve geometrically, two algebraic approaches are commonly used. The older approach, called the simplex algorithm, involves moving from one extreme point to another with lower cost until no further cost reduction is possible. A more recently developed algorithm begins in the interior of the feasible set and gropes its way toward the extreme point with lowest cost. In principle, nothing more than pencil and paper is required to apply these techniques. In practice, they are tedious to use in pencil-and-paper calculations.

Fortunately, the drudgery can be taken out of linear programming by using an appropriate computer software package. Several such packages are discussed in the appendix to this chapter. In the present section we examine just one example, MuPAD, a general-purpose computer algebra system with optimization functions that are readily adaptable to linear programming.

In MuPAD, a linear programming problem involving minimization can be expressed in the following form:

```
linopt::minimize([{I_1, I_2, ..., I_m}, F])
```

where F is the function to be minimized and $I_1, I_2, \ldots, I_m$ are the inequality constraints. For example, to enter the diet problem discussed in subsection 3.2.3, we type the following:

```
linopt::minimize([{96*x1+325*x2>=3000, 4.63*x1+7.63*x2>=70,
    266*x1+152*x2>=5000, x1>=0, x2>=0}, .3*x1+.2*x2])
```

MuPAD responds with the optimal values of the variables and the minimum cost:

```
[OPTIMAL, {x2 = 159000/35929, x1 = 584500/35929}, 207150/35929]
```

To convert the ratios to decimals, we just type `float(%)`. MuPAD responds with

```
[OPTIMAL, {x1 = 16.26819561, x2 = 4.425394528}, 5.765537588]
```

These are the answers we obtained geometrically, given to more decimal places than we cared to calculate. Naturally, MuPAD and similar software can solve linear programming problems with far more variables than we could handle geometrically.[7]

EXERCISE 3.5

Use MuPAD or another software package to verify your answer to exercise 2.

The dual problem formulated on page 36 can be solved in MuPAD by typing the following:

```
linopt::maximize([{96*v1 + 4.63*v2 + 266*v3 <= .30,
    325*v1 + 7.63*v2 + 152*v3 <= .20, v1 >= 0, v2 >= 0, v3 >= 0},
    3000*v1 + 70*v2 + 5000*v3])
```

MuPAD responds with the maximum value of the required nutrients (5.76554) and the imputed value of each nutrient (v1 = 0.000105764, v2 = 0.0, v3 = 0.00108965).

Comparing the solutions to the primal and dual, we see that the minimum calculated in the primal equals the maximum calculated in the dual (5.76554). This equality, which is characteristic of primal and dual problems, indicates that the cost of the optimal diet is exactly accounted for by the imputed value of the nutrients it provides. The imputed value of 1 calorie is about $0.0001; thus the imputed value of 100 calories is roughly $0.01 or 1 cent, as we found on page 36. The imputed value of protein is zero, confirming our solution to Exercise 3.3. The imputed value of one i.u. of vitamin A is $0.001; thus the imputed value of ten i.u.'s is $0.01, or 1 cent, as we found in Exercise 3.4.

3.4   Summary

1. To explain the convexity of isoquants, explore substitution possibilities among large sets of inputs, and predict substitution possibilities involving new inputs, economists have turned to linear programming.
2. The diet problem of linear programming is to minimize a linear function subject to linear inequality constraints, including nonnegativity conditions. Problems of this form are faced by managers in many industries.
3. Isoquants derived by linear programming are convex and piecewise linear. A least-cost diet can be found at a kink or endpoint of an isoquant.
4. Simple linear programming problems can be solved by geometric reasoning. More complicated linear programming problems can be solved by algebraic methods, implemented in readily available computer software.

3.5   Solutions to Exercises

3.1. The new protein constraint is $4.63x_1 + 7.63x_2 \geq 130$. It is satisfied by points in the first quadrant above a line segment whose horizontal and vertical intercepts are 28.1 and 17.0. This line segment and those based on the old calorie and vitamin A constraints are shown in Figure 3.8.

---

[7] For noncommercial use, MuPAD is available free of charge from http:/research.mupad.de/ . An introduction to MuPAD programming is provided by Gerhard et al. (2000).

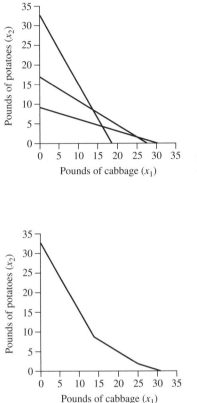

Figure 3.8 Revised protein constraint and old calorie and vitamin A constraints

Figure 3.9 Isoquant based on revised protein constraint and old calorie and vitamin A constraints

The protein and calorie constraint lines intersect at (25.0, 1.9), and protein and vitamin A constraint lines intersect at (13.9, 8.6). The outer envelope of the constraints is shown in Figure 3.9

3.2. The slope of isocost lines is still -1.5. The slope of the new protein constraint is $-4.63/7.63 = -.607$, and slopes of the other constraints are unchanged. Thus the isocost lines are steeper than the new protein constraint, as well as the calorie constraint, but flatter than the vitamin constraint. The least-cost diet is found at the intersection of the protein and vitamin constraint lines—that is, at (13.9, 8.6)—as shown in Figure 3.10. Thus the least-cost diet consists of 13.9 lbs cabbage and 8.6 lbs potatoes. It costs $0.3(13.9) + 0.2(8.6) = 5.89$.

3.3. In the diet problem on page 30, the protein constraint is not binding. Reducing the protein requirement from 70 to 69 grams has no effect on the minimum-cost diet. We still require 16.27 lbs of cabbage and 4.425 lbs of potatoes to satisfy the calorie and vitamin constraints. Our expenditure on cabbage and potatoes is unchanged. Thus the imputed value of protein is zero.

3.4. The imputed value of 10 i.u.'s of vitamin A is about 1 cent.

3.5. To enter the problem in MuPAD, use the `linopt::minimize` command given on page 37, replacing 70 with 130. MuPAD reports that the optimal diet costs $5.88541 with $x_1 = 13.8707$ and $x_2 = 8.62108$.

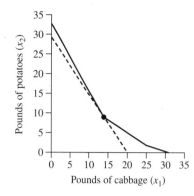

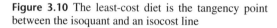

Figure 3.10 The least-cost diet is the tangency point between the isoquant and an isocost line

3.6   Problems: Something to Chew On

1. Anticipating attacks of the munchies, Mary Jane decides to prepare packets of mixed cereals to carry with her. She would like the packets to be cheap yet meet certain nutritional standards. Two cereals are available for mixing. Mary has decided that each packet should contain at least the following quantities of nutrients (b_i):

Nutrient	Minimum Requirement
Calories	400
Niacin	5 milligrams
Thiamine	1 milligram

The cereal boxes claim the following nutritional values per ounce (a_{ij}):

	Cereal	
Nutrient	1 ~~50~~	2 ~~40~~
Calories	110	120
Niacin (milligrams)	1	.25
Thiamine (milligrams)	.1	.25

Suppose that cereal 1 and cereal 2 cost 15.2 and 16.8 cents per ounce. Mary wants to minimize the cost of a packet subject to the nutritional requirements in the first table.

a. Formulate Mary's problem as a linear programming diet problem.

b. Graph the nutritional constraints and locate the feasible set of mixes.

c. Add one or more isocost lines to your diagram.

d. Determine how much of each cereal to put in a packet and how much the resulting packet costs.

2. One day Mary finds that cereals 1 and 2 have been reformulated with less sugar. Cereal 1 now has 50 calories per ounce and cereal 2 has just 40 calories per ounce. The new versions of the cereals have the same amounts of niacin and thiamine per ounce as before. Using these revised data, redo parts a–d of problem 1.

3.7 Appendix: Software for Linear Programming

Three categories of linear programming software are available: spreadsheet solvers, optimization tools in general-purpose mathematical and statistical packages, and stand-alone linear programming packages.

A spreadsheet may be the preferred software for solving a linear programming problem if the problem is simple, the coefficient values are already in spreadsheet format, or the analyst is unfamiliar with alternative software. To illustrate the use of a spreadsheet to solve simple linear programming problems, we consider how Gnumeric[8] could be used to solve the minimum-cost diet problem described in subsection 3.2.3 (starting on page 30). Coefficients, formulas, and starting values for variables must all be entered in spreadsheet cells. Row and column labels may also be entered in such cells. For example, in Figure 3.11 the coefficients of the cost function have been entered in cells B4 and C4, and those for the constraints have been entered in cells B7–B9, C7–C9, and F7–F9. Starting values (0) for the variables x_1 and x_2 have been entered in cells B3 and C3. The formula for the cost function has been entered in cell D3. While this cell is boxed, the formula appears in small windows above the spreadsheet as D3 =B3*B4+C3*C4. Because the initial values of x_1 and x_2 are zero and appear in cells B3 and C3, the formula's initial value is also zero, as shown in cell D3. Formulas for the left-hand side of nutrient constraints have been entered in cells D7–D9. Because these formulas are linear combinations of x_1 and x_2, whose initial values have been set to zero, the formulas' values initially appear as zero. Column labels have been entered in cells B2–D2 and A6–F6. Row labels appear in cells A2–A4 and A7–A9. The Solver box was opened by selecting it in the Tools menu. The greater-than-or-equal-to signs in cells E7–E9, like the column and row labels, are entered merely as reminders to users. Within the Solver box, the Parameters tab has been selected and the fields filled so as to minimize the value of the formula in cell D3 by changing the values of the variables in cells B3 and C3 while assuming a linear model with nonnegative variables.

Selecting the Constraints tab from the Solver box opens a form in which constraints can be entered. For example, the first constraint is entered as D7 >= F7. Selecting the Reports tab opens a form used to request answers and sensitivity analysis. Once all forms have been filled, clicking "Solve" will generate the requested reports. The reported answers (not shown) conform, within the limits of rounding error, to the results we obtained by hand in subsection 3.2.3 and with MuPAD in Section 3.3.

As we have seen, spreadsheets require that coefficients, variables, and formulas be identified by cell location. These cell identifiers have no natural relationship to the notation used in linear programming theory or substantive applications such as the diet problem. Merely irritating in small problems, the cell identifiers can become seriously confusing in larger problems. To avoid the cell identifiers, we can use either general-purpose mathematical or statistical programs or special-purpose linear programming packages.

General-purpose mathematical or statistical packages with linear programming capabilities include Gauss, Mathematica, Matlab, Maxima, MuPAD, R, SAS, and Scilab. The use of MuPAD was illustrated in Section 3.3. As a second example of how general-purpose packages can be used for linear programming, we next consider the case of Matlab.

A linear programming problem of our type can be entered into a Matlab program in the form

```
[x, fval] = linprog(c, ma, mb, [], [], z),
```

---

[8] Gnumeric is a free spreadsheet available at http:/www.gnome.org/projects/gnumeric/.

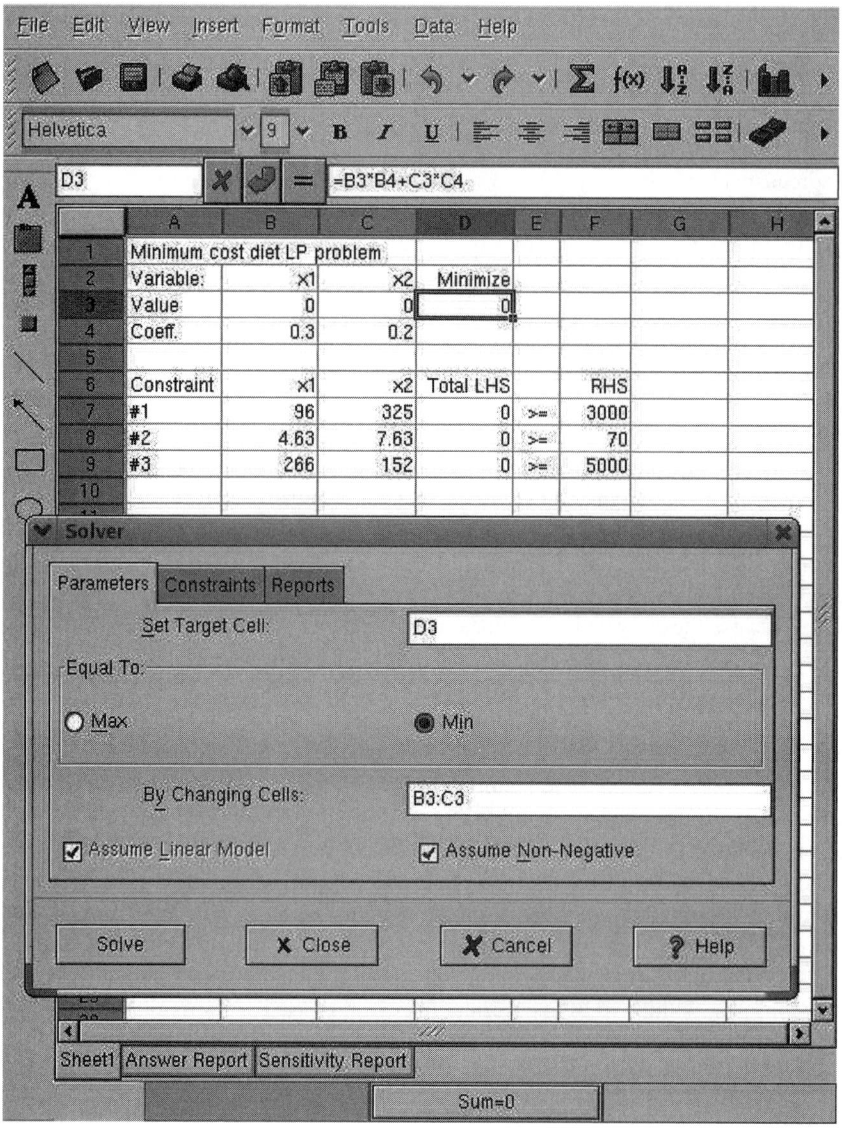

Figure 3.11 Screen shot of a linear programming diet problem expressed as a Gnumeric spreadsheet.

where x represents the variables to be chosen, $fval$ represents the optimal objective function value to be calculated, c is shorthand for the coefficients of the objective function $(c_1, c_2, \ldots, c_n)$, ma and mb pertain to the inequality constraints, and z is shorthand for the lower bounds on the variables (zeroes in our case). Matlab expects the inequality constraints to be formulated so that linear functions of the variables are *less* than or equal to constants. In contrast, in our formulation of the diet problem in subsection 3.2.2, the linear functions are *greater* than or equal to constants. To recast the diet problem in a form acceptable to Matlab, we just multiply both sides of each inequality by -1. Thus ma is shorthand for $-a_{11}, -a_{12}, \ldots, -a_{mn}$, and mb is shorthand for $-b_1, \ldots, -b_m$. The two pairs of square brackets that appear as arguments of the linprog command are place holders for coefficients of any equality constraints. (There are no equality constraints in the class of problems we are considering.) For example, to enter the diet problem discussed in subsection 3.2.3, we first supply values for the shorthand expressions and then use them in a `linprog` command. This is accomplished by the following code:

```
c = [.3; .2]
ma = [-96   -325
      -4.63 -7.63
      -266  -152]
mb = [-3000; -70; -5000]
z = [0; 0]
[x,fval] = linprog(c,ma,mb,[],[],z)
```

Matlab responds with the now familiar answers:

```
x =
      16.268
      4.4254
fval =
      5.7655
```

Stand-alone linear programming facilities include commercial products such as LINDO, freely downloadable programs such as GLPK or lp_solve, and online services such as NEOS Solvers. Detailed information on the various products and services is available from the Optimization Technology Center, http://www.ece.northwestern.edu/OTC/.

4

▉ Production and Costs

Inputs of two types are utilized in production. Some inputs are used up in the production process, for example, fuels and materials such as cement and steel. Other inputs are durable, for example, land, workers, buildings, and equipment.[1]

Output can be expressed either gross or net of the inputs used up in production. For example, if a farmer uses 1 bushel of wheat as seed to grow 60 bushels, we say that his gross output is 60 bushels and his net output is 59. **Value added** is the value of output net of the value of inputs used up in its production. For example, if an auto factory uses up $600,000 worth of steel, paint, fuel, and other such inputs while producing $1 million worth of cars, we say that its value added is $400,000. Value added is attributed to the services of durable inputs such as land, workers, buildings, and equipment.

4.2 Production Functions

A production function is an equation showing the maximum output producible, given existing technology, from each combination of inputs. Most commonly, production functions show how much net output or value added is obtained from each combination of the services of durable inputs. For simplicity, in this course we will usually work with production functions with no more than two inputs. Writing Q for value added, L for person-hours, and K for capital services (dollars-hours), we can express a production function as $Q = F(K, L)$.

Example A Cobb-Douglas production function is multiplicative in fractional powers of inputs: $Q = mK^{\alpha}L^{\beta}$, where $m > 0$, $0 < \alpha < 1$, and $0 < \beta < 1$. Increases in any of these parameters would represent technological progress.[2] The dimension of m reconciles those of Q and the right hand side variables.[3] A Cobb-Douglas production function with $\alpha = .33$ and $\beta = .67$ is illustrated in Figure 4.1.

---

[1] When speaking about the flow of services obtained from durable inputs, we should usually specify the period of time over which the services are rendered. Thus we talk about person-hours, equipment-days, building-months, land-years, and so forth. However, when the period of time is obvious or immaterial, we may leave it implicit.

[2] This function is named after Charles W. Cobb (a mathematician) and Paul H. Douglas (an economist and later U.S. senator from Illinois), who used it to model the dependence of output on capital and labor in U.S. manufacturing (Cobb and Douglas 1928). However, Cobb and Douglas were not the first to use the function. Johann Heinrich von Thünen essentially worked out this function on the basis of experiments on his farm. He published his results in 1850, 78 years before publication of Cobb and Douglas's article (Humphrey 1997; (Niehans 1990).

[3] For example, if Q is in tons, L is in hours, and K is in dollars, then m must be expressed in tons/(dollars$^{\alpha}$hours$^{\beta}$).

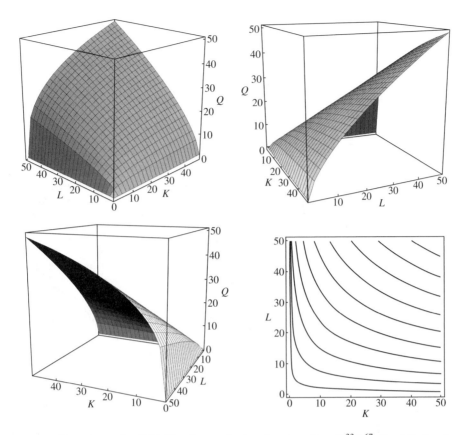

Figure 4.1 Four views of a Cobb-Douglas production function, $Q = K^{.33}L^{.67}$. Top left: function viewed from the origin; top right and bottom left: function viewed from two sides; bottom right: isoquants viewed from above

Data on the inputs and outputs of a cross section of production units seldom conform precisely to any one production function. For example, two production units with identical observed input quantities may have different observed output quantities. As a single-valued relation between inputs and output, a production function cannot fit such data. The discrepancy can be attributed to either (1) inefficiency in some production units or (2) unobserved inputs and measurement errors. In the former case, the observed output for any input combination must be less than or equal to the value of the production function at this input combination. With inputs plotted on horizontal axes and output on the vertical axis, the production function surface forms an upper envelope or frontier for the observations. We can approximate the shape of the production function by constructing a surface that passes through or above each observation. An example of such an approximation, in the case of a single input, is shown in the left panel of Figure 4.2. In the case of multiple inputs, the envelope can be constructed by an extension of linear programming known as data envelopment analysis (Charnes et al. 1994; S. Ray 2004).

Now consider the case in which all production units are equally efficient but there are unobserved inputs (such as managerial effort) or errors in measurement of output. If one production unit uses a larger quantity of an unobserved input than an otherwise identical production unit, the former will of course produce more output than the latter, with the same quantity of observed inputs. Similarly, if one production unit over- or underreports

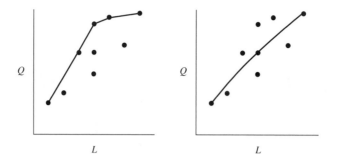

Figure 4.2 Two empirical approximations to a production function $Q = F(L)$. The dots represent the observations on labor input and the quantity of output. They are identically placed in the two panels, indicating that the same data underlie both figures. In the left panel, the function is approximated as a concave upper envelope of observed input-output combinations, drawn as a piecewise-linear curve. The vertical distance between a production unit's dot and the curve is interpreted as a measure of the production unit's inefficiency. In the right panel, the function is approximated by a curve based on an assumption of symmetrically distributed disturbances. The vertical distance between a production unit's dot and the curve is attributed to the effects of unobserved inputs and measurement errors

output, it will appear to produce more or less than an otherwise identical production unit with accurate records. In such cases, it may be reasonable to assume that observed output is scattered randomly around the true production function. Given that assumption, the production function can be easily estimated by a statistical technique known as regression analysis (Intriligator et al. 1996).

The problems we have examined—inefficiency in some production units and random errors due to unobserved inputs or measurement error—may both arise in the same data set. Whenever that combination of problems is suspected, an economist may wish to approximate the production function by using a technique that allows for both problems and attempts to disentangle their effects. This can be accomplished by using an extension of regression methods known as stochastic frontier analysis (Koop and Steel 2001; Kumbhakar and Lovell 2000).

4.3   Expansion Paths

In previous chapters we identified the cost-minimizing combination of inputs required to produce a given output as the point where an isocost line touches the appropriate isoquant without crossing it. If we vary the required level of output, we get a family of such cost-minimizing tangency points. Their locus is called an expansion path for the firm. When the inputs are capital and labor, the expansion path takes the form of a curve in (K, L) space, as in Figure 4.3.

EXERCISE 4.1

Consider the Cobb-Douglas production function $Q = mK^{\alpha}L^{\beta}$. Suppose that its isoquants are plotted with K on the horizontal axis and L on the vertical. The slope of the isoquants is $-\frac{\alpha L}{\beta K}$. (If you know calculus, you can verify that by taking the first derivative of L with respect to K, holding Q constant.) The slope of an isocost line in (K, L) space is $-r/w$, where r is the rental cost of capital and w is the wage rate. What is the equation of the expansion path? How is the slope of the expansion path affected by a change in r/w?

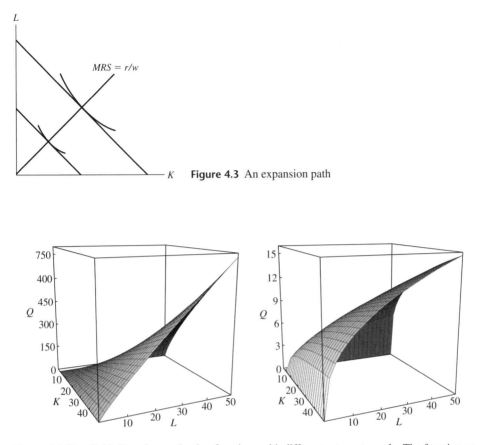

Figure 4.3 An expansion path

Figure 4.4 Two Cobb-Douglas production functions with different returns to scale. The function on the left, $Q = K^{.8}L^{.9}$, exhibits increasing returns. The function on the right, $Q = K^{.3}L^{.4}$, exhibits decreasing returns. Notice the different scales on the vertical axes

4.4 Returns to Scale

Some inputs can be varied more quickly than others. When General Motors (GM) decides to expand auto production, it can hire additional workers more quickly than it can build additional factories. For a given period of time, we say that an input is **variable** or **fixed**, depending on whether the quantity of it used in production can or cannot be changed. The longer the period in question, the larger the number of inputs that can be varied.

The **short run** is a period during which the quantity of one or more inputs is unalterable. The **long run** is a period sufficient to vary all input quantities. To save time, I shall skip over the short run, proceeding directly to the long run.

In the long run, by definition, all inputs are variable. An interesting experiment is to increase all inputs proportionately and observe whether output increases by a smaller, equal, or greater proportion. Suppose that the production function is $F(K, L)$ and we multiply all inputs by a factor c, where $c > 1$. We say that the **returns to scale** are **increasing** if $F(cK, cL) > cF(K, L)$, **constant** if $F(cK, cL) = cF(K, L)$, and **decreasing** if $F(cK, cL) < cF(K, L)$. Production functions with increasing and decreasing returns to scale are illustrated in Figure 4.4.

EXERCISE 4.2

Consider the Cobb-Douglas production function $Q = mK^\alpha L^\beta$. What value of $\alpha + \beta$ would imply constant returns to scale? What range of $\alpha + \beta$ would imply decreasing returns to scale? And what range of $\alpha + \beta$ would imply increasing returns to scale?

Increasing returns can result from either the nature of physical processes or from increasing division of labor. To take a physical example, suppose a rancher considers fencing square fields of various sizes and wants to know the relationship between the input (yards of fencing material) and the output (square yards of fenced pasture). Letting x and y denote yards of fencing material and square yards of fenced pasture, we can write $y = x^2$. This production function exhibits increasing returns to scale. Doubling the length of the fence quadruples the size of the pasture.

EXERCISE 4.3

Consider the relationship between the input and the output of beer coolers. The input is the Styrofoam (S) from which the coolers are made. To make matters simple, suppose that all coolers are shaped like cubes such as in Figure 4.5.

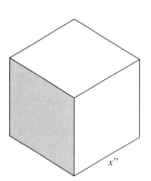

x''

Figure 4.5 Cube-shaped beer cooler

The Styrofoam used is proportional to the area of a cooler's sides. If the side is x inches, the total area is $6x^2$. Then we will need $S = 6x^2$ square inches of Styrofoam for a cooler x inches high. The output is the volume of beer kept cool. The volume of a fully packed cooler is $Q = x^3$. Write a production function relating the output Q to the input S and determine how the output responds to a doubling of the input.

Increasing returns can also be due to increasing division of labor. The effects of the division of labor on productivity were documented in the mid-1700s by the French Encyclopedists, based on direct observation of workshops such as the pin factory shown in Figure 4.6 (Kafker and Kafker 1988). Summarizing these effects, Adam Smith (1985 [1776]) argued that dividing labor among more workers increases productivity for three reasons:

1. Less time is spent in transition from one task to another, for example, changing tools.
2. Each worker develops greater skill in his or her specialty.
3. Breaking a project down into a series of simple tasks facilitates the invention of machinery to do some of the tasks.

Decreasing returns to scale might occur if raising output requires adding layers of management. For example, if 1 manager and 5 workers can produce $1000 of output a day, we can reasonably expect 1 senior manager, 5 junior managers, and 25 workers to

Figure 4.6 A room in a pin factory, as depicted in an engraving in Diderot's *Encyclopédie*. Reproduced with the permission of Dover Publications from Gillespie (1959, vol. 1, plate 184)

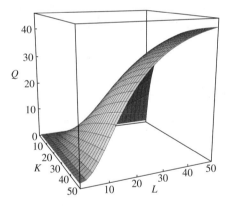

Figure 4.7 A production function exhibiting increasing returns to scale at low levels of inputs and decreasing returns at higher levels

produce $5,000 of output per day. The 5-fold increase in output requires increasing labor input by a factor of 31/6, or $5\frac{1}{6}$—hence decreasing returns.

A production function may exhibit variable returns to scale. A common pattern is for a production function to exhibit increasing returns at low input levels and decreasing returns at higher levels. A simple example of such a function,

$$Q = 50\frac{KL^2}{25^3 + KL^2},$$
(4.1)

is plotted in Figure 4.7. Several functions exhibiting first increasing and then decreasing returns, together with statistical evidence for their relevance to the transportation equipment industry, are analyzed in Zellner and Ryu (1998).

EXERCISE 4.4

Consider the production function given by Equation 4.1 and suppose that we initially choose input levels K_0 and L_0, obtaining output Q_0. If we multiply both inputs by a factor $c > 1$, we obtain a greater output, $Q_1 = 50\dfrac{c^3 K_0 L_0^2}{25^3 + c^3 K_0 L_0^2}$. (a) Express the ratio Q_1/Q_0 in terms of c and $K_0 L_0^2$ and then find the limits of this ratio as $K_0 L_0^2$ approaches 0 and ∞. Interpret your results in terms of returns to scale. (b) Setting $Q_1/Q_0 = c$, find the equation of a curve in input space along which a 1% increase in inputs would yield a 1% increase in output.

4.5 Cost Curves

The **cost** of producing something is the value of the cheapest bundle of inputs from which it can be made under specified conditions. The inputs in question include the entrepreneur's time, as well as inputs purchased from others. The conditions to be specified include the production function, the input prices, and which inputs are variable. Again, I concentrate on the long run, in which all inputs are variable.

A long-run **total cost** (TC) curve shows the cost of producing various quantities of output when all inputs are variable. If capital and labor are the only inputs, $TC(Q) = \min[rK + wL$ such that $Q = F(K, L)]$. The TC curves start from the origin because every firm in the long run has the option of going out of business and discharging all of its inputs. The TC curves are always positively sloped because increasing output costs something.

EXERCISE 4.5

In the Cobb-Douglas case, TC is proportional to $Q^{1/(\alpha+\beta)}$. Suppose Q is plotted on the horizontal axis and TC is plotted on the vertical axis. What is the shape of the total cost curve in each of the following cases: constant returns to scale, decreasing returns to scale, and increasing returns to scale?

A typical TC curve is concave in its lower reaches and convex in its upper reaches, as in Figure 4.8. The lower reaches are usually concave because a small firm commonly enjoys increasing returns to scale. The upper reaches are usually convex because the typical firm eventually runs into diminishing returns to scale, perhaps because more and more layers have to be added to the administrative hierarchy.

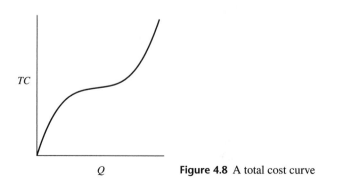

TC

Q **Figure 4.8** A total cost curve

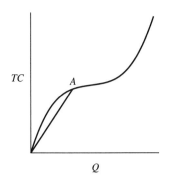

Figure 4.9 The average cost at point A is the slope of the ray from the origin to point A.

EXERCISE 4.6

The production function $Q = 50K^2L^2/(25^4 + K^2L^2)$ exhibits first increasing and then decreasing returns. It implies that total costs are $50(wr)^{1/2}(Q/(50 - Q))^{1/4}$, where w and r are the unit costs of labor and capital. (If you know calculus, you can derive the total cost function by minimizing total cost $rK + wL$ subject to the production function evaluated at a constant Q.) Assuming for simplicity that $wr = 1$, sketch the total cost function over the interval $0 \le Q \le 47$.

Average cost is total cost divided by output: $AC = TC/Q$. In geometric terms, illustrated in Figure 4.9, average cost is the slope of a ray from the origin to the total cost curve.[4]

Marginal cost is a change in total cost divided by the associated change in output: $MC = \Delta TC/\Delta Q$. In geometric terms it is the slope of the total cost curve. (For discrete changes in output, marginal cost is the slope of a chord drawn between two points on the TC curve. For infinitesimal changes in output, it is the slope of a tangent to the total cost curve.)

When the TC curve is concave for small values of Q and convex for large ones, the AC and MC curves are U-shaped and the MC curve passes through the minimum point of the AC curve, as in Figure 4.10. That makes intuitive sense because, as long as marginal cost is below average cost, producing another unit lowers average cost, but when marginal cost exceeds average cost, producing another unit raises average cost.

EXERCISE 4.7

Derive the average cost curve based on the total cost curve in Exercise 4.5, assuming that $wr = 1$. The corresponding marginal cost curve is $MC = 625/(Q^{3/4}(50 - Q)^{5/4})$. Sketch the average and marginal cost curves over the interval $2 \le Q \le 48$ in one figure and locate the point where average cost is minimized.

The shape of long-run cost curves can be important for the structure of industry. If the minimum point on the average cost curve occurs where Q is small relative to the market, the industry will consist of many small firms. However, if the minimum point on the average cost curve occurs where Q is large relative to the market, there may be room for only one or a few

---

[4] This ratio or slope is often called average *total* cost, to distinguish it from average fixed cost and average variable cost. In this text, concentrating on the long-run case, we can usually suppose all costs to be variable and thus make do with a single concept of average cost. The concept of average (total) cost came into use in business management around 1800 in Germany (Scherer 2001).

Costs

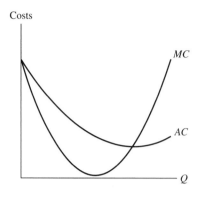

Figure 4.10 Average and marginal cost curves

firms in the industry. Smaller firms cannot match the low costs of larger firms and hence are driven out of business. Thus, industries characterized by average cost curves that decline over the relevant interval are often called **natural monopolies**. Karl Marx, among other economists, believed that declining average costs are common, and consequently capitalist evolution tends to generate monopolies (Marx 1965 [1867]).

4.6 Summary

1. Production is a process that turns inputs into valuable outputs. A production function is a mapping from inputs to maximum feasible output. Usually the inputs are services of durable resources such as capital and labor. Output is usually measured net of inputs used up in the production process; that is, output is measured as value added. In the short run, some inputs are fixed, but in the long run, all are variable.
2. The locus of minimum-cost inputs for various output levels is called a firm's expansion path.
3. A production function is said to show constant, decreasing, or increasing returns to scale depending on whether a proportional increase of all inputs raises output in equal, smaller, or greater proportion.
4. A long-run total cost curve shows the cost of producing at points along an output expansion path. The slope of a ray from the origin to a total cost curve is called average cost. The slope of the total cost curve itself is called marginal cost.

4.7 Solutions to Exercises

4.1. We can derive the equation of the expansion path as follows:

$$MRS = r/w$$

$$\frac{\alpha L}{\beta K} = r/w$$

$$L = \frac{\beta r}{\alpha w} K$$

Thus the expansion path for a Cobb-Douglas production function is a ray from the origin with slope $\frac{\beta r}{\alpha w}$. If r/w increases, so does the slope of the expansion path.

4.2. If we multiply both inputs by c, output increases by $c^{\alpha+\beta}$. Thus the Cobb-Douglas production function exhibits constant, decreasing, or increasing returns to scale, depending on whether $\alpha + \beta$ is equal to, less than, or greater than 1.

4.3. Solving the equation involving S and x for the latter variable, we get $x = (S/6)^{1/2}$. Substituting $(S/6)^{1/2}$ for x in the equation for Q, we get the production function, $Q = (S/6)^{3/2}$. If we double the amount of Styrofoam, we increase the volume of cool beer by a factor of $2^{3/2} = 2.83$.

4.4. (a) $Q_1/Q_0 = \dfrac{c^3 K_0 L_0^2}{25^3 + c^3 K_0 L_0^2} \dfrac{25^3 + K_0 L_0^2}{K_0 L_0^2} = \dfrac{c^3(25^3 + K_0 L_0^2)}{25^3 + c^3 K_0 L_0^2}$. As $K_0 L_0^2$ approaches 0, Q_1/Q_0 approaches c^3, which exceeds c. As $K_0 L_0^2$ gets arbitrarily large, Q_1/Q_0 approaches 1, which is less than c. Thus the function exhibits increasing returns for low levels of inputs and decreasing returns for higher ones. (b) $Q_1/Q_0 = c$ where $c^2(25^3 + K_0 L_0^2) = 25^3 + c^3 K_0 L_0^2$. Dropping the subscripts and solving for L, we obtain

$$L = \left(\frac{25^3(c^2 - 1)}{K(c^3 - c^2)} \right)^{1/2}.$$

Setting $c = 1.01$ to represent a 1% increase of inputs, we get $L = 175.46/\sqrt{K}$. This curve separates the region of increasing returns from the region of decreasing returns.

4.5. The total cost curve is linear, convex, or concave, depending on whether returns to scale are constant ($\alpha + \beta = 1$), decreasing ($\alpha + \beta < 1$), or increasing ($\alpha + \beta > 1$).

4.6. As an aid to sketching the total cost function, we can prepare a table of quantities and costs, such as the following:

Q	0	1	5	10	15	20	25	35	40	45	47
TC	0	18.90	28.87	35.36	40.46	45.18	50	55.33	70.71	86.60	99.48

Using the points in the table, we can sketch a total cost curve, as in Figure 4.11.

4.7. The average cost curve is $AC = TC/Q = 50/(Q^{3/4}(50 - Q)^{1/4})$. The average and marginal cost curves are shown in Figure 4.12. Average cost is minimized where the two curves intersect that is, where $Q = 37.5$ and $AC = MC = 1.755$.

4.8 Problems

1. Consider a firm whose marginal rate of substitution is $MRS = \frac{L-1}{K}$ for $L \geq 1$. Suppose that the ratio of the cost of capital to the wage rate is $r/w = 1/2$.

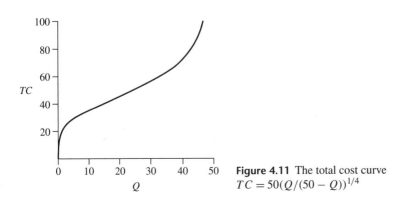

Figure 4.11 The total cost curve $TC = 50(Q/(50 - Q))^{1/4}$

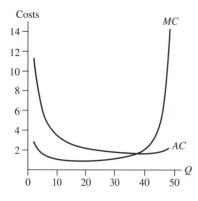

Figure 4.12 Average and marginal cost curves

  a. Sketch the expansion path.
  b. How would expansion of such a firm affect its labor-capital ratio L/K?
2. Do the following production functions exhibit constant, decreasing, or increasing returns to scale?
  a. $Q = 3K + 4L$
  b. $Q = .5KL$
  c. $Q = \min(3K, 4L)$
  d. $Q = 6K^{1/3}L^{1/3}$
3. Consider a firm whose long-run total cost curve is $TC = Q^3 - 30Q^2 + 301Q$, where Q is the quantity of output.
  a. Sketch the total cost curve for $0 \le Q \le 20$.
  b. Find the average cost curve and sketch it for $0 < Q \le 20$ in a new figure.
  c. The marginal cost curve is $MC = 3Q^2 - 60Q + 301$. (If you know calculus, verify the last equation by differentiating TC with respect to Q.) Sketch the marginal cost curve in the diagram for part b. Where do the AC and MC curves intersect?

4.9   Appendix: An Experiment with Economies of Scale and Learning by Doing

4.9.1 Background (to be read prior to the experiment)

Returns to Scale and Learning by Doing

Returns to scale are said to be constant, decreasing, or increasing, depending on whether a proportionate increase in all inputs raises output proportionately, less than proportionately, or more than proportionately. Learning by doing is said to occur when cumulative experience increases output per unit of inputs. In this experiment, we will attempt to measure returns to scale and learning by doing in the production of paper airplanes.

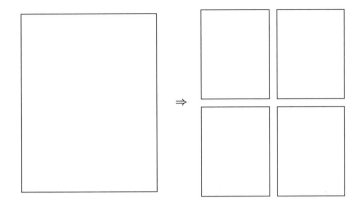

Figure 4.13 Tearing paper

Experimental Procedures

In this experiment students will be grouped into teams to make paper airplanes.[5] Teams may vary in size from 2 to 16 members. Each team member will have access to the necessary capital goods (a desk and a pen or pencil) and an ample supply of raw material (paper). Each team will be assigned a quality inspector, who will count the planes produced, tested, and shipped.

The experiment will consist of several sessions. Each session begins with a 4-minute planning period, during which teams organize their work, assigning particular tasks to individual team members. After the first session, a portion of this planning period may be used to critically assess experience in previous sessions. The second phase of each session is a 3-minute production period, during which teams make and test as many planes as possible. At the close of each session, the quality inspectors will report how many planes were shipped, your instructor will display these results, and you should copy them into your tables. We will attempt to complete four sessions.

To begin production of a plane, a team member should tear an 8.5- × 11-in. sheet of paper once crosswise and once lengthwise, making four identical small sheets, as shown in Figure 4.13.

The first steps in folding a plane are illustrated in Figure 4.14. Crease a small sheet by folding it in half lengthwise and then unfolding it. Fold down two adjacent corners to meet in the center (on the crease). Then fold down the newly formed obtuse corners so that they also meet at the center.

The next steps are shown in Figure 4.15. Fold the left side over the right side, along the central crease. Grasp the right edge of the upper flap and fold it back to align it with the left edge. Grasp the right edge of the lower flap and fold it behind the plane, so that it, too, is aligned with the left edge.

When released, the wings will spring part way back to their original position, forming a plane with a cross section like the capital letter T. Plane construction is completed by writing "MICRO GLIDER" on each wing's underside, as shown in Figure 4.16.

---

[5] The design of this experiment is adapted from Bergstrom and Miller (1997), who credit Janet Gerson with originally developing the experiment.

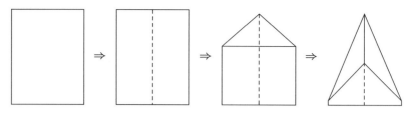

Figure 4.14 Folding paper

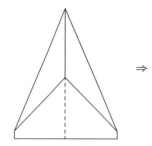 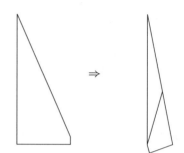

Figure 4.15 More folding

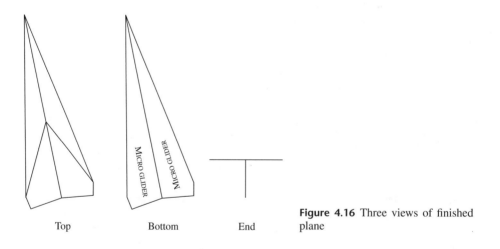

Top   Bottom   End

Figure 4.16 Three views of finished plane

After the plane is completed, a team member should test-fly it and show it to the inspector. If the inspector approves its construction, a team member should place it in a designated shipping container. The inspector should keep track of how many planes the team ships. (Planes that are not in the shipping container at the end of the 3-minute period should not be counted as part of the team's total output.)

Preparatory Exercise

Make one or two planes, following the instructions above, to make sure you understand the process.

Table 4.1 Team Sizes and Planes Shipped

Team		Number of Planes Shipped				
Name	Size	Session 1	Session 2	Session 3	Session 4	Mean
A						
B						
C						
D						
E						
F						
G						
H						
I						
Mean						

4.9.2 Lab Records (to be completed during the experiment)

During the experiment, record the size of each team and the number of planes shipped by each team in Table 4.1.

4.9.3 Data Analysis (to be done after the experiment)

Complete Table 4.1 by calculating the column and row means.

Plot the mean number of planes (right column of Table 4.1) against team size (second column of Table 4.1) in Figure 4.17 (see page 58). What does the plot suggest about returns to scale?

Plot the mean number of planes (bottom row of Table 4.1) against session number in Figure 4.18 (see page 59). What does the plot suggest about learning by doing?

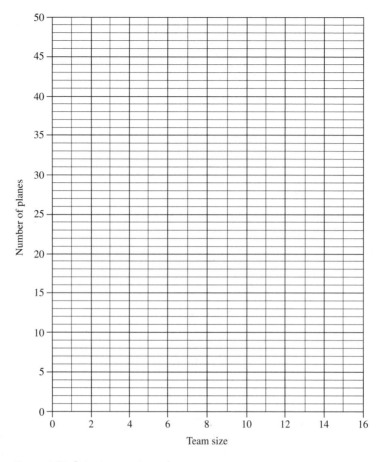

Figure 4.17 Output versus team size

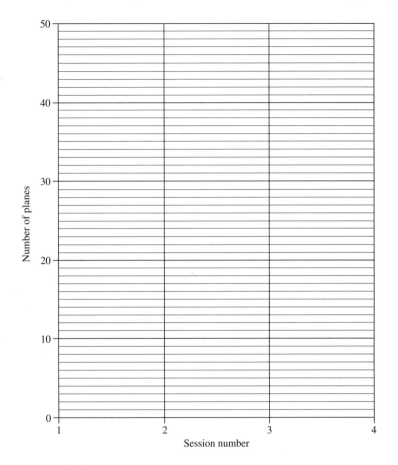

Figure 4.18 Output versus session number

5

▓ The Production Decisions of Competitive Firms

▓5.1▓ Revenue and Profit

A firm's **total revenue** (TR) is the sum of its receipts. For a firm that sells all units of output at the same price, total revenue equals the product of price (P) and quantity (Q): $TR = P \cdot Q$. **Economic profit** (Π) is total revenue minus total cost: $\Pi = TR - TC$. Recall that total cost includes the opportunity cost of using resources belonging to the firm's owner. (Costs as calculated by accountants do not always include all opportunity costs. Thus economic profit is often less than the profit reported by accountants.) When I refer to profit without any qualifying adjective, I mean economic profit. Economists usually assume that each firm acts as if it were maximizing economic profit.

What sort of behavior is entailed by profit maximization depends on market structure. There are four commonly recognized structures: perfect competition, monopoly, monopolistic competition, and oligopoly.[1] (The last two are sometimes called imperfect competition.) Perfect competition is introduced in this chapter; other structures are deferred until later chapters.

▓5.2▓ Perfect Competition

Early economists usually conceived competition as a rivalrous process in which sellers maneuver for market share and buyers jostle for bargains. Laypersons still discuss competition in such terms. However, a more impersonal concept of competition, originating with Antoine Augustin Cournot (1801–87), is now used by most professional economists (Blaug 1996; Cournot 1927 [1838]). In modern economic parlance, we say that an agent (a buyer or seller) is **competitive** in a market if the agent assumes that the market price is given— that is, independent of the agent's actions. An agent who is competitive in this sense may be called a **price-taker**. Consumers usually act as price-takers when buying gasoline at a filling station but may haggle over prices at a yard sale. Farmers usually act as price-takers when selling wheat at a commodity exchange but may dicker over prices when selling land.

Why agents are price-takers in some markets but not in others is an interesting question to which economists have proposed a variety of more or less plausible answers. Most economists would agree that the following five conditions are sufficient (if not necessary) to induce competitive behavior.

---

[1] The last three structures represent deviations from perfect competition based on the behavior of *sellers*. Parallel structures based on the behavior of *buyers* are monopsony, monopsonistic competition, and oligopsony.

1. A homogeneous (standardized) product. One gallon of 87 octane gasoline is indistinguishable from another for most consumers. In contrast, a quilt at the Jones's yard sale may be materially different from one at the Smiths's. Buyers are more price-sensitive for homogeneous products such as gasoline than for differentiated ones such as quilts. A seller of a homogeneous product who attempts to charge more than another seller is apt to lose all of his customers.

2. Numerous similar agents. If demanders can choose from many suppliers and don't care from which they buy, sellers have little bargaining power. Similarly, if suppliers face many buyers and don't care to whom they sell, buyers have little room to negotiate.

3. Free entry and exit and free mobility of resources. If new suppliers can quickly and cheaply enter a market and obtain the resources needed to start production, the incumbent suppliers would soon lose their customers if they collusively set prices above competitive levels. Similarly, if new buyers are free to enter the market, existing buyers cannot long hold prices below competitive levels.

4. Perfect information. If buyers know prices throughout a market, any seller who attempts to charge more than others is likely to lose all its customers. Similarly, if sellers know prices throughout a market, any buyer who offers less than others is likely to walk away empty-handed.

5. Negligible transaction costs in switching trade partners. An agent may be deterred from switching trade partners by costs such as fees for preparing contracts. For example, consumers of long-distance telephone services may stick with their current providers to avoid paying switching fees. If such transaction costs are negligible, a seller who tries to charge more than another seller will have trouble retaining customers.

Whether these five conditions are necessary, as well as sufficient, to induce competitive behavior is controversial. Some economists argue that the second condition (numerous similar agents) is unnecessary if the third (free entry and exit) is met. Their argument in brief is that noncompetitive behavior can be deterred by the threat of entry. A seller might conceivably be deterred from trying to raise a price by the risk that a higher price would quickly draw other sellers into the market. Similarly, a buyer might possibly be deterred from trying to lower a price by the risk that a lower price would soon attract other buyers. The effectiveness of such deterrents is debatable (Shy 1995).

Contemporary economists usually define **perfect competition** as a market structure in which all buyers and sellers are price-takers. In other words, a market is perfectly competitive if all the agents in it behave competitively (Shy 1995).[2]

5.3 Supply Curves

5.3.1 The Firm's Supply Curve

The firm chooses output Q to maximize its profit, $\Pi = TR - TC = P \cdot Q - TC$. For the competitive firm, P is a given. Thus the competitive firm's TR curve is just a ray from the origin, with slope P. The total cost curve is, as we have seen, typically shaped like a reverse S, as in Figure 5.1. To avoid losses, the firm must produce where $TC \leq TR$. To maximize profits, the firm selects from this range the Q for which the vertical distance between TR and TC is largest.

---

[2] Other definitions of perfect competition, particularly common in older texts, include lists of necessary or sufficient conditions for competitive behavior. A good example is provided by Ferguson (1969).

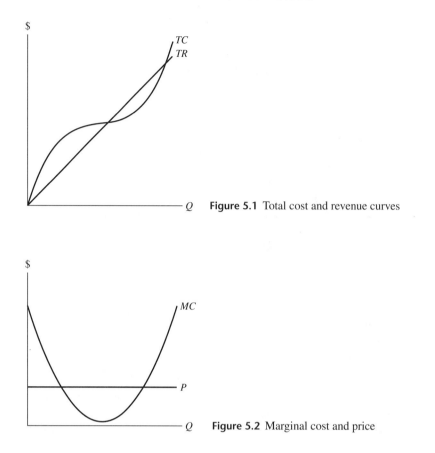

Figure 5.1 Total cost and revenue curves

Figure 5.2 Marginal cost and price

To pinpoint the profit-maximizing value of Q, let's look at the corresponding MC and P curves, shown in Figure 5.2. Price is represented by a horizontal line because it is virtually unaffected by the firm's output. Recall that marginal cost (MC) is the total cost curve's slope, $\Delta TC/\Delta Q$. It first declines and then increases. As long as $MC < P$, each additional unit produced increases the firm's profits. As soon as MC rises above P, additional units reduce the firm's profits. Thus profit attains a *local* maximum where the MC curve cuts the price line from below. (Profit also attains a *global* maximum at this point if profit is positive here. Otherwise the global maximum for profit occurs at the origin.)

The firm's profits, which we defined as $\Pi = TR - TC$, can also be expressed as $\Pi = (P - AC)Q$. As long as $P \geq AC$, the firm's MC curve is its supply curve. When $P < AC$, the firm suffers losses and has reason to shut down. Thus the firm's supply curve overlies the vertical axis up to minimum AC and coincides with the MC curve above that point. (See Figure 5.3.)

EXERCISE 5.1

Consider a firm whose total cost function is $TC = Q^3 - 6Q^2 + 15Q$. Its marginal cost function is $MC = 3Q^2 - 12Q + 15$. (If you know calculus, verify that the TC function implies the MC function.) If the price of a unit of output is 30, what is the profit-maximizing value of Q?

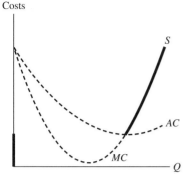

Costs

Figure 5.3 Cost and supply curves

EXERCISE 5.2

Consider a profit-maximizing firm whose average and marginal cost functions are $AC = 50/(Q^{3/4}(50 - Q)^{1/4})$ and $MC = 625/(Q^{3/4}(50 - Q)^{5/4})$. What price would induce the firm to produce $Q = 38$? (You may round the answer to the nearest cent.) How much profit would the firm make?

5.3.2 The Industry's Supply Curve

The shape of the industry's supply curve depends on the length of time available for quantity to respond to price. We will consider first the case in which the period is short enough so that the number of firms can be taken as fixed and then the case in which the period is long enough to permit free entry and exit.

No Entry or Exit

With the number of firms in the industry fixed, the industry's supply curve can be derived by simply summing the quantities supplied by individual firms. If there are n firms whose individual supplies are $q^1(p)$, $q^2(p)$, ..., $q^n(p)$, the industry supply is

$$Q(p) = \sum_{i=1}^{n} q^i(p).$$

One particularly simple special case is that in which all n firms are identical. In this instance, the industry supply is just a multiple of a firm's supply: $Q(p) = nq(p)$. In this case it is clear that the shape of the industry supply curve is qualitatively similar to that of a firm's supply curve: vertical for prices below minimum average cost and positively sloped for higher prices.

Free Entry and Exit

When the firms in an industry are making profits, entrepreneurs outside the industry have an incentive to enter. As new firms enter the industry, aggregate supply increases, reducing the equilibrium price. The price continues to fall until profits are driven to zero—that is, $P = \min(AC)$. Thus in equilibrium, with identical technology in all firms and free entry and exit, each firm will operate at the lowest point on its AC curve, as in Figure 5.4.

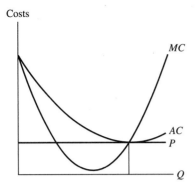

Figure 5.4 Equilibrium of the firm

Entry and exit affect an industry's aggregate output, which may in turn affect the average cost curves of industry's firms. Industries may be classified according to the long-run relationship between their output and their average costs.[3] In a **constant cost** industry, firms' minimum average costs are unaffected by the industry's aggregate output. The long-run supply curve of such an industry is horizontal at a price equal to minimum average cost.

In an **increasing-cost** industry, firms' minimum average costs rise and fall with the industry's output. This can occur if firms within the industry adversely affect each other's production functions or bid up input prices. For example, competing fishermen may deplete fish stocks (shifting production functions down) or bid up the price of inputs such as docking space. The depletion of fish stocks is an example of a **negative externality**, that is, a cost imposed by one party on another directly rather than via price changes. Bidding up dockage rates is an example of a **pecuniary diseconomy**, that is, a rise in input prices due to a rise in output. A particularly important example of a pecuniary diseconomy is provided by urban construction projects that bid up the price of land. The long-run supply curve of an increasing-cost industry is positively sloped. Evidence that the long-run supply curve for new housing is positively sloped is reported by Blackley (1999).

In a **decreasing-cost** industry, firms' minimum average costs fall as the industry expands and increase as the industry contracts. That can happen if firms within the industry favorably affect each other's production functions or act to lower input prices. For example, new farmers entering a sparsely settled territory may help control predators and weeds (shifting production functions up) or help reduce the prices of plows and wagons produced with increasing returns to scale. If a farmer's effort to control predators and weeds reduces his neighbors' costs, it is an example of a **positive externality**—that is, a benefit to parties other than those whose action caused it and that is transmitted directly rather than through price changes. A drop in farm equipment prices in a growing farm community exemplifies a **pecuniary economy**—that is, a fall of input prices due to rising output. The long-run supply curve of a decreasing cost industry is negatively sloped. Evidence that farming is in fact such an industry is reported by Castle (1989).

Although textbooks usually limit their coverage of long-run industry supply curves to those that are horizontal, monotonically increasing, or monotonically decreasing, several

---

[3] Classification schemes of this type go back at least to Marshall. Efforts to fill the classificatory categories with empirical content got off to a slow start because of difficulties in distinguishing the effects of an industry's expansion or contraction from those of concurrent technological change. Stressing these difficulties, a Cambridge University economist, John H. Clapham, likened cost-based categories to "empty boxes" (Clapham 1922). Nonetheless, economists—aided by improving data sets and statistical methods—are making progress toward filling the boxes.

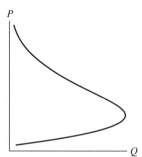

Figure 5.5 Backward bending long-run industry supply curve

studies of particular industries deal with a fourth case: a backward-bending supply curve such as shown in Figure 5.5. One thoroughly studied case is unregulated marine fisheries, where the backward bending supply curve results from open access to the seas and fish population dynamics. If fish prices are very low, incentives to fish are weak, few fish are caught, and fish populations are near their biological maxima. If fish prices are moderate, more effort is put into fishing, more fish are caught, and fish populations are reduced. If fish prices are very high, still greater effort goes into fishing, but fewer fish are caught because fish populations are badly depleted (J. Anderson 1985, 2003; L. Anderson 1986; Copes 1970). By the beginning of the twenty-first century, many fish populations had been reduced severely enough to put fisheries on the negatively sloped portion of their supply curves (Petersen et al. 2004). Other industries in which long-run supply curves are arguably backward bending include mortgages (Drake and Holmes 1997), oil (Cremer and Salehi-Isfahani 1989), and timber (Binkley 1993).

5.3.3 Price Elasticity of Supply

An elasticity is a ratio of percentage changes. Several elasticity concepts are frequently used by economists. Elasticities of supply will be considered here; discussion of elasticities of demand is deferred to Chapter 9. An **own-price elasticity of supply** is a percentage change in the quantity supplied of a good divided by the percentage change in the price of this good. A **cross-price elasticity** of supply is a percentage change in the quantity supplied of a good divided by the percentage change in the price of a different good. For example, a percentage change in the quantity supplied of wheat divided by the percentage change in the price of wheat (all other prices held constant) is the own-price elasticity of wheat, whereas the percentage change in the quantity supplied of wheat divided by the percentage change in the price of, say, barley (the price of other goods held constant) is a cross-price elasticity for wheat. An own-price elasticity involves movements along a supply curve, whereas a cross-price elasticity involves shifts of a supply curve induced by changes in the price of another good. In this text, we will be more concerned with own-price than cross-price elasticities. Own-price elasticities will turn out to be useful in understanding the price that a monopsony (sole buyer) offers to its suppliers and how buyers and sellers divide the burden of sales taxes.

An elasticity can be measured for either discrete or infinitesimal changes. An elasticity calculated for discrete changes is called an **arc elasticity**. An elasticity calculated for infinitesimal changes is called a **point elasticity**.

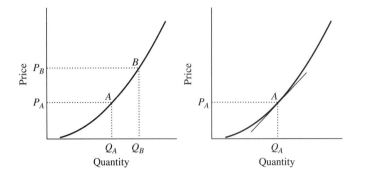

Figure 5.6 Two measures of own-price elasticity of supply. The left panel illustrates an arc elasticity; The right panel illustrates a point elasticity

An arc elasticity of supply is calculated for a move from one point to another on a supply curve. If the move is from A to B (as shown in the left panel of Figure 5.6), we can write the elasticity as follows:

$$\epsilon^s_{AB} = \frac{(Q_B - Q_A)/Q_A}{(P_B - P_A)/P_A}.$$

Letting ΔQ denote $Q_B - Q_A$ and ΔP denote $P_B - P_A$, we can simplify the expression for elasticity, as follows:

$$\epsilon^s_{AB} = \frac{\Delta Q/Q_A}{\Delta P/P_A} = \frac{\Delta Q}{\Delta P} \cdot \frac{P_A}{Q_A} = (P_A/Q_A)/(\Delta P/\Delta Q).$$

Notice that in the last expression, we divide by the slope of the supply curve. Thus the steeper the slope, the closer the elasticity is to zero.

When we want to measure the own-price elasticity of supply for infinitesimal changes—that is, in the immediate vicinity of a point on the supply curve—we draw a tangent to the supply curve at the point of interest, say A, as in the right panel of Figure 5.6. We define the point own-price elasticity of supply at A as the percentage change in quantity divided by the percentage change in price along the tangent to the supply curve at point A. Formally, we write the following:

$$\epsilon^s_A = (P_A/Q_A)/(\text{slope of demand curve at } A).$$

Notice that we are again dividing by the slope. Thus, if two supply curves pass through point A, the steeper supply curve is less price-elastic.

If two points on a supply curve are close together, the arc elasticity they determine is apt to be approximately equal to the point elasticity anywhere between them. When what we have to say pertains equally to arc and point elasticity, we simply say elasticity and write ϵ^s.

When discussing positively sloped supply curves, economists distinguish the following three cases:

- If $\epsilon^s < 1$, supply is said to be inelastic.
- If $\epsilon^s = 1$, supply is said to be unit elastic.
- If $\epsilon^s > 1$, supply is said to be elastic.

In the case of a horizontal supply curve, the change in price along the supply curve is always zero. Because division by zero is undefined, a horizontal supply curve has no own-price elasticity. In this case, economists sometimes say, in a curious turn of phrase, that supply is *perfectly* elastic.[4]

5.4 Summary

1. A firm is usually assumed to produce the quantity of output that maximizes its profit, defined as total revenue minus total cost.
2. An agent that assumes it can vary the quantity it buys or sells without affecting price is called a price-taker and is said to be competitive. An market in which all agents are price-takers is termed perfectly competitive.
3. The long-run supply curve of a competitive firm consists of the portion of the vertical axis beneath $\min(AC)$ and the portion of the MC curve above $\min(AC)$.
4. Over a period of time too short to permit entry or exit, an industry's supply curve is simply a sum of its firms' supply curves.
5. Given sufficient time, the entry and exit of firms dissipate profits and losses. The slope of an industry's long-run supply curve can be positive, negative, or zero.
6. An elasticity is a ratio of percentage changes. An own-price elasticity of supply is a ratio of a percentage change in the quantity of a good supplied to the percentage change in the price of that good.

5.5 Solutions to Exercises

5.1. The profit-maximizing level of output is found where marginal cost equals price—that is, $3Q^2 - 12Q + 15 = 30$, provided that average cost is no greater than price at this point. The roots of this equation are -1 and 5. The negative root has no economic meaning; the positive root is a quantity at which profit attains a local maximum. Here, average cost is $5^2 - 6 \times 5 + 15 = 10$. If the firm produces five units, its profit is $5(30 - 10) = 100$. Thus the firm is better off producing five units than shutting down. In other words, profit attains a global maximum at $Q = 5$.

5.2. Equating marginal cost to price, we get $625/(Q^{3/4}(50 - Q)^{5/4}) = P$. Substituting 38 for Q, we get $625/(38^{3/4}(50 - 38)^{5/4}) = P$ and thus $P = 1.83$. Average cost is $50/(38^{3/4}(50 - 38)^{1/4}) = 1.78$. Thus the firm makes a profit of $(1.83 - 1.76)38 = 2.66$.

5.6 Problems

1. Consider a firm whose total cost function is $tc = q^3 - 6q^2 + 13q$, where q is the quantity of output produced by the firm. Its marginal cost function is $mc = 3q^2 - 12q + 13$. (If you know calculus, verify that the tc function implies the mc function.)
   a. If the price of a unit of output is 13, what is the profit-maximizing value of q?
   b. Find the average cost function of the firm.
   c. What is the firm's minimum average cost?

---

[4] Use of the term "perfectly elastic" when elasticity does not exist may offend fans of the ontological argument, according to which anything perfect must exist. However, economists should prefer it to the common alternative term, "infinitely elastic," use of which is mathematically incorrect when elasticity is undefined.

    d. What is the firm's average cost when it produces the profit-maximizing quantity found in part a?

2. Consider a perfectly competitive industry in which each firm's total and marginal cost functions are as specified in Problem 1.

    a. What is the equilibrium price of output?

    b. How much does each firm produce at the equilibrium price?

    c. What is each firm's profit at the equilibrium price?

    d. Suppose the demand curve for the industry's output is $P = 34 - .1Q$, where P is price and Q is the industry's total output. Find the equilibrium value of Q.

    e. How many firms are in the industry?

6

Marginal Products and Factor Proportions

6.1 Marginal Products

When a firm increases capital input slightly while holding other inputs constant, the ratio of the increase in output to the increase in capital input is called the **marginal product of capital** (MPK). Similarly, when a firm increases labor input slightly while holding other inputs constant, the ratio of the increase in output to the increase in labor input is called the **marginal product of labor** (MPL).[1] Each marginal product is a function of all inputs.

Consider a firm that holds constant all but one factor of production. As the quantity of the variable factor increases, sooner or later its marginal product declines. A simple example is a ditch-digging operation that initially has one shovel and two laborers. Adding a second shovel may nearly double output, but adding a third shovel, without a laborer to use it, will have little effect. Similarly, a firm with two shovels and one worker will find that a second worker nearly doubles output, but a third, without a shovel, adds virtually nothing to output.

For the Cobb-Douglas production function, $Q = mK^{\alpha}L^{\beta}$, the marginal products are $MPK = \alpha m K^{\alpha-1}L^{\beta} = \alpha Q/K$ and $MPL = \beta m K^{\alpha}L^{\beta-1} = \beta Q/L$. (If you know calculus, you can derive these marginal products by differentiating Q with respect to K and L.) In this case, the marginal product curves are negatively sloped and convex, as shown in Figure 6.1.

EXERCISE 6.1

Consider the production function $Q = 6K^{1/3}L^{1/2}$. Express the marginal product of capital (MPK) and marginal product of labor (MPL) in terms of K and L.

From a production function that exhibits first increasing and then decreasing returns to scale, we can derive marginal product curves that are first concave and then may become convex. For example, the production function $Q = 50K^2L^2/(25^4 + K^2L^2)$ implies the following marginal product curves:

$$MPK = 50(25^2 2KL^2)/(25^4 + K^2L^2)^2,$$

$$MPL = 50(25^2 2K^2L)/(25^4 + K^2L^2)^2.$$

These marginal product curves are illustrated in Figure 6.2.

---

[1] If you know calculus, you can think of the marginal product of labor as the first partial derivative of output with respect to labor and think of the marginal product of capital as the first partial derivative of output with respect to capital. This interpretation of marginal products was already noted by Thünen in the first half of the nineteenth century (Blaug 1996, ch. 8).

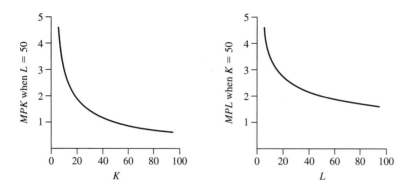

Figure 6.1 Marginal product curves for a Cobb-Douglas production function, $Q = 3K^{1/3}L^{2/3}$

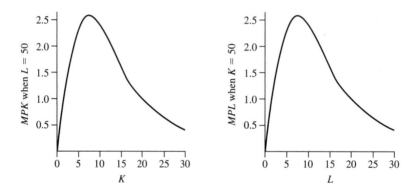

Figure 6.2 Marginal product curves for a production function exhibiting first increasing and then decreasing returns to scale

Notice that both the Cobb-Douglas and increasing-decreasing returns production functions conform to the rule, stated earlier, that increasing one factor while holding others constant will sooner or later cause the variable factor's marginal product to decline. In the Cobb-Douglas case, the decline begins immediately, whereas with increasing-decreasing returns, the decline follows an initial increase.

In the case of constant returns to scale, MPK and MPL are fully determined by K/L. In other words, proportionate changes in K and L leave the marginal products unaltered.[2] For example, if a Cobb-Douglas production function displays constant returns to scale, so that $Q = mK^{\alpha}L^{1-\alpha}$, its marginal products are as follows:

$$MPK = \alpha m(K/L)^{\alpha-1},$$
$$MPL = (1-\alpha)m(K/L)^{\alpha}. \tag{6.1}$$

---

[2] If the production function $Q = F(K, L)$ exhibits constant returns to scale, then it can be written as $Q = L \cdot F(K/L, 1)$. Defining k as K/L and $f(k)$ as $F((K/L), 1)$, we can write $Q = L \cdot f(k)$. If you know calculus, you can verify that the MPK is $\frac{\partial Q}{\partial K} = f'(k)$ and the MPL is $\frac{\partial Q}{\partial L} = f(k) - f'(k)k$. Thus the two marginal products depend solely on the capital-labor ratio k.

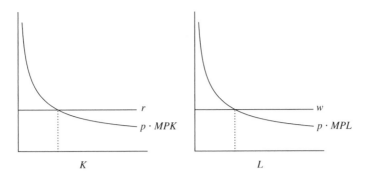

Figure 6.3 Demand for capital (left panel) and labor (right panel)

6.2   Factor Demand

A competitive firm that wants to maximize profits should adjust inputs so that the value of capital's marginal product equals the rental cost of capital and the value of labor's marginal product equals the wage rate. To express that idea mathematically, we may write

$$p \cdot MPK = r,$$
$$p \cdot MPL = w, \tag{6.2}$$

where p is the price of the firm's product, r is the rental cost of capital, and w is the wage rate.[3] To see why these conditions are necessary for profit maximization, consider the alternatives: If $p \cdot MPK < r$, the firm could make more profit by using less capital. If $p \cdot MPK > r$, the firm could make more profit by using more capital. Similarly, if $p \cdot MPL < w$, the firm could increase its profits by employing less labor, whereas if $p \cdot MPL > w$, the firm could increase its profits by employing more labor (see Figure 6.3).

Because all firms in a competitive economy face the same r, the value of capital's marginal product must be the same in all profit-maximizing firms. Similarly, because all firms in a competitive economy face the same w, the value of labor's marginal product must be the same in all profit-maximizing firms. This equality of the value of marginal products across firms is a necessary condition for efficient resource allocation. To see why, imagine that the equality did not hold. In that case, the value of aggregate output could be increased by transferring labor or capital from a firm where the value of its marginal product was below average to one where it was above average.

6.3   Factor Prices and Proportions

Dividing both sides of both equations in display 6.2 by p, we find that

$$MPK = r/p$$
$$MPL = w/p.$$

---

[3] If the marginal product curves are monotone, as in Figure 6.1, equating the value of a factor's marginal product to its price uniquely determines the amount of the factor. In contrast, if the marginal product curves rise and then fall, as in Figure 6.2, the equation of the value of a factor's marginal product to its price can have two solutions. Only the larger of these solutions would maximize profit.

Recalling that the marginal products depend on capital and labor inputs and noting that r/p is the real rental value of capital and w/p is the real wage, we can infer that factor demand is closely connected to real factor prices.

In the case of a Cobb-Douglas production function, we can write the last pair of equations as

$$\alpha m K^{\alpha-1} L^{\beta} = r/p,$$
$$\beta m K^{\alpha} L^{\beta-1} = w/p. \tag{6.3}$$

Taking logs of both sides of the equations in 6.3, we obtain

$$\begin{aligned} \log(\alpha m) + (\alpha - 1) \log K + \beta \log L &= \log(r/p), \\ \log(\beta m) + \alpha \log K + (\beta - 1) \log L &= \log(w/p). \end{aligned} \tag{6.4}$$

Given α, β, m, r, and p, Equations 6.4 represent two linear relationships between two unknowns, $\log K$ and $\log L$. After solving these equations for $\log K$ and $\log L$, we can easily obtain the corresponding values of K and L by exponentiation.[4] These values of K and L solve the firm's profit maximization problem.

EXERCISE 6.2

Suppose that $p = 4$, $r = .16$, $w = 12$, and the production function is that given in Exercise 6.1. Find the profit-maximizing values of K and L. (Refer to the appendix to Chapter 2 if you need help with logarithms.)

If a Cobb-Douglas production function has constant returns to scale, we can substitute $1 - \alpha$ for β in Equations 6.3, obtaining

$$\begin{aligned} \alpha m (K/L)^{\alpha-1} &= r/p, \\ (1 - \alpha) m (K/L)^{\alpha} &= w/p. \end{aligned}$$

(These equations could also be derived by substituting r/p for MPK and w/p for MPL in Equations 6.1.) Recalling that $0 < \alpha < 1$, we can see that an increase in the capital-labor ratio is associated with a fall in r/p and a rise in w/p. These results will be important when we get to general equilibrium analysis.

If we divide the first equation in 6.3 by the second, we get

$$\frac{\alpha L}{\beta K} = \frac{r}{w}.$$

The ratio of marginal products is equivalent to the marginal rate of substitution discussed in Chapter 2. Thus, the last equation is equivalent to the equations derived in Chapter 4, Exercise 4.1, where we noted that cost minimization requires that $MRS = r/w$ and that in the Cobb-Douglas case $MRS = \frac{\alpha L}{\beta K}$. It is worth noting again that an increase in the capital-labor ratio is associated with a fall in r/w.

EXERCISE 6.3

Given the production function in Exercise 6.1, express the marginal rate of substitution ($MRS = MPK/MPL$) in terms of K and L.

---

[4] A unique solution exists unless $\alpha + \beta = 1$, as in the case of constant returns to scale.

6.4 Summary

1. A factor's marginal product is the ratio of an increase in output to a small increase in input of that factor, other factors being held constant. When increasing quantities of a factor are employed with fixed amounts of other factors, sooner or later the marginal product of the variable factor declines.
2. In the case of constant returns to scale, marginal products depend on inputs only through factor proportions.
3. All competitive firms adjust inputs so that the value of each factor's marginal product equals the factor's price, thus ensuring that the value of each factor's marginal product is the same in all firms, a necessary condition for efficiency.
4. In equilibrium, an increase in K/L is associated with a fall in r/p, a rise in w/p, and a decrease in r/w.

6.5 Solutions to Exercises

6.1. $MPK = 2K^{-2/3}L^{1/2}$ and $MPL = 3K^{1/3}L^{-1/2}$.

6.2. Noting that $\alpha = 1/3$, $\beta = 1/2$, and $m = 6$, and substituting the given values of p, r, and w into Equations 6.4, we get

$$\begin{aligned}
\log 2 + (-2/3) \log K + (1/2) \log L &= \log(.04), \\
\log 3 + (1/3) \log K + (-1/2) \log L &= \log 3.
\end{aligned}$$

Consolidating the constant terms, we obtain

$$\begin{aligned}
(-2/3) \log K + (1/2) \log L &= \log(.02), \\
(1/3) \log K + (-1/2) \log L &= 0.
\end{aligned} \tag{6.5}$$

Adding the terms in the second line to the corresponding terms in the first, we obtain $(-1/3) \log K = \log(.02)$ and thus $\log K = -3 \log(.02)$. Exponentiating both sides, we get $K = .02^{-3}$ and hence $K = 50^3 = 125,000$. From line two of Equations 6.5, we see that $\log L = (2/3) \log K$. Exponentiating, we get $L = K^{2/3}$. Substituting 50^3 for K, we get $L = 50^2 = 2500$.

6.3. $MRS = (2/3)(L/K)$.

6.6 Problems

The problems below all refer to the production function $Q = 144K^{1/3}L^{1/2}$.

1. Does the production function exhibit constant, decreasing, or increasing returns to scale?
2. Express the marginal product of capital (MPK) and marginal product of labor (MPL) in terms of K and L.
3. Let $L = 9$. Calculate MPK for each of the following values of K: 1, 8, 27. Sketch the MPK curve.
4. Let $K = 8$. Calculate MPL for each of the following values of L: 1, 4, 9, 16. Sketch the MPL curve.
5. Express the marginal rate of substitution ($MRS = MPK/MPL$) in terms of K and L.

6. If the ratio of the rental cost of capital to the wage rate (r/w) is 0.02, what is the cost-minimizing value of L/K?

7. Suppose the price of output is $0.10 per unit, the rental cost of capital is 0.2, and the wage rate is $10.00 per hour. What are the profit-maximizing values of K and L? Calculate the profits of a firm that uses those quantities of K and L.

7

█ Comparative Advantage and Gains from Trade

7.1 Production and Comparative Advantage

7.1.1 Basic Concepts and Principles

Voluntary exchange between rational, self-interested, and fully informed individuals is generally beneficial to both parties. (If it were not mutually beneficial, such individuals would not consent to it.[1]) That is true even if we merely exchange existing goods, without producing anything new. However, the gains from trade may be considerably greater when the goods traded are produced from resources that are more productive in one use than another.

To illustrate the gains from trade that arise when goods are produced from resources with somewhat specialized uses, suppose we have two fields on which we can grow rice and wheat. One field is wet, the other dry. Rice grows better on wet ground, wheat better on dry. A hypothetical set of production possibilities for such fields is described in Table 7.1, where the quantities are expressed in physical units such as bushels.[2] Each quantity in the table represents the maximum amount of a grain that could be harvested from a field were the field entirely devoted to that crop.

We don't have to devote a field entirely to one crop. Take the wet field, for example. We could split the field in half, yielding 10 bushels of rice and 5 of wheat. The opportunity cost of a bushel of rice grown on the wet land is half a bushel of wheat. Thus we can get any combination of rice and wheat satisfying the equation $W = 10 - 0.5R$, where W stands for wheat and R for rice.[3] This equation is represented graphically by a negatively sloped line, as in Figure 7.1. The absolute value of the slope is the opportunity cost of rice in terms of wheat.

This negatively sloped line is an example of a **production possibilities frontier** (PPF), a key concept in economics. A PPF shows the maximum of one good that can be produced from available resources, given a commitment to produce a certain quantity of another good.

---

[1] Mainstream economists have traditionally assumed that most people involved in exchange are rational, self-interested, and fully informed. Of course, exceptions may exist. For example, an individual who exchanges unprotected sex for drugs of unknown purity is arguably irrational or ill informed.

[2] I've picked small round numbers for convenience. If taken literally, these numbers would imply that the fields in question are very small because wheat farmers, using modern techniques, can achieve a yield of 40 bushels per acre.

[3] If the derivation of this equation is not obvious to you, consider the following: Let f be the fraction of the field devoted to rice and $1 - f$ the fraction devoted to wheat. Thus, $R = 20f$ and $W = 10(1 - f)$. The former equation implies that $f = R/20$. Substituting $R/20$ for f in the equation for W gives us $W = 10(1 - R/20) = 10 - .5R$.

Table 7.1 Production possibilities for two crops on two fields

Crop	Fields	
	Wet	Dry
Rice	20	10
Wheat	10	20

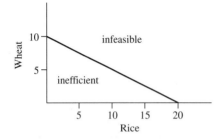

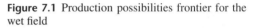

Figure 7.1 Production possibilities frontier for the wet field

Points beneath the PPF are inefficient; those above it are infeasible. The absolute value of the slope of the PPF (the opportunity cost of the good on the horizontal axis) is called the **marginal rate of transformation** (*MRT*). When we need to indicate explicitly what is transformed to what, we follow the convention of listing the good on the horizontal axis first. For example, the absolute value of the slope of the PPF in Figure 7.1 could be called the marginal rate of transformation of rice for wheat and denoted MRT_{rw}.[4] However, we can safely omit reference to the goods when they are clear from context.

The opportunity cost of a bushel of rice grown on the dry field is 2 bu of wheat. The PPF for the dry field is another negatively sloped line; this one has the equation $W = 20 - 2R$ (see Figure 7.2). How should we use each field? That depends on what we want to grow. If we want just wheat, we will, of course, plant both fields with wheat. But if we want a little rice—up to 20 bu—we should grow it on the wet land, where the opportunity cost is just half a bushel of wheat. If we want more than 20 bu of rice, we must of course grow the excess on the dry land. But as soon as we grow 20 or more bushels of rice, the opportunity cost of another bushel jumps to 2 bu of wheat. In other words, the PPF for the two fields together has two linear segments, as shown in Figure 7.3.

EXERCISE 7.1

Suppose that we acquire a third field, on which we can grow up to 15 bu of either rice or wheat. Draw the PPF for a farm consisting of the three fields.

---

[4] The terminology and notation described in this paragraph are widely but not universally used. A few economists use MRT to denote the slope of a PPF (rather than its absolute value) or list the good on the vertical axis before the good on the horizontal axis. A few others refer to a marginal rate of transformation as a "rate of product transformation" (*RPT*). It would be useful to standardize the terminology and notation; in the meantime, *caveat lector!*

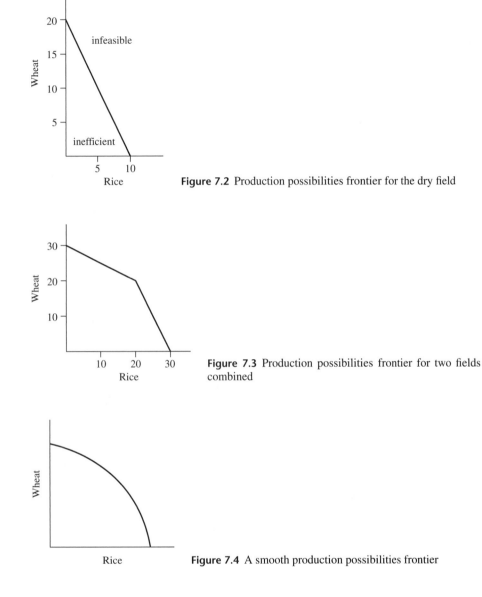

Figure 7.2 Production possibilities frontier for the dry field

Figure 7.3 Production possibilities frontier for two fields combined

Figure 7.4 A smooth production possibilities frontier

A farm with many fields with different opportunity costs for rice would have a PPF with many short linear segments, approximating a smooth concave curve such as shown in Figure 7.4.

Now suppose that the two original fields belong to different farmers. If each is an isolated, self-sufficient subsistence farmer who wants a "balanced diet" (i.e., wants to consume equal quantities of rice and wheat), each might grow $6\frac{2}{3}$ bu of each crop. Their combined output would be $13\frac{1}{3}$ bu of each crop.

If, instead, the farmer with the dry field plants just wheat and the farmer with the wet field plants just rice, the former can grow 20 bu of rice and the later 20 bu of wheat. The combined output has risen by $6\frac{2}{3}$ bu of each crop. If they exchange wheat and rice in any ratio between 1/2 and 2, both will be better off than if they had tried to be self-sufficient.

For example, if they exchange rice and wheat in a 1-1 ratio, they can each end up with 10 bu of each crop, rather than the $6\frac{2}{3}$ bu of each they could grow themselves.

EXERCISE 7.2

In the last two paragraphs we supposed that both farmers wanted their rice consumption to equal their wheat consumption. In this exercise a somewhat more general case is considered. Suppose now that each farmer wants the ratio of his wheat consumption to his rice consumption (both measured in bushels) to be X, a positive number that could be less than, equal to, or greater than one. In other words, each farmer wants his wheat consumption to be X times his rice consumption. First, assume that each individual is a self-sufficient subsistence farmer. Given this assumption, calculate each farmer's consumption of rice and wheat as functions of X. What is their combined output of each crop? Second, assume that the farmers cooperate to produce as much rice and wheat as possible subject to the constraint that wheat production is X times rice production. Given this new assumption, what quantities of wheat and rice are produced? By how much does the farmers' combined output of rice under the second assumption exceed that under the first assumption? By how much does the farmers' combined output of wheat under the second assumption exceed that under the first assumption?

The wet land is said to have a **comparative advantage** in rice production because the opportunity cost of rice is less on wet land than on dry land. Similarly, the dry land has a comparative advantage in wheat. In any model with two goods and two producers, a unit has a comparative advantage in a particular good if it can produce that good at lower opportunity cost than the other producer. In a model with two goods and more than two producers, we could say that producers have a comparative advantage in a good if their opportunity cost for producing that good is less than the good's relative price. For example, if the opportunity cost of rice in terms of wheat is 0.3 in Louisiana, 0.7 in California, 1.3 in Missouri, and 1.7 in Texas, and the relative price of rice is 1.0, we could say that Louisiana and California have a comparative advantage in rice, and Missouri and Texas have a comparative advantage in wheat. If the relative price of rice fell to 0.5, California's comparative advantage would shift from rice to wheat. Similarly, if the relative price of rice rose to 1.5, Missouri's comparative advantage would shift from wheat to rice.[5]

7.1.2 Using Comparative Advantage in Solving Space Allocation Problems

As noted in Chapter 1, Xenophon suggests using a dry room for storing grain, a cool room for storing wine, and a well-lit room for work, but he passes over in silence the more difficult problem of allocating space in a house in which the dry rooms are also cool and well lit whereas the humid rooms are warm and dark. To illustrate how the concept of comparative advantage can help solve such problems, let's consider a two-room house, in which room A is dry, cool, and sunny whereas room B is moist, warm, and dark. Space in these two rooms needs to be apportioned among three tasks: storing grain, storing wine, and drying figs. We could preserve 100 bu of grain, 100 gals of wine, or 100 lbs of figs in room A. Because of spoilage, we can preserve only 80 bu of grain, 60 gals of wine, or 40 lbs of figs in room B.

---

[5] Extending the concept of comparative advantage to models with many goods is not so simple or useful. Perhaps for that reason, comparative advantage is not stressed in texts emphasizing such models. For a more advanced treatment of cases involving many producers and/or many goods, see Jones (1961).

Table 7.2 Opportunity costs of storing three products in two rooms

| | Opportunity Costs in Room | | | | | |
| | A, in Terms of | | | B, in Terms of | | |
Product	Figs	Grain	Wine	Figs	Grain	Wine
Figs	—	1	1	—	2	3/2
Grain	1	—	1	1/2	—	3/4
Wine	1	1	—	2/3	4/3	—

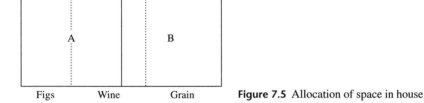

Figs   Wine   Grain   **Figure 7.5** Allocation of space in house

From that information, we can work out the opportunity cost of each product in terms of every other product, in both rooms, as shown in Table 7.2. For example, the opportunity cost in room B of a pound of figs in terms of bushels of grain is $80/40 = 2$, the number in the table's first row and penultimate column.

The opportunity cost of figs (in terms of either grain or wine) is less in room A than in room B; thus room A has a comparative advantage in figs. The opportunity cost of grain (in terms of either figs or wine) is greater in room A than in room B; thus room B has a comparative advantage in grain. The opportunity cost of wine in terms of figs is lower in room B, but the opportunity cost of wine in terms of grain is lower in room A. (Wine is more sensitive to storage conditions than grain but less sensitive than figs.)

Suppose we need to preserve 50 lbs of figs, 60 bu of grain, and as much wine as possible. Where should we put the products and how much wine can we preserve? Because room A has a comparative advantage in figs, we preserve the figs there, using 50/100, or 0.5 of its space, as shown in Figure 7.5. Because room B has a comparative advantage in grain, we preserve the grain there, using 60/80, or 0.75 of its space. In the remaining space in rooms A and B we can preserve $0.5(100) + 0.25(60)$ or 65 gals of wine. A toast to comparative advnatage!

The problem of allocating space in two rooms for storing three goods can be expressed in terms of linear programming[6] as follows: Let f_a, f_b, g_a, g_b, w_a, and w_b denote the pounds of figs, bushels of grain, and gallons of wine preserved in rooms A and B. Our problem is to maximize $w_a + w_b$, subject to the fig and grain constraints

$$f_a + f_b = 50,$$
$$g_a + g_b = 60,$$

---

[6] This technique was introduced in Chapter 3.

the space constraints

$$\frac{1}{100}f_a + \frac{1}{100}g_a + \frac{1}{100}w_a \leq 1,$$

$$\frac{1}{40}f_b + \frac{1}{80}g_b + \frac{1}{60}w_b \leq 1,$$

and nonnegativity constraints on f_a, f_b, g_a, g_b, w_a, and w_b.

If we had to solve this problem without computer assistance, we would want to use substitution to eliminate some variables and geometry to help identify feasible and optimal values for the remaining variables. The problem is solved in this manner in the appendix to this chapter.

A quicker solution can be obtained with computer assistance. For example, to solve the problem in MuPAD, we would type the following:

```
linopt::maximize([{fa+fb=50, ga+gb=60, fa+ga+wa<=100,
    fb/40 + gb/80 + wb/60 <= 1, fa>=0, fb>=0, ga>=0, gb>=0,
    wa>=0, wb>=0}, wa+wb])
```

MuPAD responds with the optimal values of the variables and the maximum of the objective function:

```
[OPTIMAL, {fb = 0, ga = 0, wb = 15, fa = 50, gb = 60, wa = 50}, 65]
```

These are the answers we obtained by reasoning in terms of comparative advantage and geometry. Of course, MuPAD can solve allocation problems with more variables than we could handle unassisted.

7.2 Revenue Maximization

A PPF presents a producer with a menu of output choices. To maximize revenue subject to the PPF, a producer selects a point on the frontier that is worth, at market prices, as much or more as any other feasible point. To visualize how this is done, we couple a PPF with an **isorevenue line**, defined as a set of points in output space that all yield the same revenue.[7] If the possible outputs are rice and wheat, with prices p_r and p_w and quantities q_r and q_w, the isorevenue line for revenue level c is the set (q_r, q_w), such that $p_r q_r + p_w q_w = c$. The line's intercepts on the q_r and q_w axes are c/p_r and c/p_w, as shown in Figure 7.6. Its slope is $-p_r/p_w$. Output combinations on the line are worth more, at market prices, than those below it but less than those above it.

An output combination represented by a point at which the PPF is crossed by an isorevenue line cannot maximize revenue. For example, consider point A in Figure 7.7. It generates no more revenue than point B, which lies under the PPF. Moving from B to C, we increase output of both goods and thereby increase revenue above the level attained at A or B.

An output combination that maximizes revenue must be located where an isorevenue line touches the PPF without crossing it. If this point lies where the PPF runs into the horizontal axis, $MRT \leq p_r/p_w$, as in the left panel of Figure 7.8. If this point lies where the PPF runs into the vertical axis, $MRT \geq p_r/p_w$. These points are corner solutions to the revenue maximization problem.

---

[7] An isorevenue line is sometimes called a trade line.

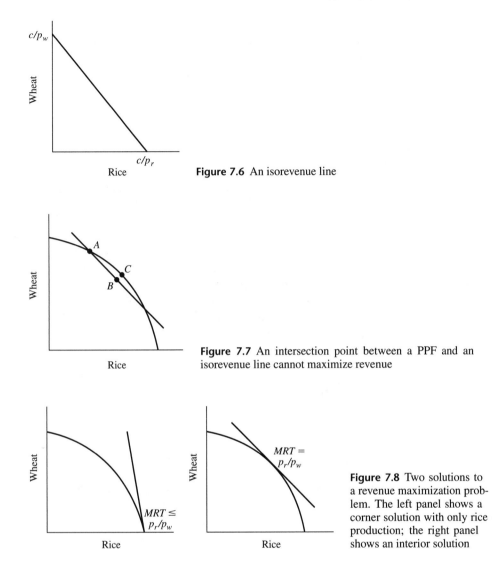

Figure 7.6 An isorevenue line

Figure 7.7 An intersection point between a PPF and an isorevenue line cannot maximize revenue

Figure 7.8 Two solutions to a revenue maximization problem. The left panel shows a corner solution with only rice production; the right panel shows an interior solution

A corner solution is particularly likely if the PPF is linear. For example, recall the dry and wet fields introduced in Subsection 7.1.1. If the relative price of rice p_r/p_w is less than 1/2, revenue would be maximized on both the dry and the wet fields by producing just wheat. If $1/2 < p_r/p_w < 2$, revenue maximization requires producing wheat on the dry field but rice on the wet field. Finally, if $p_r/p_w > 2$, revenue would be maximized on both fields by producing rice.

If the point where the PPF and an isorevenue line touch without crossing is located in the interior of the first quadrant, it is called an interior solution. At such a solution, the PPF could be either smooth or kinked. If the PPF is smooth at an interior solution, $MRT = p_r/p_w$, as in the right panel of Figure 7.8. This implies that two producers facing the same value for p_r/p_w and producing both goods will have the same MRT.

When two producers making the same pair of goods have smooth PPFs and hence well-defined MRTs, equality of their MRTs is a necessary condition for efficiency. To see why, imagine a situation in which two farmers are each growing both rice and wheat but with different MRTs. In this case, if the farmer with the higher MRT_{rw} reduced output of rice by one unit, using the released resources to increase wheat production, and the farmer with the lower MRT_{rw} reduced wheat production just enough to increase rice production by one unit, the net result would be unchanged rice production and increased wheat production. Clearly the initial situation, with different MRTs for different farmers, was not efficient.

EXERCISE 7.3

Suppose the PPF consists of output combinations satisfying the equation $q_w = \sqrt{200 - q_r^2}$. The MRT for this PPF is q_r/q_w. (If you know calculus, verify the MRT by differentiating q_w with respect to q_r along the PPF.) Suppose the relative price of rice is $p_r/p_w = 1$. Calculate the output combination that maximizes revenue subject to the PPF.

To illustrate an interior solution at a kink in a PPF, we can reconsider the farm with two fields, one dry and one wet, illustrated in Figure 7.3. At the kink where the two line segments meet, the PPF has no well-defined slope or MRT. The MRT to the left of the kink is that on the wet field, and the MRT to the right of the kink is that on the dry field. Denoting these as MRT^w and MRT^d, we can characterize an interior solution at the kink by the following chain of inequalities: $MRT^w < p_r/p_w < MRT^d$.

EXERCISE 7.4

The task of maximizing revenue on the farm whose PPF is shown in Figure 7.3 can be formulated as a linear programming problem as follows: Maximize $p_w W + p_r R$ subject to

$$W + .5R \le 30$$
$$W + 2R \le 60.$$

The first inequality is the basis for the upper-left segment of the PPF. Similarly, the second inequality is the basis for the lower-right segment of the PPF. Solve this linear programming problem for the case in which $p_r = p_w = \$4$. How much revenue can the farm generate?

7.3   International Trade

If a country can produce a good at lower opportunity cost (i.e., at lower cost in terms of forgone production of other goods) than the marginal producer, it is said to have a comparative advantage in that good. Notice that the definition is couched in terms of opportunity cost, not resources consumed. Thus, in a two-good model, even a country with backward, wasteful technologies in both industries must have a comparative advantage in one industry.

The idea of comparative advantage as a basis for gains from international trade was first introduced by Ricardo (Figure 7.9) in the early nineteenth century. At the time Britain had high tariffs on imported food, under the so-called corn laws. Arguing for the abolition of these tariffs, Ricardo (1963 [1817], p. 71) offered the following example of gains from trade due to comparative advantage. Suppose England imports wine from Portugal, paying for it by exporting cloth. Suppose, for simplicity, that wine and cloth are each produced

Figure 7.9 David Ricardo. (The image comes from and is used with the permission of The Warren J. Samuels Portrait Collection at Duke University.)

Table 7.3 Labor requirements for cloth and wine in England and Portugal

Country	Labor requirements (person-years)	
	Cloth	Wine
England	100	120
Portugal	90	80

by labor alone. Let the amounts of labor required for the two goods in the two countries be as shown in Table 7.3. According to Ricardo's assumptions, Portugal can produce both wine and cloth with less labor than England.[8] Ricardo assumed, realistically, that although cloth and wine could move between countries, workers could not; immigration controls and language barriers prevented English workers from moving to Portugal. In this case, the differences in labor productivity could persist, shaping the pattern of trade.

Ricardo argued that England could obtain its wine more cheaply by importing it than by producing it at home. His reasoning was as follows: If England imports the wine and transportation costs are negligible, it pays with cloth that takes 100 person-years to produce. If, in contrast, England produced the wine at home, 120 person-years would be required. Thus England saves 20 person-years by importing the wine.

Similarly, Portugal is better off importing cloth than producing it at home. The reason? Provided that transportation costs are negligible, the cloth Portugal imports is paid for by

[8] Economists traditionally say that in this example Portugal has an "absolute advantage" in both goods. More generally, a country that can produce a good from a smaller quantity of resources than its potential trade partner is said to have an absolute advantage in that good. In this usage, "absolute" is a technical term having none of the positive connotations it carries in ordinary speech. It would be a mistake to suppose that absolute advantage is more important than comparative advantage in determining optimal trade patterns.

wine that took 80 person-years to produce. If Portugal produced the cloth domestically, 90 person-years would be needed. Thus Portugal saves 10 person-years by importing cloth. Evidently, this pattern of trade is mutually advantageous.

The opportunity cost of producing the cloth in England is $100/120 = 5/6$ of the wine. The opportunity cost of producing the cloth in Portugal is $90/80 = 9/8$ of the wine. Hence, Ricardo said, England had a comparative advantage relative to Portugal in cloth despite England's lower labor productivity. Portugal has a comparative advantage relative to England in wine. Generally, both countries gain when each exports the good in which it has a comparative advantage.[9]

A country, like a farm, can maximize its income by producing at a point on its PPF that is touched but not crossed by an isorevenue line. The slope of a country's isorevenue line is determined by relative prices on the world market. At an interior solution to a country's revenue maximization problem, the world market relative price of the good on the horizontal axis equals the country's MRT.

The determinants of comparative advantage can be classified under two broad headings: natural and acquired. Natural endowments include land, broadly construed, and labor in its raw, uneducated form. The United States, for example, is well endowed with fertile land in a temperate climate and as a result has a comparative advantage in crops like wheat and soy beans. Saudi Arabia is well endowed with oil and thus has a comparative advantage in petroleum and petroleum products. India is abundant in unskilled labor and so exports labor-intensive manufactures.

Acquired endowments include physical and human capital. Physical capital is acquired by investment in equipment and structures. Such investments by Japan have given it a comparative advantage in capital-intensive manufactures. Human capital is acquired by investment in education and work experience. A large population of engineers and scientists gives the United States a comparative advantage in several high-technology industries, including aircraft, medicines, and organic chemicals.[10]

7.4   Summary

1. A production possibilities frontier (PPF) shows the maximum feasible output of one good consistent with producing a specified quantity of another good. The absolute value of the slope of a PPF (the opportunity cost of the good on the horizontal axis) is the marginal rate of transformation (MRT).

2. Gains from trade are particularly large when producers specialize in the goods in which they have a comparative advantage, that is, those they can produce at lower opportunity cost than other producers.

---

[9] Notice that a country has a comparative advantage *relative to* a specified trade partner. It is quite possible that England might have a comparative advantage relative to Portugal in cloth but a comparative advantage relative to Iceland in wine. Similarly, Portugal might have a comparative advantage relative to England in wine but a comparative advantage relative to France in cloth. To determine a country's comparative advantage relative to the rest of the world, domestic relative costs can be compared to world market relative prices, as in Subsection 7.1.1.

[10] Foundations for modern discussions of trade were laid by Ohlin (1935). Following World War II, interest in the determinants of international comparative advantage grew in parallel with the volume of international trade. Recent works on this subject include Leamer (1984) and Burkett (2000).

3. To maximize revenue subject to a PPF, a producer chooses an output combination at a point where an isorevenue line touches the PPF without crossing it. If all producers of two products face the same relative price and maximize revenue, then all will have the same marginal rate of transformation, a necessary condition for efficiency.

4. International trade, no less than domestic trade, can yield welfare gains. In free international trade, a country's exports and imports reflect its comparative advantage as shaped by its natural and acquired endowments.

7.5   Solutions to Exercises

7.1. The PPF has three linear segments, as shown in Figure 7.10.

7.2. When each farmer is self-sufficient, the farmer with the wet field solves the following pair of equations: $W = 10 - 0.5R$ and $W = XR$. Thus the farmer with the wet field produces and consumes $R = 10/(X + 0.5)$ and $W = 10X/(X + 0.5)$. The farmer with the dry field solves another pair of equations: $W = 20 - 2R$ and $W = XR$. Hence the farmer with the dry field produces and consumes $R = 20/(X + 2)$ and $W = 20X/(X + 2)$. The two farmers' combined output is $R = 10/(X + 0.5) + 20/(X + 2) = 30(X + 1)/[(X + 0.5)(X + 2)]$, $W = 10X/(X + 0.5) + 20X/(X + 2) = 30X(X + 1)/[(X + 0.5)(X + 2)]$.

When the farmers cooperate to maximize rice and wheat production subject to the constraint $W = RX$, there are two cases to consider. If $X \leq 1$, the line $W = RX$ cuts the lower segment of the PPF shown in Figure 7.3. Points in this segment of the PPF satisfy the equation $W = 20 - 2(R - 20)$; that is $W = 60 - 2R$. The pair of equations the farmers solve is thus $W = 60 - 2R$ and $W = RX$. The solution is $R = 60/(2 + X)$, $W = 60X/(2 + X)$. In this case, the farmers' combined output of rice under the second assumption exceeds that under the first assumption by $60/(2 + X) - 30(X + 1)/[(X + 0.5)(X + 2)] = 30X/[(X + 0.5)(X + 2)]$, which is positive for all $0 < X \leq 1$. Because $W = XR$ under both assumptions, the excess of wheat production under the second assumption over that under the first assumption is obviously $30X^2/[(X + 0.5)(X + 2)]$ and thus positive.

If $X \geq 1$, the line $W = RX$ cuts the upper segment of the PPF shown in Figure 7.3. Points in this segment of the PPF satisfy the equation $R = 30 - 0.5W$. The pair of

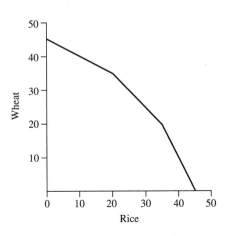

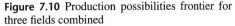
Figure 7.10 Production possibilities frontier for three fields combined

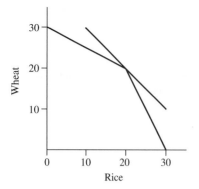

Figure 7.11 An interior solution to a revenue maximization problem

equations solved by the farmers in this case is $R = 30 - 0.5W$ and $W = RX$. The solution in this case is $R = 30/(X + 0.5)$, $W = 30X/(X + 0.5)$. The farmers' combined output of rice under the second assumption exceeds that under the first assumption by $30/(X + 0.5) - 30(X + 1)/[(X + 0.5)(X + 2)] = 30/[(X + 0.5)(X + 2)]$, which is positive for all $1 < X \leq \infty$. Because $W = XR$, the excess of wheat production under the second assumption over that under the first assumption is $30X/[(X + 0.5)(X + 2)]$, which is also positive.

7.3. We can look for an interior solution by equating the MRT and the relative price of rice. If the resulting quantities are both positive, we have found an interior solution. If one is negative, we should look for a corner solution. In our case, looking for an interior solution involves solving the equations $q_r/q_w = 1$ and $q_w = \sqrt{200 - q_r^2}$. The first implies that $q_r = q_w$. Substituting q_r for q_w in the equation of the PPF, we get $q_r = \sqrt{200 - q_r^2}$. Squaring both sides, we get $q_r^2 = 200 - q_r^2$, which implies that $q_r = 10$. Substituting 10 for q_r in the equation of the PPF, we get $q_w = 10$. Thus the revenue-maximizing combination of outputs is (10, 10).

7.4. The relative price of rice is $p_r/p_w = 4/4 = 1$. Thus the slope of an isorevenue line is -1. An isorevenue line with this slope drawn through the kink in the PPF will lie above the PPF at all other points, as shown in Figure 7.11. Thus the kink is an interior solution to the revenue maximization problem. Its coordinates are (20, 20). Thus revenue is maximized by producing 20 bu of each rice and 20 bu of wheat. The maximum revenue the farm can generate is $20 \cdot 4 + 20 \cdot 4 = \$160$.

7.6 Problems

1. Suppose that land in Maine and Rhode Island can be used to grow either potatoes or sod (turf). The production possibilities are shown in the following table, where quantities are in tons.

	Maine	Rhode Island
Maximum output of potatoes	300	100
Maximum output of sod	300	300

   a. Draw the production possibility curves for Maine and Rhode Island separately.

b. If each state devotes half its land to potatoes and half to sod, how much of each crop is produced in total?

c. What is the opportunity cost of potatoes in each state?

d. Which state has a comparative advantage in potatoes? Sod?

e. Draw the production possibility curve for Maine and Rhode Island together.

f. If the two states together produce 200 tons of potatoes, how many tons of sod can they produce? Comparing your answer to that in part b, find the gains from exploiting comparative advantage.

2. Abe, Ben, and Carl can each make wine and cheese. Their output per day is indicated in the following table:

	Abe	Ben	Carl
Maximum kilograms of cheese	2	3	5
Maximum liters of wine	5	3	2

a. Draw a production possibilities curve for each brother.

b. What is the opportunity cost of cheese made by each brother?

c. Abe, Ben, and Carl found ABC Foods Inc. Draw their firm's production possibility curve.

d. If the firm makes 6 kg of cheese a day, how should each brother spend his time?

3. Recalling Xenophon's problem of allocating rooms to alternative uses, consider a house with just two rooms. Room A is cool, dry, and sunny and thus ideal for storing wine or grain or drying raisins. Room B is warm, humid, and dark and thus inferior to A in all uses. In room A we can preserve 20 lbs of raisins, 30 bu of grain, or 40 gals of wine. In room B, because of spoilage, we can preserve only 10 lbs of raisins, 10 bu of grain, or 10 gals of wine.

a. Complete the following table, showing the opportunity costs of each product in terms of every other product in both rooms. (You can leave the bank the entries for the opportunity cost of a good in terms of itself.)

	Opportunity Costs in Room					
	A, in Terms of			B, in Terms of		
Product	Raisins	Grain	Wine	Raisins	Grain	Wine
Raisins	—	3/2		—		
Grain		—			—	
Wine			—			—

b. Which room has a comparative advantage in raisins? Which room has a comparative advantage in wine?

c. Suppose you must preserve 8 lbs of raisins, 8 bu of grain, and as much wine as possible. Where would you preserve the raisins and grain? How much wine could you preserve?

d. Suppose you must preserve 12 lbs of raisins, 9 bu of grain, and as much wine as possible. Where would you preserve the raisins and grain? How much wine could you preserve?

7.7   Appendix: A Linear Programming Solution to a Space Allocation Problem

As a first step in solving the problem formulated in Subsection 7.1.2, we can eliminate all variables except f_a and f_b as follows: From the fig, grain, and nonnegativity constraints, we see that

$$f_a \leq 50, \tag{7.1}$$

$$g_a \leq 60. \tag{7.2}$$

From the space constraint on room A and the nonnegativity constraint on w_a, we see that

$$g_a \leq 100 - f_a. \tag{7.3}$$

From the space coc nstraint on room B and the nonnegativity constraint on w_b, we find that

$$g_b \leq 80 - 2f_b.$$

Using the fig and grain constraints, we can replace in the last inequality f_b by $50 - f_a$ and g_b by $60 - g_a$, getting

$$g_a \geq 80 - 2f_a. \tag{7.4}$$

Considering inequalities 7.1, 7.2, 7.3, and 7.4, we see that feasible choices are limited to the shaded region in Figure 7.12.

One of the five corners of this region must maximize $w_a + w_b$. To see which, we use the space constraints to write

$$w_a \leq 100 - f_a - g_a, \tag{7.5}$$

$$w_b \leq 60 - 1.5f_b - .75g_b. \tag{7.6}$$

Summing the last two lines, we get

$$w_a + w_b \leq 160 - f_a - 1.5f_b - g_a - .75g_b.$$

Substituting out f_b and g_b, we get

$$w_a + w_b \leq 40 + .5f_a - .25g_a. \tag{7.7}$$

Thus to maximize the quantity of wine stored, we want to make f_a as large as possible and g_a as small as possible. Considering the fig constraint and the nonnegativity constraints,

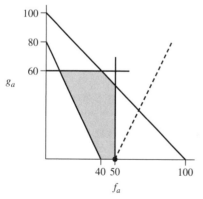

Figure 7.12 Geometry of the linear programming approach to the space allocation problem

we set $f_a = 50$ and $g_a = 0$. Substituting those values into inequalities 7.5 and 7.7 and letting w_a and w_b be as large as possible consistent with these inequalities, we get $w_a = 50$, $w_a + w_b = 65$, and thus $w_b = 15$, the same results as we obtained by reasoning in terms of comparative advantage. The set $\{(f_a, f_b)$ such that $65 = 40 + .5f_a - .25g_a, g_a \geq 0\}$ is plotted as a dashed line in Figure 7.12. This line makes contact with the feasible set only at $(50, 0)$. Points to the left of the line yield less wine. Points to the right would yield more wine but are infeasible. Thus the point $(50, 0)$ yields more wine than any other feasible point. In other words, we have found the unique solution to the problem.

8

▓▓▓▓ Allocation of Factors in Competitive Markets

▓8.1▓ Introduction to General Equilibrium

Until now we have studied one market at a time. Now we are ready to consider formally the interconnection among markets. The study of one market at a time is called **partial equilibrium analysis**. The study of several markets as an interconnected system is called **general equilibrium analysis**. Its pioneers were Léon Walras (1834–1910) and his protege Vilfredo Pareto (1848–1923). General equilibrium analysis of factor markets is introduced in this chapter; general equilibrium analysis of markets for final goods is deferred until Chapter 10.

▓8.2▓ General Equilibrium in Factor Markets

Consider a society with fixed quantities of the factors of production. Suppose there are two factors of production, labor (L) and capital (K), allocated to two competitive industries, say, clothing (C) and food (F). To be concrete, suppose that the economy is endowed with 200 units of capital and 100 units of labor. Initially, let us say, 150 units of capital and 25 units of labor are allocated to the clothing industry, with the rest allocated to the food industry. We can depict the initial allocation of factors to industries in a box diagram named after one of its early users, Francis Ysidro Edgeworth (1845–1926; Figure 8.1). Let us put capital on the horizontal axis and labor on the vertical, as in Figure 8.2. We shall measure the capital and labor used in the clothing industry from the southwest corner and the factors used in the food industry from the northeast corner.

Suppose the industries have isoquants that are smooth and convex to their origins. One isoquant for each industry is drawn through the initial allocation point in Figure 8.3. The lens-shaped region enclosed by the pair of isoquants consists of allocations that enable each industry to produce more than it could with its initial endowment.

All profit-maximizing firms adjust their factor proportions so that their $MRS = r/w$. Because firms in both industries face the same factor-price ratio, they will all have the same MRS.[1] Recalling that MRS is the absolute value of the slope of an isoquant, we infer that

---

[1] In this paragraph, I have implicitly assumed that MRS (a) is a continuous function of factor proportions and (b) equals r/w for some positive quantities of capital and labor. If assumption (a) is false, isoquants could be kinked as those we examined when considering the linear-programming approach to diet problems. At a kink, the slope of the isoquant is not well defined. The coordinates of the kink represent a cost-minimizing combination of inputs if along the isoquant $MRS \geq r/w$ to the left of the kink and $MRS \leq r/w$ to the right of it. If assumption (b) is false, the cost minimization problem has a corner solution, in which the firm uses no capital or no labor. If the firm uses no capital, $MRS \leq r/w$. If the firm uses no labor, $MRS \geq r/w$.

Figure 8.1 Francis Ysidro Edgeworth (The photograph is used with the permission of the Econometric Society.)

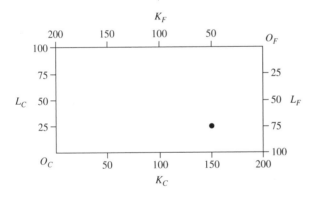

Figure 8.2 Edgeworth box, showing initial allocation

the isoquants of the two industries are tangent to one another at an equilibrium point in the interior of the Edgeworth box, as in Figure 8.4.

At allocation points where isoquants touch without crossing, there are no further possibilities for reallocating factors to increase output in both industries. Thus each industry is producing as much as possible, given the other's output. Such allocations are said to be **technically efficient, Pareto efficient**, or **Pareto optimal**. The set of Pareto optimal allocations is called the **Pareto set**.[2] As seen in Figure 8.5, the Pareto set[3] of allocations of capital and labor is $\{(K_C, L_C)$ such that $MRS_c = MRS_f\}$.

---

[2] Some authors refer to the Pareto set as the contract curve. However, the latter term is reserved by other authors for a *segment* of the Pareto set lying between specified isoquants for the two industries (Mas-Colell et al. 1995).

[3] Credit for first constructing such a figure may belong to Abba P. Lerner (Niehans 1990). A nice example appears in one of his 1933 papers, reprinted in Lerner (1953).

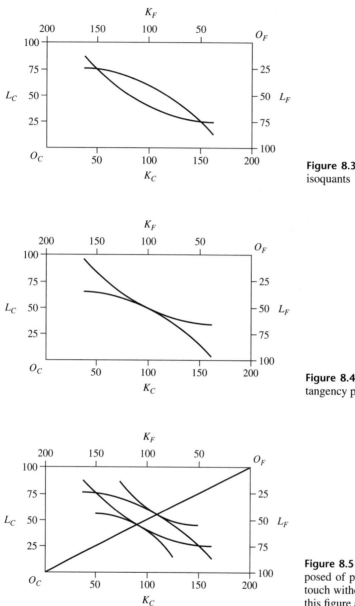

Figure 8.3 Edgeworth box with isoquants

Figure 8.4 Edgeworth box with tangency point

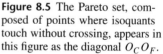

Figure 8.5 The Pareto set, composed of points where isoquants touch without crossing, appears in this figure as the diagonal $O_C O_F$.

EXERCISE 8.1

Consider an economy with 20 units of capital and 10 units of labor to be allocated between the clothing and food industries. Suppose that the marginal rates of substitution in the clothing and food industries are $MRS_c = \frac{L_c}{2K_c}$ and $MRS_f = \frac{L_f}{K_f}$. Derive an equation satisfied by points in the Pareto set, expressing L_c as a function of K_c. Sketch the Pareto set.

The Pareto set has both a positive and a normative interpretation. In positive terms, it is the set of equilibrium allocations that could be reached through trade. Hence, points in the

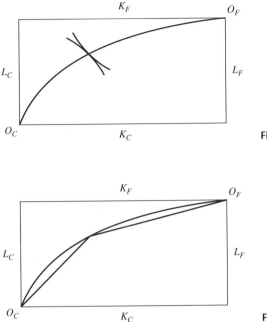

K_F O_F

L_C L_F

O_C K_C

Figure 8.6 A concave Pareto set

K_F O_F

L_C L_F

O_C K_C

Figure 8.7 Slopes of rays are L/K ratios

Pareto set are sometimes said to represent competitive equilibria. In normative terms, the Pareto set is the class of allocations that cannot be changed without reducing the output of at least one industry.

Because the Pareto set represents both equilibrium allocations and Pareto optimal allocations, we can say that all competitive equilibria are Pareto optimal and all Pareto optimal allocations are competitive equilibria. This result is the analytical foundation for many economists' conviction that free markets and efficient production go hand in hand. Whether the optimality of resource allocation carries over to more realistic models of market economies is an interesting question that is addressed in several longer or more advanced texts—for example, Nicholson (1995) and Mas-Colell et al. (1995).

The shape of a Pareto set indicates how factor proportions differ between industries. Take, for example, a concave[4] Pareto set, illustrated in Figure 8.6. To explore the implications of its shape, let us draw rays from each origin to an allocation in the Pareto set, as in Figure 8.7. The slope of the ray from O_C is the labor-capital ratio in the clothing industry. The slope of the ray from O_F is the labor-capital ratio in the food industry. We see that the slope of the first ray is greater than that of the second, meaning that the clothing industry has a greater labor-capital ratio. We say that the clothing industry is more labor-intensive or, equivalently, that it is less capital-intensive.

The Edgeworth production box is a useful tool for studying the effect of a shift in demand in product markets on factor markets. Suppose demand shifts from clothing to food. To accommodate the shift in demand, productive factors must be shifted from clothing to food production. We represent this reallocation by moving away from O_F toward O_C along the Pareto set. Note that as we move the allocation point, the slope of a ray from O_C to the allocation point increases, as in Figure 8.8, meaning that the labor-capital ratio rises in

---

[4] Recall that a curve is called concave if its chords lie below its arcs.

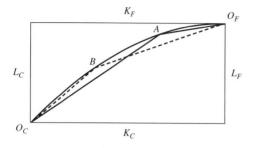

Figure 8.8 Expansion of food industry from A to B raises L/K ratios in both industries

clothing manufacture. The same is true in food production. This rise in labor intensity is necessary to avoid idling labor as the more labor-intensive sector (clothing) contracts.

Individual businesses are, of course, interested in maximizing profits, not maintaining full employment of productive factors. What, then, motivates them to increase their labor-capital ratio? As the labor-intensive clothing industry contracts and the capital-intensive food industry expands, if factor prices remain constant, excess demand for capital and excess supply of labor result. Excess demand for capital and excess supply of labor drive up the cost of capital relative to the cost of labor. In response to this change in relative factor prices, firms in both industries increase their labor-capital ratio. This is an instance of a more general proposition: *Expansion of an industry that uses a factor intensively raises the relative price of that factor and makes all industries try to substitute now cheaper factors.*

A shift in demand in product markets affects not only the ratio of factor prices but also real factor prices—that is, factor prices divided by commodity prices. To examine these effects in a simple context, let us focus on two industries—say, clothing and food—each assumed to use just capital and labor and to exhibit constant returns to scale. Given these assumptions, we can build on two ideas developed in Chapter 6. First, under constant returns to scale, an industry's marginal products depend solely on its labor-capital ratio. Second, competitive firms hire capital and labor in amounts such that each factor's marginal product equals its real price. Hence, changes in labor-capital ratios imply changes in real factor prices.

To apply these ideas to an economy producing just clothing and food, we can use the following notation. Let p_c and p_f denote the prices of clothing and food, and MPK_c, MPK_f, MPL_c, and MPL_f denote the marginal products of capital and labor in the clothing and food industries. In this notation, we can describe competitive factor markets by the following equations:

$$
\begin{aligned}
MPK_c &= r/p_c, \\
MPK_f &= r/p_f, \\
MPL_c &= w/p_c, \\
MPL_f &= w/p_f.
\end{aligned}
\tag{8.1}
$$

If the labor-capital ratio rises in both industries (because of, say, an expansion of the capital-intensive industry and a contraction of the labor-intensive industry), MPK_c and MPK_f rise while MPL_c and MPL_f fall. Given Equations 8.1, we can infer that r rises relative to both product prices, whereas w falls relative to both product prices. In other words, capital owners become unambiguously better off, and workers become unambiguously worse off.

8.3 Applications

General equilibrium theory has found many applications in public finance, international trade, and other fields.

8.3.1 Public Finance

Public finance is a branch of economics that focuses on taxes and government expenditure. Economists have been interested in tax incidence (distribution of the burden of taxes) at least since the time of Adam Smith. Early analysis of tax incidence was conducted in a *partial* equilibrium framework. Starting with the pioneering work of Arnold Harberger (1959, 1962), economists have increasingly relied on *general* equilibrium theory for analysis of tax incidence. Problem 2 in the problem set for this chapter provides one illustration.

As another illustration of the application of general equilibrium theory to public finance, suppose a state adopts a sales tax on luxuries but none on necessities.[5] This sounds like a populist measure to "soak the rich." But is it? The tax causes the luxury goods industry to contract and the industry that produces necessities to expand. Luxuries are often produced in small batches, using labor-intensive methods, in contrast to necessities, which tend to be produced on a larger scale, using more capital-intensive methods. Thus the contracting luxury goods industry is likely to be more labor-intensive than the expanding industry that produces necessities. As long as wages and the cost of capital are unchanged, the result is unemployment and excess demand for capital goods. Unemployment tends to lower wages, and excess demand for capital goods tends to raise the cost of capital. Thus the tax on luxuries may tend to redistribute income from workers to capital owners. Furthermore, the fall in the relative price of labor induces a rise in labor-capital ratios. If the industries exhibit constant returns to scale, the result is a fall in the real wage in both industries—that is, a fall in workers' purchasing power. That may not be what the advocates of the tax had intended.

8.3.2 International Trade

Pioneering applications of general equilibrium theory to international trade were made by James E. Meade (1952), Bertil Ohlin (1935), and Paul Samuelson (1948), all of whom subsequently won Nobel prizes.[6] Some interesting features of their work can be illustrated in a simple model with two countries, two goods, and two factors. Let us assume that the industries producing the two goods, say, clothing and food, exhibit constant returns to scale.[7] For simplicity, let us further assume that the two countries have the same tastes and technology (isoquants) and that factors—say, capital and labor—are mobile between industries but not between countries.

---

[5] As economists use these terms, a "luxury" is a good whose income elasticity of demand exceeds 1; a "necessity" is a good whose income elasticity of demand is less than 1. In other words, a 1% increase in income raises demand for luxuries by more than 1% and raises demand for necessities by less than 1%.

[6] Samuelson won the prize in 1970; Ohlin and Meade shared the prize in 1977.

[7] An alert student may ask whether this assumption is consistent with the U-shaped cost curves that we have taken to be typical of firms in perfectly competitive industries. The answer is that in equilibrium each firm operates at the lowest point on its average cost curve. In a small interval around this point, returns to scale are approximately constant for the firm. Furthermore, if we double the amount of the two factors—capital and labor—available to the industry, we can double the number of firms in the industry and thereby double the industry's output. Thus the industry may exhibit constant returns to scale even though the firms composing it exhibit returns to scale that first increase and then decrease.

Import Tariffs and Income Distribution

The **Stolper-Samuelson theorem** asserts that if an import tariff raises the relative price of the imported good, the price of the factor used intensively in its production will rise relative to both commodity prices, whereas the price of the other factor will fall relative to both commodity prices. Given the assumptions used in this chapter, we can prove the Stolper-Samuelson theorem as follows: The rise in the relative price of the imported good provides an incentive to expand the industry that produces import-competing goods. The import-competing industry bids capital and labor away from the export-oriented industry. At the old factor prices, there will be excess demand for the factor used intensively in the import-competing industry and excess supply of the other factor. Hence the price of the factor used intensively by the import-competing industry rises and that used intensively in the export industry falls. Managers in both industries respond by substituting some of the now cheaper factor for some of the now more expensive factor. When the adjustment process is completed, the marginal products of the factor used intensively in the import-competing industry will have risen and those of the other factor will have fallen. Hence the price of the factor used intensively in the import-competing industry must have risen relative to the prices of both goods, while the price of the other factor must have fallen relative to the prices of both goods.

As an example of Stolper-Samuelson theorem, let us suppose that the United States produces both clothing and food, imports some clothing, and exports some food. Suppose further that clothing is labor-intensive and food is capital-intensive. Imposing a tariff on clothing imports would allow the U.S. clothing industry to expand and force the food industry to contract. Given the initial factor prices, the immediate result would be excess demand for labor and excess supply of capital goods. To restore factor market equilibrium, the wage would have to rise relative to the cost of capital. Managers would then substitute capital for labor. The fall in the labor-capital ratios would raise the MPL and lower the MPK in both industries. Recalling Equations 8.1, we can conclude that the wage rate would rise relative to the prices of both goods, whereas the cost of capital would fall relative to the prices of both goods.

Removing the tariff on clothing imports would reverse the process. Fear of such a reversal may have underlain the opposition that U.S. unions expressed to the North American Free Trade Agreement (NAFTA), which was expected to increase clothing imports and food exports, and their continued opposition to giving the president "fast track" authority to negotiate similar trade deals with other countries.

Trade Policy Implications

We have seen that removing tariffs between two countries tends to increase consumption possibilities in both countries and redistribute income within each country. In capital-abundant countries such as the United States, tariff reductions are likely to decrease wages for unskilled workers and increase the return to (physical and human) capital, whereas the opposite is true in less capital-abundant countries.

Most economists support free trade in the interest of achieving an efficient international division of labor. However, recognizing that income distribution under free trade could be very unequal, many economists recommend combining free trade with supplemental measures to curb inequality. Among these supplemental measures might be retraining programs to assist workers displaced from import-competing industries in acquiring the skills needed to get good jobs in other industries.

8.3.3 Other Fields

General equilibrium analysis is having a growing impact in several fields. It has been used to study economic growth (Johnson 1971); market imperfections, technical progress, and money (Baldry 1980); the effects of financial disturbances, energy price increases, and foreign investment (Scarf and Shoven 1984); trends in skilled and unskilled labor (Burkett 1989); and the effects of price controls (Shoven and Whalley 1992). For complex applications, the two-sector models illustrated in this chapter are now commonly supplemented with numerical methods described by Shoven and Whalley.

EXERCISE 8.2

Consider an economy that uses capital and labor to produce guns and butter. Suppose gun production is more capital-intensive than butter production. If an increase in military expenditure causes the gun industry to expand and the butter industry to contract, what would the consequences be for the wage and the rental cost of capital?

8.4   Summary

1. If producers are free to trade inputs, they will swap inputs until MRS is the same for all producers. These allocations form the Pareto set for factor allocations. These allocations are technically efficient in the sense that any reallocation of inputs would reduce output of at least one good.
2. General equilibrium analysis has important and sometimes surprising applications in public finance, international trade, and other fields. Graphical analysis of the two-sector model can be supplemented with numerical techniques capable of handling larger dimensions.

8.5   Solutions to Exercises

8.1. At all points in the Pareto set, $MRS_c = MRS_f$, and thus $\frac{L_c}{2K_c} = \frac{L_f}{K_f}$. Substituting $20 - K_c$ for K_f and $10 - L_c$ for L_f, we get $\frac{L_c}{2K_c} = \frac{10-L_c}{20-K_c}$, and thus $L_c = \frac{20K_c}{20+K_c}$. The Pareto set is the curve in Figure 8.9.

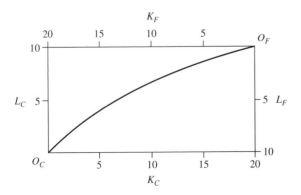

Figure 8.9 The Pareto set for this exercise is slightly concave

8.2. At the initial equilibrium wage and rental cost of capital, the expansion of gun production and reduction of butter production would create excess demand for capital and excess supply of labor. To restore equilibrium, the rental cost of capital would have to rise and the wage would have to fall.

8.6   Problems

1. Consider a country that has 20 units of capital and 10 units of labor and two industries: food and clothing. Draw an Edgeworth box with the origin for the clothing industry in the lower left corner and capital measured on the horizontal axis. Suppose the isoquants for the clothing industry have slope $-L_c/K_c$ and those for the food industry have slope $-L_f/K_f$, where L and K denote labor and capital and the subscripts c and f indicate clothing and food industries. Describe the Pareto set by an equation giving L_c as a function of K_c. Sketch the Pareto set in the Edgeworth box diagram.

2. Suppose the corporate and noncorporate sectors each employ two factors: capital and labor. Assume the corporate sector is more capital-intensive. Draw an Edgeworth box diagram showing the Pareto set. Suppose the corporate income tax causes the corporate sector to contract and the noncorporate sector to expand. At the old wage-rental ratio, is labor in excess demand or supply? How about capital? What happens to the equilibrium wage-rental ratio? What happens to the labor-capital ratio in each industry?

3. Suppose that the production functions in the clothing and food industries are $Q_c = K_c^{1/4}L_c^{3/4}$ and $Q_f = K_f^{1/2}L_f^{1/2}$. The corresponding marginal products are $MPK_c = \frac{1}{4}(L_c/K_c)^{3/4}$, $MPL_c = \frac{3}{4}(K_c/L_c)^{1/4}$, $MPK_f = \frac{1}{2}(L_f/K_f)^{1/2}$, and $MPL_f = \frac{1}{2}(K_f/L_f)^{1/2}$. (If you know calculus, check these results by partial differentiation of the production functions.) The corresponding marginal rates of substitution are $MRS_c = \frac{L_c}{3K_c}$ and $MRS_f = \frac{L_f}{K_f}$. (If you know calculus, you can check those results by totally differentiating the production functions, setting the differentials equal to zero, and solving for the derivatives of labor with respect to capital.) Assume that $L_c + L_f = 1$ and $K_c + K_f = 1$.

   a. Find the equation of the Pareto set for the production box diagram.

   b. Suppose that a rise in the relative price of clothing stimulates a flow of resources from food to clothing production. If the shift in resources involves increasing K_c from 0.25 to 0.75, what is the corresponding change in L_c?

   c. Given the shift noted in part b, find the initial and terminal values of r/p_c, r/p_f, w/p_c and w/p_f, where r and w are the rental cost of capital and the wage rate and p_c and p_f are the prices of clothing and food.

   d. What theorem do parts b and c illustrate?

9
Consumer Choice and Demand

9.1 Introduction

In the late nineteenth century, economists developed a theory about households' choices of consumer goods that has strong parallels to the now familiar theory of competitive firms' choices of inputs. Alfred Marshall (1842–1924), who did much to systematize the theory of consumer choice, listed Cournot and Thünen, pioneers of the theory of the firm, as the chief influences on his work.[1] The analogy between households and firms has proved useful, although—as shown in the next chapter—it has its limitations. It is a central feature of influential theories developed by **neoclassical** economists such as Marshall, Edgeworth, Walras, Pareto, Stigler, and Samuelson. Utilizing the analogy allows us to compress the fundamental elements of these theories into a single chapter[2]

9.2 Budget Constraints

Consider a very simple economy in which only two consumer goods are available. An ordered pair of quantities for the two goods, (q_1, q_2), is called a **consumption bundle**. If the prices of the goods are p_1 and p_2, a household that has Y dollars to spend over some period can buy any consumption bundle such that $p_1 q_1 + p_2 q_1 \leq Y$, $q_1 \geq 0$, $q_2 \geq 0$. The set of consumption bundles satisfying those inequalities, $\{(q_1, q_2)$ such that $p_1 q_1 + p_2 q_2 \leq Y$, $q_1 \geq 0$, $q_2 \geq 0\}$, is called the household's **opportunity set**. For a more concise notation, we may replace "such that" by "s.t." The set of consumption bundles defined by replacing the $\leq$ sign by an equality, $\{(q_1, q_2)$ s.t. $p_1 q_1 + p_2 q_2 = Y$, $q_1 \geq 0$, $q_2 \geq 0\}$, is called the **budget constraint**.[3] If the prices are independent of the quantities consumed, the opportunity set

---

[1] "Under the guidance of Cournot, and in a less degree of Thünen, I was led to attach great importance to the fact that . . . the demand for a thing is a continuous function, of which the 'marginal' increment is, in stable equilibrium, balanced against the corresponding increment of its cost" (Marshall; quoted in Blaug 1996, p. 301). In another context, Marshall states that he learned his analytical technique from Cournot and his economics from Thünen (Niehans 1990, p. 175).

[2] Fuller expositions of these theories and many examples of their application can be found in several texts. Good microeconomics texts with extentsive treatment of consumer choice and demand, listed in order from elementary to advanced, include Stiglitz (1997), Frank (2003), Nicholson (1995), and Mas-Colell et al. (1995). A classic monograph in this field is Deaton and Muellbauer (1980).

[3] The concepts of consumption bundle, opportunity set, and budget constraint are easily generalized to apply to choice among n goods, where n is any integer greater than 1. In this general case, the consumption bundle is an $n-$tuple $(q_1, q_2, \ldots, q_n)$. The opportunity set is $\{(q_1, \ldots, q_n)$ s.t. $\sum_{i=1}^{n} p_i q_i \leq Y$, $q_1 \geq 0, \ldots, q_n \geq 0\}$, where $\sum_{i=1}^{n} p_i q_i$ is shorthand for $p_1 q_1 + p_2 q_2 + \ldots + p_n q_n$. To obtain a definition of the budget constraint, we would just replace the $\leq$ sign by an equality.

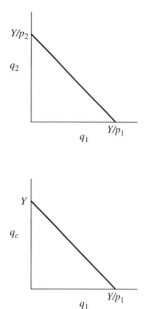

Figure 9.1 For a household with Y dollars to spend on two goods with prices p_1 and p_2, the opportunity set is a right triangle and the budget constraint is its hypotenuse

Figure 9.2 A budget constraint for a specific good and a composite good

is a right triangle and the budget constraint is its hypotenuse, as shown in Figure 9.1. The absolute value of the slope of the hypotenuse is p_1/p_2, the relative price of the good on the horizontal axis.

The budget constraint of a household is formally similar to an isocost line for a firm. However the two concepts are used somewhat differently. In elementary treatments of consumer choice, we usually take household income and the associated budget constraint as *given*, whereas in the theory of the firm we have assumed that a firm *chooses* its inputs and the associated isocost line to maximize profits.

EXERCISE 9.1

Consider a consumer who has $100 to spend on goods 1 and 2. Good 1 costs $8 per unit and good 2 costs $4 per unit. Letting q_1 and q_2 denote quantities of the two goods, write an expression for the consumer's opportunity set. Characterize the consumer's budget constraint by writing q_2 as a function of q_1.

Our simple two-dimensional model can be applied in a world of many goods if we think of a consumer as choosing between one specific good and a collection of other goods. This collection is usually called either a **composite good** or **Marshallian money**, in honor of Marshall, who introduced the concept.

To illustrate the analytic uses of the concept of a composite good, let us consider a consumer who can spend up to Y \$/week. If the consumer buys q_1 units of good 1 at price p_1, then he or she has remaining $Y - p_1q_1$. Suppose the consumer spends this remainder on a composite good. By appropriate choice of the unit of measurement for the composite good, we make its price equal to $1. Let's denote the quantity purchased of the composite good by q_c. Clearly, $q_c = Y - p_1q_1$. Now we can construct a two-dimensional figure showing the consumer's budget constraint. We plot q_1 on the horizontal axis and q_c on the vertical axis, as in Figure 9.2. If the consumer spends Y entirely on good 1, the consumption bundle is a point on the horizontal axis: $(Y/p_1, 0)$. If the consumer spends nothing on good 1, the consumption bundle is a point on the vertical axis: $(0, Y)$. Because the price of the composite good is \$1, the slope of the budget constraint is simply $-p_1$.

9.3 Consumer Preferences

There are two common approaches to consumer preferences. In the ordinal utility approach, we assume that consumers can rank all possible consumption bundles in preference order, from worst to best. In the cardinal utility approach, we make a stronger (more restrictive) assumption—that people can make statements such as "bundle B is half as good as bundle A," or in more operational terms, "I'm indifferent between getting B for sure and a 50-50 chance to get A." Let's first work through the ordinal utility approach before seeing what cardinal utility has to offer.

9.3.1 Ordinal Utility

The utility of a consumption bundle to an individual is its subjective value to that individual. In the ordinal utility approach, we assume that each consumer can rank all bundles in terms of increasing utility, that is, in order of preference. Such a ranking is called a **preference ordering**. Five assumptions about preference orderings serve to define the ordinal utility approach to consumer preferences. Four of these assumptions can be stated immediately. The fifth must be postponed until we introduce an additional concept.

1. We assume each consumer's preference ordering is **complete** in the sense that he or she can rank not just some but all possible bundles of goods. Thus for every pair of bundles A and B, we suppose that the consumer can reach one of the following judgments.

> "I prefer A to B," denoted $A \succ B$.
> "I prefer B to A," denoted $A \prec B$.
> "I am indifferent between A and B," denoted $A \sim B$.

The completeness assumption is unlikely to be completely accurate for a consumer faced with thousands of different goods. The consumer may be unable to confidently rank unfamiliar bundles. However, in practice the assumption is usually applied to a restricted set of bundles that are well known to their potential consumers.

2. We assume that preferences are **transitive**[4] in the sense that for any three bundles A, B, and C the following three propositions hold:

> If $A \succ B$ and $B \succ C$ then $A \succ C$.
> If $A \sim B$ and $B \sim C$ then $A \sim C$.
> If $A \succ B$ and $B \sim C$ then $A \succ C$.

Why should people have transitive preferences? One possible answer is that intransitivity could be expensive. Indeed, a sharp trader who first identifies a consumer with intransitive preferences might make a quick and easy profit at the consumer's expense. Suppose, for example, that I have A and state the following intransitive preferences: $A \prec B \prec C \prec A$. Noticing my inconsistency, a trader offers me B in exchange for A and a little money. I accept. Then he offers me C in exchange for B and a little money. I accept. Finally, he offers me A in exchange for C and a little money. Accepting this offer, I end up with what

---

[4] Preferences that are complete and transitive constitute what various economists term a *rational preference relationship*, a *weak order*, or a *complete preorder*.

I started with, minus some money.[5] I have fallen for a **money pump**, which is defined as "a sequence of trading opportunities offered to a particular individual such that, if all those opportunities are accepted, the resulting sequence of trades generates an unambiguous gain for the trader who offers the opportunities and an unambiguous loss for the person who accepts them" (Sugden 2004, p. 1029).

One interpretation of the story is that to avoid falling victim to money pumps, I should make sure my preferences are transitive. However, a money pump is a form of arbitrage, and as noted in Chapter 1, opportunities for profitable arbitrage tend to be competed away. If the trader who first notices my inconsistency makes a dime on each trade, another is likely to offer trades with a nine-cent profit margin, and so forth. If I have a choice among many traders and pick the cheapest, my intransitivity may cease to be profitable for the traders and become nearly costless to me (Sugden 2004).

A simpler and arguably stronger justification for transitive preferences is that they are necessary for choice of the best among three or more alternatives. To see why intransitive preferences impede choice, suppose that I again have intransitive preferences such as $A \prec B \prec C \prec A$. If asked to choose the best of the three, I would be unable to comply because each alternative appears inferior to another (Varian 1992).

3. We shall assume that increasing the quantity of any good in a consumption bundle makes the bundle more attractive. In other words, if the quantity of each good in bundle A is greater than or equal to that in B and the inequality is strict for at least one good, then A is preferred to B. This assumption is sometimes called the **nonsatiation** axiom; preferences that satisfy it are said to be **monotone**. For some goods this assumption seems a little too strong. After all, there is a limit to how many potatoes we want to consume per week. However, our consumption of a good usually stops short of satiation. In the neighborhood of most actual consumption bundles, the nonsatiation assumption is likely to be true. When a weaker axiom is needed, we may be willing to assume that more is no worse than less. This weaker assumption is true whenever disposal is free.

4. We shall assume **continuity**, in the sense that a strict preference for one consumption bundle over another is not reversed by an infinitesimally small change in either bundle. This is a plausible assumption for many consumer choices. Consider, for example, a consumer choosing bundles composed of chocolate and marzipan. Let (q_1, q_2) denote a bundle composed of q_1 lbs of chocolate and q_2 lbs of marzipan. Suppose that a consumer prefers $(1\frac{1}{n}, 1)$ to $(0, 2)$ for all $n = 1, 2, 3, \ldots$. In this case, if the consumer's preferences are continuous, he will not reject $(1, 1)$ in favor of $(0, 2)$.

The continuity assumption rules out **lexicographic preferences**, which rank bundles first on one dimension and then on another, as a dictionary orders words by their first letter, then their second letter, and so on. A consumer who has lexicographic preferences and orders bundles primarily according to their first element will prefer a bundle (a_1, a_2) to a bundle (b_1, b_2) if $a_1 > b_1$ or if $a_1 = b_1$ and $a_2 > b_2$. This consumer prefers (b_1, b_2) to (a_1, a_2) if $a_1 < b_1$ or if $a_1 = b_1$ and $a_2 < b_2$. She is indifferent between the bundles only when they are identical—that is, $a_1 = b_1$ and $a_2 = b_2$. To see why lexicographic preferences are not continuous, consider again a consumer who has lexicographic preferences and gives priority to the first good. For this consumer $(1\frac{1}{n}, 1) \succ (1, 2)$ for all $n = 1, 2, 3, \ldots$ but $(1, 1) \prec (1, 2)$. Implausible as they may seem when applied to two candies, lexicographic preferences may have more appeal when the two goods appear qualitatively different from each other. Suppose, for example, the first good is years of life remaining and the second is again marzipan. Some people who would be happy, other things being equal, to accept

---

[5] This story is adapted from Frank (2003).

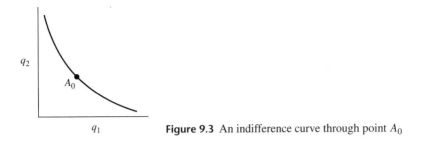

Figure 9.3 An indifference curve through point A_0

an extra pound of marzipan would not knowingly give up any fraction of their life to get it.

These four assumptions (completeness, transitivity, nonsatiation, and continuity) suggest a graphical representation of a consumer's preferences in a two-good model. Consider an arbitrary point A_0 in (q_1, q_2) space. Let's try to construct the set of all points that some consumer values just as highly as A_0—that is, the locus consisting of all bundles A_i such that $A_i \sim A_0$. Let's call this locus A. In standard set theoretic notation, $A = \{A_i \text{ s.t. } A_i \sim A_0\}$. It is easy to establish that A must be a curve with a negative slope. Nonsatiation implies that A_0 is preferable to points to its southwest but inferior to points to its northeast. Thus any bundles just as good as A_0 must lie to its northwest or southeast. The same argument can be repeated for each point in A, establishing that A is a negatively sloped curve, as illustrated in Figure 9.3.

The set A is an example of an **indifference curve**.[6] Generally, an indifference curve is defined as a set of consumption bundles among which a person is indifferent.[7] Note that an indifference curve separates the space of goods into two regions. All points to the right and above of an indifference curve are preferred to any point on it. All points on the curve are preferred to any point below and to the left of the curve.[8]

Indifference curves occupy a position in the theory of households roughly analogous to that of isoquants in the theory of firms. Both show various combinations of inputs (goods for households; factors of production for firms) that yield equivalent outcomes (equal levels of satisfaction for households; equal levels of production for firms). However, the shape of indifference curves is not as easily observed as that of isoquants. Thünen experimentally determined the form of some agricultural production functions—from which what we now call isoquants could be easily derived—in the early 1800s, although that term was not coined

---

[6] By assuming continuity, we have ruled out lexicographic preferences. However, it is worth recalling that a consumer with lexicographic preferences is never indifferent between two distinct consumption bundles. For such a consumer, the set A is a "singleton"—that is, contains just a single element, namely, A_0.

[7] Indifference curves first appeared in Edgeworth's *Mathematical Psychics*, published in 1881 (Blaug 1996; Niehans 1991).

[8] The assumption of nonsatiation and the implied negative slope of indifference curves seem to rule out two types of goods. First, there are goods we dislike. Perhaps we should call these bads rather than goods. The point can be illustrated by an old story about Brighton, an English resort town that had an unpleasant reputation when the story first circulated. According to this story, the winner of a contest received a week's vacation in Brighton and the runner up received two weeks. For people who feel that way about Brighton, less is better. To make such cases consistent with our axiom of nonsatiation, we can simply redefine the good. Instead of considering the obnoxious product a good, we can treat its absence as a good. Thus absence of pollution, freedom not to go to Brighton, and so on can be treated as goods for which we have a nonsatiated demand. Second, there are so-called neutral goods—items that we neither like nor dislike. Such items can simply be ignored for most purposes, thus reducing the dimension of our goods-space.

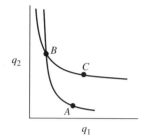

Figure 9.4 Intersecting curves cannot represent the indifference curves of a rational consumer

until the 1930s (Humphrey 1997, pp. 61–63; Niehans 1991, p. 331). In contrast, the form of indifference curves was largely a matter of theoretical discussion prior to recent experiments (discussed starting in Chapter 11).

The completeness assumption implies that every consumption bundle lies on some indifference curve. A set of indifference curves representing a person's preferences is called an **indifference map**.

The transitivity and nonsatiation assumptions imply that no two indifference curves belonging to a single consumer's indifference map can intersect. To prove this proposition, we show that if two indifference curves were to cross, then under our assumptions a logical contradiction would result. Suppose points A and B are on one indifference curve and points B and C are on another intersecting curve, as in Figure 9.4. Let C represent a point that dominates A in the sense that at C we have more of both goods. Then the consumer whose preferences are represented by this indifference map would be indifferent between A and C by transitivity yet prefer C to A by nonsatiation. To avoid such contradictions we must not allow indifference curves to intersect.

If preferences are complete, transitive, monotone, and continuous, they can be represented by a continuous **utility function**—a continuous mapping from the space of goods into the real numbers, $U = U(q_1, \ldots, q_n)$, such that bundle A is preferred to bundle B if and only if the utility function evaluated at A exceeds the utility function evaluated at B.[9] Nonsatiation implies that U is an increasing function of each of its n arguments. For example, if the space of goods is two-dimensional and the indifference curves are rectangular hyperbolas, the preferences could be represented by a utility function $U = q_1 q_2$.

The ordinal utility approach to consumer choice is only concerned about the ranking of alternatives. Hence preferences that can be represented by a utility function $U()$ could equally well be represented by any increasing function of $U()$. For example, preferences represented by $q_1 q_2$ are equally well represented for present purposes by $(q_1 q_2)^{.5}$ or $(q_1 q_2)^{.25}$.

In the context of consumer choice, the **marginal rate of substitution** (MRS) between two goods at a point in goods-space is the rate at which a consumer is willing to substitute one for the other at that point. In the two-dimensional case, the MRS at any point is intimately related to the indifference curve passing through this point. Indeed, the MRS is simply the absolute value of the curve's slope at this point.[10] Because indifference curves are typically nonlinear, when we speak of the slope of an indifference curve at a point we mean the slope

---

[9] For a proof, see Mas-Colell et al. (1995, pp. 47–48).

[10] The expression "marginal rate of substitution" was introduced by Hicks and Allen (1934) in the context of consumer demand. Recall that in the context of production, we defined the marginal rate of substitution as the rate at which one input could be substituted for another while holding output constant—that is, the absolute value of the slope of an isoquant. To distinguish these two concepts, some economists use the term "marginal rate of *technical* substitution" in the context of production.

of a line *tangent* to the curve at that point. When we must explicitly distinguish a *MRS* from its reciprocal, we can use the convention introduced in Chapter 2, listing the good on the horizontal axis first. Thus the absolute value of the slope of the indifference curve in Figure 9.3 could be called the marginal rate of substitution between good 1 and good 2 and denoted by MRS_{12}. Usually, however, the inputs will be clear from context.

The fifth assumption that characterizes the ordinal utility approach to consumer preferences is that the *MRS* between good i and good j diminishes as the amount of good i consumed rises and as the amount of good j falls. The economic intuition behind this assumption is that consumers value variety in the sense that if they have relatively little of one good they are reluctant to part with it in exchange for another good with which they are better provided. In the two-dimensional case, a diminishing *MRS* is represented by indifference curves that are convex. Accordingly, the supposition of a diminishing *MRS* is often called the **convexity assumption** of consumer theory.

9.3.2 Cardinal Utility

The cardinal utility approach to consumer choice is concerned with not only rankings of alternatives but also quantitative comparisons of the utilities associated with these alternatives. For purposes of making such quantitative comparisons, it is important to know certain features of the utility function that were inessential to the ordinal approach. For example, suppose we were considering increasing the quantity of two consumer goods from (0,0) to (1,1) and then from (1,1) to (2,2). If we wanted to quantitatively compare the gains in utility from the first increment to those from the second increment, we would not be content to be told that utility is some function of the form $(q_1q_2)^\alpha$, where α is an unspecified positive number. We would need to determine the value of α. Depending on whether α is less than, equal to, or greater than $1/2$, the utility gains from the second increment will be less than, equal to, or greater than the gains from the second increment.

If all the parameters of a utility function are known, we can calculate the utility associated with any consumption bundle. When there are no more than two goods, the utility function can be displayed graphically. If we put the two goods on the horizontal axes, utility will be on the vertical axis. A typical utility surface looks like a side of a hill. On this hill, a contour of constant elevation represents points of equal utility. If we project such a contour down on the goods plane, we get an indifference curve. Indeed, an indifference map is much like a topographic map of the utility hill. On topographic maps, the contour lines represent elevation. On an indifference map derived from a utility function, the indifference curves represent utility levels.[11] For example, if the only variables affecting utility (U) were quantities of clothing (C) and food (F) and if the utility function had the Cobb-Douglas form familiar from the theory of production, we could write $U = mC^\alpha F^\beta$. The case where $m = 1, \alpha = .4$, and $\beta = .3$ is illustrated in Figure 9.5

Utility functions play a role in the theory of consumption somewhat analogous to that played by production functions in the theory of the firm. Note, however, that while consumers are presumed to maximize utility, firms are supposed to maximize profit rather than production.

[11] Given that a utility function can be used to derive an indifference map, it is natural to ask whether the process can be reversed. That is, can we use an indifference map to derive a utility function? The answer in general is no. The typical indifference map is not labeled with cardinal utility levels. An unlabeled indifference map corresponds to an infinite number of utility functions. If $U()$ is a utility function and V is any increasing function, then $U()$ and $V(U())$ give rise to the same unlabeled indifference map.

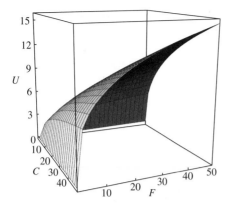

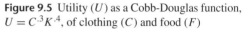

Figure 9.5 Utility (U) as a Cobb-Douglas function, $U = C^{.3}K^{.4}$, of clothing (C) and food (F)

9.4   Constrained Optimization

Given a budget constraint and an indifference map or utility function, we can easily determine the best feasible consumption bundle.

Because of nonsatiation, the best feasible bundle falls on the budget constraint rather
than in the interior of the opportunity set. The problem is thus reduced to finding the best
point on the budget constraint. In the two-dimensional case, the solution is easy to see. If
any segment of an indifference curve passes under the budget constraint, no point on this
curve can represent the best feasible bundle. (A point at the intersection of an indifference
curve and the budget constraint is no better than the points on the same indifference curve
in the interior of the opportunity set. Nonsatiation implies that these points are inferior to
some on the budget constraint.) Hence the best feasible bundle must be at a point where an
indifference curve touches but does not cross the budget constraint.

9.4.1 Interior Solutions

If this point occurs where positive quantities of both goods are consumed, it is called an
interior solution because it lies in the interior of the first quadrant. If the budget constraint
and the indifference curve both have well-defined slopes at an interior solution, that is, if
neither is kinked at this point—the slopes are equal. In this case, if the budget constraint is
linear, $MRS = p_1/p_2$ at the interior solution, as in Figure 9.6.

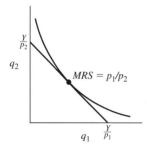

Figure 9.6 An interior solution to the consumer's maximization
problem

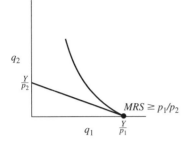

Figure 9.7 A corner solution to the consumer's maximization problem

9.4.2 Corner Solutions

If there is no interior solution, the point where an indifference curve touches the budget constraint without crossing it must be found in one of the corners of the budget triangle. Such a point is called a corner solution. If this point occurs on the horizontal axis, the *MRS* at this point will be greater than or equal to the absolute value of the slope of the budget constraint, as in Figure 9.7. If the corner solution occurs on the vertical axis, the *MRS* at this point will be less than or equal to the absolute value of the slope of the budget constraint.

EXERCISE 9.2

Consider a consumer whose budget constraint satisfies the equation $q_2 = 40 - 2q_1$. Suppose the consumer's indifference curves have the slope $-q_2/q_1$. Calculate the optimal consumption bundle for the consumer.

9.5 Demand

9.5.1 Individual Demand

In Chapter 1 we noted that demand curves usually slope down. Now that we have examined the theory of rational consumer choice, we are in a position to see why. A demand curve can be derived from a preference ordering by varying the price of the good and hence the slope of the budget constraint. The derivation may be done graphically by putting the good of interest on the horizontal axis and the composite good on the vertical axis, drawing an indifference map, and then drawing a family of budget constraints corresponding to various prices for the good on the horizontal axis. For example, in Figure 9.8, the price of good 1 increases from p_1' to p_1'', shifting the horizontal intercept of the budget constraint from Y/p_1' to Y/p_1'', moving the optimal consumption bundle from b' to b'', and reducing the quantity demanded of the first good from q_1' to q_2''. The demand curve is sketched in the lower panel by connecting the points (q_1', p_1') and (q_1'', p_1'').

It is sometimes useful to decompose the change in the quantity demanded into two components called income and substitution effects. The **substitution effect** of a price change is the alteration in the quantity demanded due to the change in relative prices, with real income or utility held constant. To show the substitution effect graphically, we compare the tangency point between the original budget constraint and an indifference curve with the point where this indifference curve has a slope matching that of the new budget constraint. The substitution effect of a price increase is always negative in the sense that

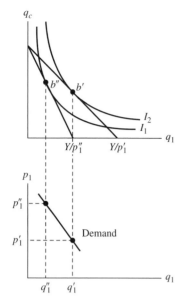

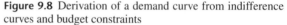

Figure 9.8 Derivation of a demand curve from indifference curves and budget constraints

a price increase reduces the quantity demanded when utility is held constant. That occurs because indifference curves are convex.

The **income effect** of a price increase is the change in the quantity demanded due to the loss of real income or utility. To graphically depict the income effect, we compare the point where the original indifference curve slopes downward just as steeply as the new budget constraint with the tangency point between the new budget constraint and an indifference curve. An increase in the price of a normal good has a negative income effect. An increase in the price of an inferior good has a positive income effect.

All normal goods have negatively sloped demand curves because for normal goods a price increase has a negative income effect, as well as a negative substitution effect. In the case of inferior goods, a price increase has a positive income effect, which partially offsets the negative substitution effect. The substitution effect almost always predominates, making nearly all demand curves negatively sloped.[12] However, in principle, the positive income effect could outweigh the negative substitution effect, resulting in a positively sloped demand curve. Those very rare inferior goods that have positively sloped demand curves are called **Giffen goods**, after a British economist and statistician, Robert Giffen.[13]

9.5.2 Market Demand

Summing the quantities demanded at a particular price by all the buyers in a market gives us the total quantity demanded in this market. The relationship between price and the total quantity demanded is called market demand. If there are n buyers whose individual demands

---

[12] The "law of demand" is an ambiguous expression that refers sometimes to the *analytical* statement that (given fixed preferences) all *normal* goods have negatively sloped demand curves and sometimes to the *empirical* statement that nearly all *observed* demand curves are negatively sloped.

[13] We have derived a demand curve under the assumption that changes in prices alter consumers' budget constraints but not their preferences. If changes in prices alter preferences, even some normal goods may have positively sloped demand curves. For example, cutting the price of a good could conceivably reduce its snob appeal so much as to reduce the quantity demanded (Leibenstein 1950).

Table 9.1 Individual and market demand

| Price | Quantities Demanded | | |
	q^1	q^2	$Q = q^1 + q^2$
$5	0	1	1
4	0	2	2
3	0	3	3
2	1	4	5
1	2	5	7

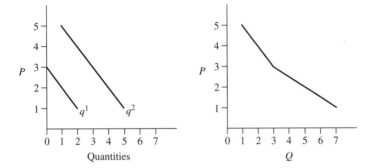

Figure 9.9 Individual demand curves (left panel) and market demand curve (right panel)

are $q^1(p), q^2(p), \ldots, q^n(p)$, the market demand is

$$Q(p) = \sum_{i=1}^{n} q^i(p).$$

As a simple numerical example, suppose there are two buyers in the market, demanding quantities as shown in the first two columns of Table 9.1 and the left panel of Figure 9.9. The total quantity demanded is shown in the last column of the table. The market demand curve is shown in the right panel of the figure.

9.5.3 Elasticity of Demand

As noted in Chapter 5, an elasticity is a ratio of percentage changes. An elasticity of demand is a percentage change in a quantity demanded divided by a percentage change in some variable influencing this quantity. Based on the variable whose percentage change appears in the denominator, we distinguish three kinds of elasticity of demand. An **own-price elasticity of demand** is a ratio of a percentage change in the quantity of good demanded to a percentage change in the price of this good. Own-price elasticity of demand will be important in understanding how a firm with monopoly power prices its product and how buyers and sellers share the burden of a sales tax. A **cross-price elasticity of demand** is a ratio of a percentage change in the quantity of a good demanded to a percentage change in the price of some other good. For example, a percentage change in the quantity of coats demanded divided by the percentage change in the price of coats is the own-price elasticity for coats, and a percentage change in the quantity of coats demanded divided by the percentage change in the price of sweaters is a cross-price elasticity for coats. An

income elasticity of demand is a percentage change in a quantity demanded divided by a percentage change in the demanders' income. Own-price elasticities of demand relate to movements along a demand curve. Cross-price and income elasticities pertain to shifts of demand curves.

EXERCISE 9.3

What are the signs of the cross-price elasticities of demand for complements and substitutes? (Refer, if need be, to the definitions of complements and substitutes in Chapter 1 and the Glossary.)

EXERCISE 9.4

What are the signs of the income elasticities of demand for normal and inferior goods? (If necessary, review the definitions of these goods in Chapter 1 and the Glossary.)

As in the case of elasticities of supply, elasticities of demand can be measured for either discrete or infinitesimal changes. As noted in Chapter 5, arc and point elasticities are calculated in the discrete and infinitesimal cases, respectively. An arc own-price elasticity of demand for a price decrease from P_A to P_B, as shown in the left panel of Figure 9.10, can be calculated by using the following formula:

$$\epsilon^d_{AB} = \frac{(Q_B - Q_A)/Q_A}{(P_B - P_A)/P_A}.$$

This elasticity can also be expressed in terms of first differences, as follows:

$$\epsilon^d_{AB} = \frac{\Delta Q/Q_A}{\Delta P/P_A} = \frac{\Delta Q}{\Delta P} \cdot \frac{P_A}{Q_A} = (P_A/Q_A)/(\Delta P/\Delta Q).$$

In the last expression, the slope of the demand curve appears in the denominator. Hence the steeper the demand curve, the closer the elasticity is to zero.

A point own-price elasticity of demand at point A in the right panel of Figure 9.10 can be calculated as follows:

$$\epsilon^d_A = (P_A/Q_A)/(\text{slope of demand curve at } A).$$

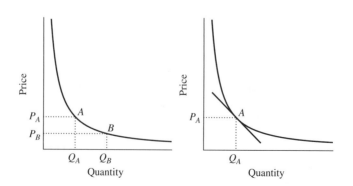

Figure 9.10 Two ways of measuring the own-price elasticity of demand. The left panel illustrates an arc elasticity for a cut in price from P_A to P_B. The right panel illustrates a point elasticity.

Notice that the slope again appears in the denominator. Thus if two demand curves pass through point A, the steeper demand curve is less price-elastic.

When two points on a demand curve are close together, the arc elasticity they define is usually about the same as the point elasticity anywhere between them. When what we have to say pertains equally to arc and point elasticity, we simply say elasticity and write ϵ^d.

For a negatively sloped demand curve, the own-price elasticity is negative. When the negative sign can be understood from context, it is sometimes omitted. Thus if an economist says that the own-price elasticity of demand for bananas is 1.5, he or she almost surely means that it is -1.5.

The jargon for price elasticities of demand is as follows:

If $|\epsilon^d| < 1$, demand is said to inelastic.
If $|\epsilon^d| = 1$, demand is said to be unit elastic.
If $|\epsilon^d| > 1$, demand is said to be elastic.

In the case of a horizontal demand curve, own-price elasticity is not defined; nonetheless such a curve is sometimes said to be "perfectly elastic."

In equilibrium, at the intersection of a demand and a supply curve at a point A, the price-quantity ratio P_A/Q_A that appears in the definitions of the elasticities is the same for demand and supply. This means that the elasticities of demand and supply differ only because of the difference in slopes of the demand and supply curves. That's a handy fact; it enables us to tell at a glance whether demand or supply is more elastic at the equilibrium point. The steeper curve is less elastic.

A good may be classified as a **necessity** or a **luxury**, depending on whether its income elasticity of demand is less than or greater than one.

9.6 Consumer Surplus

When rational, self-interested, and well-informed individuals buy goods, they benefit from their purchases; otherwise they would not have made the purchases. We sometimes want to measure *how much* consumers benefit from purchases of a particular good.

Consumer surplus is the name economists give to a monetary measure of consumers' gains from their purchases. The most commonly used such measure is that devised by Jules Dupuit (1804–1866), a French engineer and economist (Ekelund and Hébert 1999). This measure was subsequently popularized by Marshall and is now generally known as "Marshallian consumer surplus."[14] Dupuit and Marshall regarded buyers' gains from a transaction as the difference between the most they were willing to pay and what they actually paid. Their idea is best represented graphically. If consumers choose to buy Q units of a good when its price is P, as in Figure 9.11, then the Marshallian consumer surplus is the area beneath the demand curve to the left of Q and above P.

As a measure of the benefits a consumer gets from access to a market for a particular good, Marshallian consumer surplus is exact if the income elasticity of demand for the good is zero; otherwise it is an approximation. In most cases, this approximation is close enough for practical purposes (Willig 1976). For cases in which the approximation is not satisfactory, alternative measures have been suggested by Hausman (1981) and Vartia (1983).

---

[14] This usage conforms to Stephen Stigler's (1980, p. 147) law of eponymy: "No scientific discovery is named after its original discoverer."

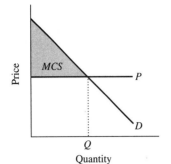

Figure 9.11 Marshallian consumer surplus is the shaded area beneath the demand curve and above the price line

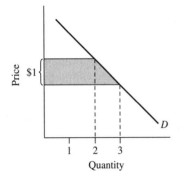

Figure 9.12 Loss of Marshallian consumer surplus

EXERCISE 9.5

Consider a market in which the demand function is $P = 10 - .2Q$, where P and Q represent price and quantity, and the equilibrium price is 4. Calculate the Marshallian consumer surplus.

A typical use of consumer surplus concepts is in figuring out how consumers would be affected by public policies. For example, suppose Congress is considering a bill to impose a tariff on coffee imports. The tariff is expected to raise the retail price of coffee by $1 a pound. Consider a consumer who has been buying 3 lbs of coffee a month. Suppose the slope of this consumer's demand curve is -1, meaning that this consumer would respond to a $1/lb price increase by cutting consumption by a pound per month. What is the loss of consumer surplus? It is represented by a rectangle plus a triangle, as in Figure 9.12. The area of the rectangle is ($1/lb)(2 lbs) = $2. The area of the triangle is ($1/lb)(1 lb)/2 = $0.50. Hence the loss of consumer surplus for this individual is $2.50 per month. To make an economically rational decision about the tariff, we should aggregate the loss of consumer surplus of all U.S. coffee drinkers and weigh this cost against any benefits the tariff might have.

9.7 Summary

1. A consumer's budget constraint consists of all the consumption bundles that cost precisely as much as he or she can spend. If prices do not depend on quantities, then the budget constraint can be represented as an equation that is linear in quantities.

2. A consumer's preferences can be represented by a utility function or by a preference map. Under our usual assumptions, preference orderings are characterized by completeness, transitivity, nonsatiation, continuity, and a diminishing MRS.

3. The best feasible bundle is a point where an indifference curve touches but does not cross the budget constraint. If the best possible bundle contains positive quantities of all goods, it is called an interior solution. Otherwise, it is called a corner solution. If the budget constraint and indifference curve are smooth and the solution is an interior one, then it is found where the MRS is equal to the absolute value of the slope of the budget constraint.

4. An individual demand curve can be derived from a budget constraint and an indifference map. The demand curve shows how the price of a good influences the quantity demanded. It almost always is negatively sloped. Market demand for a good is the relationship between the good's price and the sum of the quantities of the good demanded by all buyers. A market demand curve is a horizontal sum of individual demand curves.

5. An own-price elasticity of demand is a percentage change in a good's quantity demanded divided by the percentage change in the same good's price. A cross-price elasticity is a percentage change in a good's quantity demanded divided by the percentage change in the price of a different good. An income elasticity of demand is a percentage change in a good's quantity demanded divided by the percentage change in the income of the demanders.

6. Marshallian consumer surplus is a commonly used measure of the benefits consumers derive from having an opportunity to buy a good at a particular market price. It is simply the area beneath a demand curve to the left of the quantity consumed and above the price paid.

9.8   Solutions to Exercises

9.1. The opportunity set is $\{(q_1, q_2)$ s.t. $8q_1 + 4q_2 \leq 100, \quad q_1 \geq 0, \quad q_2 \geq 0\}$. The equation characterizing the budget constraint is $q_2 = 25 - 2q_1$.

9.2. At a tangency between the budget constraint and an indifference curve, the slopes are equal, implying that $q_2 = 2q_1$. Substituting $2q_1$ for q_2 in the equation for the budget constraint, we get $2q_1 = 40 - 2q_1$. Solving that equation, we get $q_1 = 10$. Substituting 10 for q_1 in either the budget constraint equation or the tangency equation, we get $q_2 = 20$. Thus the optimal consumption bundle is (10, 20).

9.3. The cross-price elasticities of demand are negative for complements and positive for substitutes.

9.4. The income elasticity of demand for a normal good is positive. The income elasticity of demand for an inferior good is negative.

9.5. The Marshallian consumer surplus is the area below the demand curve and above the price line, which in this exercise is that of a triangle with height $10 - 4 = 6$ and base $Q = 5(10 - P) = 30$. The area of this triangle is $6 \times 30/2 = 90$.

9.9   Problems

1. Ann has \$4 to spend on goods 1 and 2. Good 1 costs \$2 per unit and good 2 costs \$1 per unit. Letting q_1 and q_2 denote quantities of goods 1 and 2, write Ann's budget

constraint, that is, an equation showing how q_2 depends on q_1. What is the slope of the budget constraint?

2. Suppose Ann has indifference curves whose slopes are $-q_2/q_1$ when q_1 is plotted on the horizontal axis and q_2 on the vertical axis. Given the budget constraint derived in Problem 1, find the best feasible bundle of goods for Ann. Is this bundle a corner solution or an interior solution?

3. Bob has $10 to spend on goods 1 and 2. The price of good 1 is $1 and the price of good 2 is $2. What is Bob's budget constraint? What is the slope of the constraint? What are the horizontal and vertical intercepts?

4. Suppose Bob has indifference curves whose slopes are $-(q_2 + 6)/q_1$. Given the budget constraint derived in Problem 3, what is the best feasible bundle of goods for Bob? Is this bundle a corner solution or an interior solution?

5. Carol has $30,000 to spend on all goods. Good 1 costs $3 per unit. Denoting the quantity of good 1 purchased as q_1 and expenditure on all other goods as q_c, write Carol's budget constraint, that is, an equation showing how q_c depends on q_1. What is the slope of the budget constraint?

6. Suppose Carol has indifference curves with slope $-q_c/(q_1 + 9900)$. Given the budget constraint derived in Problem 5, what is the optimal consumption bundle for Carol? Is this bundle a corner or an interior solution?

7. Dick has 10 lbs of cornmeal and 4 lbs of oatmeal. Jane has 2 lbs of cornmeal and 8 lbs of oatmeal. The utility function for each individual is $x \cdot y$, where x is cornmeal consumed and y is oatmeal consumed.
   a. What are Dick's and Jane's utility levels if they consume the cornmeal and oatmeal they have on hand?
   b. The utility function implies that the marginal rate of substitution (MRS) is y/x. What is the numerical value of each individual's MRS if he or she consumes what is on hand?
   c. If Dick gives Jane 3 lbs of cornmeal in exchange for an equal amount of oatmeal, what are Dick and Jane's new utility levels?
   d. After the exchange, what are Dick's and Jane's new marginal rates of substitution?
   e. Sketch indifference curve diagrams for Dick and Jane and use the diagrams to show how the exchange made both individuals better off.

8. Elmer has $200 to spend on goods 1 and 2. His marginal rate of substitution is $MRS = q_2/q_1$, where q_1 and q_2 are the quantities of goods 1 and 2 that he consumes. Denoting the prices of goods 1 and 2 as p_1 and p_2, derive Elmer's demand curve for good 1—that is, an equation showing how q_1 depends on p_1. Sketch the demand curve in a diagram with q_1 and p_1 on the horizontal and vertical axes.

9. Frank's demand for food is $q_f = y/(2p_f)$, where y is Frank's income and p is the price of food. Along his demand curve, $\frac{\Delta q_f}{\Delta p_f} = -y/(2p_f^2)$.
   a. What is Frank's own-price elasticity of demand for food?
   b. When q_f is plotted against y, the slope of the curve is $\frac{\Delta q_f}{\Delta y} = \frac{1}{2p_f}$. What is Frank's income elasticity of demand for food?
   c. Any income Frank has left over after buying food is spent on clothing. What is Frank's cross-price elasticity of demand for food?

10. Greg's demand for food is $q_f = y^{.75} p_f^{-.50} p_c^{-.25}$, where y is income, p_f is the price of food, and p_c is the price of clothing. The slopes of q_f with respect to the right-side variables are $\frac{\Delta q_f}{\Delta y} = .75 \frac{q_f}{y}$, $\frac{\Delta q_f}{\Delta p_f} = -.5 \frac{q_f}{p_f}$, and $\frac{\Delta q_f}{\Delta p_c} = -.25 \frac{q_f}{p_c}$. Calculate
    a. the income elasticity of demand for food,
    b. the own-price elasticity of demand for food,
    c. the cross-price elasticity of demand for food.

11. Mickey's demand for cheese (lb/week) is $q_c = 10 - 2p_c$.
    a. Express his Marshallian consumer surplus as a quadratic function of p_c.
    b. Assuming that $p_c = \$3/\text{lb}$, calculate the numerical value of his Marshallian consumer surplus.

12. Suppose that demand for a good by individual i ($i = 1, \ldots, n$) is $q_i = \sqrt{y_i}/p$, where y_i is the income of individual i and p is the price of the good.
    a. Write an equation showing how market demand depends on incomes and the price.
    b. Let $p = 1, n = 4$, and $\sum_{i=1}^{n} y_i = 400$. What would market demand be if income were equally distributed among the four individuals?
    c. Continue to assume that $p = 1$, $n = 4$, and $\sum_{i=1}^{n} y_i = 400$. What would market demand be if all income went to one of the four individuals?

10

▓▓▓ Exchange and Product Assortment

General equilibrium theory was introduced and applied to factor markets in Chapter 8. The concept of indifference curves, covered in Chapter 9, enables us to now extend general equilibrium theory to markets for consumer goods. We will do so by first considering the exchange of existing goods between consumers and then analyzing how product assortment is determined in competitive markets.

▓▓▓ 10.1 Exchange

Consider an economy endowed with fixed quantities of several goods. No more of any good can be produced within the period in question. The goods are initially in the hands of several consumers, but not necessarily in the hands of the consumers who most value them. We want to examine how the consumers exchange goods among themselves.

To boil the problem down to essentials, suppose there are just two goods, say Kandinskys[1] and Leonardos.[2] Also for simplicity, suppose there are just two consumers, Carl and Francis. The economy is endowed with 200 Kandinskys and 100 Leonardos. Initially, let us say, Carl is allocated 150 Kandinskys and 25 Leonardos, and Francis is allocated the rest. We can depict the initial endowments in a box diagram analogous to those used in Chapter 8 to represent allocation of factors between industries. Let us put Kandinskys on the horizontal axis and Leonardos on the vertical, as in Figure 10.1, a reproduction of Figure 8.2. We shall measure the number of Kandinskys and Leonardos in Carl's possession (K_C, L_C) from the southwest corner and those in Francis's possession (K_F, L_F) from the northeast corner.

Will Carl and Francis be content with their initial endowments, or will they swap Kandinskys and Leonardos with each other? That, of course, depends on their preferences, which, as usual, can be represented by indifference curves. If the indifference curves are fixed and smooth, as we assumed in Chapter 9, they can play the same role in explaining the allocation of consumer goods that isoquants played in explaining the allocation of factors in Chapter 8. One indifference curve for each consumer is drawn through the initial endowment point in Figure 10.2. The lens-shaped region enclosed by the pair of indifference curves consists of allocations that both consumers prefer to their initial endowment.

If allowed to trade, the consumers will swap Kandinskys and Leonardos until they reach an allocation at which their indifference curves touch without crossing. Here, the possibilities for mutually advantageous exchange have been exhausted. Thus each consumer is as well satisfied as possible, given the other's level of satisfaction. Such allocations are

---

[1] Paintings by Vassily Kandinsky, 1866–1944.
[2] Paintings by Leonardo da Vinci, 1452–1519.

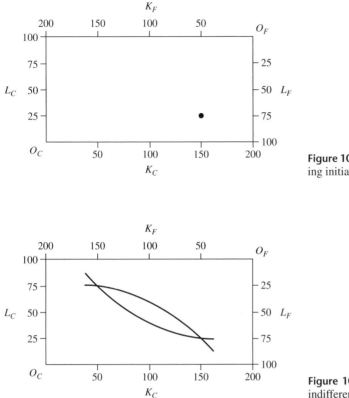

Figure 10.1 Edgeworth box, showing initial allocation

Figure 10.2 Edgeworth box with indifference curves

said to be **Pareto optimal** or **Pareto efficient**. The set of Pareto optimal allocations is called the **Pareto set**.[3]

Consider the two indifference curves tangent at a Pareto optimal allocation in the interior of an Edgeworth box. If the curves have well-defined slopes at the tangency point, these slopes are equal, as are the corresponding marginal rates of substitution. Under these conditions, a Pareto set could be described as a set of allocations at which the marginal rates of substitution are the same for all consumers. As illustrated in Figure 10.3, the Pareto set for exchange between Carl and Francis is $\{(K_C, L_C)$ such that $MRS_C = MRS_F\}$.

As with factors of production, so too with consumer goods—the Pareto set has both a positive and a normative interpretation. In positive terms, it is the set of equilibrium allocations that could be reached through trade. Hence points in the Pareto set are sometimes said to represent competitive equilibria. In normative terms, the Pareto set is the class of allocations that can't be changed without harming at least one party.

Because the Pareto set represents both equilibrium allocations and Pareto optimal allocations, we can say that all competitive equilibria are Pareto optimal and all Pareto optimal allocations are competitive equilibria. This result is part of the analytical foundation for economists' traditional view that free markets and material well-being go hand in hand.

---

[3] Some authors refer to the Pareto set as the contract curve. However, the latter term is reserved by other authors for a *segment* of the Pareto set lying between specified indifference curves for the two consumers (Mas-Colell et al. 1995).

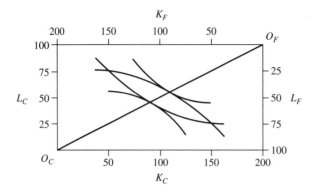

Figure 10.3 The Pareto set, composed of points where indifference curves touch without crossing, appears in this figure as the diagonal $O_C O_F$. (In other cases, the Pareto set might not be straight and might not run through the origins.)

Whether the optimality of resource allocation carries over to more realistic models of market economies is, as we noted in Chapter 8, an interesting question that is addressed in many longer or more advanced texts, for example, Nicholson (1995) and Mas-Colell (1995).

EXERCISE 10.1

Consider a country in which there are 200 Kandinskys and 100 Leonardos, some owned by old collectors and others by young collectors. The MRS of Leonardos for Kandinskys is $(3/2)L_y/K_y$ for young collectors and $(2/3)L_o/K_o$ for old collectors, where K_o, L_o, K_y, and L_y denote Kandinskys and Leonardos owned by old and young collectors. Derive the Pareto set—that is, an equation showing how L_o varies with K_o. Sketch the Pareto set in an Edgeworth box diagram.

10.2 Product Assortment

An economy could achieve Pareto efficiency in allocation of consumer goods and technical efficiency in production of the goods and yet ill serve consumers if it produced an unwanted assortment (mix) of goods. For example, something seems amiss in an economy that produces many more right shoes than left shoes or lots of shoelaces but no shoes.

As an aid to formalizing our intuition that the product mix should match the pattern of consumer demand, we recall remarks in Chapter 7 about production possibilities frontiers. A production possibilities frontier (PPF) is the set of outputs that corresponds to the set of technically efficient input allocations. In other words, a PPF shows the maximum amount of one good that can be produced as a function of output of other goods. If there are just two goods, a production possibilities frontier is easily sketched. Let us put the quantity of clothing (C) on the horizontal axis and the quantity of food (F) on the vertical axis. For each level of clothing production, the PPF indicates the maximal possible level of food production. All feasible combinations of clothing and food production lie on or beneath the frontier. The frontier is simply the Pareto set translated from input to output space.

As I have drawn this frontier in Figure 10.4, it is concave. This shape will usually occur when some resources are relatively well adapted to producing one good and others to producing the other good. (Recall the agricultural example introduced in Chapter 7: Wet land has a comparative advantage in production of rice, whereas dry land has a comparative advantage in the production of wheat. The result was a piecewise linear PPF that was concave downward.) Another possible reason for the concavity of the PPF is decreasing returns to scale.

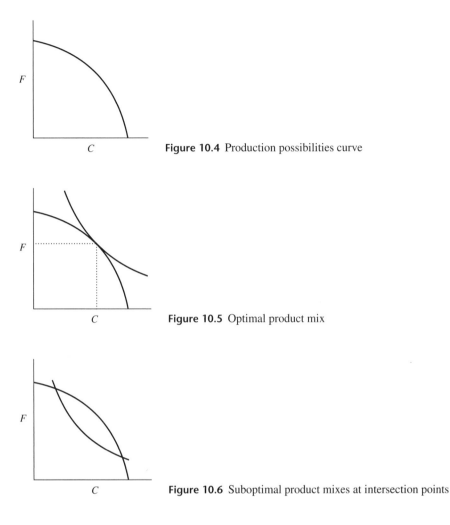

Figure 10.4 Production possibilities curve

Figure 10.5 Optimal product mix

Figure 10.6 Suboptimal product mixes at intersection points

An important proposition in welfare economics is the following:

A point on the PPF represents an optimal product mix if and only if MRS = MRT at that point.

Let us first prove the "if" part of the statement. Consider a point on the PPF where *MRS = MRT*. Recall that *MRS* is just the absolute value of the slope of the indifference curve through this point. The rest of the indifference curve lies above the PPF, provided that the PPF is concave and the indifference curve is convex, as usually assumed. Thus all other feasible points are inferior to the one we are considering. In other words, the point where *MRS = MRT* is indeed optimal (see Figure 10.5).

Now let us prove the "only if" part of the statement. Consider a point on the PPF where *MRS ≠ MRT*. The indifference curve through this point passes through the interior of the set of feasible points. Points in the interior are inferior to points on the frontier to their northeast, according to the axiom of nonsatiation. Thus the point we were considering cannot be optimal (see Figure 10.6).

Finally, we can ask whether a competitive economy tends to select an efficient product mix. An affirmative answer is easily derived from two now familiar facts. First, as seen in Chapter 7, Section 3, perfectly competitive firms adjust their production so that the *MRT* is equal to the ratio of product prices. Thus if we have food on the vertical axis, in equilibrium $MRT = P_C / P_F$. Second, as we saw in Chapter 9, Section 4, consumers adjust their consumption so that the marginal rate of substitution is equal to the ratio of product prices. Thus if *MRS* is the rate at which consumers are willing to exchange food for clothing, we have $MRS = P_C/P_F$. Combining our two facts, we get the important result that

$$MRT = \frac{P_C}{P_F} = MRS.$$

We have now established that a perfectly competitive economy is efficient in product assortment, as well as in production and (when preferences are fixed) exchange.

EXERCISE 10.2

Consider a production possibilities frontier diagram with food on the vertical axis and clothing on the horizontal. Suppose the production possibilities frontier has slope $-X_c/X_f$ and consumers' indifference curves have slope $-4D_f/D_c$, where X and D represent production and consumption and the subscripts c and f indicate the clothing and food industries. What is the equilibrium relative price of clothing?

10.3 Summary

1. If consumers are free to trade, they will swap goods until they exhaust the possibilities for mutually beneficial exchange. Any allocation that consumers choose to maintain, given freedom to trade, is a point in a Pareto set—a point such that no reallocation could make one consumer better off without making another worse off, given their preferences. If preferences are fixed, trade thus makes a consumer as well satisfied as possible, given other consumers' levels of satisfaction. If indifference curves are smooth, in equilibrium the *MRS* is the same for all consumers.
2. If consumers and producers are free to trade with each other, the product mix will adjust so that a representative indifference curve touches the production possibilities curve without crossing it. If the two curves are smooth, the result is that *MRS* = *MRT*. This mix is preferred by a representative consumer to any other feasible bundle of goods.

10.4 Solutions to Exercises

10.1. Equating the marginal rates of substitution for the two groups of collectors, we get

$$MRS_o = MRS_y$$
$$(2/3)L_o/K_o = (3/2)L_y/K_y$$
$$(2/3)L_o/K_o = (3/2)(100 - L_o)/(200 - K_o)$$
$$L_o(200 - K_o) = (9/4)K_o(100 - L_o)$$
$$200L_o - L_oK_o = (900/4)K_o - (9/4)L_oK_o$$
$$200L_o + (5/4)L_oK_o = 225K_o$$
$$L_o(200 + (5/4)K_o) = 225K_o$$
$$L_o = \frac{225K_o}{200 + (5/4)K_o}.$$

The Pareto set is graphed in Figure 10.7.

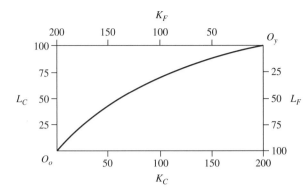

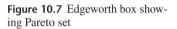
Figure 10.7 Edgeworth box showing Pareto set

10.2. Equating the slopes of the PPF and the indifference curves, we get $X_c/X_f = 4D_f/D_c$. Noting that in a closed economy the quantities produced and consumed must be the same, we substitute X_f for D_f and X_c for D_c, getting

$$X_c/X_f = 4X_f/X_c$$

$$(X_c/X_f)^2 = 4$$

$$X_c/X_f = 2.$$

Recalling that the absolute value of the slope of the PPF is the relative price of clothing, we conclude that the relative price of clothing is 2.

10.5 Problems

1. Consider a country in which there are 200 Kandinskys and 100 Leonardos, some owned by old collectors and others by young collectors. The MRS of Leonardos for Kandinskys is $2L_y/K_y$ for young collectors and $0.5L_o/K_o$ for old collectors, where K_o, L_o, K_y, and L_y denote Kandinskys and Leonardos owned by old and young collectors.
   a. Derive the Pareto set—i.e., an equation showing how L_o varies with K_o.
   b. Suppose that accelerating technological change enriches the young collectors relative to the old ones. As young collectors buy paintings from old collectors, K_o falls from 100 to 40 and L_o from 80 to 50. What is the price of a Kandinsky (relative to a Leonardo) before and after the shift?

2. Consider a production possibilities frontier diagram with food on the vertical axis and clothing on the horizontal. Suppose the production possibilities frontier has slope $-X_c/X_f$ and consumers' indifference curves have slope $-D_f/D_c$, where X and D represent production and consumption and the subscripts c and f indicate the clothing and food industries. What is the equilibrium relative price of clothing?

11

▊▊ Loss Aversion and Reference-dependent Preferences

11.1 Evidence That Assets Can Affect Preferences

In the last two chapters, we assumed—as is traditional in economics—that preferences are independent of current assets. Thus we drew indifference curves without reference to endowments. However, this view of preferences has been challenged by **behavioral economists**—researchers who, sharply distinguishing between normative and positive theories, seek positive theories of economic behavior with "realistic psychological foundations" (Camerer and Loewenstein 2004, p. 3). In the view of many behavioral economists, a growing body of experimental evidence suggests that under some circumstances (1) preferences are influenced by assets and (2) indifference curves are sharply bent in the vicinity of the current endowment.

People often exhibit a **status quo bias**, that is, a tendency to retain rather than exchange the goods initially in one's possession. For example, a survey at Harvard found that existing employees are less likely than new employees to adopt a newly offered medical plan (Tversky and Kahneman 1991). In some instances, status quo bias could be caused by decision costs, transaction costs, or reluctance to alter prior choices (Samuelson and Zeckhauser 1988; Tversky and Kahneman 1991). In other instances, status quo bias could indicate that acquiring a good increases the value of the good to its new owner. Such an increase in value is called an **endowment effect**.[1] In an effort to isolate and measure the endowment effect, economists have tried to design experiments in which other possible causes of status quo bias would be reduced to negligible proportions.

A pioneering experiment by Jack L. Knetsch (1989) focused on choice among goods. In this experiment, students in three classes were given opportunities to choose a coffee mug or a large chocolate bar. The choice was framed differently in each class. In one class, students were initially given mugs and later allowed to swap them for chocolate bars. In a second class, students were initially given chocolate bars and later allowed to swap them for mugs. In a third class, students were simply allowed to choose a mug or a chocolate bar. The proportion of students who chose a mug over a chocolate bar was 89% in the first class, 10% in the second, and 56% in the third. Thus students who were initially given a mug or a chocolate bar were much more likely to show a preference for it than those who chose before receiving either good, an outcome that suggests a strong endowment effect.

Many experiments concerned with the endowment effect have involved contrasts between the terms on which people are willing to buy and sell goods. A particularly influential

---

[1] The term was introduced by Richard H. Thaler (1980), who observed that giving up a good you own is an out-of-pocket cost, but doing without a good you never possessed is not. To the extent that people overemphasize out-of-pocket costs relative to other opportunity costs, they are apt to exhibit an endowment effect.

Figure 11.1 Daniel Kahneman. (The photograph is from Princeton University, Office of Communications.)

set of experiments was conducted by Daniel Kahneman (a winner of the 2002 Nobel Prize in Economic Sciences; Figure 11.1), Jack L. Knetsch, and Richard H. Thaler. The subjects in their first experiment, which we will call KKT1, were 44 Cornell undergraduates. After three practice "trials," or rounds intended to verify that the subjects understood the experimental procedures, one out of every two subjects was given a Cornell coffee mug.[2] The subjects were asked to examine a mug (their own or a neighbor's) and were then informed that the remainder of the experiment would consist of four trials, one of which would determine what they got to keep. In every trial each subject who had been given a mug would indicate the minimum price at which he was willing to sell his mug, and each subject without a mug would indicate the maximum price at which she was willing to buy one. A market-clearing price would be calculated. All mug owners who had declared a willingness to sell at that price or lower would be recorded as having agreed to sell at the market-clearing price. Similarly, buyers who had declared a willingness to buy at or above the market-clearing price would be recorded as having agreed to buy a mug at the market-clearing price. After the four rounds were completed, one would be randomly selected as "binding" in the sense that all purchases and sales agreed to during this round, and no others, would be executed. Given this information, subjects had an incentive in each trial to specify with care the prices at which they were willing to trade because any round might turn out to be binding.

Subjects with mugs were given the following instructions:

You now own the object in your possession. You have the option of selling it if a price, which will be determined later, is acceptable to you. For each of the possible prices below indicate whether you wish to: (1) sell your object and receive this price, or (2) keep your object and take it home with you. (Kahneman et al. 1990, p. 1331, © 1990 by The University of Chicago. All rights reserved)[3]

---

[2] At the time of the experiment, the university bookstore was selling the mugs for $6.

[3] The instructions refer generally to an "object" rather than specifically to a mug because the same instructions were also used in an experiment involving ballpoint pens.

The possible prices ranged from $0.25 to $8.75 in $0.50 increments. Subjects without mugs were given analogous instructions:

> You do not own the object that you see in the possession of some of your neighbors. You have the option of buying one if a price, which will be determined later, is acceptable to you. For each of the possible prices below indicate whether you wish to: (1) pay this price and receive an object to take home with you, or (2) not buy an object at this price. (Kahneman et al. 1990, p. 1331, ©1990 by The University of Chicago. All rights reserved)

Considering the large number of subjects, none could realistically expect to have much influence on the market-clearing price. As a first approximation, the subjects could be assumed to be price-takers. On that assumption, it was in each subject's interest to honestly state the range of prices over which he or she was willing to do business.[4] Indeed, subjects were told that it was in their interest to respond honestly to the questions about acceptable prices.

On the conventional view that individuals know their preferences and these are independent of endowments, we would expect the sellers' minimum acceptable prices and the buyers' maximum acceptable prices—both of which may be called **reservation prices**—to be similar. Reservation prices might vary widely for both buyers and sellers, but the distribution of these prices would be expected to be similar on both sides of the market. In particular, we would expect a measure of central tendency, such as the median, to be about the same for the reservation prices of buyers and sellers. That being the case, the lowest 50% of sellers' reservation prices would on average be below the top 50% of the buyers' reservation prices. Thus about half of the buyers and half of the sellers would want to trade. Without barriers to trade, the number of trades would be about half of the number of objects to be traded. For example, in an experiment with 22 mugs, the predicted number of trades would be 11, as illustrated in the left panel of Figure 11.2.

In contrast, if an endowment effect exists, the reservation prices of mug owners are raised relative to those of mug buyers. As a result, the number of trades is less than half the number of mugs, as shown in the right panel of Figure 11.2. This "undertrading" could be viewed as a market-level analog of the status quo bias in individual choice. Like that bias, undertrading may result from an endowment effect or other causes.

The results of this experiment are shown in Table 11.1. Notice that the median reservation price for buyers is lower than for sellers, and this discrepancy persists from trial to trial. Referring to a buyer's reservation price as **willingness to pay** (*WTP*) and a seller's reservation price as **willingness to accept** (*WTA*), we could restate this result by saying that in this experiment median *WTP* was persistently less than *WTA*.[5] Notice also that the number of trades is persistently well below 11. Clearly, KKT1 is consistent with the existence of a substantial endowment effect.

Kahneman et al. (1990) report seven additional experiments. Particularly relevant to issues arising later in this text are their experiments 5 and 6, which we will call KKT5 and KKT6. Each was designed to remove an uncertainty about the interpretation of KKT1.

---

[4] If a seller overstated his minimum acceptable price and the market-clearing price turned out to below his stated minimum but above his true minimum, he would miss a chance to make to gain from trade. If a seller understated his minimum price and the market-clearing price fell between his stated and true minimums, he would be forced to sell for less than the mug was worth to him. Similarly, if a buyer overstated her maximum acceptable price, she could be forced to pay more than a mug was worth to her. If she understated her maximum acceptable price, she could miss a opportunity to gain from trade.

[5] The term "willingness to pay" is easily understood. In contrast, "willingness to accept" can be confusing. A high *WTA* indicates that the seller insists on a high price, not that he is highly willing to accept any offer.

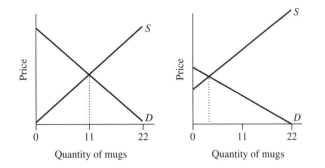

Figure 11.2 The left panel illustrates the case in which reservation prices are distributed in the same way for buyers as for sellers. In this case, demand and supply curves are mirror images, and the number of trades in an experiment with randomly allocated mugs is half the number of mugs. The right panel illustrates the case in which reservation prices for sellers are shifted up relative to those for buyers. In this case, the number of trades is less than half the number of mugs.

Table 11.1 Results of experiment KKT1

Trial [a]	Trades	Median Reservation Price Buyers	Sellers
4	4	$2.75	$5.25
5	1	2.25	5.25
6	2	2.25	5.25
7	2	2.25	5.25

[a] The trials listed here are numbered four through seven because they were preceded by three practice trials.

Recall that in KKT1 trades occurred at market prices, which were calculated from the reservation prices chosen by buyers and sellers. This arrangement might have suggested to subjects that they could manipulate market prices by misstating their reservation prices. To avoid this problem, KKT5 used an alternative approach to eliciting reservation prices, the **Becker- DeGroot-Marschak (BDM) procedure**.[6] In this procedure, buyers and sellers know that trades will occur at random prices, unrelated to their stated reservation prices. After subjects state their reservation prices, a random price is announced. Buyers whose reservation prices are greater than or equal to the announced price buy at the announced price. Others buy nothing. Similarly, sellers whose reservation prices are less than or equal to the announced price sell at the announced price, whereas others sell nothing. Thus the BDM procedure gives subjects no reason to believe they can manipulate market prices and no incentive to misstate their reservation prices.

The participants in KKT5 were 59 students at Simon Fraser University, 30 of whom, chosen at random, were given mugs. Possible prices ranged from $0.00 to $9.50 in $0.50 steps. If preferences were independent of endowments and subjects understood what they were doing, we would expect median reservation prices for buyers and sellers to be similar and the number of trades to be around 14 or 15. Instead, the median reservation prices

---

[6] This procedure is named after the authors of an article, Becker et al. (1964), in which it is expounded.

for buyers and sellers were $2.25 and $5.75, respectively, and only 6 trades occurred. The experimenters interpret this as further evidence of "a large and significant endowment effect" (Kahneman et al. 1990, p. 1338).

The excess of *WTA* over *WTP* could be due to reluctance to sell (part with goods), reluctance to buy (part with money), or both. The relative size of these factors was assessed in experiment KKT6. This was similar to KKT1 except that the participants (77 Simon Fraser students) included not only buyers and sellers but also a third group, whose members were asked to choose either mugs or money. After being randomly assigned to these three groups, the subjects were given instructions appropriate to their roles. Subjects in each group were asked to consider a series of prices ranging from $0.00 to $9.25. As in earlier experiments, each subject who had received a mug was asked to indicate at which of these prices she would be willing to sell her mug. Similarly, each subject in the buyers group was asked to indicate at which prices he would be willing to purchase a mug. Each subject in the third group, called "choosers," was asked to choose, at each possible price, between a mug and its cash equivalent.

The median reservation prices were $7.12 for sellers and $2.87 for buyers. The number of trades was 3, rather than the 12 or 13 that would be expected if preferences were independent of endowments and subjects were free of misconceptions.

The median valuation of mugs by choosers was $3.12. Because the choosers did not have to give up anything in their possession, they should not exhibit any endowment effect. Assuming that all subjects understood their incentives, we could take the choosers as a neutral baseline and calculate the share of the *WTA-WTP* gap due to reluctance to sell as $(7.12 - 3.12)/(7.12 - 2.87) = .9412$ and the share due to reluctance to buy as $(3.12 - 2.87)/(7.12 - 2.87) = .0588$. In short, reluctance to sell appears far stronger than reluctance to buy.

Experiment KKT6 also provides information pertinent to another question that could be raised about earlier experiments. In KKT1 and KKT5 we might expect sellers to be one mug richer than buyers on average. After all, random assignment of subjects to groups should ensure that average wealth in the two groups was roughly equal before mugs were distributed. After distribution, of course, each potential seller was one mug richer than before, whereas the potential buyers were stuck with their initial wealth. The slightly greater average wealth of potential sellers might induce them to state slightly higher reservation prices for mugs. In other words, an "income effect" (in this case more accurately termed a "wealth effect") could account for some part of the *WTA-WTP* gap in KKT1 and KKT5. To eliminate this possibility in KKT6, we can compare potential sellers to choosers. We would expect them to be equally wealthy on average. (Each had a mug or entitlement to a mug or its cash equivalent.) Facing the same decision problem (mug vs. money), sellers and choosers should on average value mugs equally, if there are no misconceptions and endowment effects. The fact that sellers valued mugs more highly than choosers shows that income effects are not sufficient to explain observed *WTA-WTP* gaps (Kahneman et al. 1990).

There are more experiments documenting a status quo bias and a *WTA-WTP* gap than can be summarized here. However, lest it appear that the bias and gap are a syndrome peculiar to North Americans overexposed to mugs and dollars, we should note in passing that the bias and gap have also been found in experiments with other subjects, goods, and currencies. Consider, for example, an experiment, conducted in England, that focused on marginal rates of substitution between Coca-Cola and pounds sterling. Some subjects in this experiment were given £3.00 (about $4.50) and two cans of Coke, while others were given £2.20 (about $3.30) and six cans of Coke. Subjects in the first group were asked how much they would pay for four extra cans of Coke. Subjects in the second group were asked at what price they would sell four cans of Coke. The responses indicated that 60.0% of the subjects in the first group preferred to keep their £3.00 rather than pay £0.80 for four cans of Coke, but only 15.8% of the subjects in the second group were willing to sell four cans of Coke for £0.80. In short, under the conditions of this experiment, consumers again exhibit a status quo bias and *WTP* again falls short of *WTA* (Bateman, et al. 1997).

In summary, a substantial body of evidence supports the existence of a status quo bias and a *WTA-WTP* gap and is consistent with the existence of an endowment effect. This evidence suggests that we should take seriously the possibility that individuals' preferences may depend on reference points based at least in part on their current endowment.

11.2   A Theory of Reference Dependence

To model the kind of behavior examined in the previous section, we can begin by indexing the preference relationships $\succ$ and $\prec$ and the indifference relationship $\sim$ (introduced in Chapter 9) by reference points. Thus $A \succ_r B$ means that A seems better than B when judged from reference point r, $A \prec_r B$ means that A seems inferior to B from reference point r, and $A \sim_r B$ means that A seems just as good as B from reference point r. The standard theory, surveyed in the last chapter, is a special case based on an assumption of reference independence—that is, that if one consumption bundle is preferred to another from one reference point, then it will be preferred to the other from all possible reference points—an assumption seemingly violated in the experiments described in the last section.

Indifference curves often seem to be kinked at a point corresponding to the current endowment, as in Figure 11.3. The marginal rate of substitution changes discontinuously at the reference point. An indifference curve kinked at the current endowment is suggestive of **loss aversion**—a disinclination to accept a small loss of any good without large compensation in terms of other goods.[7] From the reference point r a movement to the southeast along the indifference curve involves forfeiting a small amount of good 2 in exchange for a large amount of good 1, whereas a movement to the northwest along the same indifference curve involves forfeiting a small amount of good 1 in exchange for a large amount of good 2.

Kinked indifference curves can arise from utility functions indexed by reference points. Letting r_i denote a reference point's i^{th} coordinate, we can write out a simple example of such a utility function for the two dimensional case as follows:

$$U_r(q_1, q_2) = R_1(q_1) + R_2(q_2), \text{ where } R_i(q_i) = \begin{cases} q_i - r_i & \text{if } q_i \geq r_i \\ 2(q_i - r_i) & \text{if } q_i < r_i \end{cases} \qquad (11.1)$$

Indifference curves for that utility function are shown in Figure 11.4. A notable feature of the diagram is that although the indifference curve through the reference point has one kink, those for lower and higher levels of utility have two kinks each—one where $q_1 = r_1$ and another where $q_2 = r_2$.

EXERCISE 11.1

Consider the utility function given by Equation 11.1 and suppose that the reference point is $(r_1, r_2) = (5, 10)$. Calculate the utility of the reference point and then the utility of $(10, 5)$. Which point is preferred?

---

[7] Although loss aversion has only recently become a focus of formal economic theory, related ideas were expressed as early as 1759, when Adam Smith noted that "we suffer more . . . when we fall from a better to a worse situation, than we ever enjoy when we rise from a worse to a better" (quoted in Camerer et al. 2004, p. 5).

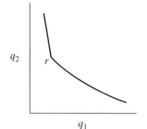

q_2

r

q_1

Figure 11.3 A kinked indifference curve through reference point r

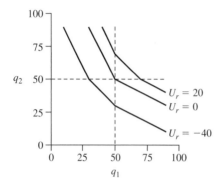

q_2

$U_r = 20$
$U_r = 0$
$U_r = -40$

q_1

Figure 11.4 Indifference curve map for utility function with reference point $r = (50, 50)$

EXERCISE 11.2

Consider again the utility function given by Equation 11.1 but now suppose that the reference point has shifted so that $(r_1, r_2) = (10, 5)$. Recalculate the utility of the (5, 10) and (10, 5). Which point is now preferred? Explain the contrast between the preferences in the two exercises.

11.3 Boundaries of Loss Aversion, the Endowment Effect, and the *WTA-WTP* Gap

Although arguably common, loss aversion, the endowment effect, and the *WTA-WTP* gap are not ubiquitous. As noted in a pioneering exposition, "no endowment effect would be expected . . . when goods are purchased for resale rather than for utilization" (Kahneman et al. 1990, p. 1328). For the reseller, the goods are just potential money.[8] More generally, loss aversion and its consequences are likely to be absent when an individual contemplates exchanging one item for another that is to him in all respects at least as useful as the original. In such cases, the individual can easily see the net value of the exchange. For example, if the individual considers exchanging one sewing kit for another that has one more needle but is otherwise identical, he can immediately see a net gain of one needle and need not be concerned about any loss. Still more generally, loss aversion and its results are unlikely when "the gains and losses associated with a transaction are mentally *integrated* prior to evaluation, rather than being evaluated separately. When a loss and an equal and opposite

---

[8] In the terminology of classical political economy, the reseller cares about the goods' exchange value, not their use value.

gain are integrated in this way, painful perceptions of loss do not arise" (Bateman et al. 2003, p. 7). The conditions in which losses and gains are integrated are not fully understood. Hence several questions remain open concerning the range of circumstances under which loss aversion, the endowment effects, and the *WTA-WTP* gap are important.

11.3.1 Loss Aversion and Buying

Do consumers commonly experience loss aversion when considering exchanging money for goods? An affirmative response is implied by the **current endowment hypothesis**, according to which an individual's reference point is her current endowment, including money, as well as goods. A negative response is provided by the **no loss in buying (NLB) hypothesis**, according to which consumers, viewing money as potential goods, believe that by purchasing goods they are not losing money but realizing its potential.

Evidence about these hypotheses is thus far mixed. On the one hand, experiments such as KKT6 have found very little difference between the valuation of goods by subjects who may buy goods and those who may choose between goods and money. On the other hand, a recent experiment conducted collaboratively by supporters of the current endowment hypothesis and a supporter of the NLB hypothesis produced evidence that subjects perceive money spent in buying goods as losses (Bateman et al. 2003).

11.3.2 Endowment Effects and Market Experience

Do consumers become less prone to the endowment effect as they gain experience with markets? Given the neoclassical assumption that preferences are independent of endowments, people who exhibit the endowment effect are making costly mistakes, that is, missing opportunities for gains from trade. In that case, as people learn from market experience they should become less apt to exhibit the endowment effect. In contrast, if preferences depend on reference points that are affected by current assets, people who exhibit the endowment effect are not necessarily making mistakes. In this view, the endowment effect need not be attenuated by market experience. Although several experiments have been conducted with the aim of clarifying this issue, a consensus has not yet emerged.

William T. Harbaugh, Kate Krause, and Lise Vesterlund conducted experiments with subjects in kindergarten, third grade, fifth grade, and college. Finding "no evidence that the endowment effect decreases with age," they interpret their findings as "supporting the hypothesis that people have reference-dependent preferences that are not changed by repeated experience getting and giving up goods" (Harbaugh et al. 2001, pp. 175, 181).

A somewhat different perspective is offered by a John A. List, a researcher who conducted surveys and experiments at sports-card shows and a market for collector pins. Like Harbaugh et al., List (2003, 2004) finds no evidence that the endowment effect diminishes with age. However, to supplement the age data, List also asked his subjects how many years they had participated in markets for sports cards or collector pins and how many trades they had made in the previous year. The probability that a subject accepted a trade offered by List turns out to be unrelated to the number of years of market experience but positively related to the number of trades in the previous year. Only people who traded little in the past year exhibited a strong endowment effect in List's experiments. One possible interpretation is that trades made within the past year helped subjects avoid mistakes in deciding whether to accept the trades List offered. Perhaps trades made more than a year ago did not play the same role because of lapses of memory. However, other interpretations are possible. The number of trades in the past was not under experimental control but rather chosen by the subjects themselves. It is conceivable that the degree of loss aversion varies over individuals but is somewhat persistent over time. In this case, the number of trades individuals made last year could accurately predict their probability of accepting a new trade offer even if market experience fails to attenuate the endowment effect.[9]

11.3.3 *WTA-WTP* Gaps and Experimental Design

Are the *WTA-WTP* gaps revealed in experiments due to endowment effects or to something else, such as instructions or procedures that might leave subjects with misconceptions about their incentives? In an interesting article addressing this question, Charles R. Plott and Kathryn Zeiler (2005) surveyed reports of 39 experiments published between 1984 and 2002. Of these experiments, 27 produced *WTA-WTP* gaps and 12 did not. A wide variety of controls to avert misconceptions had been employed, suggesting a lack of consensus among experimenters about what constitutes a sufficient set of controls.

To check the sensitivity of *WTA-WTP* gaps to experimental procedure, Plott and Zeiler (2005) first replicated KKT5 and then conducted three new experiments—which we will call PZ1, PZ2, and PZ3—using more controls to avert subjects' misconceptions. The subjects in their replication experiment were 58 undergraduates at the California Institute of Technology. Half of them were given mugs with the Caltech logo.[10] Following procedures similar to those in KKT5, the experimenters elicited reservation prices from the mug owners and the potential mug buyers. The median *WTA* was $4.50 whereas the median *WTP* was $1.50. Thus this experiment, like KKT5, produced evidence of a substantial *WTA-WTP* gap.

The subjects in PZ1 and PZ2 were law students at the University of Southern California; those in PZ3 were undergraduates at Pasadena City College. Each of these experiments was designed to ensure subject anonymity and "consisted of a detailed training session, two unpaid practice rounds, fourteen paid rounds using lotteries and one paid round using mugs" (Plott and Zeiler 2005, p. 536).

The training sessions for PZ1, PZ2, and PZ3 were the same for all participants and covered optimal strategies for both buyers and sellers. Detailed suggestions were given regarding how a potential buyer can determine the maximum she is willing to pay and how a potential seller can determine the minimum he is willing to accept. The practice rounds involved buying and selling lottery tickets rather than mugs. All subjects got practice on both sides of the market.

Two different sequences of paid rounds were tried. In PZ1 and PZ3, the 14 rounds involving lotteries preceded the round involving mugs. In PZ2, the lottery rounds followed the mug round.

The results of the mug rounds in the three experiments are displayed in Table 11.2. In no case is a mug's median reservation price higher for potential sellers than for potential buyers. Pooling observations across the three experiments, Plott and Zeiler (2005) find that the median *WTP* and *WTA* are $6 and $5 respectively. In this pooled sample the *WTA-*

---

[9] In an effort to narrow the range of plausible interpretations, List (2003) supplemented his initial cross-sectional data with a follow-up study of some of his original subjects 11 months after the first study. Twenty-seven subjects in the follow-up study recalled increasing their trading frequency since the last interview. Of these, 13 had declined an offer to trade in the first experiment but accepted an offer to trade in the second. Twenty-six subjects recalled a stable or decreased trade frequency. Of these, only 3 switched from no-trade to trade responses from the first to the second experiment. List interprets this as evidence that increased trade reduces the endowment effect. Another possible interpretation is that an individual's degree of loss aversion rises or falls gradually, making trade frequency in the recent past better than that in the distant past as a predictor of current willingness to trade, even if market experience has no causal influence on the endowment effect.

[10] At the time of the experiment, the mugs were being sold in a campus bookstore for about $7.00.

Table 11.2 Results of Plott and Zeiler's (2005) experiments

Experiment	Median Reservation Price Buyers	Sellers
PZ1	$5.00	$5.00
PZ2	6.50	5.10
PZ3	8.00	4.25

WTP gap is negative, the opposite of what would be expected if the endowment effect were operative. However, because of wide variation in both individual *WTA* and individual *WTP*, the sample medians for *WTA* and *WTP* are not (in a statistical sense) significantly different from each other. In other words, the evidence is consistent with the hypothesis that there is no difference between *WTA* and *WTP* in the population from which the subject sample was drawn.

The contrast between the results in KKT5 and its replication, on the one hand, and those in PZ1–3 on the other hand, is open to several possible interpretations.[11] Two examples follow:

1. The *WTA-WTP* gap could be confined to cases in which subjects misstate their reservation prices, possibly because of misconceptions about their incentives. Perhaps some subjects in KKT5 and its replication mistakenly believed that they were bargaining over prices. In this case, potential buyers might have imagined that they could secure better bargains by stating low reservation prices. Similarly, some sellers might have imagined that they could get better deals by stating high reservation prices. Perhaps subjects in PZ1–3 were protected from similar misconceptions by extra training and practice. In this interpretation, the *WTA-WTP* gap is evidence not of an endowment effect but of confusion and strategic misstatement of values.

2. The *WTA-WTP* gap could stem from an endowment effect that operates when subjects think of mugs as consumer goods for personal use but not when they think of them as commodities for trade. In KKT5 and its replication, each subject was either a potential buyer throughout or a potential seller throughout. No subjects switched roles. In contrast, each subject in PZ1–3 received preliminary training in both buying and selling, got practice on both sides of a lottery market,[12] and was told that "you will switch between the roles of buyer and seller" (Plott and Zeiler 2005, on-line appendix, http://www.e-aer .org/data/june05_app_plott.pdf, p. 14). Perhaps this training, practice, and orientation with respect to both buying and selling conditioned subjects to view mugs as tradable commodities rather than goods for use.

---

[11] Five interpretations are discussed by Plott and Zeiler.

[12] The effect of practice with lotteries on decisions about mugs depends on the extent to which attitudes acquired in one situation transfer to another. List (2004) reports that the more experience people have trading sports cards and memorabilia the more apt they are subsequently to make trades involving mugs and candy bars. This evidence is consistent with the idea that attitudes acquired in one situation may be transfered to another. However, it is also consistent with the idea that, across situations and over time, some people are consistently more loss-averse than others. More research is needed to determine the extent of transfer.

These interpretations are not mutually exclusive. Some *WTA-WTP* gaps could arise from confused attempts at bargaining, and others stem from an endowment effect. Further experimentation is needed to assess the relative importance of various factors contributing to *WTA-WTP* gaps. However, it is already clear that decisions about prices to offer and accept are influenced by not only wealth and preferences but also the decision context. Seemingly small differences in how alternatives are presented can have surprisingly large effects on behavior. More evidence on the importance of context will be surveyed in Chapter 12.

11.4 Economic Implications of Loss Aversion

11.4.1 Consumer Demand

Durables

If a consumer's indifference curve is kinked at the point representing her current endowment of durable goods, then small changes in the relative price of a good (the absolute value of the slope of the budget constraint) may have no effect on the bundle of durables selected. In Figure 11.5, the budget constraint shifts from Bb to $B'b'$ without inducing the consumer to move away from the reference point. For example, an increase in the price of housing relative to automobiles rotates the budget constraints of individuals who own houses and cars around their endowment points but rarely induces the owners to move into smaller quarters to finance the purchase of more or bigger cars.[13]

Nondurables

If a consumer's indifference curve is kinked at the point representing his initial consumption of nondurable goods, then small changes in the price of a good, with no change in income or the prices of other goods, may have no effect on his allocation of income among goods. In Figure 11.6, the price of the second good rises relative to both income and the price of the first good. As a result, the budget constraint shifts from Bb to $B'b$. The quantity of the first good consumed is unaffected. For the second good, the quantity consumed falls just enough to offset the price increase. As a result, expenditure on each good remains constant. In other words, the own-price elasticity of demand is -1 and the cross-price elasticity of demand is 0. For example, consider a consumer who divides his income between food and entertainment. If the price of entertainment rises while his income and the price of food remain constant, he may maintain his food consumption while reducing the quantity of entertainment just enough to offset the increase in the price of entertainment. This behavior is consistent with evidence that many people maintain mental accounts, allocating fixed fractions of their income to specific categories of consumption. For example, the majority of MBA students in one study kept separate budgets for clothing, entertainment, and food (Thaler 1999).

11.4.2 Preference Change

When a change in an individual's budget constraint induces a change in consumption, a shift in the individual's reference point is apt to ensue. In cases like this, in which indifference curves change their shape or position in response to changes in consumption

---

[13] For discussion of other effects of loss aversion in housing markets, see Genesove and Mayer (2001).

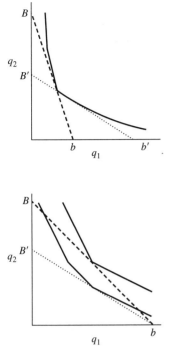

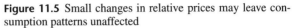

Figure 11.5 Small changes in relative prices may leave consumption patterns unaffected

Figure 11.6 Small changes in the price of the second good, with income and the price of the first good held constant, may leave expenditure on each good unchanged

or other economic variables, economists say that preferences are **endogenous**.[14] Although peripheral to the concerns of most neoclassical economists, endogenous preferences have been a focus of interest for institutional economists such as Thorstein Veblen (1857–1929), radical economists such as Samuel Bowles, behavioral economists such as Richard Thaler, and cognitive psychologists such as Daniel Kahneman. Their writings contain suggestions that reference points may be influenced not only by current endowments but also by "aspirations, expectations, norms, and social comparisons" (Tversky and Kahneman 1991, pp. 1046–47).

Once the reference point has changed, a return of the budget constraint to its original position will not necessarily induce the consumer to return immediately to his original consumption bundle. Marketers show an intuitive understanding of endogenous preferences when they give away samples or offer deep discounts to first-time customers, hoping—in effect—to shift the consumers' reference points to boost sales. An extreme case is that of drug dealers who know that inducing addiction can turn occasional users into regular customers.

11.4.3 General Equilibrium and Welfare

Exchange

If past and current assets influence tastes, as evidence surveyed above suggests, then the location of the Pareto set may depend on the initial allocation. In a variation on an

---

[14] More generally, economic theorists say a variable is endogenous in a model if its values are determined within the model. These variables are contrasted to exogenous variables, whose values are taken as given. (A somewhat different usage of the terms prevails in econometrics.)

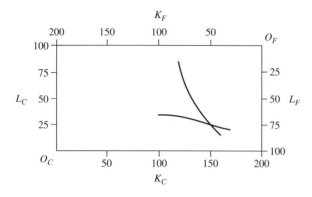

Figure 11.7 Edgeworth box with kinked indifference curves

example from the previous chapter, Carl and Francis may be strongly averse to losing any paintings in their initial allocation of Kandinskys and Leonardos. In other words, their indifference curves may be sharply kinked at the initial allocation. In that case, the lens-shaped area representing mutually advantageous reallocations may be reduced or eliminated. Two kinked indifference curves touching at the initial allocation are shown in Figure 11.7.

The traditional view has been that through trade consumers get what they prefer. An alternative view suggested by the literature on loss aversion is that consumers come to prefer what they happen to have. In this alternative view, the Pareto set is conditional on a reference point. Although an allocation in the Pareto set makes one consumer as well satisfied as possible, given the other's level of satisfaction and current tastes, some other allocation, outside the current Pareto set, might make both consumers better satisfied once their preferences had adapted to the new allocation. (For a survey of economic research related to endogenous preferences, see Bowles 1998.)

Product Assortment

Even if preferences adapt to consumption patterns, we can still characterize an equilibrium product assortment as a point where a representative consumer's indifference curve touches the production possibilities frontier (PPF) without crossing it. However, if the indifference curve is kinked at the point of contact, it has no well-defined marginal rate of substitution at this point. Thus we cannot characterize the equilibrium as an equality between consumers' marginal rate of substitution and producers' marginal rate of transformation. More important, the equilibrium product assortment does not necessarily represent a unique long-run welfare maximum. A different product assortment might yield equal or higher levels of welfare once preferences adjusted to it.

11.5 Summary

1. As viewed by many behavioral economists, a growing body of experimental evidence suggests that, under some circumstances, preferences depend on a reference point. When the reference point is the current endowment, choice exhibits a status quo bias.
2. In a theory of reference dependence, developed to fit the experimental evidence, indifference curves are kinked at the coordinates of a reference point. Decision makers with such indifference curves exhibit loss-aversion, a disinclination to accept a small loss of any good without large compensation in other goods.

3. The boundaries of loss aversion, the endowment effect, and the *WTA-WTP* gap are still uncertain. Mapping them clearly will probably require more experiments.

4. When preferences are reference-dependent, changes in budget constraints can induce changes in preferences. The Pareto set retains its interpretation as an equilibrium locus but loses its status as a set of optimal allocations. Similarly, the product assortment found where a PPF touches but does not cross an indifference curve retains its interpretation as an equilibrium but loses its claim to optimality.

11.6   Solutions to Exercises

11.1. The utility of (5, 10) is $(5 - 5) + (10 - 10) = 0$. The utility of (10, 5) is $(10 - 5) + 2(5 - 10) = -5$. The first point is preferred.

11.2. The utility of (5, 10) is now $2(5 - 10) + (10 - 5) = -5$. The utility of (10, 5) is now $(10 - 10) + (5 - 5) = 0$. The second point is preferred. The choice has been reversed because the reference point shifted. In each case, the consumer preferred the reference point to the alternative.

11.7   Problems: Economics Gets Kinky

Suppose that Amos has \$100 to spend on goods 1 and 2 and that his tastes are represented by the indifference curve map below. Let p_1 and p_2 denote the prices of goods 1 and 2. Suppose that initially $p_1 = p_2 = \$1$. When working on the questions below, you may find a straight edge useful for representing a budget constraint.

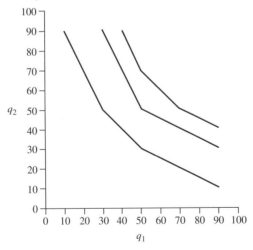

1. At the initial prices described above, what quantities of goods 1 and 2 would Amos buy? Judging from the shape of his indifference curves, would you think those quantities are the coordinates of his reference point? (In other words, do you think Amos is used to buying those quantities?)

2. If p_1 rose to \$1.67 and p_2 remained at \$1.00, what quantities of goods 1 and 2 would Amos buy? If he got used to consuming these new quantities, do you think the shape of his indifference curves would change? If so, how? If not, why not?

3. If p_1 remained at $1.00 while p_2 rose to $1.67, what quantities of goods 1 and 2 would Amos buy? If Amos got used to consuming these new quantities, what do you think his indifference curves would look like?

4. If p_1 and p_2 both rose to $1.25, what would you predict would happen to the quantities of goods 1 and 2 purchased by Amos?

5. If p_1 fell a little below $1.00 while p_2 remained at $1.00, what do you think would happen to the quantities of goods 1 and 2 purchased by Amos?

12
The Context and Framing of Choice

Having learned in the last chapter that preferences can depend on a reference point that shifts with endowments, we now consider two other possible influences on preferences: the context in which choices are made and the framing or description of alternatives.

12.1 Context

The context of choice has two components: The **background** context consists of the tradeoffs that the decision maker has previously observed and may now take as points of comparison for the tradeoffs currently faced. The **local** context is the decision maker's current opportunity set.

12.1.1 Background Context

Consider a consumer faced with a choice between two products that differ in two attributes. Examples of such pairs include two brands of tires differing in price and length of warranty, two apartments differing in size and proximity to campus, or two bicycles differing in weight and number of gears. The choice is easy if one of the products **dominates** the other in the sense of being preferable in both respects. When neither product dominates, the consumer has to evaluate the tradeoff between attributes. Is the extra length of warranty worth the price? Is the extra space worth the extra travel time? Are the extra gears worth the extra weight?

The consumer may compare the available tradeoff to his or her marginal rate of substitution or willingness to pay, as assumed in neoclassical economic theory. In this case, the consumer chooses the tires with the longer warranty if and only if the cost for the extra warranty length is less than his or her willingness to pay. However, consumers who are uncertain about their preferences (or concerned about justifying their choices to acquaintances with different tastes) may try to evaluate the currently available tradeoff by comparison to analogous tradeoffs previously encountered. Is the cost of the extra warranty now lower than before? If so, some consumers may regard that as a reason for buying the higher priced tires. Although it is clearly not a *good* reason, it may or may not be an *influential* one. To determine just how influential such tradeoff comparisons are, marketing specialists and psychologists have conducted a series of experiments.

Experimenters typically divide subjects into two groups. Subjects in each group are asked to make two successive choices under different tradeoffs between attributes. The tradeoffs involved in the first choice provide background contexts for the second. The second, or "target," tradeoff is the same for both groups, but the background tradeoffs differ. For example, in an experiment conducted by Itamar Simonson and Amos Tversky

137

Figure 12.1 Amos Tversky (used with the permission of Professor Barbara Tversky)

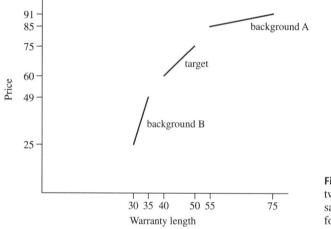

Figure 12.2 Tradeoffs between warranty length (thousand miles) and price (dollars) for tires

(1937–96, Figure 12.1) both groups were given a choice in the second round between tires with warranties for 40,000 or 50,000 miles at prices of $60 or $75. To establish different background contexts, experimenters in the first round offered the 111 subjects in group A a choice of tires with warranties for 55,000 or 75,000 miles at prices of $85 or $91 while offering the 109 subjects in group B a choice of tires with warranties for 30,000 or 35,000 miles at prices of $25 or $49. These three tradeoffs are shown in Figure 12.2

Faced with the target tradeoff, the subjects chose as follows: In group A, 57% preferred the cheaper tires and 43% the more expensive ones. In group B, by contrast, 33% chose the cheaper tires and 67% the more costly ones.[1] Apparently, the subjects exposed to background A felt that the target tradeoff was too steep, whereas those exposed to background B found the target tradeoff more appealing. Similar results were obtained with other products (books, CDs, computers, dental insurance, and paper towels) and experimental designs (Simonson and Tversky 1992; Tversky and Simonson 1993). Taken together, these experiments strongly support the hypothesis that choices are affected by their background context.

12.1.2 Local Context

In neoclassical theory, consumers' preference orders (utility functions) and opportunity sets are independent. Faced with any opportunity set, a consumer selects the element that maximizes his or her utility. According to this view, consumers' choices exhibit **independence of irrelevant alternatives**, meaning that a consumer's preference between two consumption bundles does not depend on what other bundles are in his or her opportunity set. In other words, the consumer's preference between two alternatives is assumed to be independent of the local context.[2]

Independence of irrelevant alternatives is normatively appealing. Indeed, transparent violations of independence can seem ridiculous. Imagine, for example, overhearing the following dialogue in a restuarant:[3]

> Waiter: Would you care for a desert?
> Diner: Do you have pie?
> Waiter: Certainly. Apple or cherry?
> Diner: Apple, please.
> Waiter: Oh, I just recalled, today we also have pecan pie.
> Diner: In that case, I'll have a piece of the cherry pie.

Few people are as patently inconsistent as the diner in that dialogue. However, we should not dismiss the possibility of subtler violations of the independence assumption without empirical inquiry.[4] Because such inquiry typically uses data aggregated over many individuals, we must begin by asking about the aggregate level implications of independence.

Although independence of irrelevant alternatives is an assumption about individual choice, it has a direct and important implication for aggregate demand for any given product or consumption bundle. This implication, known as the **regularity condition**, is that the fraction of people choosing a given product cannot be raised by adding new alternatives to the existing ones. In other words, the market share of a product cannot be boosted by giving consumers additional choices.

---

[1] The difference between the two groups is statistically significant at the .01 level.

[2] The definition of independence of irrelevant alternatives given in this section is standard in the literature on bargaining (Binmore 1992; Bowles 2004; Luce and Raiffa 1989 [1957]) and deterministic individual choice (Luce 1959; Rubenstein 1998; Tversky and Simonson 1993). Two other definitions are customary in the literatures on social choice and probabilistic individual choice. The various meanings have a common ancestor in Huntington (1938) and are surveyed by P. Ray (1973).

[3] This example is a minor variation on stories appearing in several sources including Binmore (1992) and Frank (2003).

[4] Nor should we overlook the possibility that some seeming violations of the independence assumption are consistent with rational behavior. Being offered a third alternative might provide some new information about the first two Sen (1993). For example, the restaurant in the story might employ two cooks on alternate days; one of whom makes a good apple pie, a poor cherry pie, and no pecan pie; the other makes a poor apple pie, a good cherry pie, and a mediocre pecan pie. In that case, learning that pecan pie is available would change the diner's expectations regarding the quality of the apple and cherry pies.

To test the regularity condition, marketing researchers have performed several experiments (Huber et al. 1982; Simonson 1989; Simonson and Tversky 1992). The experimental design for one such study is summarized by the researchers as follows:

> Subjects were informed that some of them, selected randomly, would receive $6. They were further told that the winners would have the option of trading the $6 for a pen. Subjects were asked to examine the available pens and indicate whether they would like to trade the $6 for a pen. Later, 10% of participants received either $6 or the pen they had chosen.
>
> In one version of the questionnaire, subjects were presented an elegant Cross pen. In the other version, subjects were given an additional option—a lesser known brand name that was selected specifically for its unattractiveness. (Simonson and Tversky 1992, p. 287. Quoted with permission of the American Marketing Association.)

Of the 106 subjects offered only $6 or the Cross pen, 36% chose the pen. Of the 115 subjects offered $6 or either pen, 46% chose the Cross pen.[5] This result is a violation of the regularity condition and suggests, as the researchers note, that willingness "to pay cash for a good can be increased by the introduction of an inferior alternative" (Simonson and Tversky 1992, p. 287). A plausible interpretation is that some subjects supposed that they had found a reason for choosing the Cross pen when they noted that it, unlike $6, obviously dominated the other pen. Cases like this are called instances of **asymmetric dominance**. This reason for choosing the Cross pen is illogical, in that it has no bearing on the question of whether acquiring the pen or $6 would do more to raise utility. Nonetheless, this reason seems to have swayed some subjects.

12.2 Invariance and Framing

Neoclassical economists assume that all informationally equivalent descriptions of alternatives elicit identical choices. This presumption—known as the **invariance assumption**—is accurate in many cases. For example, our willingness to purchase a box of doughnuts is not likely to be affected by whether it claims to contain "twelve" or "one dozen" doughnuts.[6] However, subtler violations of the invariance assumption cannot be ruled out a priori.

Opposing the invariance assumption, some psychologists and economists have argued that differently worded but logically equivalent descriptions of alternatives could elicit different responses. Their argument, in brief, is as follows: Choices are based on mental representations of alternatives. The process of forming these mental representations is called **framing** and seems to be governed by two rules of mental economy, known as segregation and acceptance. According to the **segregation rule**, people frame decision problems by focusing on the acts, outcomes, and contingencies that appear to them most directly relevant to the choice under consideration, while ignoring other acts, outcomes, and contingencies, some of which might play a role in utility maximization. A prime example of segregation of outcomes is the nearly universal practice of thinking about choice problems in terms of gains and losses, rather than in terms of full consumption bundles. Focusing on different aspects of the same alternatives could lead people to make different choices. According to the **acceptance rule**, given a reasonable formulation of a choice problem, decision makers are prone to accept the problem as presented to them and do not spontaneously generate

---

[5] The difference in percentages is statistically significant at the .10 level.

[6] In logic, a term's **extension** is the class of objects to which it refers. "Twelve" and "one dozen" share the same extension. The invariance assumption is sometimes called the **extensionality** assumption.

alternative representations. Differing descriptions of given alternatives could induce people to focus on different aspects of the alternatives and thus to make different choices.

Empirical evidence suggests that invariance may be violated when a difference can be made to appear large or small by comparison to alternative initial quantities. The following two examples are representative of the experimental literature.

The first example involves two groups of subjects who were presented with alternative versions of a problem hinging on price differences. One group was given the following version:

> Imagine that you are about to purchase a jacket for $125 and a calculator for $15. The calculator salesman informs you that the calculator you wish to buy is on sale for $10 at the other branch of the store, located 20 minutes drive away. Would you make the trip to the other store? (Excerpted with permission from Amos Tversky and Daniel Kahneman, The Framing of Decisions and the Psychology of Choice, *Science* 211, p. 457. Copyright 1981 AAAS)

Of the 93 respondents, 68% indicated they would make the trip to save the $5.

The version given to the second group was the same except that the prices of the jacket and calculator were interchanged, so the question was whether to make the 20-minute trip to buy a calculator for $120 rather $125. Of the 88 respondents to this version, only 29% indicated willingness to make the trip to save the $5.

Under the invariance assumption, consumers should make the trip if and only if the cost of a 20-minute trip is less than $5. The proportion of people making the trip should be unaffected by the base price of the calculator. Thus the experiment's results are inconsistent with the invariance assumption. A reasonable interpretation is that consumer sensitivity to a price difference decreases as the base price rises. Consistent with this interpretation, economists have noted that the store-to-store variation (standard deviation) of prices for a given product rises with the mean price of the product (Pratt et al. 1979). For example, the standard deviation of prices across outlets is likely to be much less for pencils than for pianos.

The second example of a violation of the invariance assumption involves two groups of subjects presented with a policy choice involving percentages expressed in different ways. One group was given the following problem:

> Political decision making often involves a considerable number of trade-offs. A program that benefits one segment of the population may work to the disadvantage of another segment. Policies designed to lead to higher rates of employment frequently have an adverse effect on inflation. Imagine you were faced with the decision of adopting one of two economic policies.
>
> If program *J* is adopted, 10% of the work force would be unemployed, while the rate of inflation would be 12%. If program *K* is adopted, 5% of the work force would be unemployed, while the rate of inflation would be 17%. The following table summarizes the alternative policies and their likely consequences:

Policy	Work Force Unemployed (%)	Rate of Inflation (%)
Program *J*	10	12
Program *K*	5	17

> Imagine you were faced with the decision of adopting program *J* or program *K*. Which would you select? (Quattrone and Tversky 2000 [1988], pp. 461–62. Quoted with permission of Cambridge University Press)

Of the 126 subjects given this question, 36% selected program *J* and 64% selected program *K*.

The problem given to the second group was identical except that the labor market conse-quences of the programs were described in terms of employment rather than unemployment. Thus the table presented to the second group was as follows:

Policy	Work Force Unemployed (%)	Rate of Inflation (%)
Program *J*	90	12
Program *K*	95	17

Of the 133 subjects given this version of the problem, 54% chose program *J* and 46% chose program *K* (Quattrone and Tversky 2000 [1988], p. 462. Quoted with permission of Cambridge University Press)

Because the unemployed and the employed, expressed as percentages of the work force, necessarily sum to 100, the two versions of the problem are strictly equivalent. Thus the reversal of the modal response is a clear violation of the invariance assumption. A plausible interpretation is that a 5 percentage point difference looked large compared to a 5 or 10% unemployment rate but small when compared to a 90 or 95% employment rate.

These and similar experimental results indicate that, contrary to the invariance assump-tion, various ways of framing a given problem can induce different decisions. Faced with such evidence, a growing number of researchers have sought to develop a positive theory of choice surpassing neoclassical utility theory in predictive accuracy. A key component of a successful positive theory now appears to be a model of value comparison, as described in the next section.

12.3   Value Comparison

When people cannot spot a dominant alternative, they seem to make choices by comparing subjective values. In accordance with the segregation rule, outcomes are expressed in terms of gains and losses—that is, positive and negative deviations from a neutral reference outcome that is assigned a value of zero. A mapping from gains and losses to subjective values, known as a **value function**, is typically of the form

$$v(x) = \begin{cases} x^\alpha & \text{if } x \geq 0, \\ -\lambda(-x)^\beta & \text{if } x < 0 \end{cases} \tag{12.1}$$

where α and β are in the interval $(0, 1)$, $\lambda > 1$, and x represents gains when it is positive and losses when it is negative. Such a function is illustrated in Figure 12.3 for the case in which $\alpha = \beta = .758$ and $\lambda = 3.11$.[7]

According to Kahneman and Tversky, the value function is usually concave above the reference point and convex below it. Thus the difference in subjective value between a gain of $100 and a gain of $200 is greater than the difference in subjective value be-tween a gain of $1100 and a gain of $1200. The same relation between value differences holds for the corresponding losses. The value function indicates that the effect of a mar-ginal change decreases with the distance from the reference point in either direction. The

---

[7] These parameter estimates are based on econometric analysis of financial markets (Shumway 1997). Similar estimates ($\alpha = \beta = .88$, $\lambda = 2.25$) have been obtained from analysis of controlled experiments (Tversky and Kahneman 1992).

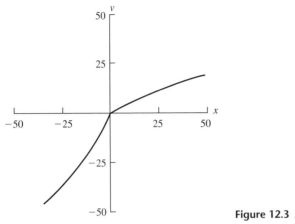

Figure 12.3 A value function

shape of the value function is consistent with the psychological **principle of diminishing sensitivity**: The impact of a change diminishes with the distance from the reference point.

Both branches of Equation 12.1 are power functions.[8] The point elasticity of v with respect to x is α for gains and $-\beta$ for losses. For small gains and losses, the arc elasticities are also approximately α and $-\beta$.

EXERCISE 12.1

Suppose $\alpha = .8$. Calculate the arc elasticity from $x = 100$ to $x = 101$.

The slope of the value function is greater for losses than for gains. This feature of the value function represents **loss aversion**—the tendency to take losses more seriously than gains of equal size. The common reluctance to accept a fair bet on the toss of a coin suggests that the displeasure of losing a sum of money exceeds the pleasure of winning the same amount.

Business people sometimes seem to have an intuitive understanding of loss aversion. For example, the credit card lobby has preferred that any price difference between cash and card purchases should be labeled a cash discount rather than a credit surcharge (Thaler 1980). Similarly, businesses that want to temporarily reduce a price frequently do so by offering discounts or rebates rather than by cutting the list price. Customers may be expected to frame cancellation of a rebate as a gain forgone but frame an explicit price increase as a loss.

---

[8] The idea that the subjective value of monetary gains and losses is given by a power function with an exponent between 0 and 1 has been traced back to a letter written by Gabriel Cramer in 1728 Bernoulli (1954 (1738)). Modern experimental psychologists have found that power functions describe the dependence of sensation on stimulus in many domains of experience. For example, the sensation of sweetness is related to the amount of saccharine by a power law with exponent .8. In general, "the power law has become one of the best established empirical relations in psychology" (Gescheider 1997, p. 306). It has largely replaced the older logarithmic relationship know as the Weber-Fechner law (Gescheider 1997, p. 298).

EXERCISE 12.2

Consider the following value function:

$$v(x) = \begin{cases} x^{.8} & \text{if } x \geq 0 \\ -3(-x)^{.8} & \text{if } x < 0 \end{cases}.$$

Using this value function, calculate $v(-10) - v(-15)$ and $v(-120) - v(-125)$. How do your calculations help explain the behavior of subjects in the experiment involving the purchase of a calculator, described on page 141?

EXERCISE 12.3

Using the value function in the previous problem, calculate $v(-5) - v(-10)$ and $v(95) - v(90)$. How do your calculations help explain the behavior of subjects in the experiment involving policies affecting labor markets and inflation, described starting on page 141?

12.4 Summary

1. Choice can be influenced by background and local context. People are more likely to buy a good at a given price if the background context is one of higher rather than lower prices. Contrary to the principle of independence of irrelevant alternatives, people are more likely to buy a given good if its local context includes a good it dominates than otherwise.

2. Neoclassical theories of household behavior have assumed that all informationally equivalent descriptions of alternatives elicit the same choice. However, recent experiments have shown that this invariance assumption is often violated when informationally equivalent descriptions suggest different reference points. Evidence of such preference reversals has prompted closer scrutiny of how individuals frame alternatives and then choose among them. The most important features of framing are acceptance and segregation. Acceptance is the tendency to accept a plausible description of a problem rather than rephrase it. Segregation is the tendency to isolate some acts, contingencies, and outcomes and ignore others. The most important example of segregation is the tendency to think in terms of gains and losses rather than complete consumption bundles.

3. If no dominant alternative is obvious, people act as if they were calculating the overall value of each alternative, using an S-shaped value function defined on gains and losses. The function is steeper for losses than gains, indicating loss aversion.

12.5 Solutions to Exercises

12.1. The arc elasticity is

$$\frac{\Delta v}{\Delta x}\frac{x_0}{v_0} = (101^{.8} - 100^{.8})\frac{100}{100^{.8}} = .7992.$$

12.2. Using the given value function, we calculate that $v(-10) - v(-15) = 7.25$ but $v(-120) - v(-125) = 4.58$. If the subjects in the experiment had value functions similar to the one in this problem and framed outlays as losses, they would have felt that reducing an outlay from \$15 to \$10 represented a greater change in value than reducing an outlay from \$125 to \$120.

12.3. Using the value function, we find that $v(-5) - v(-10) = 8.06$ whereas $v(95) - v(90) = 1.62$. If the subjects in the experiment had value functions similar to this one and framed unemployment as a loss and employment as a gain, they would have felt that a reduction of unemployment from 10 to 5% represented a greater change in value than an increase in employment from 90 to 95%.

12.6 Problems

1. Consider a consumer who is shopping for a bicycle. Other things being equal, the consumer prefers a bicycle with more speeds, less weight, and a lower price. Do any of the following models dominate all the others? If so, which?
   a. 15 speeds, 25 lbs, \$300
   b. 18 speeds, 28 lbs, \$275
   c. 21 speeds, 23 lbs, \$325
   d. 10 speeds, 22 lbs, \$270
   e. 18 speeds, 24 lbs, \$280

2. Consider an individual to whom the invariance assumption is applicable. Between which of the following alternatives would the individual express indifference?
   a. A pound of chocolates or 16 ounces of chocolates
   b. An operation with a 99% survival rate or an operation with a 1% fatality rate
   c. A lottery with a 5% chance of winning or a lottery with a 95% chance of not winning
   d. A score of cookies or a dozen cookies
   e. A gallon of milk or 4 quarts of milk

3. Consider an individual whose value function is

$$v(x) = \begin{cases} x^{.5} & \text{if } x \geq 0 \\ -2(-x)^{.5} & \text{if } x < 0 \end{cases},$$

where a positive x represents gains and a negative x represents losses.
   a. Using this value function, calculate $v(-10) - v(-15)$ and $v(-120) - v(-125)$. How do your calculations help explain the behavior of subjects in the experiment involving the purchase of a calculator?
   b. Using the value function in the previous problem, calculate $v(-5) - v(-10)$ and $v(95) - v(90)$. How do your calculations help explain the behavior of subjects in the experiment involving policies affecting labor markets and inflation?

13

▨ Labor Supply

13.1 Consumption vs. Leisure

A decision to work a certain number of hours is a decision to forgo that amount of free time in order to increase income. Time not spent working or sleeping will be called **leisure**. Assuming that an individual needs to sleep 8 hours a day, we suppose that he has 16 hours to divide between work and leisure.[1]

The individual faces a tradeoff between leisure and income. This tradeoff can be described by a budget constraint. Assuming for simplicity that all income is spent rather than saved, we can interpret the tradeoff between leisure and income as a tradeoff between leisure and consumption. Viewing the labor supply decision as a choice of the best combination of leisure and consumption, we can reuse the—now familiar—apparatus of budget constraints and indifference curves. Consider an individual who has no unearned income but may work any number of hours (up to 16 a day) at a constant wage rate w. If we denote daily income or consumption by C and leisure measured in hours by Le, we can write the individual's budget constraint as $C = w(16 - Le)$. When Le is plotted on the horizontal axis, the slope of the budget constraint is $-w$.

The individual's preferences between leisure and income can, as usual, be described by an indifference map. Since both consumption and leisure are goods, the indifference curves are negatively sloped.[2]

Optimal allocation of time is represented by a point where an indifference curve touches the budget constraint without crossing it. If at this point leisure and consumption are strictly positive and the indifference curve and the budget constraint are smooth, then the wage rate w equals the marginal rate of substitution (MRS), as in Figure 13.1. For example, if the

---

[1] For simplicity, we assume in this chapter that all work is for wages; that is, no time is spent on domestic chores such as gardening and sewing that augment consumption outside the marketplace. Given this assumption, time not devoted to work or sleep can reasonably be called "leisure." However, in a more advanced treatment of labor supply, we might subdivide time not devoted to wage work or sleep into time consumed by home chores and time devoted to recreation. In that case, the aggregate of time spent on chores and recreation would be more appropriately called "nonmarket time" rather than "leisure."

[2] Recent empirical studies suggest that, for a typical worker, indifference curves for leisure and consumption are sharply curved near the point representing the worker's current position. This finding can be understood as an instance of Tversky and Kahneman's (1991) principle of loss aversion. Workers seem to require a large gain in leisure to compensate for any loss in consumption and a large gain in consumption to compensate for any loss in leisure (Dunn 1996). Given that workers are loss-averse, we should expect that changes in their reference points may alter their preferences with regard to leisure and consumption.

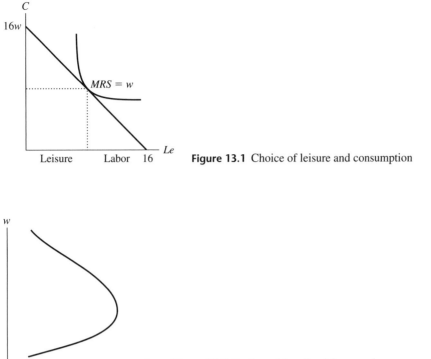

Figure 13.1 Choice of leisure and consumption

Figure 13.2 Backward-bending labor supply curve

budget constraint has the form described and the indifference curves have slope $-C/Le$, then at a tangency point $-w = -C/Le$, or $w \cdot Le = C$. Note that for an individual who derives all his income from labor, $C = w \cdot La$, where $La = 16 - Le$ is labor time. Hence at the tangency point we find that $w \cdot Le = w \cdot La$ or $Le = La$, that is, the individual divides the day equally between work and leisure. This particular individual works 8 hours regardless of the wage rate. We would say that this individual's labor supply is completely price-inelastic.

13.2 Labor Supply Curve

The quantity of labor supplied may be affected by the wage.[3] However, there is no general rule about the direction of the effect. Some people's labor supply is an increasing function of the wage; some people's labor supply is a decreasing function of the wage. Still other people's labor supply may be a nonmonotonic function of the wage. Backward-bending labor supply curves, as in Figure 13.2, are rather common, at least in textbooks. Labor supply curves shaped like an inverted S have been discussed in the development economics literature (Sharif 2003).

---

[3] Here, quantity of labor can be interpreted as duration. The pace of labor will be discussed in Section 13.4.

Mike sleeps 8 hours a day and divides the remaining 16 hours between labor (La) and leisure (Le). He can work up to 16 hours a day at a wage rate of $\$w$/hr. He consumes his entire income. When leisure is plotted on the horizontal axis and consumption (C) on the vertical, Mike's indifference curves have slope $-(C + 48)/Le$. Mike's wages are his only income. Thus his budget constraint for consumption and leisure is $C = w(16 - Le)$.

  a. Derive Mike's labor supply function, that is, an equation showing how La depends on w.
  b. At what wage does Mike enter (or leave) the labor force; that is, at what wage does Mike want to work zero hours?
  c. As the wage rate increases, what is the limit toward which La tends?
  d. Sketch Mike's labor supply curve.

We have been assuming that there is only one kind of labor and the only alternative to labor is leisure. These assumptions are appropriate if we are analyzing total work time. However, if we wanted to analyze the amount of time an individual devotes to a particular occupation, say, carpentry, we would need to consider the wage rates in that and alternative occupations. If an individual has a choice of several kinds of work, his supply of any particular kind of labor is almost sure to be directly related to the wage for that kind of work and inversely related to the wages in other occupations.[4] The flow of workers from low-paying to higher paying jobs tends to narrow wage differentials between jobs requiring the same skills. However, this flow does not completely obliterate wage differences even among jobs requiring identical skills. One reason for the persistence of wage differences is that they compensate for nonpecuniary (nonmonetary) job differences. For example, garbage collectors may earn more than florists because their jobs literally stink. Economists say that jobs that are less attractive must pay **compensating differentials**, that is, higher wages to counterbalance their unattractive nonpecuniary characteristics.

The market supply curve is obtained by horizontally summing individual supply curves. The market supply curve for any particular occupation is almost sure to be upward sloping because higher wages for it will draw workers away from other occupations. The market supply curve for all types of labor taken together, however, is not necessarily positively sloped.

13.3   Nonlinear Budget Constraints

Thus far we have assumed that an individual has no unearned income but may work any number of hours at a constant wage rate w. These assumptions allowed us to draw a linear budget constraint. Other assumptions, however, may lead to nonlinearities. We will consider three cases: unearned income, involuntary unemployment and underemployment, and overtime pay.

---

[4] Similarly, if a forward-looking individual has a choice of working at various times, his supply of labor at a particular time should be an increasing function of the wage at that time measured relative to wages at other times. "Make hay while the sunshines" is good economic advice. Whether most people follow that advice is an empirical question that we'll examine in the chapters on intertemporal choice.

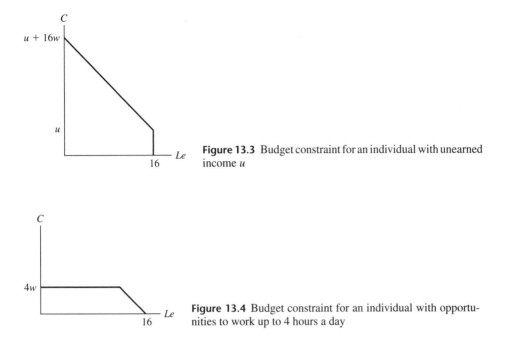

Figure 13.3 Budget constraint for an individual with unearned income u

Figure 13.4 Budget constraint for an individual with opportunities to work up to 4 hours a day

13.3.1 Unearned Income

The budget constraint for an individual who has an unearned income of u dollars a day is shifted up by that amount, as in Figure 13.3. If an indifference curve passes through the kink at $(16, u)$ without dipping under the budget constraint, then the individual will not enter the labor force.

13.3.2 Involuntary Unemployment and Underemployment

If employers, governments, or unions set wages above market-clearing levels, some people will be unable to work as long as they would like.[5] If they cannot find jobs, their budget constraints lack negatively sloped segments. If they may work a few hours a day, but not 16, their opportunity sets are truncated above. For example, Figure 13.4 shows the budget constraint of an individual who has opportunities to work up to 4 hours a day. If an indifference curve passes through the kink at $(12, 4w)$ without dipping below the budget constraint, the individual will work 4 hours but might prefer to work more.

EXERCISE 13.2

Graph the budget constraint for an individual whose daily unearned income is $15 and who has the opportunity to work up to 6 hours a day at $10 an hour.

---

[5] Employers may set wages above market clearing levels in order to have their pick of a large applicant pool, boost worker morale and productivity, or discourage shirking and labor turnover. Governments and unions may set wages above market clearing levels in industries where they believe labor demand is inelastic, in hopes of raising average earnings.

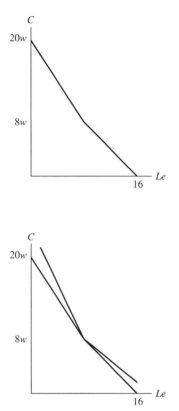

Figure 13.5 Budget constraint for an individual offered overtime pay for working more than 8 hours

Figure 13.6 A kinked budget constraint and a more sharply kinked indifference curve

13.3.3 Overtime Wages

In many industries, wage rates vary with hours worked. In a typical case, the wage rate for hours in excess of 40 a week is 1.5 times the wage rate for hours up to 40 a week. Such overtime pay arrangements result in budget constraints that are piecewise linear and convex. For example, Figure 13.5 shows the budget constraint for an individual who is paid at a hourly rate $\$w$ for up to 8 hours a day and then at a rate $\$1.5w$ for additional hours. If this individual worked 16 hours, she would earn $8w + 8(1.5w) = 20w$. The slope of the budget constraint changes discontinuously at the point $(8, 8w)$.

If all indifference curves were smooth, none could pass through the kink in the budget constraint without passing under some segment of the constraint. Thus no individual would voluntarily stop working at the moment an overtime premium starts. Yet a large majority of hourly wage workers stop working at just that point (Dunn 1996). In some cases the workers may want overtime work but are denied the opportunity. They are involuntarily underemployed, as in Subsection 13.3.2. However, in other cases, workers may choose to stop work just as overtime rates become applicable because their indifference curves are more sharply kinked at this point than is their budget constraint. Tversky and Kahneman (1991) report evidence suggesting that indifference curves are commonly 2–2.5 times steeper above the reference point than below it. The corresponding factor for budget constraints is typically just 1.5 (Dunn 1996). This case is illustrated in Figure 13.6.

How does a worker's reference point come to be located just where overtime pay begins? Two possibilities spring to mind. One is that the worker initially wanted to work overtime but was not allowed to do so. Eventually the worker adapted to the limited employment opportunities by filling her spare time with gardening, cooking, and so on. A second possibility is that the individual initially wanted part-time employment but found that the only available jobs were full time. The individual took a full-time job and adapted to it by giving up hobbies, finding a babysitter, and getting used to eating at fast-food joints. In either case, her indifference curves became kinked at the point representing her habitual schedule.

13.4 Pace and Motivation

Workers may have choices about the pace, as well as the duration, of labor. Offered higher pay for faster work, rational workers would adjust their pace until the marginal disutility of faster work just equaled the marginal utility of higher income.

The question of how managers should motivate workers to maintain an appropriate pace was raised by Xenophon and continues to be discussed. The right answer may depend on (1) whether the pace of work has to be synchronized among workers and (2) how closely a manager can monitor the pace or results of work.

A piecework system may be adopted if the pace of work does not have to be synchronized among workers and the results of individual work can be easily measured by a manager. In this case, workers individually set their own pace. Fruit and vegetable picking are classic examples.

Hourly wage rates and a uniform pace of work may be adopted where synchronization matters and work is readily observed. An assembly line exemplifies this case. Workers who do not keep up with the line speed can be quickly identified and fired.

A more complicated case arises when synchronization matters but individual performance is not subject to continuous monitoring. Many offices fit this description. Even when office managers can see who is at work, they cannot always see who is making timely progress. Managers undertake occasional performance reviews to identify and dismiss shirkers. However, that leaves the problem of how to motivate workers between reviews. One possibility is that employers may set wages above market-clearing levels to make the threat of firing a serious deterrent to shirking.[6]

13.5 Human Capital and Education

The amount of goods people can produce depends not only on how long and hard they work but also on their skills, or as economists often say, **human capital**. Just as investment in plant and equipment creates physical capital, investment in education and training produces human capital. Capital is often measured as the sum of past investments, discounted for depreciation. Measured in this way human capital exceeds physical capital in the United States by a margin of two or three to one.

An individual invests in physical or human capital hoping to increase his income. Governments encourage investment in physical and human capital hoping to raise national

---

[6] Employers may also set pay rates above market-clearing levels to reduce labor turnover or (in less developed countries) to promote good nutrition as a prerequisite to high productivity. Any pay rate set above the market-clearing level for the benefit of the employer may be termed an *efficiency wage*. Such wages are analyzed in Akerlof and Yellen (1986).

output. Individuals who invest in education certainly enjoy higher average incomes than those who do not. The median income of individuals who completed 4 years of college is 63% more than that of individuals who completed high school but did not attend college. The median income of individuals with doctorates is 42% higher than that of individuals who got bachelor's degrees but did not attend graduate school (Snyder and Hoffman 2003).

The gap between the wages of unskilled and skilled workers widened in the 1970s and 1980s because employers' demand for skilled labor rose relative to their demand for unskilled labor. Many economists attribute this shift in demand to technological change that has increased the productivity gap separating workers with different levels of education. Another possible explanation for the shift in demand is the growth of international trade. American firms found it increasingly difficult to compete with foreign producers in industries that make intensive use of unskilled labor, for example, apparel and shoes. American firms found their comparative advantage in industries that make intensive use of skilled labor, for example, aircraft and chemicals.[7]

Why are employers willing to pay higher wages to individuals with more education? One possible explanation for the positive correlation of education and income is that education produces skills for which employers are willing to pay high wages. Another possible explanation is that smart and persevering individuals are more likely to get college and graduate school degrees than are stupid and shiftless individuals. Employers who need smart and persevering individuals may want to hire individuals with advanced degrees even if their education imparts no productive skills. In other words, schools screen individuals, and degrees signal their possessors' abilities.[8]

If employers use college degrees as a signal of high productivity, students have an incentive to stay in school even if they are not learning productive skills. They become engaged in what is called **credentials competition**.

From a student's standpoint, it makes little difference whether advanced education raises income because it raises productivity or because it identifies highly productive individuals. However, from society's standpoint, the distinction is important. To the extent that education raises productivity, it surely merits support. But if education merely sorts individuals into productivity groups, some cheaper sorting system might be better. A week of testing I.Q.s and personality traits might substitute for 4 to 8 years of college.

13.6 Summary

1. Decisions about how long to work are decisions about how much leisure and how much material consumption to enjoy. Rational individuals choose a combination of leisure

---

[7] A large gap between the wages of skilled and unskilled workers may induce some unskilled workers to seek additional training. Certainly it increases the incentives to young people to stay in school. Thus we might expect the supply of unskilled labor to gradually contract and the supply of skilled labor to expand. These shifts in supply should diminish the spread between the wages of the skilled and unskilled.

[8] Supporters of this interpretation sometimes cite the following pattern of wage increases: 1 to 3 years of college raises wages by 14.8% over wages of high-school graduates; a college degree raises wages 37.6% over wages of persons with 1 to 3 years of college. This pattern—sometimes called "the sheepskin effect"—is consistent with the idea that employers regard a college degree as a sign of perseverance and likely productivity (Murphy and Welch 1989). However, if students who dropped out of college were learning less per year than those who graduated, the pattern is also consistent with the idea that employers value education for the skills it imparts.

and consumption that lies on their budget constraint where it is touched but not crossed by an indifference curve.

2. As the wage varies, individuals may respond by increasing or decreasing the hours they work. The relationship between wages and hours is shown by a labor supply curve.

3. Budget constraints are nonlinear when individuals have unearned income, are involuntarily unemployed or underemployed, or face wage rates that vary with hours worked.

4. Workers may have choices about how fast to work, as well as how long. To motivate workers to maintain an appropriate pace, managers can choose between piecework and hourly rates, with the better choice depending on whether pace needs to be synchronized among workers and whether individual performance can be closely monitored.

5. Education creates human capital. In America, human capital considerably exceeds physical capital in value. Workers with more education get higher wages. The wage gap between skilled and unskilled workers widened over the last 20 years because of shifts in labor demand. One explanation for why employers offer higher wages to better educated workers is that they believe that education imparts productive skills. Another explanation is that they believe that more productive individuals tend to get more education.

13.7 Solutions to Exercises

13.1.

  a. The tangency condition is $(C + 48)/Le = w$. Solving it for C, we obtain $C = wLe - 48$. Substituting $wLe - 48$ for C in the budget constraint, we get $wLe - 48 = w16 - wLe$, which implies that $Le = 8 + \frac{24}{w}$. Mike's time constraint is $La = 16 - Le$. Substituting $8 + \frac{24}{w}$ for Le in the previous equation, we get $La = 8 - \frac{24}{w}$.

  b. Solving the labor supply function for w, we get $w = 24/(8 - La)$. Thus $w = 3$ when $La = 0$.

  c. The limit is

$$\lim_{w \to \infty} La = \lim_{w \to \infty} \left(8 - \frac{24}{w}\right) = 8.$$

  d. Mike's labor supply curve is shown in Figure 13.7

13.2. The graph of the budget constraint is shown in Figure 13.8.

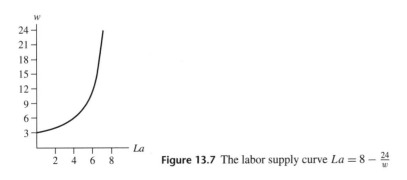

Figure 13.7 The labor supply curve $La = 8 - \frac{24}{w}$

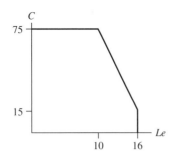

Figure 13.8 Budget constraint for an individual who has $15 in unearned income and an opportunity to work up to 6 hours at $10 an hour

13.8 Problems

Al sleeps 8 hours a day and divides the remaining 16 hours between labor (La) and leisure (Le). He can work up to 16 hours a day at a wage rate of $\$w/hr$. He consumes his entire income. When leisure is plotted on the horizontal axis and consumption (C) on the vertical, Al's indifference curves have slope $-(C + 32)/Le$.

1. Al's wages are his only income. Thus his budget constraint for consumption and leisure is $C = w(16 - Le)$.
   a. Derive Al's labor supply function, that is, an equation showing how La depends on w.
   b. At what wage does Al enter (or leave) the labor force—that is, at what wage does Al want to work zero hours?
   c. As the wage rate increases, what is the limit toward which La tends?
   d. Sketch Al's labor supply curve.
2. Thanks to a bequest from a rich uncle, Al starts getting interest income amounting to $16/day.
   a. What is Al's new budget constraint for consumption and leisure? Derive Al's new labor supply curve.
   b. At what wage does Al now enter the labor force?
   c. As the wage rate increases, what is the limit toward which La now tends?
   d. Sketch Al's new labor supply curve.
   e. At any given wage, does Al now supply more or less labor than before? Explain the difference.
3. After blowing the bequest at a casino, Al is back to relying on his earnings. To deepen his gloom, the government now requires him to pay a 25% income tax.
   a. Taking the tax into account, write Al's new budget constraint for consumption and leisure. Derive his new labor supply curve.
   b. At what wage does Al now enter the labor force?
   c. What is the limit toward which La tends as the wage rises?
   d. Sketch Al's new labor supply curve.
   e. At any given wage, does Al supply more or less labor than before he was taxed? Explain the difference.

14

▓ Monopoly and Monopsony Power

14.1 Monopoly

If a product has no close substitutes[1] and a single seller, economists say that its market is a **monopoly** and its seller is a **monopolist**.[2] Profits accruing to a monopolist normally constitute an incentive to outsiders to enter the industry and thereby destroy the monopoly. Thus when a profitable monopoly persists, economists suspect that potential entrants are kept at bay by circumstances that make entry costly or impossible (entry barriers) or by the monopolist's expected reaction to competitive threats (entry deterrence).

14.1.1 Entry Barriers

Identifying circumstances that prevent entry is a subtle and controversial problem of great interest to policymakers and economists specializing in industrial organization.[3] More consensus exists with regard to some possible barriers than others.

Most economists agree that entry barriers exist when potential entrants face restrictions or costs that the monopolist has never encountered. Important examples include the following:

1. A government may restrict or prohibit entry in various ways. (a) Patents give a temporary monopoly to inventors. In the United States patents last 20 years from the patent application filing date. They are granted in hopes of strengthening incentives for inventive activity. (b) Government licenses or franchises can create monopolies. At times some governments have used monopolies as revenue collection or patronage devices. Currently in the United States, government sanction for monopolies is usually given only in exceptional cases; for example, some states authorize a single restaurant or gas station at freeway rest stops. Similarly, some states have created alcoholic beverage control boards with monopoly powers. For a would-be entrant, overcoming government-imposed restrictions and prohibitions may either be impossible or entail costly lobbying and litigation.

2. Information may be concentrated in ways that hinder entry. A firm that has exclusive understanding of how to make a certain good will have temporary monopoly power,

---

[1] Recall that two goods are said to be substitutes if a rise in the price of one causes an increase in demand for the other. How strong this effect must be to make goods *close* substitutes is a matter of judgment. Rather than drawing an arbitrary dividing line between monopolies and competitive firms, many economists prefer to recognize a range of variation in monopoly power, a topic we shall examine in Subsection 14.1.5.

[2] Some authors use "monopoly" to refer to a monopolist as well as the market in which it sells.

[3] Classic works addressing this problem include Bain (1956), G. Stigler (1968), and von Weizsäcker (1980).

whether or not its understanding is protected by patents. Considerable expense might be required to crack commercial secrets such as the recipe for Coca-Cola.

3. A monopoly may have exclusive control over essential inputs. For example, the De Beers Group has at times enjoyed nearly exclusive control over raw diamonds. A would-be entrant might have to incur great expense to discover an alternative source or invent a substitute.

4. Customers who know and trust the monopolist may exhibit brand loyalty, that is, be unwilling to try the products of a new entrant unless offered deep discounts. Thus initial promotional expenses could be an entry barrier.

Controversies have arisen over proposals to extend the list of entry barriers to include difficulties in financing entry, economies of scale that allow large firms to produce more cheaply than small ones, and irreversible investments such as incorporation expenses. A promising recent suggestion for resolving the controversies is offered by McAfee et al. (2004), who argue that none of these factors in isolation is an entry barrier but each may combine with other circumstances to form such a barrier. They further argue that circumstances that fail to permanently block entry may nonetheless delay it long enough to be of concern to public officials in charge of antitrust policy.

14.1.2 Entry Deterrence

A monopolist may be able to deter entry by making a credible threat to take hostile action against any entrant. Three such actions are the following: First, a monopolist might frustrate an entrant's plans by locking up patent rights to crucial technologies. Second, a monopolist could act to raise its rival's costs. For example, if the rival uses a more labor-intensive technology, the monopolist might agree with a union to raise wages, hoping the union would then impose a similar contract on its rival. In the same vein, the monopolist might lobby for regulations or taxes that would be more onerous to the entrant than to itself. Third, a monopolist might respond to an entry attempt by signing contracts with the entrant's likely customers, freezing it out of the market (Shy 1995; Viscusi et al. 2000). How such threats might be made credible is a question that falls in the domain of game theory, a topic that will be introduced in Chapter 21.[4]

14.1.3 Objectives

What is the objective of a monopolist? The owners of a monopoly, like the owners of a perfectly competitive firm, would presumably want it to maximize profit. However, monopolies tend to be large firms in which many people hold stock. Frequently, stockholders lack tight control over the behavior of managers. This lack of tight control does not make much difference in the case of perfectly competitive firms because managers must in any case maximize profits just to break even and survive in the long run. In contrast, a lack of shareholder control over a monopoly might give its manager some discretion about which objectives to pursue.[5]

---

[4] Unless a threat is credible, it is not an effective deterrent. Consider, for example, a monopolist's excess capacity, which has sometimes been seen as a threat to respond to entry by flooding the market with cheap goods. This threat lacks credibility when implementing it would reduce the monopolist's profits (Shy 1995). Empirical evidence suggests that monopolists rarely build excess capacity with the aim of deterring entry (Liberman 1987).

[5] One possibility is that the manager of a monopoly may be inclined to empire building and wish to maximize revenue subject to a minimum profit constraint Baumol (1967).

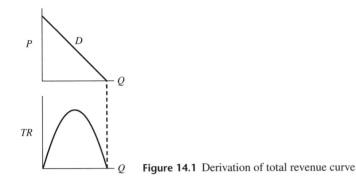

Figure 14.1 Derivation of total revenue curve

However, there are two good reasons to believe that monopolists usually behave much as if they were profit maximizers. First, owners generally structure compensation packages to make the income and benefits of top managers vary with profits. Second, if a manager fails to maximize profits, the price of his company's stock will be depressed, making the company a tempting target for a hostile takeover (Frank 1994). Thus the assumption of profit-maximization is probably nearly as as accurate for monopolies as for perfectly competitive firms.[6] We will make that assumption for the remainder of our discussion of monopolies.

14.1.4 Behavior

It is useful to distinguish between two types of monopolists: A nondiscriminating monopolist sells identical products at identical prices. In the case of similar products sold by a nondiscriminating monopolist, ratios of prices match corresponding ratios of marginal costs. For example, if the marginal cost of a good delivered to Hawaii is 1.2 times that of an otherwise identical good delivered to Illinois, the ratio of prices is 1.2. In contrast, a discriminating monopolist sells identical products at different prices or, in the case of similar products, sets prices in ratios that do not correspond to ratios of marginal costs. We will deal with the nondiscriminating monopolists first.

Nondiscriminating Monopolists

Because a monopolist by definition is the sole producer of a good, it cannot take the price of the good as given but rather has to choose a price and quantity combination consistent with the market demand curve. Faced with a negatively sloped demand curve, a monopolist must charge less to sell more. Let us write profits as $\Pi(Q) = P(Q) \cdot Q - TC(Q)$, where $P(Q)$ is the demand curve. To get a feeling for what the profit function looks like, let us start by plotting total revenue $TR = P \cdot Q$. Supposing that $P(Q)$ cuts both axes, we can see that $P \cdot Q$ must be zero for $Q = 0$ and for Q such that $P(Q) = 0$. In between, $P \cdot Q$ is positive (see Figure 14.1).

---

[6] Senbongi and Harrington (1995) show that owners of monopolies and competitive firms (unlike owners of some oligopolies) can devise compensation plans to induce managers to maximize profits. Brandenburger and Polak (1996) note an interesting qualification to the argument that stock markets enforce profit maximization: The market valuation of a firm is based on publicly available information about future profits. A manager who maximizes the market value of his firm may act differently than one who uses private as well as public information to maximize expected profits.

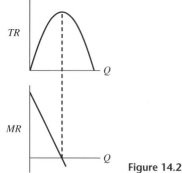

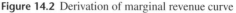

Figure 14.2 Derivation of marginal revenue curve

The slope of a tangent to the *TR* curve is called **marginal revenue** (*MR*). When *TR* is at its maximum, *MR* is zero (see Figure 14.2). A nondiscriminating monopolist's marginal revenue can be shown to have a simple relationship to the price it charges and its buyers' own-price elasticity of demand:[7]

$$MR = P\left(1 + \frac{1}{\epsilon^d}\right). \tag{14.1}$$

This formula for *MR* implies that if a demand curve is linear, the corresponding *MR* curve has the same vertical intercept but twice the slope. To derive this implication, consider the linear demand curve $P = a - bQ$, where a (the vertical intercept) and b (the absolute value of the slope) are positive constants. The reciprocal of the slope of this demand curve is $\frac{\Delta Q}{\Delta P} = -\frac{1}{b}$ and the own-price elasticity of demand is $\epsilon^d = \frac{\Delta Q}{\Delta P}\frac{P}{Q} = -\frac{1}{b}\frac{a-bQ}{Q}$. Substituting the right side of the last equation for ϵ^d in the formula for *MR*, we find that $MR = P(1 - \frac{bQ}{a-bQ}) = P(\frac{a-bQ-bQ}{a-bQ}) = a - 2bQ$. Comparing the demand curve and the *MR* curve, we see that their vertical intercepts are the identical but the slope of the *MR* curve $(-2b)$ is twice that of the demand curve.

The *TC* curve is positively sloped. As you probably recall, the slope of a tangent to the *TC* curve is called marginal cost (*MC*). Profit is the vertical difference between the *TR* and *TC* curves. Profit attains a local maximum where $MR = MC$. The monopoly produces at this point (Q^*) provided that profits (the net area below the *MR* curve and above the *MC* curve to the left of Q^*) are nonnegative; otherwise it shuts down (see Figure 14.3). Note that for a perfectly competitive firm $MR = P$, so the perfectly competitive firm's rule for profit maximization ($MC = P$) is a special case of the monopolists rule ($MC = MR$).

Note also that the profit-maximizing monopolist does not have a supply curve in the sense of a unique Q for every P. The profit-maximizing value of Q depends not only on P but also on the shape of the demand curve.

Given that Equation 14.1 holds for a nondiscriminating monopolist and that $MR = MC$ when profit is maximized, we see that a profit-maximizing, nondiscriminating monopolist

---

[7] Recall from Chapter 9 that an own-price elasticity of demand ϵ^d is a percentage change in the quantity divided by a percentage change in the price for movements along the demand curve. The relationship of *MR* to P and ϵ^d is most easily derived by using elementary calculus:

$$MR = \frac{dTR}{dQ} = P + Q\frac{dP}{dQ} = P\left(1 + \frac{Q}{P}\frac{dP}{dQ}\right) = P\left(1 + \frac{1}{\epsilon^d}\right).$$

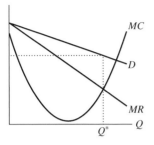

Figure 14.3 Monopolist sets $MC = MR$

sets its product's price based on its marginal cost and the own-price elasticity of demand:

$$P = MC \left(1 + \frac{1}{\epsilon^d} \right)^{-1} \tag{14.2}$$

For example, if $\epsilon^d = -5$ then $P = 1.25MC$ but if $\epsilon^d = -1.1$ then $P = 11MC$. In general, as the elasticity falls in absolute value, the markup of price over marginal cost increases.[8]

EXERCISE 14.1

Consider a monopoly whose total cost function is $TC = Q^3 - 30Q^2 + 302Q$, whose marginal cost function is $MC = 3Q^2 - 60Q + 302$, whose demand function is $P = 329 - 30Q$, and whose marginal revenue function is $MR = 329 - 60Q$, where Q is output and P is price. (If you know calculus, verify the marginal revenue function given above by differentiating the total revenue function $TR = P \cdot Q = 329Q - 30Q^2$ with respect to Q.) Assume that the firm maximizes profit but cannot practice price discrimination. (a) How much does the firm produce? (b) How much does the firm charge? (c) How large are the firm's profits?

Discriminating Monopolists

Price discrimination is the practice of selling identical products at different prices or similar products at price ratios that diverge from the corresponding ratios of marginal costs. To engage in price discrimination, a firm needs to be able to (a) set prices, (b) sort buyers (or induce buyers to sort themselves) according to price elasticity of demand, and (c) thwart resale.

Analysis of price discrimination was initiated in the mid nineteenth century by Jules Dupuit (1804–66) and other French engineers concerned with bridges, roads, and similar public works. Dupuit noted that the cost of operating some bridges and roads exceeded the revenue that could be generated by a uniform toll but could nonetheless be covered by revenue from a system of varied tolls. For example, consider a new bridge that might be used by workers commuting between their homes and jobs and by wealthier tourists. If the toll on the new bridge is low, many workers will use it in preference to an existing distant but free bridge. However, if the toll on the new bridge is high, the workers will avoid it

---

[8] Profit-maximizing nondiscriminating monopolists pick a point on their demand curve where $\epsilon^d < -1$. A point where $-1 < \epsilon^d$ could not maximize profit because moving up the demand curve (raising price and cutting output) would raise revenue and lower costs.

Table 14.1 Bridge tolls, use, and revenue

| Toll | Crossings by | | Revenue from | | |
	workers	tourists	workers	tourists	all
$1	500	280	$500	$280	$780
2	200	200	400	400	800
3	0	130	0	390	390

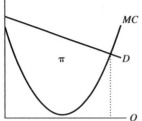

Figure 14.4 First-degree price discrimination

by continuing to use the old bridge. The wealthy tourists are less price sensitive. Suppose maintenance and interest on construction costs amount to $850 a day, independent of the number of users. Can these costs be covered from tolls? Let us assume that the daily number of bridge crossings depends on the toll, as shown in Table 14.1.

None of the three tolls in the table, applied uniformly, generates as much as $850 daily. However, before writing off the bridge as a money-losing project, let us consider charging $1 to workers and $2 to tourists. That combination would raise $900, more than enough to cover expenses. It illustrates how price discrimination can boost revenue Dupuit 1962 (1849). Note that the toll is set higher for the users with the less elastic demand.[9] Of course, to implement this price discrimination, the toll collector would have to distinguish workers from tourists by some procedure—for example, checking photo IDs issued to workers.

Forms of price discrimination are often classified using terminology introduced by a British economist, A. C. Pigou (1877–1959). In this classification, first-degree or perfect price discrimination is a hypothetical case in which a seller charges the maximum the buyer is willing to pay for each unit. In this case, MR is the price of the last unit sold, that is, the lowest price charged on any unit. Equating MR and MC means, in this case, producing where the MC curve crosses the demand curve. A monopolist who achieved first-degree price discrimination would capture all the gains from trade. Note that the monopolist practicing first-degree discrimination produces more than the nondiscriminating monopolist (see Figure 14.4).

Second-degree price discrimination was originally defined as a hypothetical case that would apply "if a monopolist were able to make n separate prices, in such wise that all units with a demand price greater than x were sold at a price x, all with a demand price less than x and greater than y at a price y, and so on" (Pigou 1932, p. 279). However, contemporary

---

[9] From the data in Table 14.1, we see that the arc price elasticity of demand, as the toll rises from $1 to $2, is .60 for workers and .29 for tourists.

economists generally say that a firm practices second-degree or indirect price discrimination when it sets a price schedule under which the unit price paid by a buyer depends on the quantity or quality purchased by this buyer, with prices not proportional to marginal cost. In selecting a quantity or quality, a buyer simultaneously selects a price. Thus second-degree price discrimination is said to rely on "self-selection" to match buyers with prices.

Important instances of the use of quantity in second-degree price discrimination are quantity discounts and two-part tariffs. Quantity discounts are exemplified by breakfast cereals that are cheaper per ounce in larger boxes and software licenses that are cheaper per user for larger sites.[10] A **two-part tariff** consists of an entry fee and a usage charge. For example, an amusement park may charge for admission and for each ride. At a park charging $20 for entry and $1 for each ride, the total cost per ride is $11 for a consumer who takes two rides but $3 for a consumer who takes ten rides.

Quality based price discrimination can rely on quality differences in consumption or purchasing. Quality differences in consumption are important to airline and software pricing. Airline tickets are are often cheaper when subject to restrictions such as advance purchase and Saturday night stay-overs. These restrictions are designed to be more inconvenient for business travel than for personal travel. Business travelers, with a low price elasticity of demand, are thus induced to buy expensive unrestricted tickets, while personal travelers, with higher price elasticities, rearrange their lives to use cheaper restricted tickets. Similarly, software often comes in a cheap "student" edition and a costly "professional" edition. The former, a crippled version of the latter, is usually capable of handling small-scale homework exercises but not large-scale business problems. Crippling the student edition does not reduce the vendor's costs but increases its revenue by forcing business users buy the more expensive edition.[11]

Quality differences in purchasing are exemplified by products that can be purchased with or without coupons. Purchase without coupons is quick and simple but expensive. Purchase with coupons requires more time and planning but saves money. Sellers that issue coupons do so in the hope that people who can afford to purchase a good without a coupon will do so, while those who would not buy the good at its regular price will take the time required to use a coupon. In other words, the sellers hope that people whose price elasticity of demand is low in absolute value will buy without using coupons while those with elasticities higher in absolute value will use coupons to buy products they would otherwise would not consume. Evidence consistent with these hopes has been reported in several studies. For example, Silva-Risso and Bucklin (2004) find that the price elasticity of demand for ketchup is -1.243 among coupon users and -0.978 among non users. Similarly, the price elasticity of demand for detergent is -1.816 among coupon users and -0.893 among non users.

Third-degree or multi-market price discrimination occurs when a seller distinguishes two or more groups of buyers and offers them identical goods at different prices or similar goods at prices not proportional to marginal costs. A seller practicing third- (as contrasted to second-) degree price discrimination actively matches buyers with price offers rather than relying on buyers' self-selection. The seller attempts to group together buyers with similar price elasticities, offering low prices to buyers with elasticities that are high in absolute value and high prices to buyers with elasticities that are low in absolute value. For example,

---

[10] More accurately expressed, the pricing of cereals and software constitutes price discrimination if it is not based on variation in marginal cost such as might arise from packaging and distribution.

[11] Likewise, some software companies target non-business and third-world users with selectively disabled "home" or "starter" editions.

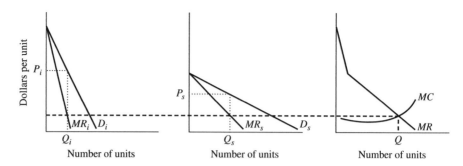

Figure 14.5 Third-degree price discrimination between two groups of buyers

a profit- or revenue-maximizing bridge operator, faced with the data in Table 14.1 would, as we have seen, set a lower toll for workers than wealthy tourists.

The relationships involved in third-degree price discrimination are illustrated in Figure 14.5. The monopolist distinguishes two groups of buyers. The group that is relatively insensitive to price has demand curve D_i and marginal revenue curve MR_i, as show in the diagram on the left. The group that is relatively price-sensitive has demand curve D_s and marginal revenue curve MR_s, shown in the the center diagram. The monopolist horizontally sums the two marginal revenue curves, getting the aggregate marginal revenue curve MR, shown on the right of the figure. The intersection of the marginal revenue curve and the marginal cost curve (also shown on the right) establishes the profit-maximizing values of aggregate output Q and marginal cost, indicated with dashed lines. The intersections of the dashed marginal cost line with the disaggregate marginal revenue curves MR_i and MR_s, shown in the left and center diagrams, fix the profit-maximizing quantities to sell in the two markets, Q_i and Q_s, indicated with dotted lines. The intersection of a vertical line at Q_i with the demand curve D_i determines the profit-maximizing price P_i, shown on the left. The intersection of a vertical line at Q_s with the demand curve D_s establishes the profit-maximizing price P_s, shown in the center diagram. Note that $P_i > P_s$.

Contemporary examples of third-degree price discrimination are provided by publishers and pharmaceutical makers. Publishers of many journals charge different prices to subscribers grouped by characteristics thought to be indicative of price elasticity: Libraries are charged more than individuals; subscribers in rich countries are charged more than subscribers in poor countries; professors are charged more than students.

Similarly, pharmaceutical makers have tried to sell drugs at high prices to buyers presumed to have elasticities low in absolute value. Until the late 1990s the drug manufacturers sold at higher prices to retail pharmacies than to hospitals, health maintenance organizations, and pharmacy benefit management firms, which (unlike retail pharmacies) have substantial influence over prescriptions. In response to an antitrust lawsuit by retail pharmacists, pharmaceutical makers agreed in 1996 to abandon this form of price discrimination (Scherer 1997). However, drug makers continue to sell their products at higher prices in the U.S. than in countries with lower per capita incomes or more cost-sensitive national health systems. This practice has lead to discussions at state and federal levels of U.S. government about whether to permit re-importation of drugs from countries where they can be purchased more cheaply (Pecorino 2002).

EXERCISE 14.2

Consider a monopolist that practices first-degree price discrimination but is otherwise identical to the firm in Exercise 14.1. (a) How much does the firm produce? (b) What is the lowest price the firm charges for any unit? (c) How large are the firm's profits? (d) Contrast your results in Exercises 1 and 2, parts a–c, and explain the differences.

Community Standards of Fairness

Although economists usually talk about firms as though they faced a given demand curve and cost curves, there is evidence that firms' behavior can sometimes affect these curves. The most conspicuous example of firms attempting to shift their demand curves is advertising. However, in the current section we shall focus on a different channel through which firms can influence their demand and cost curves.

An important link between behavior and demand and cost curves is provided by community standards of fairness. When people feel that a firm is acting unfairly they have a variety of ways of retaliating. Consumers may boycott the firm, thus shifting its demand curve down. Workers may refuse to work for it. Citizens may mobilize politically to impose onerous taxes or regulations. People with no other recourse may vandalize the firm's property. These actions can shift the cost curves up significantly.

Monopolies tend to be more in the public eye than smaller, more competitive firms. Thus they are peculiarly sensitive to public opinion and need to appear compliant with community standards of fairness. Survey research indicates that community standards of fairness are based largely on recent precedents. For example, people who are used to paying $2.00 a gallon for gasoline feel that it is fair for gasoline companies to go on charging $2.00 a gallon unless rising production costs dictate a higher price. Most people are hostile to price hikes based on increases in monopoly power. For example, respondents to a survey "were nearly unanimous in condemning a store that raises prices when its sole competitor in a community is temporarily forced to close" (Kahneman et al. 1986, p. 735).

Firms sometimes take such sentiment into account. A rustic example was chronicled by Laura Ingals Wilder in *The Long Winter*. When blizzards cut off a small town in the Dakota territories from food supplies, the merchant with the last remaining wheat tried to raise its price to three times its cost. But after the angry locals threatened to boycott his store when alternative sources of food became available, he relented and sold the wheat at cost. A second example is drawn from events during the spring and summer of 1920, when there was a severe gasoline shortage on the West Coast, where Standard Oil of California was the dominant supplier. The firm was vertically integrated, so it could not blame suppliers if it decided to raise gasoline prices. In deference to public opinion, Standard Oil maintained previous prices and introduced a rationing scheme (Olmstead and Rhode 1985; cited by Kahneman et al. 1986). A contemporary example is provided by the hotels that in peak season fill up and turn away potential customers rather than raising their rates to market-clearing levels. Hotel proprietors say they are afraid that if they jacked up rates to market-clearing levels during the peak season, customers would be so offended that they wouldn't return during the slack season (Kahneman et al. 1986).

Price discrimination sometimes provokes public hostility. For example, price discrimination by U.S. railroads in the nineteenth century sparked a populist backlash that contributed to the passage of the Interstate Commerce Act of 1887, which prohibits personal discrimination and higher charges for short hauls than long hauls. More recently, Coca Cola tried programming vending machines to make prices an increasing function of temperature. After encountering a hostile public reaction, Coca Cola abandoned this form of price discrimination (Odlyzko 2003).

Popular objections to price discrimination rest in part on a perception of unfairness in price increases based solely on changes in demand. In one survey, 91% of respondents condemned as unfair a rent increase occasioned by a tenant taking a nearby job and thus becoming less willing to move (Kahneman et al. 1986). The tenant's price elasticity had presumably decreased in absolute value, making a rent increase profitable, but not, apparently, socially acceptable.

Price discrimination is sometimes concealed by **barter** (exchange of goods for other goods rather than money) or **bundling** (pricing bundles of products rather than their components). To make overt price discrimination more palatable to loss-averse consumers, firms generally frame it in terms of discounts rather than surcharges (Kimes and Wirtz 2003, Odlyzko 2003).

14.1.5 Measurement of Monopoly Power

Monopoly power is usually conceived as the ability to sell goods at prices above their marginal cost. A convenient measure of this ability for a nondiscriminating monopolist, the **Lerner index**, is the excess of price over marginal cost expressed as a fraction of price, $(P - MC)/P$ (Lerner 1934). To calculate a similar index for a discriminating monopolist, we could replace the P in Lerner's formula by an average of the various prices it charges.

When a nondiscriminating monopolist maximizes profit, its Lerner index equals the reciprocal of the absolute value of the own-price elasticity of demand:

$$\frac{P - MC}{P} = \frac{1}{|\epsilon^d|} \tag{14.3}$$

This result follows from Equation 14.2 and the fact that ϵ^d is negative. Equation 14.3 implies that a firm facing a horizontal demand curve (as in perfect competition) has zero monopoly power. As the demand curve gets steeper, the absolute value of the price elasticity of demand drops and monopoly power rises.

EXERCISE 14.3

Using the information in Exercise 14.1, calculate (a) the Lerner index $\frac{P-MC}{P}$ and (b) the reciprocal of absolute value of the price elasticity of demand $\left| \frac{P}{Q} \frac{\Delta Q}{\Delta P} \right|^{-1}$ at the profit-maximizing values of P and Q. Are your answers the same?

14.1.6 Welfare Implications

Some forms of monopoly involve a loss of efficiency compared to perfect competition. The nondiscriminating monopolist produces where $MC = MR < P$. Thus there are potential buyers who are willing to pay more than the marginal cost of production but who are not able to buy the product. That is an inefficient restriction of output.

The efficiency loss can be represented in a diagram featuring a production possibilities frontier and an indifference curve map for a representative consumer. Equilibrium under perfect competition in a closed economy is represented by a tangency point between the production possibilities curve and an indifference curve. Monopoly in one of the two industries restricts output in this industry. Displaced resources find employment in the

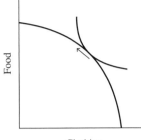

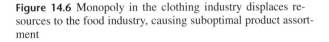

Figure 14.6 Monopoly in the clothing industry displaces resources to the food industry, causing suboptimal product assortment

competitive sector. Thus the product mix is distorted, reducing consumer welfare. (See Figure 14.6.)

Discriminating monopoly may or may not be inefficient, depending on its form. First-degree (perfect) discrimination would involve no inefficiency because everyone willing to pay the marginal cost of production would get the product. Were a monopolist able to practice perfect price discrimination, any objections would be on grounds of equity rather than efficiency: The monopolist would appropriate all the gains from trade, some of which would constitute Marshallian consumer surplus under perfect competition.

The effects of second-degree price discrimination may depend on the method of implementation and the cognitive abilities of buyers. Even in favorable cases, a monopolist practicing second-degree price discrimination may reduce social welfare by producing a nonoptimal quantity and/or misallocating goods among consumers (Katz 1983). Further inefficiencies can ensue if the discrimination is implemented by degrading product quality—e.g., crippling software or imposing Saturday-night stay-over requirements on air travel (Wilson 1993). Yet another type of inefficiency results when second-degree price discrimination confronts boundedly rational buyers. In this case, complex price schedules may impose decision-making costs and/or induce errors (Varian 1989). For example, many buyers are confused by airfares, which have grown complicated enough to challenge even experienced travel agents.[12]

Third-degree price discrimination may or may not mitigate the inefficiency characteristic of nondiscriminating monopoly. The favorable case occurs if the price discrimination allows a monopoly to profitably sell to a group of demanders to whom it would otherwise sell nothing. In other cases third-degree price discrimination comes no closer to efficiency than does nondiscriminating monopoly (Varian 1989).

14.1.7 Policy Issues

What should be done about monopolies? The answer may depend on their origins. If a monopoly is based solely on exclusive control of an input, a government license, or entry deterrence, breaking up the monopoly through antitrust action may result in efficiency gains.

---

[12] I once encountered a travel agency headed by a man with a Ph.D. in math from U.C. Berkeley. He wrote computer software based on graph theory to find the bargains that airlines had concealed in their maze of fares. The encounter left me wondering (a) how much brainpower is occupied in devising and deciphering needlessly complicated fare structures and (b) what this brainpower could accomplish if redirected to research on, say, fusion power, genetic engineering, or global warming.

Other sources of monopoly are less attractive targets for antitrust action. We may be better off putting up with monopolies based on patents or commercial secrets than doing without the inventions stimulated by the possibility of profiting from them.

Antitrust action against a monopoly with economies of scale may be inappropriate because the advantages of eliminating monopolistic distortions of product assortment may be more than counterbalanced by the disadvantages of forgoing economies of scale. Unfortunately, the government does not always have enough information to tell whether significant economies of scale exist. The authors of U.S. antitrust laws (such as the Sherman Act of 1890 and the Clayton Act of 1914) feared that evidence of economies of scale would be fabricated if such evidence were allowed to be a basis for legal mergers. Consequently, U.S. antitrust law makes no provision for allowing mergers that result in cost savings. In practice, the Justice Department uses its discretion in deciding which cases to prosecute.

We have seen that monopolies are frequently inefficient and virtually always appropriate consumer surplus, yet breaking up natural monopolies results in loss of economies of scale. The alternatives are public ownership, regulation, or contracting.

A publicly owned monopoly could be instructed to operate at the point where its marginal cost curve cuts its demand curve. If its MC curve lies below its AC curve (as in a firm with economies of scale), it will earn negative profits at this point. The loss can be made up by a subsidy provided from general tax revenue, as in Figure 14.7. Abba P. Lerner (1944) explained in detail how public ownership should work. How well it works in practice may depend on political institutions and the quality of the civil service. Opponents of public ownership argue that it has two flaws. First, managers of public enterprises may ignore their mandate to produce efficiently and instead inflate their costs. Second, political pressures may influence plant location decisions; for example, the former Yugoslavia's "political factories" were situated far from suppliers and customers.

Public regulation of privately owned monopolies has a long and complex history in the United States. Regulatory methods first applied to railroads in the late nineteenth century were subsequently adapted to other services such as electricity, gas, and telecommunications. For several decades the most common method was **rate-of-return regulation** (also known as **cost-of-service regulation**) under which regulators first set an allowed rate of return on capital, typically somewhat higher than the opportunity cost of capital, and then set output prices consistent with this allowed rate of return. The effectiveness of such regulation in keeping prices near competitive levels depends, naturally, on whether the regulatory agency is responsive to consumers or captured by the monopolist. Capture may

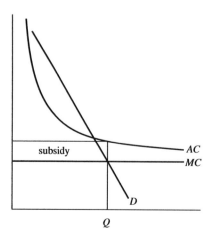

Figure 14.7 A subsidy equal to $Q(AC - MC)$ enables a monopoly with falling average costs to break even where $MC = P$.

occur because the regulated firms are among the most likely future employers of the erst-while regulators. Aware that their career prospects are affected by their regulatory decisions, regulators may be tempted to oblige the firms they nominally oversee.

By reducing uncertainty about profits, rate of return regulation reassured potential investors and lenders and thus probably lowered the cost of capital to regulated monopolists. These effects were particularly important for the growth of capital-intensive industries such as electric power generation (Hausman and Neufeld 2002).

Economists have found two theoretical reasons to question the efficiency of rate-of-return regulations. First, an assured rate of return on capital in excess of the cost of capital provides an incentive to use more than the efficient amount of capital. If the quantity and quality of output is given, the excess capital would displace labor or other productive inputs (Averch and Johnson 1962; Kolpin 2001). If the monopolist has some discretion in choosing the quantity and/or quality of output, it may raise them to inefficient levels in order to use more capital and thus earn higher profits (Abel 2000 cited in Banerjee 2003). Second, a monopolist who reduced production costs would reap no lasting gain under rate-of-return regulation. Sooner or later the regulators would cut the output price to match the cost savings. Thus rate-of-return regulation embodies a ratchet effect, which blunts incentives to reduce costs (Ai and Sappington 2002). The empirical evidence about these theoretical concerns' relevance to regulation as practiced in the United States is mixed (Banerjee 2003; Frank 2003; Viscusi et al. 2000).

In recent years, rate-of-return regulation has been replaced in some industries by other forms of regulation. In the telecommunications industry, for example, the number of U.S. states using rate-of-return regulation declined from 50 in 1985 to 12 in 1999. One of the most widely used replacements is **price-cap regulation**, under which a regulator sets a moving upper bound on the price of a firm's output. The rate of growth in this cap is calculated as the inflation rate minus the expected rate of productivity growth for similar firms. Subject to this cap, the regulated firm is free to choose its inputs to maximize its profits. Thus price-cap regulation, unlike rate-of-return regulation, provides incentives to use only efficient levels of capital and to cut costs when possible. Developed in Britain in the 1980s, price-cap regulation has spread rapidly in the United States. The number of U.S. states applying price-cap regulation to telecommunications rose from 0 in 1989 to 35 in 1999 (Ai and Sappington 2002). The change from rate-of-return to price-cap regulation appears to have increased efficiency in U.S. telephone service (Resende 2000).

A final alternative for dealing with a natural monopoly is for the government to invite firms to compete to become the monopolist, a procedure known as **competitive tendering** or **franchise bidding**. To implement this procedure, a government could (at least in simple cases) specify the product and solicit bids to produce it. The firm offering the lowest bid would be awarded a contract making it the sole supplier within the government's jurisdiction. Competitive bidding should drive the price to a level at which the monopolist just breaks even.[13] Compared to regulation, this approach is attractive, when feasible, because (a) the government can implement it without knowing the cost curves of producers and (b) the government and the monopolist have little opportunity to collude to set high prices at the expense of consumers or taxpayers (Demsetz 1968).

Thinking about implementation of franchise bidding, some economists suspect "the devil is in the details," particularly if the details are numerous, subtle, or uncertain. Such details may be encountered when attempting to specify product quality, set procedures for adjusting

---

[13] If a two-part tariff is used, the price can be driven down to marginal cost, with entry fees covering any excess of average over marginal cost. If two-part tariffs are excluded, the price would be driven to equal average cost.

prices to accommodate future shifts in demand or cost curves, or arrange the transfer of assets from one period's franchise holder to its successor (Williamson 1976).

Notable policy experiments with franchise bidding include cable television in the United States and municipal services in the United Kingdom. Cable TV is arguably a natural monopoly in the sense that, in a typical locale, cable service can be provided more cheaply by one system than by overlapping systems. Hence consumers may benefit from monopoly provided the monopolist is forced, by some procedure such as franchise bidding, to sell at cost. In many parts of the United States local governments have experimented with auctioning rights to operate cable TV service. Contracts, typically lasting fifteen years, specified certain aspects of service quality, such as the number of channels, and left others, such as program content, to the discretion of the service provider. Detailed specification of program content would have been not only tedious for the regulators but unconstitutional under the First Amendment. After obtaining a contract, cable operators were able to use their discretion to switch to cheaper programming (Viscusi et al. 2000).

During the life of a fifteen year contract, a cable operator's costs could change enough to require reconsideration of rates charged to consumers. In many cases, operators proposed rate increases, which government authorities then approved or rejected. Thus regulation, which franchise bidding was supposed to replace, returned to supplement incomplete long-term contracts. Frustration with program quality and cable rates led policy makers in the late 1990s to look for alternatives to franchise bidding and rate regulation. Current interest focuses on creating competition among providers of TV signals over cable, direct broadcast satellite systems, and telephone line systems (Viscusi et al. 2000).

In the United Kingdom many local services were routinely performed until the late 1980s by government workers. This pattern was changed by the Local Government Act of 1988, which required that services including building and street cleaning, garbage collection, grounds and vehicle maintenance, and school and welfare catering be provided under contracts awarded through competitive tendering. Government workers interested in performing the services were grouped into Direct Service Organizations (DSO) to compete with private firms for contracts (Bivand and Szymanski 2000). The Act required local governments to award a contract to the lowest bidder, regardless of the bidder's employment practices or wage rates. Thus the Act forced the DSO workers to risk losing their jobs or accept wages and benefits as low as those paid by the lowest-cost private contractors (Pinch and Patterson 2000).

Competitive tendering helped to reduce the cost of local services, particularly in areas with multiple bidders. For example, in the case of garbage collection, econometric estimates suggest cost saving of at least 6.7% for two bids, 10.4% for three bids, 13.0% for four bids, and 14.9% for five bids (Gómez-Lobo and Szymanski 2001). The cost savings were achieved by some combination of increased productivity, reduced pay for service workers, and degraded service quality. Productivity gains and/or service degradation are suggested by reports that employment in services subjected to competitive tendering dropped about 12.5% (Pinch and Patterson 2000). Economists who have studied the matter tend to believe that the cost cuts came more at the expense of service workers than at the expense of service quality (Bivand and Szymanski 2000). However, when the Labour government elected in 1997 moved away from competitive tendering, its stated reasons had more to do with service quality than workers' interests (Pinch and Patterson 2000).

The experiences of the United States and the United Kingdom both suggest that franchise bidding is difficult to implement satisfactorily and loses political support rather quickly. Unless better implementation methods are found, franchise bidding seems likely to remain no more than one of several imperfect instruments in policy makers' toolkits.

Figure 14.8 Joan Violet Robinson

14.2 Varieties of Imperfect Competition

Imperfect competition comprises market structures involving two or more firms but failing to meet the conditions for perfect competition. It is subdivided into monopolistic and monopsonistic competition (covered in Sections 14.3 and 14.5) and oligopoly and oligopsony (introduced in Chapter 15 and revisited in Chapter 21).

14.3 Monopolistic Competition

Monopolistic competition is a market structure with two defining characteristics: (1) Firms produce branded or otherwise differentiated goods, which are imperfect substitutes for each other. Each good is produced by a single firm, which thus has some monopoly power. (2) Firms freely enter and exit the industry, with new entrants producing new goods. Examples of enterprises that may be monopolistically competitive include PC-clone makers, restaurants, bars, massage parlors, vendors of term papers, fortune-tellers, and econometric forecasters.

In models of monopolistic competition based on the work of Edward Hastings Chamberlin (1899–1967) and Joan Violet Robinson (1903–83, Figure 14.8), each firm competes against all others in its industry (Chamberlin 1936; Robinson 1965 [1933]).[14] Because each firm produces a slightly different product, it faces a downward-sloping demand curve. Because there are many firms, each competing against all others, each firm feels lost in an anonymous crowd. In other words, each firm takes its demand curve as given, ignoring decisions by other firms in its industry.

---

[14] This is in contrast to so-called spatial models, based on the work of Harold Hotelling (1929), in which each firm competes principally with the firms that produce products most similar to its own.

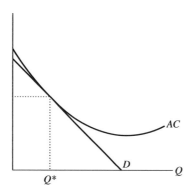

Figure 14.9 Monopolistic competition

14.3.1 Short run

We know that a profit-maximizing firm produces a quantity such that $MC = MR$, provided that profits are nonnegative; otherwise, it shuts down and sells its assets as soon as it can. The demand schedule of a monopolistically competitive firm is negatively sloped; hence, the MR curve lies below the demand curve. In the short-run, the monopolistically competitive firm may earn positive or negative economic profits. Note that the short-run behavior of monopolistically competitive firms is similar to that of monopolists.

14.3.2 Long Run

In the long run, positive economic profits stimulate entry into the industry, and losses force firms to exit from the industry. Entry shifts the demand curves of existing firms to the left. Exit shifts the demand curves of the remaining firms to the right. Entry or exit continue until the demand curve is tangent to the AC curve: $\Pi = (P - AC)Q = 0$. When the demand curve reaches this position, the best a firm can do is to break even. If it produces more or less than the profit-maximizing output Q^*, it suffers a loss. Because Q^* is the profit-maximizing level of output, $MC = MR$ at Q^* (see Figure 14.9).

EXERCISE 14.4

Consider a monopolistically competitive firm whose total and marginal cost functions are $TC = Q^3 - 30Q^2 + 301Q$ and $MC = 3Q^2 - 60Q + 301$. Suppose its demand function is $P = 157 - 6Q$ and its marginal revenue function is $MR = 157 - 12Q$. (a) How much does the firm produce? (b) How much does the firm charge? (c) How large are the firm's profits? (d) If all firms in the industry are identical to this firm, is the industry in equilibrium?

14.3.3 Fixed Costs and Market Structure

A firm's **fixed costs** (FC) are, by definition, the same at all positive levels of output. They often include the maintenance costs on the firm's headquarters and essential machinery. In technologically dynamic industries, fixed costs are commonly interpreted to include research and development (R&D) outlays.

Large fixed costs tend to give a cost advantage to large firms. Indeed, if marginal costs (MC) are constant, then the existence of fixed costs implies that average cost (AC) declines

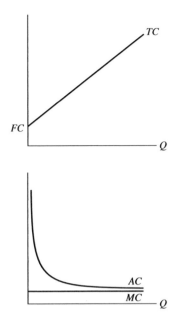

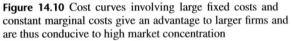

Figure 14.10 Cost curves involving large fixed costs and constant marginal costs give an advantage to larger firms and are thus conducive to high market concentration

as output increases: If total cost is $TC = FC + MC \cdot Q$, then $AC = FC/Q + MC$ and

$$\lim_{Q \to \infty} AC = MC.$$

(See Figure 14.10.) Thus industries with large fixed costs tend to be highly concentrated. The chemical industry, for example, is characterized by both large fixed costs (including substantial R&D expenses) and high market concentration.

EXERCISE 14.5

Consider a monopolistically competitive industry in which each firm has fixed cost f, marginal cost 4, and demand curve $p = 844 - 4Nq$, where N is the number of firms in the industry. The slope of its average cost curve is $-fq^{-2}$. Express the equilibrium value of N as a function of f. Evaluate the function for $f = 20, 30, 50, 70, 100$. Sketch the graph of the function.

EXERCISE 14.6

Do you think the firms described in the previous problem would go on acting as monopolistic competitors if f rose to 22050?

14.3.4 Welfare Implications and Policy Issues

In a monopolistically competitive industry, the equilibrium price exceeds minimum average cost. Thus sales are smaller than they would be if price equaled minimum average cost, as under perfect competition. Just as in the case of a monopoly, resources are displaced to the competitive sector, resulting in a suboptimal product mix.

Monopolistic competition has not been a major public policy issue. Policymakers may be deterred from regulatory action by three considerations. First, the efficiency losses associated with restricted output and greater than minimum average costs may be partially compensated by welfare gains associated with greater product variety. Second, the large number of monopolistically competitive firms implies that any attempt to make them behave more like perfect competitors would involve significant administrative costs. Third, public policy is driven more by politics than economic theory. In the political arena, populist sentiment usually condemns monopolies but condones small monopolistically competitive firms. The former are viewed as robber barons, whereas the latter are portrayed as family enterprises already overburdened with government regulations.

14.3.5 Caveat

Although the simplicity of Chamberlin and Robinson's model of monopolistic competition is appealing, identifying industries to which it can be realistically applied has proved difficult. Many economists today are inclined to believe that, contrary to the Chamberlin-Robinson model, firms producing similar goods make decisions based on conjectures about each others' actions and reactions. To model strategic interactions among firms, economists are increasingly turning to ideas drawn from game theory, elements of which we will examine in connection with oligopoly.

Monopolistic competition remains an important theoretical concept in fields such as international trade and macroeconomics for researchers who want to model imperfectly competitive economies without getting bogged down in details of rivalry between individual firms.[15]

14.4 Monopsony

A monopsony is a market with just one buyer, termed a **monopsonist**.[16] We will examine a monopsonist that buys from many suppliers and sells its product in a perfectly competitive market. A classic example is a mining firm that is the sole employer of men in an isolated company town.[17] As a monopsonist in its labor market, this firm can select any combination of wage (W) and labor quantity (L) from the supply curve, which we will assume to be positively sloped. The firm's **total expenditure** on labor is $TE = WL$, the area of a rectangle with its southwest corner at the origin and its northeast corner on the supply curve, as illustrated in Figure 14.11.

If the firm increases its labor input by $\Delta L = L_1 - L_0$, pushing the wage up by $\Delta W = W_1 - W_0$, total expenditure rises by $\Delta TE = W_0 \Delta L + L_0 \Delta W + \Delta L \Delta W$, as shown in Figure 14.12.

The rate of change in TE as L varies is called **marginal expenditure** or **marginal expense** (ME). For discrete changes in L, $ME = \frac{\Delta TE}{\Delta L} = W_0 + L_0 \frac{\Delta W}{\Delta L} + \Delta W$, where $\frac{\Delta W}{\Delta L}$ is the slope of the labor supply curve. Assuming that the labor supply curve is continuous, we see that as ΔL approaches 0, ΔW also approaches 0, and $\frac{\Delta TE}{\Delta L}$ approaches $W + L \frac{\Delta W}{\Delta L}$,

---

[15] Examples of interesting works using monopolistic competition in this manner include Blanchard and Kiyotaki (1987) and Bergstrand (1989).

[16] The term "monopsony" is also sometimes applied to a product's only buyer, that is, a monopsonist.

[17] Another example of monopsony is an isolated hospital that is the sole local employer of registered nurses. In this case, the nurses may have other opportunities to work—for example, as store clerks—but not in their profession and not at wages close to those they earn at the hospital. The voluminous literature on monopsony in the nursing market includes Currie et al. (2002), Staiger et al. (1999), and Sullivan (1989).

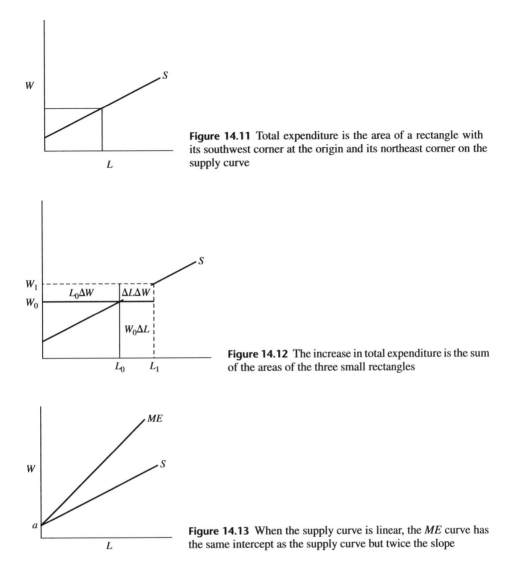

Figure 14.11 Total expenditure is the area of a rectangle with its southwest corner at the origin and its northeast corner on the supply curve

Figure 14.12 The increase in total expenditure is the sum of the areas of the three small rectangles

Figure 14.13 When the supply curve is linear, the *ME* curve has the same intercept as the supply curve but twice the slope

where subscripts have been omitted because changes between initial and final values are now negligibly small. Thus for small changes in L, we can interpret ME as $W + L\frac{\Delta W}{\Delta L}$. (If you know calculus, you will recognize this expression as a discrete approximation to the first derivative of *TE* with respect to L.) It is clear that $ME > W$ as long as $L > 0$.

The case of a linear supply curve provides a simple illustration. Suppose the supply function is $W = a + bL$ with slope $\frac{\Delta W}{\Delta L} = b$. Then $ME = W + bL = a + 2bL$. Note that when the supply function is linear, the ME function has the same intercept (a) but twice the slope, as illustrated in Figure 14.13.

14.4.1 Behavior and Implications

If the firm increases its labor input by ΔL, the rate of change in its profits is $\frac{\Delta \pi}{\Delta L} = P\frac{\Delta Q}{\Delta L} - ME$. The first term on the right is the value of the marginal product of labor ($VMPL$), which we expect to decrease as L increases, at least beyond a certain point. The second term

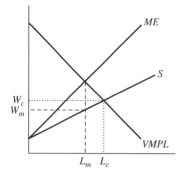

Figure 14.14 To maximize profit, a monopsonistic employer hires just enough labor (L_m) so that the value of labor's marginal product (*VMPL*) equals the marginal expenditure *ME* on labor. It sets the wage rate (W_m) just high enough to attract that quantity of labor. In contrast, in a competitive labor market, the wage rate (W_c) and employment (L_c) would both be higher

on the right is the marginal expenditure on labor, which we expect to increase as L increases. Thus $\Delta \pi / \Delta L$ decreases as L increases. To maximize profit, the firm increases labor input just up to the point at which $\Delta \pi / \Delta L = 0$ and $VMPL = ME$, as illustrated in Figure 14.14. This quantity of labor is less than that which would equate *VMPL* and W, as would be done in a competitive labor market. The monopsonistic employer sets the wage rate just high enough to attract the amount of labor that it wants to employ. This wage rate is lower than that which would prevail in competitive labor markets.

The monopsonistic equilibrium is inefficient because there are people who are willing to work for a wage rate (such as W_c in Figure 14.14) that is less than the value of their marginal product but who are refused jobs.

14.4.2 Measurement of Monopsony Power

Monopsony power is usually conceived as the ability to purchase inputs for less than the value of their marginal product. A convenient measure of this ability is the difference between the value of the marginal product and the input's price as a fraction of that price. When the input is labor, its price is, of course, the wage rate, and the measure of monopsony power is $\frac{VMPL-W}{W}$, where *VMPL* is the value of the marginal product of labor and W is the wage rate. This measure of monopsony power is sometimes called the **rate of exploitation**.[18]

When a monopsonistic employer maximizes profits, the rate of exploitation is equal to the reciprocal of the **wage elasticity of labor supply**, defined as a percentage change in labor divided by the percentage change in the wage rate for movements along the labor supply curve. (This can be proved as follows: Recalling that a profit-maximizing monopsonist chooses an employment level at which $VMPL = ME$ and that for small changes $ME = W + L\frac{\Delta W}{\Delta L}$, we see that $VMPL = W + L\frac{\Delta W}{\Delta L}$ and hence $\frac{VMPL-W}{W} = \frac{L}{W}\frac{\Delta W}{\Delta L}$. The expression on the right is just the reciprocal of the wage elasticity of labor supply.) Thus factors whose supply is more elastic are subject to a lower rate of exploitation.

14.4.3 Countervailing Actions

Faced with a monopsonistic employer, workers may be able to increase both the wage rate and employment by either unionizing or persuading government to impose a minimum wage. If the union wage or legal minimum wage is set at the competitive level, then the

---

[18] Use of the term "exploitation" to refer to the gap between *VMPL* and W was introduced by Pigou (1932). The same term had previously been used in a different sense by Marx (1965 [1867]).

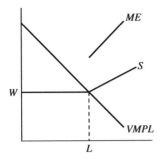

Figure 14.15 If a union contract or minimum wage law flattens the labor supply at the level of the competitive wage up to the competitive level of employment, the monopsonist can be induced to increase employment up to the point where $VMPL = W$

monopsonist will find that the labor supply curve is horizontal up to the competitive level of employment. In this case ME coincides with W up to that employment level, as in Figure 14.15. The monopsonist responds by increasing employment until $VMPL = W$. This is one of the few cases in which union or government actions can raise wages without causing adverse side effects such as unemployment.

14.5 Monopsonistic Competition

Monopsonistic competition has three defining characteristics: (1) numerous buyers compete for a good or service, (2) each buyer faces a positively sloped supply curve, and (3) buyers are free to enter and exit. Important examples of monopsonistic competition are found in labor markets (Bhaskar et al. 2002; Manning 2003).

Employers may commonly face positively sloped labor supply curves because, as Robinson observed in 1933,

> there may be a certain number of workers in the immediate neighborhood and to attract those from further afield it may be necessary to pay a wage equal to what they can earn near home *plus* their fares to and fro; or there may be workers attached to the firm by preference or custom and to attract others it may be necessary to pay a higher wage. (Robinson 1965 [1933], p. 296)

In the short run, a monopsonistic competitor behaves like a monopsonist. However, in the long run, entry and exit drive output prices and input supply curves to positions such that monopsonistic competitors just break even.

14.6 Summary

1. A monopoly is a market for a product sold by a single supplier and lacking close substitutes. Profitable monopolies are sustained by entry barriers and entry deterrence. Most economists assume that monopolies, like other firms, maximize profits.
2. A nondiscriminating profit-maximizing monopoly produces the quantity for which its marginal cost equals its marginal revenue, provided that at this quantity profits are positive. Otherwise, it shuts down and sells its assets as soon as possible. A nondiscriminating monopoly restricts output to less than the level that would be produced by a perfectly competitive industry faced with the same demand and cost conditions. Resources displaced from a monopolized industry may be absorbed by competitive industries. Thus presence of monopoly in any industry may distort resource allocation throughout the economy.

3. Various forms of price discrimination may help a monopoly appropriate all or part of what would have been Marshallian consumer surplus under perfect competition.

4. Possible policy responses to monopoly include antitrust action, public ownership, regulation, and franchise bidding.

5. Monopolistic competition is a market structure in which numerous firms produce goods that are close but imperfect substitutes and in which there is free entry and exit.

6. In the models of Chamberlin and Robinson, each firm competes against all others in its industry. Each faces a downward-sloping demand curve. In the short run, each behaves like a monopolist. In the long run, entry and exit drive economic profit to zero in a monopolistically competitive industry. In long-run equilibrium, each firm produces a quantity such that its demand curve is tangent to its AC curve.

7. High fixed costs and constant or declining marginal costs allow larger firms to produce at lower average cost than their smaller rivals and thus are conducive to high market concentration.

8. A monopsony is a market with a single buyer—for example, a labor market with a single employer, as in a company town.

9. To maximize profit, a monopsonist employer hires just enough labor so that the value of labor's marginal product equals the firm's marginal expenditure on labor. It pays a wage just high enough to elicit the desired quantity of labor. The resulting employment and wage are both lower than in a corresponding competitive labor market.

10. Faced with a monopsonistic employer, workers can raise both the wage rate and employment by flattening the labor supply curve at the competitive wage rate, either by means of a wage contract or a legal minimum wage.

11. Monopsonistic competition is a market structure in which a large number of buyers compete for an input, each buyer faces an upward-sloping supply curve, and buyers have freedom to enter and exit the input market. Labor markets often closely approximate this market structure because in a typical case many employers compete for workers, potential workers prefer the location or other nonwage characteristics of some employers to those of others, and barriers to employers' entry and exit are minor.

12. In the short run, a monopsonistic competitor behaves like a monopsonist. In the long run, entry and exit drive the economic profits of monopsonistic competitors to zero.

14.7 Solutions to Exercises

14.1. (a) Setting $MC = MR$, we get $3Q^2 - 60Q + 302 = 329 - 60Q$ and thus $Q = 3$. (b) Substituting 3 for Q in the demand equation, we get $P = 239$. (c) Recalling that profit is $PQ - TC$, where $P = 239$, $Q = 3$, and $TC = Q^3 - 30Q^2 + 302Q$, we find that profit is 54.

14.2. (a) Setting MC equal to the lowest price charged, as given by the demand function, we get $3Q^2 - 60Q + 302 = 329 - 30Q$ and thus $Q = 10.83$. (b) Substituting 10.83 for Q in the demand function, we get $P = 4.07$. (c) Profit is, as usual, $TR - TC$. The only novelty is that TR is the area under the demand curve to the left of 10.83. This consists of a triangle above 4.07 and a rectangle below 4.07. The area of the triangle is $(329 - 4.07)10.83/2 = 1759.50$. The area of the rectangle is $4.07 \times 10.83 = 44.08$. Thus $TR = 1803.58$. Substituting 10.83 for Q in the TC function, we get $TC = 1022.23$. Thus profit is $1803.58 - 1022.23 = 781.35$. (d) The discriminating monopoly, in comparison to its nondiscriminating counterpart, produces more, charges less for the marginal unit, and makes a greater profit. It can do that because price discrimination makes MR equivalent to the price of the last unit sold.

14.3. (a) The Lerner index is $\frac{239-149}{239} = 90/239$. (b) The reciprocal of the absolute value of the price elasticity of demand is $\left| \frac{239}{3} \frac{1}{-30} \right|^{-1} = 90/239$. The answers are the same.

14.4. (a) Equating MC and MR, we get $3Q^2 - 60Q + 301 = 157 - 12Q$, which implies that $Q = 12$. (b) Substituting 12 for Q in the demand function, we get $P = 85$. (c) Profit can be calculated as $Q(P - AC) = 12[85 - (12^2 - 30 \times 12 + 301)] = 0$. (d) Yes, because when all firms are breaking even, there is no incentive to exit or enter the industry.

14.5. In a monopolistically competitive industry, equilibrium is characterized by two equations. One says that average cost equals price. In our case, $f/q + 4 = 844 - 4Nq$. Subtracting 4 from both sides and multiplying both sides by q, we get

$$f = 840q - 4Nq^2. \tag{14.4}$$

The other equilibrium condition says that the slope of the average cost curve equals the slope of the demand curve. In our case,

$$fq^{-2} = 4N. \tag{14.5}$$

Multiplying both sides of the last equation by q^2, we get $f = 4Nq^2$. Substituting f for $4Nq^2$ in Equation 14.4, we get $f = 840q - f$, which implies that $q = f/420$. Substituting $f/420$ for q in Equation 14.5, we get $f(f/420)^{-2} = 4N$, which simplifies to $N = 44100/f$. Evaluating this function at the indicated values of f, we get the following table:

f	N
20	2205
30	1470
50	882
70	630
100	441

Sketching a curve through the tabulated points, we get Figure 14.16, which illustrates the idea that an increase in fixed costs tends to reduce the number of firms.

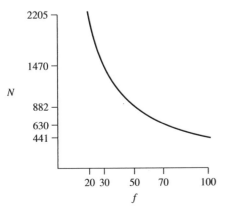

Figure 14.16 Relationship between the fixed cost f and the number of firms in the industry N

14.6. If the fixed costs rose to 22050 and firms continued to act in a monopolistically competitive manner, the equilibrium number of firms would drop to two. But the two remaining firms would very likely stop acting like monopolistic competitors (taking their demand curves as given and ignoring each other) and start acting like duopolists, which, as we will see in Chapter 15, involves conditioning one's actions on those of one's rival.

14.8   Problems

1. Consider a monopolist whose total cost function is $TC = Q^3 - 30Q^2 + 301Q$, whose marginal cost function is $MC = 3Q^2 - 60Q + 301$, whose demand function is $P = 1501 - 30Q$, and whose marginal revenue function is $MR = 1501 - 60Q$, where Q is output and P is price. (If you know calculus, verify the marginal revenue function given above by differentiating the total revenue function $TR = P \cdot Q = 1501Q - 30Q^2$ with respect to Q.) Assume that the firm maximizes profit but cannot practice price discrimination.
   a. How much does the firm produce?
   b. How much does the firm charge?
   c. How large are the firm's profits?
   d. Assuming that the firm chooses its quantity and price to maximize profit, calculate the own-price elasticity of demand and the Lerner index of monopoly power.
2. Consider a monopolist that practices first-degree price discrimination but is otherwise identical to the firm in the previous problem.
   a. How much does the firm produce?
   b. If the firm produces $Q = 25$, what is the lowest price it charges for any unit?
   c. If the firm produces $Q = 25$, how large are its profits?
   d. Contrast your results in Problems 1 and 2, parts a–c, and explain the differences.
3. Consider a monopsonist employer facing a labor supply function $W = 3 + 0.1L$, where W is the hourly wage rate and L is the number of workers.
   a. Derive the monopsonist's marginal expenditure function; that is, show how the monopsonist's marginal expenditure on labor depends on the number of workers it employs.
   b. Suppose the value of the marginal product of labor is $VMPL = 15 - 0.1L$. How many workers must the monopsonist employ to maximize its profits?
   c. What wage rate must the monopsonist offer to attract the number of workers determined in part b?
   d. Assuming that the firm chooses the number of workers and the wage rate to maximize profit, calculate the wage elasticity of labor supply and the rate of exploitation.
   e. Suppose a union contract or legal minimum wage prevents the monopsonist from hiring anyone for less that $9 per hour. The new labor supply curve is flat at $9 for $L \le 60$ and coincides with the old labor supply curve for $L > 60$. How many workers will the monopsonist employ?
4. Consider a monopolistically competitive firm whose total and marginal cost functions are $TC = Q^3 - 30Q^2 + 301Q$ and $MC = 3Q^2 - 60Q + 301$. Suppose its demand function is $P = 201 - 10Q$ and its marginal revenue function is $MR = 201 - 20Q$.
   a. How much does the firm produce?
   b. How much does the firm charge?
   c. How large are the firm's profits?
   d. If all firms in the industry are identical to this firm, is the industry in equilibrium?

5. Consider a monopolistically competitive industry in which each firm has fixed cost f, marginal cost 100, and demand curve $p = 2100 - Nq$, where N is the number of firms in the industry. The slope of its average cost curve is $-fq^{-2}$.
   a. Express the equilibrium value of N as a function of f.
   b. Evaluate the function for $f = 100, 1000, 10000$.
   c. Sketch the function.
6. Consider a firm that hires labor in a monopsonistically competitive market. The firm's labor supply curve is $W = 0.5L$, where W is the wage rate and L is employment. Its total revenue is $TR = 16L^{1/2}$ and the value of the marginal product of labor is $VMPL = 8L^{-1/2}$.
   a. What is the profit-maximizing value of L?
   b. What wage rate does the firm pay?
   c. What is the wage elasticity of labor supply? What is the rate of exploitation?
   d. If the firm's total costs are $TC = 24 + WL$, what are its profits? If all firms in the labor market are identical to this firm, is the market in equilibrium?

15

Oligopoly and Oligopsony: Classic Models

Oligopoly

Oligopoly is a market structure in which a few suppliers account for all or nearly all the sales. The profits of each seller depend materially on the actions of other major sellers, as well as its own actions. Thus strategic interaction between sellers is an important feature of oligopoly. For simplicity we will concentrate on the case in which there are just two sellers, a market structure called **duopoly**.[1] One example of duopoly is provided by large commercial aircraft, which are manufactured almost exclusively by Airbus and Boeing. Another example is provided by auctions of art and antiques, most of which are conducted by Christie's or Sotheby's. The goods produced by oligopolists may be either homogeneous or differentiated, as in monopolistic competition. For simplicity, we shall generally assume that the goods are homogeneous.

15.1.1 Three Classic Models of Oligopolistic Behavior

Three simple models of duopoly go by the names of their originators: Cournot, Bertrand, and Stackelberg. An interesting feature of this trio is that although the differences in assumptions seem small, the differences in conclusions are dramatic. Another interesting feature is that these models, although quite old, anticipate in some ways modern game theory, a branch of mathematical economics that is usually said to have its origins in Von Neumann and Morgenstern (1944).

Cournot

The first important model of duopoly was introduced in 1838 by a French economist and mathematician, Antoine Augustin Cournot (1801-77; Figure 15.1), who assumed that each duopolist chooses its quantity of output to maximize its profits, given its rival's output quantity. Consider, for example, a duopoly facing a market demand curve $P = a - b(Q_1 + Q_2)$, $a > 0$, $b > 0$, where Q_1 and Q_2 are the quantities produced by firms 1 and 2.[2] Taking Q_2 as given, firm 1 considers that the demand curve for its output is $P = (a - bQ_2) - bQ_1$. Its marginal revenue curve is $MR_1 = (a - bQ_2) - 2bQ_1$. (This equaiton can be derived from the demand curve for firm 1 by using the rule, introduced

---

[1] In this and most other modern texts, "oligopoly" is defined broadly enough to include duopoly as a special case. In contrast, a few texts apply the term "oligopoly" only to markets in which three or more sellers compete.

[2] Most of the notation in this section comes from R. Frank (2003). However, Frank assumes marginal cost to be zero, whereas in this section it may be any nonnegative value M.

Figure 15.1 Antoine Augustin Cournot. Used with the permission of the Econometric Society

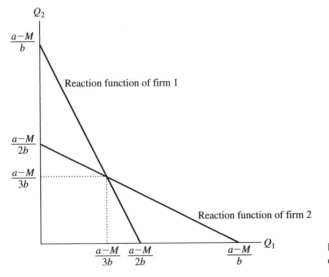

Figure 15.2 Reaction functions of Cournot duopolists

in Subsection 14.1.4, that a linear demand function implies a linear MR function with the same vertical intercept but twice the slope.)

Suppose that each firm has constant marginal cost M. To maximize profits, firm 1 must set $M = (a - bQ_2) - 2bQ_1$. To solve for its output, we write $2bQ_1 = a - bQ_2 - M$, or $Q_1 = (a - M - bQ_2)/(2b)$. This equation is called firm 1's **reaction function** because it shows how firm 1 reacts to firm 2's output. Analogously, firm 2's reaction function is $Q_2 = (a - M - bQ_1)/(2b)$. The intersection of these reaction functions determines how much each firm produces, as shown in Figure 15.2. Solving the two equations simultaneously, we find that $Q_1 = Q_2 = (a - M)/(3b)$. Total output is, of course, $Q = Q_1 + Q_2 = (2/3)(a - M)/b$.

The market price is

$$P = a - bQ$$
$$= a - b(2/3)(a - M)/b$$
$$= a - (2/3)(a - M)$$
$$= (1/3)a + (2/3)M.$$

This is a weighted average of the maximum possible price a and the marginal cost M.
The profit of firm i ($i = 1, 2$) is

$$\pi_i = (P - M)Q_i$$
$$= (1/3)(a - M)(a - M)/(3b) = \frac{1}{9b}(a - M)^2.$$

This duopoly is a special case of Cournot's remarkably general model of imperfect competition. In the general case, it can be shown that as the number of firms increases, the price falls toward marginal cost and each firm's profit falls toward zero; that is, the price and profit levels approach those expected in perfect competition.

Bertrand

A French mathematician, Joseph Louis François Bertrand (1822–1900), assumed that each firm would take its rival's price, rather than quantity, as given. Let us continue to suppose that each firm produces at constant marginal cost M. Furthermore, suppose there are no fixed costs—that is, costs that are the same at all positive levels of output and thus cannot be avoided without going out of business. Under these suppositions, marginal and average costs are equal. If firm 2 initially charges more than M, firm 1, taking this price as given, will set a slightly lower price in hopes of capturing the entire market. Firm 2 will retaliate by setting a price slightly below that of firm 1. The price war will continue until price is driven down to marginal cost M, which, of course, is lower than the price in the Cournot model. Using the demand curve $P = a - bQ$, we see that $bQ = a - M$, or $Q = (a - M)/b$; this quantity exceeds that in the Cournot model by 50%. Profits are zero for both firms. Thus Bertrand duopolists behave like perfect competitors.

Stackelberg

A German economist, Heinrich von Stackelberg (1905–46), considered an asymmetrical duopoly in which one firm knows that the other follows a specific Cournot reaction function. In a book published in 1934, Stackelberg argued that the firm that knows its rival's reaction function would maximize its own profits subject to that function. Suppose for example that firm 2 is the Cournot duopolist. Its reaction function, as we have seen, is $Q_2 = (a - M - bQ_1)/(2b)$. Taking this reaction function into account, firm 1 (called the Stackelberg leader) sees that its demand curve is

$$P = a - b(Q_1 + (a - M - bQ_1)/2b)$$
$$= a - bQ_1 - (a - M - bQ_1)/2$$
$$= (a + M - bQ_1)/2.$$

Its marginal revenue curve is $MR_1 = (a + M)/2 - bQ_1$. Setting $MC = MR_1$, we get $M = (a + M)/2 - bQ_1$ or $bQ_1 = (a - M)/2$, or $Q_1 = (a - M)/(2b)$.

The second firm (known as the Stackelberg follower) produces

$$Q_2 = (a - M - bQ_1)/(2b)$$
$$= (a - M - (a - M)/2)/(2b)$$
$$= (a - M)/(4b),$$

half as much as the leader.

Total output is

$$Q = Q_1 + Q_2$$
$$= (a - M)/(2b) + (a - M)/(4b)$$
$$= (3/4)(a - M)/b,$$

more than in the Cournot model $[(2/3)(a - M)/b]$ but less than in the Bertrand model $[(a - M)/b]$. The price is

$$P = a - b(3/4)(a - M)/b$$
$$= a - (3/4)(a - M)$$
$$= (1/4)a + (3/4)M.$$

Note that the Stackelberg price is below the Cournot price $[(1/3)a + (2/3)M]$ but above the Bertrand price $[M]$.

The profit of the Stackelberg leader is

$$\pi_1 = (P - M)Q_1$$
$$= \frac{1}{4}(a - M)(a - M)\frac{1}{2b}$$
$$= \frac{1}{8b}(a - M)^2.$$

The profit of the follower is

$$\pi_2 = (P - M)Q_2$$
$$= \frac{1}{4}(a - M)(a - M)\frac{1}{4b}$$
$$= \frac{1}{16b}(a - M)^2.$$

Because the leader makes a larger profit than the follower, each firm would like to be the leader. If the firms choose their quantities simultaneously, one possible outcome is a **Stackelberg disequilibrium**, in which each firm (falsely) assumes the other obeys a Cournot reaction function. In our example, this disequilibrium outcome would entail each firm's producing $(a - M)/(2b)$, driving the price down to M and profits down to zero, as in Bertrand's model.

If the firms choose their quantities sequentially and the first mover's choice is known to the second mover, then the latter's best choice is given by its Cournot reaction function. Anticipating this, the first mover sees that its best choice is to act as the Stackelberg leader. The ability of the first mover to obtain extra profits by acting as the Stackelberg leader is known as a **first-mover advantage**. An incumbent typically has a first-mover advantage over a new entrant.

15.1.2 Collusion and Cartels

Were the firms in an oligopoly to agree to act as a monopoly, they could raise their aggregate profits. For example, if the two firms analyzed in the previous section acted as a profit-maximizing monopoly, their joint profits would be $\frac{1}{4b}(a - M)^2$, which is more than that obtained in Cournot, Bertrand, or Stackelberg duopolies.[3] A secret agreement to act in this manner is called collusion. (Secrecy is to be expected where agreements to act as a monopoly are illegal.[4]) An organization to coordinate the actions of sellers trying to obtain monopoly profits is called a cartel. (The best-known cartel is the Organization of Petroleum Exporting Countries, OPEC.) Agreements to act as a monopoly, whether secret or open, are difficult to sustain because each party to such an agreement has an incentive to cheat by selling more than the agreed-upon quantity.

EXERCISE 15.1

Suppose that the two duopolists discussed in the previous section agree to act as a profit-maximizing monopoly. According to the agreement, each firm is entitled to sell $\frac{1}{4b}(a - M)$ units. Suppose that firm 1 is prepared to cheat but believes that firm 2 will abide by the agreement. What is the profit-maximizing quantity for firm 1?

15.1.3 Welfare Implications and Policy Issues

As we have seen, oligopolies can generate a variety of outcomes, ranging from (Bertrand duopolists') replication of perfectly competitive equilibrium to (collusive oligopolists') replication of monopoly restrictions. Those outcomes that restrict output below the level attained in perfect competition typically involve some welfare loss.[5]

Neither economists nor public policymakers have a firm understanding of why particular oligopolies behave as they do. However, there is a widespread suspicion that output restriction and welfare losses are likely to become more severe as the degree of market concentration increases. One of the most widely used measures of market concentration is the **Herfindahl-Hirschman index** (*HHI*), defined as the sum of the squares of the market shares of individual firms. (If, for example, a market is divided among 10 firms of equal size, so each has 10% of the market, $HHI = 10(10^2) = 1000$. If two such firms were to merge, the change in the *HHI* would be $20^2 - 2 \cdot 10^2 = 200$.)

In the United States, under the Clayton Act of 1914, mergers or acquisitions that would substantially lessen competition are illegal. The Federal Trade Commission (FTC) and the Department of Justice (DOJ) have the legal authority to monitor mergers and acquisitions and to request the courts to block those that threaten competition.

In practice, firms with assets or sales in excess of $100 million must report acquisitions of assets valued in excess of $15 million. A merger does not take place until the FTC or the DOJ

---

[3] One way to obtain these profits is for each firm to produce the quantity it would produce as a Stackelberg follower, that is, $(a - M)/(4b)$.

[4] A recent instance of collusion involved Christie's and Sotheby's. In 1993 these firms, according to the U.S. Department of Justice, began colluding to set commissions. In 2002 the European Commission found that their collusion violated European competition rules. In the same year a U.S. court convicted Sotheby's former chairman of price fixing. His counterpart at Christie's has declined to leave England to stand trial in the United States.

[5] An exception may arise if an oligopolistic restriction of output offsets other distortions. For example, a restriction on output of goods with strong negative externalities could be welfare enhancing.

determines the competition effects of such an acquisition. With this procedure, very few cases are brought to courts since in most cases the FTC evaluation is sufficient for providing the signals to the acquiring firm about whether it should proceed with the acquisition or call it off. (Shy 1995, p. 210)

Under guidelines issued in 1992 by the FTC and the DOJ, a merger goes unchallenged if it satisfies any of the following conditions:

1. Postmerger *HHI* < 1000.
2. Postmerger *HHI* < 1800 and ΔHHI < 100.
3. ΔHHI < 50.

A merger that does not meet any of these criteria is apt to be challenged unless entry of new competitors is easy or the merger seems likely to bring large gains in efficiency (Viscusi et al. 2000).

EXERCISE 15.2

Under FTC and DOJ guidelines, which of the following mergers would go unchallenged? (a) A merger between two firms, each of which has 10% of the market, the remaining 80% divided equally between 10 firms, each with 8% of the market. (b) A merger of two firms, each of which has 5% of the market, with the remaining 90% divided among 10 firms, each of which has 9% of the market.

15.1.4 Case Study: The Pharmaceutical Industry

Cournot models of oligopoly and empirical studies suggest that profits tend to rise with seller concentration. Where in the spectrum of profitability and concentration does the pharmaceutical industry lie? Data on profits suggest an oligopoly with a high level of seller concentration. From the late 1980s to the early 2000s, the rate of return on conventionally measured assets was 2.9 to 11.4 percentage points higher for drug companies than for manufacturers on average (Santerre and Neun 2004, p. 467).

In contrast, data on seller concentration suggest, on first inspection, that the industry is rather competitive. If we take 1994 sales of all prescription drugs in the United States as our unit of analysis, we find that the largest seller, Merck, had only 7.3% of the market. Furthermore, the top four firms held only 27.4% of the market (Viscusi et al. 2000, p. 820). The Herfindahl-Hirschman index for pharmaceutical preparations in 1997 was just 462, well below the threshold of concern (1000) established in the guidelines of the FTC and the DOJ (Santerre and Neun 2004). Moving from the U.S. to the world market, we find even less evidence of higher seller concentration. In 1998, Astra Zeneca, the largest drug company, held only 4.2% of the world market (*New York Times*, November 5, 1999, p. 1). How can the data on profits and structure be reconciled?

Profits

Part of the answer is that the rates of return cited earlier omit from the denominator two intangible capital assets that are particularly important in the pharmaceutical industry: knowledge and goodwill. Knowledge capital is produced by investment in R&D, and goodwill is produced by promotional efforts, including advertising and the work of detailers (sales staff). If these intangibles were added to the physical capital stock, the rate of profit would be substantially lowered.[6] The Office of Technology Assessment estimated that "correcting pharmaceutical industry profit rates for investment in intangible capital reduces rates of return by roughly 20 to 25 percent" (cited in Viscusi et al. 2000, p. 831). However, even after that adjustment, the rate of return in the late 1980s and early 1990s was more than two and a half times higher for drug companies than for manufacturers on average.

Another part of the answer is that a higher than average rate of return is required to induce risk-averse individuals to invest in an industry with higher than average risks. Investment in the drug industry is particularly risky because many of its R&D ventures fail for each one that results in a profitable new drug.

> For every 5,000 compounds evaluated, five enter human trials, and only one is approved for use by the Food and Drug Administration (FDA). The odds of making a profit on an approved drug are even lower with only 30 percent generating enough sales to cover average R&D expenditures. (Henderson 1999, p. 399)

However, according to one study based on data for 1976–87, pharmaceutical makers enjoyed rates of return 2 to 3 percentage points above that of other firms in similarly risky industries (Schweitzer 1997, p. 25).

Market Structure

To understand why the rate of return in pharmaceuticals is above average, even after adjusting for intangible capital and unusual risks, we must note that the market for drugs is segmented into noncompeting therapeutic categories like antibiotic, cardiovascular, neurological, and respiratory drugs. Within each category, one or a few firms may have large market shares. Indeed, a study published in 1983 indicated that on average the top four firms in any therapeutic category held 70% of the market. Similarly, a 1993 study that divided ailments into 141 symptom groups found that "the number of drugs per symptom group ranged from one to 50 with a median of five drugs and mean of 6.04" (Scherer 2000, pp. 1319–20). High levels of market concentration are sustained in several therapeutic categories by barriers to entry of three types: patents, brand loyalty, and economies of scale.

Patents have been important barriers to entry to some therapeutic categories since 1948, when the U.S. Patent Office ruled, in the case of streptomycin, that chemically modified and purified forms of natural materials could be patented.[7] Patent holders sometimes attempt to deter rivals from marketing close substitutes by threatening them with patent infringement suits. Defending themselves against such suits can be a costly burden for relatively small companies.[8]

Brand loyalty is a second barrier to entry. Until recently, doctors were the key figures in deciding whether brand name or generic drugs would be prescribed. Doctors tended, for

---

[6] The pharmaceutical industry is notable for its R&D intensity. The R&D/sales ratio in 1997 was 12.3% in the pharmaceutical industry as compared to 4.2% for all industries (National Science Foundation 1999).

[7] A would-be entrant can overcome a patent barrier by developing "chemically distinct substitutes for the original product" (Viscusi et al. 2000, p. 821). An important illustration is a family of antiulcer drugs that work by blocking secretion of stomach acids. One of the first drugs in this family was introduced to the U.S. market by SmithKline, under the brand name Tagamet. By 1980 it had become the world's best selling drug. However, a rival firm, Glaxo, discovered a slightly different drug that allegedly had fewer side effects and did not need to be taken as frequently. In 1978 Glaxo got a patent for this drug, which it called Zantac. Nine years later Zantac displaced Tagamet as the world's best-selling drug.

[8] Executives at Teva Pharmaceuticals U.S.A. and Watson Pharmaceuticals, two generic drug makers, complained that "their annual legal expenses had swelled to about $4 million each" (*New York Times*, October 12, 1999, p. C2).

four reasons, to continue prescribing brand name drugs even after cheaper generics became available. First, with about 22,000 drugs already on the market in the 1970s, doctors had plenty of pharmaceutical information to remember without taking note of new entrants. Second, switching from a known drug to a new generic substitute entails risks of delayed recovery, harmful side effects, and possible malpractice suits. Third, makers of brand name drugs invest heavily in maintaining brand loyalty. "Promotion expenditures can run as high as 20 to 30 percent of sales for many research-based pharmaceutical companies" (Santerre and Neun 2004, p. 453). Fourth, doctors had no financial incentive to prescribe the cheapest safe and effective drug. These factors made it difficult for cheap generic drugs to take market share from better known but more costly brand names.

Although pharmaceutical companies have profitably cultivated brand loyalty among fee-for-service physicians, they have had less success with hospitals and health maintenance organizations (HMOs), which have been more alert to opportunities to substitute cheap generic drugs for costly brand name products. As HMOs have taken on a larger role in the U.S. health care system, generic drugs have been able to accelerate their market penetration. Thus the share of drug markets captured by generics within 2 years of entry rose from 45% in the mid-1980s to 73% in the early 1990s (Viscusi et al. 2000, p. 823).

The difference in brand loyalty between fee-for-service doctors, on the one hand, and hospitals and HMOs, on the other, has had a curious consequence for drug pricing. The maker of a brand name drug commonly reacts to entry by competing generic drugs by *raising* the price of its product. Evidently, the brand name maker expects to lose the price-sensitive segment of the market (hospitals and HMOs) to the generics. The brand name maker's remaining market segment (patients of fee-for-service doctors) is less price-sensitive than the total market was prior to the entry of generics. This diminished price sensitivity makes a price increase profitable for the brand name maker (Frank and Salkever 1995).

Barriers to entry of the third type are formed by economies of scale connected with fixed costs. Research and Development can be viewed as a fixed cost because the cost of inventing a product is the same whether you sell one unit or a billion. Expenditures for R&D are unusually large in the pharmaceutical industry. The U.S. Office of Technology Assessment found that the "average aftertax R&D . . . outlay for each new drug that reached the market in the 1980s" was about $194 million (Viscusi et al. 2000, p. 824). The R&D costs are this large in part because the Food and Drug Administration (FDA) requires extensive testing before approving a new drug.

Pursuit of scale economies and risk hedging in R&D is one factor behind the recent wave of mergers in the industry. These include the American Home Products' 1994 takeover of American Cyanamid; Glaxo Holdings' 1995 acquisition of Wellcome; Hoechst's 1995 takeover of Marion Merrell Dow; Pharmacia's 1995 merger with Upjohn, its 1999 acquisition of Sugen, and its 2000 merger with Monsanto; the 1996 merger of Ciba-Geigy and Sandoz to create Novartis; the 1998 merger of Hoechst and Rhône-Poulenc; the Zeneca Group's 1998 purchase of Astra (*New York Times*, March 8, 1996, pp. D1, D4; December 10, 1998, pp. C1–2; and April 23, 2000, p. 20); the 2003 merger of Pfizer and Pharmacia; and Baxter's 2003 acquisition of ESI Lederle.

Some proposed acquisitions and mergers would have substantially increased market concentration for particular drugs. For example, Baxter's planned acquisitions would have raised the *HHI* for pancuronium by 2496 points. The Federal Trade Commission conditioned its approval of Baxter's 2003 acquisition on divestiture of assets related to that drug (FTC Docket No. C-4068 Decision and Order, February 3, 2003).

In short, the pharmaceutical industry is segmented into several therapeutic categories within which a few firms have large market shares protected by substantial barriers to entry. It can be appropriately called a differentiated oligopoly (Santerre and Neun 2004, p. 470).

15.2 Oligopsony

Oligopsony is a market structure in which there are only a few major buyers. The profits of each buyer depend materially on the actions of other major buyers, as well as its own actions. Hence strategic interaction between buyers is a key feature of oligopsony. For simplicity we will concentrate on the case in which there are just two buyers.

15.2.1 Behavior

It is possible to build models of oligopsony analogous to those for oligopoly, covered in Section 15.1. To illustrate this possibility, let's construct a model, analogous to a Cournot duopoly, of two employers competing for labor. Suppose the market-level labor supply function is $W = a + b(L_1 + L_2)$, where W is the wage rate, L_1 and L_2 are the quantities of labor employed by firms 1 and 2, and a and b are positive parameters. Taking L_2 as given, firm 1 considers that it faces the labor supply curve $W = (a + bL_2) + bL_1$, and thus the marginal expenditure function $ME = (a + bL_2) + 2bL_1$. Suppose that the value of the marginal product of labor in firm 1 is $VMPL_1 = c - dL_1$ and that in firm 2 is $VMPL_2 = c - dL_2$, where c and d are positive parameters. To maximize profits, firm 1 must choose L_1 so that $ME = VMPL_1$ or equivalently $(a + bL_2) + 2bL_1 = c - dL_1$. Solving the last equation for L_1, we obtain the first firm's reaction function:

$$L_1 = \frac{c - a - bL_2}{d + 2b}.$$

Symmetrically, the reaction function for the second firm is

$$L_2 = \frac{c - a - bL_1}{d + 2b}.$$

The intersection of the reaction functions, as shown in Figure 15.3, determines how much labor each firm employs. Solving the two reaction functions for employment, we find that

$$L_1 = L_2 = \frac{c - a}{3b + d}.$$

EXERCISE 15.3

Suppose that the two employers are unaware that their employment decisions affect the wage. Suppose further that they employ just enough labor to equate the value of labor's marginal product with the wage. Calculate the competitive equilibrium wage and employment levels in terms of the parameters a, b, c, and d. Contrast these with the wage and employment levels generated by the Cournot oligopsony.

EXERCISE 15.4

By analogy to Bertrand's model of duopoly, suppose that two employers take each other's wage as given and believe that all workers will seek employment with the firm that offers the higher wage. What level of wages and employment would you expect to result?

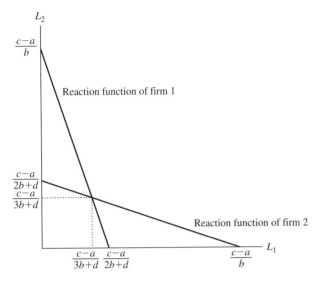

Reaction function of firm 1

Reaction function of firm 2

Figure 15.3 Reaction functions of oligopsonists

15.2.2 Countervailing Actions

Workers facing an employers' oligopsony that holds employment and wages below competitive levels (like workers facing a monopsonist) may be able to increase both employment and wages by either unionizing or persuading government to impose a minimum wage. If the union wage or legal minimum wage is set at the competitive level, then the oligopsonists will find that the labor supply curve is horizontal up to the competitive level of employment. In this case ME coincides with W up to that employment level. The oligopsonists respond by increasing employment until $VMPL = W$.

15.3 Summary

1. Oligopoly is a market structure in which there are only a few important sellers. In such markets, firms are rivals and strategic interaction is important.
2. The special case in which there are only two sellers is called duopoly. Early models of duopoly include those of Cournot, Bertrand, and Stackelberg. Cournot duopolists take each other's output as given. Bertrand duopolists take each other's price as given. A Stackelberg follower takes the Stackelberg leader's output as given, while the leader knows the follower's reaction function.
3. As the degree of market concentration increases, many economists suspect that competition becomes less likely and collusion more likely. To avert such dangers, governments in some countries, including the United States, prohibit mergers and acquisitions that would substantially lessen competition.
4. An interesting example of oligopoly is provided by the pharmaceutical industry. The rate of profit is higher in this industry than in most other industries, even after adjusting for intangible assets. This industry can sustain above average profits in part because it is segmented into several therapeutic categories, within which a few firms have large market shares protected by substantial barriers to entry.

5. Oligopsony is a market structure in which there are only a few important buyers. The profits of each buyer depend materially on the actions of other major buyers, as well as its own actions.

6. There are models of oligopsony analogous to those of oligopoly. In the Cournot case, oligopsony tends to hold input quantities and prices below competitive levels.

7. Faced with an employers' oligopsony, workers may be able to raise both employment and wages by setting a union wage or getting government to set a legal minimum wage at the competitive level.

15.4 Solutions to Exercises

15.1. Firm 1, believing that its marginal revenue is function is $(a - \frac{a-M}{4}) - 2bQ_1$, maximizes profit by selling $\frac{3}{8b}(a - M)$ units, thus exceeding its quota.

15.2. (a) The first merger does not meet any of the criteria for escaping challenge. (b) The second merger meets criteria 1 and 2 for escaping challenge.

15.3. If the employers hired just enough labor to equate the value of labor's marginal product with the wage, their total labor demand would be $L^d = 2(c - w)/d$, where w is the wage rate. Labor supply is $L^s = (w - a)/b$. Equating demand and supply, we find that the competitive equilibrium wage is $w = \frac{ad+2bc}{2b+d}$ and the competitive equilibrium employment is $L = \frac{2(c-a)}{2b+d}$. In contrast, the oligopsony's employment level, as we saw above, is $\frac{2(c-a)}{3b+d}$. Clearly the oligopsony holds employment below its competitive equilibrium. Because the labor supply curve is positively sloped, the restricted employment under oligopsony implies a depressed wage.

15.4. Starting from a situation in which both firms pay the same wage and this wage is below the value of labor's marginal product, we can see that each employer will try to bid workers away from the other. Wages will rise to equal the value of labor's marginal product, at which point neither firm has any incentive to try to increase employment. Thus this Bertrand-like oligopsony results in the same levels of wages and employment that would be found in a perfectly competitive industry.

15.5 Problems

1. Suppose the market demand curve for widgets is $P = 36 - 3Q$, where P is price and Q is output for the industry. The industry is a duopoly, with firm 1 producing Q_1 and firm 2 producing Q_2; thus $Q_1 + Q_2 = Q$. Marginal cost and average cost for each duopolist are 18. Thus the profits of firm 1 are $\pi_1 = (P - 18)Q_1$, with an analogous equation holding for firm 2.
   a. If the firms behave as Cournot supposed, what are the values of Q_1, Q_2, P, π_1, and π_2?
   b. If the firms behave as Bertrand supposed, what are the values of Q, P, π_1, and π_2?
   c. If firm 1 is a Stackelberg leader and firm 2 is a follower (behaving as Cournot supposed), what are the values of Q_1, Q_2, P, π_1, and π_2?
   d. If firms 1 and 2 collude and act as a monopolist, what are the values of Q and P?

2. Suppose the labor supply curve is $W = 5 + 0.1L$, where W is the wage rate and L is employment. The labor market is a duopsony, with firms 1 and 2 employing L_1 and

L_2 units of labor; thus $L = L_1 + L_2$. The value of the marginal product of labor is $VMPL_1 = 17 - 0.1L_1$ in firm 1 and $VMPL_2 = 17 - 0.1L_2$ in firm 2.

  a. If the firms behave as a Cournot duopsony, what are the values of L_1, L_2, and W?
  b. If the firms behave as a Bertrand duopsony, what are the values of L_1, L_2, and W?
  c. If the reaction function for firm 2 is $L_2 = 40 - \frac{1}{3}L_1$, and firm 1, knowing that, acts as a Stackelberg leader, what are the values of L_1, L_2, and W?
  d. If the two firms collude and act as a monopsonist, what are the values of L and W?

15.6 Appendix: An Experiment with Duopoly

15.6.1 Background (to be read prior to experiment)

Economic theory identifies several kinds of equilibria that could emerge in a duopoly. We have studied the Cournot, Bertrand, and Stackelberg cases. However, economic theory has comparatively little to say about which of these possible equilibria is most likely to occur. Our experiment is intended to throw some light on that issue.

Imagine that two rival student clubs hold bake sales, offering identical cakes. By using a fraternity or sorority kitchen, a club avoids fixed costs. The marginal cost is $8 a cake. The total market demand curve for cakes is $P = 20 - Q_1 - Q_2$, where P is price and Q_1 and Q_2 are the number of cakes produced by club 1 and club 2. A club can either announce a price and then sell as many cakes as are demanded at that price, or it can bake a certain number of cakes and sell them at whatever price it can get. Cakes get stale quickly; hence storing them for sale at a later date is not feasible. Unable to collude, the clubs make their decisions independently.

If both clubs announce prices, and these prices happen to be identical, they will sell equal quantities. For example, if both price their cakes at $10, they will each sell $(20 - 10)/2 = 5$ cakes. If the two clubs set different prices, the club with the lower price sells as many cakes as are demanded at that price whereas the club with the higher price sells none. For example, if clubs 1 and 2 price their cakes at $9 and $10, respectively, club 1 will sell 11 cakes and club 2 will sell none.

If both clubs bake cakes and then sell them at whatever price they can get, the price will be determined by the demand curve. For example, if club 1 bakes 4 cakes and club 2 bakes 5 cakes, then cakes will sell for $20 - 9 = 11$ each.

If one club bakes a certain number of cakes while the other announces a price for its cakes, then the former club will sell all its cakes at the announced price or whatever the market will bear, whereas the latter club will sell as many cakes as it can at the announced price. For example, if club 1 bakes 4 cakes and club 2 prices cakes at $10, then club 1 will sell 4 cakes while club 2 sells $20 - 4 - 10 = 6$ cakes. However, if club 1 bakes 11 cakes and club 2 prices cakes at $10, then club 1 will sell 11 cakes at $9 each but club 2 sells none. In general, if club i bakes $Q_i \leq 20$ cakes while club j announces price P_j, then club i gets revenue $Q_i \min(P_j, 20 - Q_i)$ while club j gets revenue $\max(0, P_j(20 - P_j - Q_i))$.

Considering that each club could choose any price between $8 and $20 or any quantity between 0 and 12, and assuming that each price is an integer number of dollars, we see that each club has 26 possible strategies. If we tried to present all possible combinations of strategies, we would get a 26×26 matrix. That's too big for convenient display or analysis. However, we may get some insights from considering just strategies that emerge as equilibria in the three classic models of duopoly. In Cournot equilibrium, each club produces $(1/3)(20 - 8) = 4$ cakes. In Bertrand equilibrium, each club sets its price at $8. In

Table 15.1 Strategy combinations and the corresponding profits

		Club 2			
		Cournot ($Q_2 = 4$)	Bertrand ($P = 8$)	Leader ($Q_2 = 6$)	Follower ($Q_2 = 3$)
Club 1	Cournot ($Q_1 = 4$)	16 16	0 0	12 8	15 20
	Bertrand ($P = 8$)	0 0	0 0	0 0	0 0
	Leader ($Q_1 = 6$)	8 12	0 0	0 0	9 18
	Follower ($Q_1 = 3$)	20 15	0 0	18 9	18 18

Stackelberg equilibrium, the leader and follower bake $(20 - 8)/2 = 6$ and $(20 - 8)/4 = 3$ cakes, respectively. The profits resulting from these strategies are shown in Table 15.1.

EXERCISE 15.5

Circle the cells in Table 15.1 that are Cournot, Bertrand, or Stackelberg equilibria.

To keep clubs small enough so all members can participate in decision making, we may need to divide the class into more than two clubs. The lab record sheets below are constructed on the assumption that four clubs will exist, with two making angelfood cake and two making devilsfood cake. The pair making angelfood cake form one duopoly and the pair making devilsfood cake form another. We will assume that the two types of cake are neither complements nor substitutes. Using an obvious notation, we can write the demand for angelfood and devilsfood cakes as $P_a = 20 - Q_{a1} - Q_{a2}$ and $P_d = 20 - Q_{d1} - Q_{d2}$. Thus the clubs making angelfood need to think about each others' decisions but can ignore the clubs making devilsfood. Similarly, the clubs making devilsfood should consider each others' choices but can disregard the clubs making angelfood.

We shall attempt to conduct five rounds of experimentation. A round begins with each club deciding at what level to set price or quantity. (Remember, a club can choose price or quantity but not both. The market determines the other variable.) Clubs submit their decisions in writing to the market manager (a.k.a. professor). We then calculate each club's profits before beginning another round. By the fifth round we may observe convergence to an equilibrium.

To provide an incentive to maximize profits, a professor may give each club member extra credit points proportional to the profits earned by his or her club. To ensure that its members get the extra credit points, each club should compile a list of its members' names and identification numbers and hand it in before the end of class.

15.6.2 Lab Records (to be completed during the experiment)

After each round, fill in the corresponding line of Table 15.2.

Table 15.2 Decisions and profits

| Round | Angelfood | | | | Devilsfood | | | |
| | Club 1 | | Club 2 | | Club 1 | | Club 2 | |
	P or Q	Profit	P or Q	Profit	P or Q	Profit	P or Q	Profit
1								
2								
3								
4								
5								

Table 15.3 Equilibria and other combinations of strategies

Round	Angelfood	Devilsfood
1		
2		
3		
4		
5		

15.6.3 Data Analysis (to be completed after the experiment)

Referring to Table 15.2 for data, complete Table 15.3 by writing C, B, or S in each cell that was a Cournot, Bertrand, or Stackelberg equilibrium and leaving other cells blank.
Referring to Tables 15.2 and 15.3, answer the following questions.

1. Once a duopoly reached a Cournot, Bertrand, or Stackelberg equilibrium, did it ever depart from it? If so, suggest a reason for the departure.
2. Did any pair of decisions that was not a Cournot, Bertrand, or Stackelberg equilibrium persist from one round to another? If so, suggest a reason for the persistence.
3. If the combination of decisions for a duopoly in the last round was a Cournot, Bertrand, or Stackelberg equilibrium, suggest a reason why that equilibrium rather than some other emerged. If the combination of decisions in the last round was none of those equilibria, suggest why none occurred.
4. What does the experiment suggest about the likely frequency of Cournot, Bertrand, and Stackelberg equilibria in the real world?

16

■■■ Economics of Time

Interest

16.1.1 Basic Concepts

An interest rate is a price for the use of money for a period of time, just as ground rent is a price for the use of land for a period of time or a wage rate is a price for using a worker's abilities for a period of time. If I pay $7 to borrow $100 for a year, the interest rate for the loan is $7/100 = 0.07$, or 7%.[1]

Interest rates establish an equivalency between different sums of money at various times. You are probably well familiar with this equivalency in the context of savings deposits. If you deposit $100 in a savings account that pays 6% compounded annually, at the end of 1 year you have $100(1.06) = 106. If you leave the $106 in the bank for a second year and the interest rate remains 6%, at the end of the second year you have $106(1.06) = 112.36. However, if the interest rate for the second year was 7%, you'd have $106(1.07) = 113.42.

■ **EXERCISE 16.1**

You put $100 into a savings account for 3 years. The account pays 5% interest during the first year, 3% during the second, and 4% during the third. At the end of each year you add the interest to your account. How much do you have in the account at the end of the 3 years?

16.1.2 Nominal and Real Interest Rates

When the prices of goods and services are subject to change, a distinction should be made between the growth rate of the nominal value of an interest-earning asset and the growth rate of its purchasing power over goods and services. Economists call the former the nominal interest rate and the latter the real interest rate.

For example, if a savings account has a nominal interest rate of 6% and the prices of goods and services rise 2% a year, an individual who puts $100 in a savings account will find that after 1 year the purchasing power of her account (expressed in constant prices) is $100(1.06)/(1.02) = 103.92. In other words, she would be able to purchase 3.92% more

---

[1] How interest rates are determined and how they affect savings and investment behavior are difficult questions, which we will skip over here. Some considerations relevant to these questions will be discussed later in this text. Others are discussed in macroeconomics.

goods and services with the money in the savings account at the end of the year than at the beginning. Thus the real interest rate was 3.92%.

The rate of change in the prices of goods and services is called the **inflation rate**.[2] Letting i, n, and r denote the inflation rate, the nominal interest rate, and the real interest rate (all in decimal form), we note that $1 + r = \frac{1+n}{1+i}$ and hence $r = \frac{n-i}{1+i}$. When i is close to zero, a good approximate formula is $r \approx n - i$. For example, if $n = 0.06$ and $i = 0.02$, then $r = 0.0392 \approx 0.04$.

16.2 Present and Future Value

Generalizing from the examples in Subsection 16.1.2, let's suppose you deposit in a bank a sum we'll call the present value and denote by PV; in our previous illustrations, PV was $100. Suppose you leave the money in the bank for T years and the interest rates in decimal form for those years are $r_1, r_2, \ldots, r_T$; then at the end of the T years you have a sum we'll call the future value at time T and denote by FV_T. This amount is

$$FV_T = PV(1 + r_1)(1 + r_2) \cdots (1 + r_T).$$

This is a fundamental relationship,[3] worth committing to memory. If the interest rates are the same for all periods, that is, if $r_1 = r_2 = \cdots = r_T = r$, then this formula simplifies to

$$FV_T = PV(1 + r)^T.$$

This equation involves four variables. If we know any three, we can use the equation to compute the fourth. For example, if we know that $PV = \$100$, $r = 0.05$ and $T = 3$, then we can calculate $FV_3 = \$100(1.05)^3 = \$115.76$. If the interest rate rose to 10%, we would calculate $FV_3 = \$100(1.1)^3 = \$133.10$. More generally, the higher the interest rate, the higher the future value, given the present value.

If we know FV_T, r, and T, we can calculate PV:

$$PV = \frac{FV_T}{(1 + r)^T}.$$

This expression comes in handy when trying to appraise an investment that yields a payoff after T years. For example, a bond that will be worth $10,000 in 5 years but provides no income in the meantime has a present value of $\frac{\$10,000}{(1+r)^5}$. If the rate of interest on alternative assets[4] is $r = 0.06$, then the present value is $\frac{\$10,000}{(1.06)^5} = \$7472.58$. Given the future value, an increase in the interest rate would lower the present value. Incidentally, this kind of bond is exceptional: Whereas most bonds pay their owners a fixed annual amount called the **coupon** until maturity, the bond we discussed pays nothing. Because it has no coupon value, it is called a zero-coupon bond, or a "zero" for short.

---

[2] When prices are falling, the inflation rate is negative and its absolute value is called the *deflation* rate. The prices of various goods and services typically change at different rates. In this case, an inflation or deflation rate is defined in terms of the rate of change in the cost of a bundle of many different goods and services.

[3] If the interest rates in this relationship are real (as the notation suggests), the present and future values refer to purchasing powers at constant prices. If the interest rates are nominal, the present and future values are also nominal, that is, not adjusted for inflation.

[4] The interest rate on alternative assets, such as bank deposits, is the opportunity cost of holding the bond; hence that interest rate can be used to calculate the bond's present value.

If we know PV, FV_T, and T, we can calculate r:

$$r = \left(\frac{FV_T}{PV}\right)^{1/T} - 1.$$

For example, if the bond that will be worth $10,000 in 5 years is currently selling for $7000, then investors must believe that the average annual interest rate for the next 5 years will be $r = \left(\frac{10,000}{7,000}\right)^{1/5} - 1 = 0.0739$.

If we know PV, FV_T, and r, we can calculate T:

$$T = \frac{\log(FV_T/PV)}{\log(1+r)}.$$

For instance, if we have $100 to invest at 5% and want to know how long we must wait until our investment is worth $300, we can write $T = \frac{\log(3)}{\log(1.05)} = 22.5$. An increase in the interest rate would reduce the time we have to wait for our wealth to triple.

If we anticipate a sequence of payments and a constant interest rate r, we can easily figure the present value of the sequence just by dividing each payment by the appropriate power of $1 + r$ and then summing the quotients. Let's denote the payment received t years from now as FV_t. For example, a payment received now is FV_0 and one received in 5 years is FV_5. In this notation, we can express the present value of the sequence of payments over the next T years as

$$FV_0 + \frac{FV_1}{(1+r)} + \cdots + \frac{FV_T}{(1+r)^T} = \sum_{t=0}^{T} \frac{FV_t}{(1+r)^t}.$$

For example, suppose we expect the interest rate to be 8% and we anticipate the following sequence of payments:

t	payment
1	$100
3	200
6	100

The present value of this sequence is $\frac{100}{1.08} + \frac{200}{1.08^3} + \frac{100}{1.08^6} = 92.59 + 158.77 + 63.02 = 314.38$.

If in some periods we must make payments, these outlays can be recorded as negative receipts. For example, when the interest rate is 8%, the present value of a project that involves paying out $100 with a delay of 1 year and receiving $200 with a delay of 3 years is $\frac{-100}{1.08} + \frac{200}{1.08^3} = -92.59 + 158.77 = 66.18$. To emphasize that discounted outlays have been netted out of discounted receipts, we often call such a sum *net* present value (*NPV*).

EXERCISE 16.2

A zero will be worth $1000 when it matures in 3 years. Buyers and sellers of bonds believe that the interest rate on other assets (the opportunity cost of holding the zero) will be 4% in the first year and 5% in the second and third years. What is the present value of the zero?

EXERCISE 16.3

An investment project involves spending $2 million now and $2 million a year from now. Starting 2 years from now, the project will yield $1 million a year for 5 years. What is the net present value of the project if the interest rate is 5%?

EXERCISE 16.4

A zero will be worth $1000 when it matures in 3 years. It is now selling for $863.84. What is the implied interest rate? (In other words, what average annual interest rate makes $863.84 the present value of $1000 3 years in the future?)

16.3 Implications for Schooling and Work

The economics of time can be applied to decisions about when to make the transition from school to work. To briefly illustrate the application, let us make three simplifying assumptions.

1. Let the number of years to be worked be a constant, $n + 1$. Thus staying in school an extra year entails postponing retirement, as well as the start of work, by 1 year.
2. Suppose that the only cost of schooling is postponing earnings.
3. Assume that earnings are constant over a career although they may vary with schooling. Let Y_x denote the annual earnings of a person with x years of schooling.

Given those simplifying assumptions, the present value of earnings for any given length of schooling is easily calculated. Consider, for example, an individual who gets only 8 years of school. When he leaves school for work, the present value of his earnings is

$$PV_8 = Y_8 \sum_{t=0}^{n}(1+r)^{-t}, \tag{16.1}$$

whereas the present value (as of the same date) for a person who plans to remain in school an additional s years is

$$PV_{8+s} = Y_{8+s} \sum_{t=0}^{n}(1+r)^{-(t+s)}. \tag{16.2}$$

Individuals can choose s to maximize the present value of their earnings. Thus far the analysis has been normative; however, it can be given a positive twist, as we shall now see.

If everyone had the opportunity to get as many years of schooling as desired and if people were indifferent between school and work, then the present value of earnings would be the same regardless of years of schooling. That would mean, for example, that $PV_8 = PV_{8+s}$ for all s. From equations 16.1 and 16.2 we can infer that

$$Y_8 \sum_{t=0}^{n}(1+r)^{-t} = Y_{8+s} \sum_{t=0}^{n}(1+r)^{-(t+s)}. \tag{16.3}$$

Simplifying the last equation, we get

$$Y_{8+s} = Y_8(1+r)^s. \tag{16.4}$$

Thus each year of additional education would multiply annual earnings by a factor equal to one plus the interest rate r (Mincer 1974).

The assumptions leading to Equation 16.4 are by no means fully realistic. Thus we should not expect the equation to provide a perfect fit to data on earnings and schooling. Nonetheless, several empirical studies indicate that each year of schooling tends to multiply earnings (adjusted for experience and gender) by a constant factor, which in the United States is about 1.1. In other words, each year of education raises earnings in this country by about 10% (Krueger and Lindahl 2001). That is higher than the usual value of the real rate of interest in the United States, which is not surprising considering that the model understates the costs of education in terms of both forgone earnings and out-of-pocket expenses.

16.4 Summary

1. An interest rate is a price for the use of money for a period of time.
2. If a sum called the present value (PV) is invested at a constant annual interest rate r for T years, its future value is $FV_T = PV(1+r)^T$. Given values for any three of the four variables in this equation, we can solve for the fourth.
3. The net present value of a sequence of future receipts ($FV_t > 0$) and outlays ($FV_t < 0$), with a constant interest rate r, is

$$NPV = \sum_{t=0}^{T} \frac{FV_t}{(1+r)^t}.$$

4. Present value calculations can help individuals decide when to make the transition from school to work. A simple model suggests that each year of schooling may raise earnings by a fixed percent. Empirical evidence indicates that in the United States each additional year of schooling raises earnings (adjusted for experience and gender) by about 10%.

16.5 Solutions to Exercises

16.1. At the end of 3 years, you have $\$100(1.05)(1.03)(1.04) = \$112.48$.

16.2. The present value of the zero is $\frac{1000}{(1.04)(1.05)(1.05)} = 872.14$.

16.3. The net present value of the project, expressed in millions of dollars, is $(-2) + (-2/1.05) + 1/1.05^2 + 1/1.05^3 + 1/1.05^4 + 1/1.05^5 + 1/1.05^6 = (-2) + (-1.905) + 0.907 + 0.864 + 0.823 + 0.784 + 0.746 = 0.219$.

16.4. The interest rate is $\left(\frac{1000}{863.84}\right)^{1/3} - 1 = 0.05$.

16.6 Problems

1. You put $100 into a savings account for 3 years. The account pays 5% interest during the first year, 7% during the second, and 6% during the third. At the end of each year you add the interest to your account. How much do you have in the account at the end of the 3 years?
2. A zero (a bond that has no coupons but is sold at a discount from its face value) will be worth $1000 when it matures in 2 years. Buyers and sellers of bonds believe that the

interest rate on other assets will be 6% in the first year and 10% in the second. What is the present value of the zero?

3. An investment project involves spending $1 million now and $1 million a year from now. Starting 2 years from now, the project will yield $1 million a year for 3 years. What is the present value of the project if the interest rate is 10%?

4. A zero will be worth $1000 when it matures in 2 years. It is now selling for $873.44. What is the implied interest rate? (In other words, what average annual interest rate makes $873.44 the present value of $1000 2 years in the future?)

5. If you put $1000 in a savings account that pays 5% compounded annually, how many years would you have to wait to have the balance grow to $2000?

17

▨ Saving Behavior

Intertemporal Choice

The decision to save rather than to spend a portion of income is in effect a decision to consume in the future rather than in the present. Thus economists look at savings decisions as problems in intertemporal choice. Intertemporal choice based on consistent preferences can be represented by the same conceptual apparatus we used for analyzing choice between consumer goods in the present: a budget constraint and indifference curves. If we consider only two periods, we can illustrate our arguments with a two-dimensional diagram, plotting present consumption c_0 on the horizontal axis and future consumption c_1 on the vertical axis.

▨ 17.2 Budget Constraints

The form of consumers' intertemporal budget constraints depends on their opportunities to borrow. Banks usually regard as poor credit risks individuals who lack property that could be put up as collateral. Unable to borrow, such individuals cannot consume in the present period more than their present income y_0. However, these individuals may be able to save and lend. Let r_s denote the real interest rate that an individual can earn on her savings.[1] By reducing her current consumption c_0 by \$1 and depositing the \$1 in her savings account, she can increase her consumption next year by \$1 + r_s. Indeed, if she saved her entire current income, she could consume next year up to $y_0(1 + r_s) + y_1$, where y_1 is her noninterest income for next year. Thus her intertemporal budget constraint would be chisel-shaped, as in Figure 17.1.

An indifference curve could be tangent to the upper portion of the budget constraint. In this case, the marginal rate of substitution (MRS) of future for present consumption equals the absolute value of the slope of the upper portion of the budget constraint $(1 + r_s)$. The only other possible places for an indifference curve to touch the budget constraint without crossing are at the kink (y_0, y_1) and the corner $(0, y_1 + y_0(1 + r_s))$. The latter is very unlikely because it would mean consuming nothing in the first period. Many people with chisel-shaped budget constraints end up at the kink, consuming their current income each period. In this case, $MRS \geq 1 + r_s$.

If we can borrow at a real interest rate r_b and lend at an interest rate r_s, where $r_b > r_s$, then our budget constraint will look like a boomerang, as in Figure 17.2. The upper portion has

---

[1] Recall from Chapter 16 that a real interest rate r is calculated from a nominal interest rate n and an inflation rate i as follows: $r = \frac{n-i}{1+i}$, where all rates are expressed in decimal form.

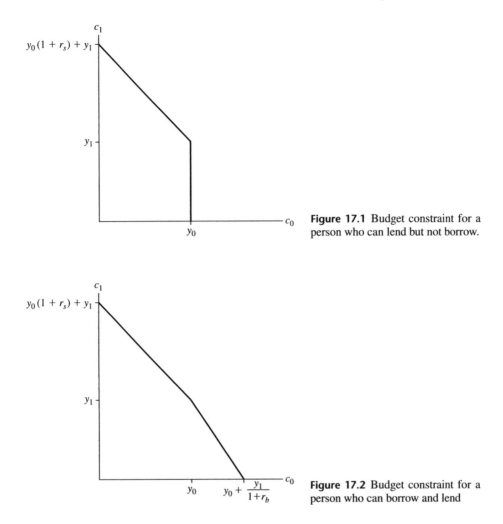

Figure 17.1 Budget constraint for a person who can lend but not borrow.

Figure 17.2 Budget constraint for a person who can borrow and lend

slope $-(1 + r_s)$ and the lower portion $-(1 + r_b)$. Again, there is a kink at (y_0, y_1), but now the angle is more oblique. An individual who was willing to abstain from consumption in the second period might borrow in the present period any amount up to the present value of his future income, $\frac{y_1}{1+r_b}$. Hence the budget constraint's horizontal intercept is at $y_0 + \frac{y_1}{(1+r_b)}$. There can be tangencies either above the kink (where $MRS = 1 + r_s$) or below it (where $MRS = 1 + r_b$). However, some people find that at the kink $1 + r_s \leq MRS \leq 1 + r_b$. These people simply consume their current income, as if following Polonius's advice to his son: "neither a borrower, nor a lender be" (Shakespeare, *Hamlet*, act I, scene III).

The reason that the rate of interest on savings is generally lower than on money we borrow is twofold. First, banks have to cover administrative costs out of the spread between the two interest rates. Second, individuals are more likely to fail to repay a bank than a bank is to fail to repay an individual. Thus the risk premium is higher on loans to individuals than on bank deposits.

Most individuals in the United States face boomerang-shaped budget constraints. Hence this is the case on which we will concentrate when we discuss the effects of interest rates on saving and borrowing. However, before we get to that, there is one last budget constraint shape to be mentioned, if only for completeness.

If we were lucky enough to be able to borrow and lend at the same rate of interest r, our budget constraint would be a straight line with slope $-(1 + r)$. The absolute value of this slope can be interpreted as the relative price of present consumption in terms of future consumption. An indifference curve could be tangent to the budget constraint at any point. Corner solutions are conceivable but most unlikely because they would mean zero consumption in one period. An interior solution, which is more likely, implies that $MRS = 1 + r$. The linear budget constraint is rarely met in practice. However, it is nonetheless interesting for two reasons. First, it is a limiting case, showing what happens as the spread between borrowing and lending rates decreases. Second, it is a convenient simplification and acceptably accurate when the spread is small.

A change in interest rates alters the slopes of both segments of a boomerang-shaped budget constraint: An increase in interest rates makes both segments steeper. An increase in interest rates may be thought of as an increase in the relative price of present consumption. In response to this relative price change, people tend to substitute future for present consumption.

An increase in interest rates increases the income of lenders and the expenses of borrowers. The former can increase consumption; the latter must curtail consumption. An increase in interest rates could theoretically cause total personal saving to either rise or fall. The range of uncertainty has been only modestly narrowed by empirical research. A survey of evidence from developing countries finds no statistically significant effect of interest rates on household saving (Schmidt-Hebbel et al. 1992). A survey focusing on evidence from the United States concludes that (a) the short-run interest elasticity of aggregate household saving is probably positive but cannot be precisely estimated, and (b) the long-run effects of interest rates on household saving are still more difficult to estimate (Elmendorf 1996).

EXERCISE 17.1

Fortunata expects to earn \$30,000 this year and \$55,000 next year. Her marginal rate of substitution of future for present consumption is c_1/c_0, where c_1 denotes future consumption and c_0 denotes present consumption. The interest rate at which she can lend is 0.05. (a) If Fortunata cannot borrow, what is her optimal current consumption? (b) If she can borrow at an interest rate of 0.10, what is her optimal current consumption?

17.3   Causes of Low Saving Rates

Household saving rates in the United States today are low in comparison to either the earlier U.S. experience or other rich countries. The household saving rate fell from 11.2% of disposable income in 1982 to 1.0% in 2004 (*Economic Report of the President* 2005, table B30). The saving rate in the United States is now well below that in many other industrial countries. Low saving rates are a matter of concern because if we do not save, we cannot invest. If do not invest, our capital stock will dwindle and our incomes fall. Four possible explanations for the low saving rates now prevalent in the United States are the following:

First, preferences may have changed in favor of immediate gratification. Old people, who remember the Great Depression of the 1930s, are used to the idea that the stock market can crash and millions can lose their jobs. People who live in fear of another great depression tend to save a large fraction of their current income, in order to have something to fall back

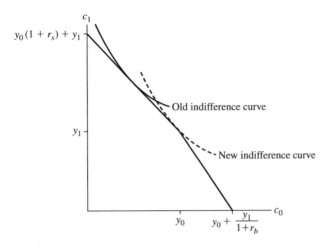

Figure 17.3 A change in tastes

on in hard times.[2] Younger people, who grew up during postwar prosperity, have difficulty imagining a great depression. They may tend to be less frugal because they are less fearful.[3] A change in tastes in favor of immediate gratification is represented by drawing new, steeper indifference curves, tangent to the budget constraint further to the right, as in Figure 17.3.

Second, the shape of budget constraints has been altered by financial innovations including home equity loans, credit cards, and federal student loan programs. Home equity loans, which allow homeowners to borrow as much as 80% of the market value of a house, were widely offered and vigorously promoted by lenders beginning in the late 1980s (Canner et al. 1998). Credit cards, which have been aggressively marketed in recent years, facilitate borrowing by people whom bankers might deem uncreditworthy. When credit card companies increase credit limits, credit card debt immediately rises (Gross and Souleles 2002). Similarly, federal student loan programs make credit available to people who might otherwise be denied it. These loan programs include federally guaranteed private loans (Federal Family Education Loans) authorized under the Higher Education Act of 1965 and direct federal loans authorized by the Higher Education Amendments of 1992. Both programs expanded rapidly. The number of federally guaranteed loans rose from 89,000 in fiscal 1966 to 6,745,000 in fiscal 1994. The number of borrowers under the Federal Direct Loan Program rose from 162,000 in fiscal 1994 to 2,506,000 in fiscal 2000 (U.S. Department of Education 2002). These changes in capital markets are represented by replacing a chisel-shaped budget constraint by a boomerang-shaped one. People who were at the kink may have moved down into the lower slope of the boomerang.[4]

Third, the growth of disposable (after-tax) income slowed after about 1974. It may be that when incomes rise, particularly when they rise unexpectedly, people take some time to decide how to spend the extra income. In the interim, their saving rates may be high. In

---

[2] James Michner, for example, became rich from writing best-selling historical novels. However, recalling the Great Depression, he could never bring himself to spend much of his newly acquired wealth.

[3] One might suspect that increased advertising is another cause of diminished frugality. However, empirical studies have generally found no evidence that advertising affects *aggregate* consumer expenditure. Advertising seems to mainly affect how consumers apportion their expenditure among competing products (Berndt 1991, pp. 393-400).

[4] The capital market changes may have increased borrowing, particularly by people who have difficulties carrying out plans. Such difficulties, which were already familiar to Xenophon, will be discussed further in the next chapter.

contrast, when incomes are stagnant, people may find them easy to spend in habitual ways; hence saving rates may be lower (Schmidt-Hebbel et al. 1998).

Fourth, booming stock markets in the 1980s and 1990s made many Americans feel richer even when their measured disposable incomes stagnated. Believing that their existing investments were adequate to finance retirement needs, they may have seen little need to save out of disposable income. The dip in stock prices starting in the spring of 2000 has coincided with a slight rise in the household saving rate.

17.4 Policies to Stimulate Saving

To stimulate saving, the government could try to raise real after-tax interest rates. For purposes of discussion, let's separate the programs to raise the rates faced by savers and borrowers.

The real after-tax interest rate received by savers could be raised by cutting taxes on interest income. The idea is understandably popular with rich people, who have large interest incomes. However, others raise two objections to the proposed tax cut. First, it would be inequitable, in the sense that most of the benefits would go to a wealthy few. Second, it is likely to be ineffective in raising savings. Remember that raising the interest rate on savings has a negative substitution effect but a positive income effect on current consumption. The net effect is small and even its sign is uncertain.

The real after-tax interest rate paid by borrowers could be raised by eliminating the federal income tax deduction for interest payments. To a considerable extent, that has been done under the 1986 Tax Reform Act. Before that law, most personal interest payments, including those on loans to buy automobiles, on credit cards, and on charge accounts, could be deducted from taxable income. After 1986 this deduction was phased out. Starting with the 1991 tax year, personal interest payments are not deductible. The elimination of the deduction in effect raises the after-tax interest rate, rotating inward the lower segment of the budget constraint, discouraging borrowing, and tending to raise national saving rates. One category of interest payments remained deductible: interest on mortgage debt including home equity loans.[5]

EXERCISE 17.2

Zlatna is in the 36% tax bracket and can borrow at an interest rate of 8%. (a) When interest payments were deductible from taxable income, what was the after-tax cost to Zlatna of borrowing? (In other words, what nondeductible interest rate would be the equivalent of the deductible 8%?) (b) What effect did the elimination of the interest deduction have on her optimal borrowing?

17.5 Summary

1. Decisions about how much to save are in effect decisions about consuming now or later. These decisions can be analyzed by using a budget constraint and indifference curves

---

[5] This loophole contributed to a change in the composition of household borrowing, involving a switch from auto loan and credit card debt to mortgage debt (Stango 1999). The share of home owners with home equity loans rose from seven percent in 1983 to thirteen percent in 1997 (Canner et al. 1998).

relating to present and future consumption. Typically the interest rate at which we can borrow is higher than the interest rate at which we can lend. As a result the intertemporal budget constraint is typically kinked at the point representing current and future income.

2. Indifference curves may touch the budget constraint either at a tangency point in one of the linear segments or at the kink. In the latter case, present consumption equals present income and saving is zero.

3. A rise in real interest rates reduces borrowing and may either increase or decrease saving. The net effect on aggregate household saving is probably small but positive.

4. The savings rate among U.S. households is now low by comparison both to earlier U.S. experience and to other wealthy countries. A low savings rate is a matter of concern because it can result in a low capital stock and income.

5. The government could try to stimulate savings by raising the real after-tax interest rate, particularly that faced by borrowers. Eliminating the income tax deduction for personal interest was a step in that direction.

17.6 Solutions to Exercises

17.1. (a) With Fortunata unable to borrow, her budget constraint is chisel-shaped and her current consumption cannot exceed $30,000. The absolute value of the slope of the upper segment of the budget constraint is 1.05. The MRS at (30000, 55000) is $55/30 = 11/6$. Because $1.05 < 11/6$, Fortunata will consume $30,000 this year.

(b) With Fortunata now able to borrow at an interest rate of 0.10, her budget constraint is boomerang-shaped. Points on the lower segment of the budget constraint satisfy the equation $c_1 = 55000 - (1.1)(c_0 - 30000)$, which can be more simply expressed as $c_1 = 88000 - 1.1c_0$. A tangency point between the lower segment of the budget constraint and an indifference curve can be characterized by the equation $c_1/c_0 = 1.1$, which can be rewritten as $c_1 = 1.1c_0$. Equating the right sides of the two equations for c_1, we get $1.1c_0 = 88000 - 1.1c_0$. Solving that equation for current consumption, we get $c_0 = 40000$.

17.2. (a) The after-tax cost to Zlatna of borrowing was $(1 - .36)8\% = .64 \times 8\% = 5.12\%$.

(b) Elimination of the interest deduction reduced her optimal borrowing.

17.7 Problems

1. Ann expects to earn $30,000 this year and $33,000 next year. She can borrow at an interest rate of 0.10 and lend at an interest rate of 0.05. Sketch her intertemporal budget constraint.

2. Joe expects to earn $30,000 this year and $40,000 next year. His marginal rate of substitution of future for present consumption is C_1/C_0, where C_1 denotes future consumption and C_0 denotes present consumption. The interest rate at which he can lend is 0.05.

   a. If Joe cannot borrow, what is his optimal current consumption?

   b. If Joe can borrow at an interest rate of 0.10, what is his optimal current consumption?

3. Josephine is in the 31% tax bracket and can borrow at an interest rate of 10%.

   a. When interest payments were deductible from taxable income, what was the after-tax cost to Josephine of borrowing? (In other words, what nondeductible interest rate would be the equivalent of the deductible 10%?)

    b. What effect did the elimination of the interest deduction have on her optimal borrowing?

4. Old MacDonald has $500,000 that he could consume or leave as a bequest to his son, Callow Mac. Plotting his consumption on the horizontal axis and the bequest on the vertical axis, the old man finds that his indifference curves have slope $-\frac{3B}{2C}$. The old man does not trust banks, so he keeps his wealth in the form of gold buried under his barn. Thus his wealth earns no interest but is protected from inflation.

    a. Draw the budget constraint showing the tradeoff between the old man's consumption and the bequest.

    b. What does the old man consume and how much does he leave to his son?

18
Inconsistent Intertemporal Choice

18.1 Preferences

In the first chapter we noted that Ischomachos, as recalled by Xenophon, believed that many knowledgeable managers fail because they lack the strength of character to implement their plans. Their problems involve unsteady intertemporal preferences. For example, a farm manager may prefer at fall harvest time to save grain for the spring planting but prefer in late winter to eat the grain immediately.

Intertemporal preferences are **consistent** if plans made at one moment are still attractive at all subsequent moments when steps must be taken to implement them. Preferences are **inconsistent** if the mere passage of time makes individuals regret or abandon their previously adopted plans. A person who resolves every morning to stay sober and get to bed by 11 p.m. but who every evening goes drinking until 1 a.m. suffers from an acute form of inconsistent preferences.

18.2 Additivity, Consistency, and Exponential Discounting

An individual's lifetime utility depends on her present and future consumption. To represent this dependence, we may write $U = U(c_0, c_1, c_2, \ldots)$, where U denotes lifetime utility and c_t denotes consumption t periods in the future. The consumer's decision problem and economists' predictive problems are simplified if the lifetime utility function can be written as a sum of discounted instantaneous utilities, $U = u(c_0) + u(c_1)\delta(1) + u(c_2)\delta(2) + \cdots$, where $u(c_t)$ is the instantaneous utility function evaluated at c_t and $\delta(t)$ is the discount function evaluated at t. (For an impatient consumer, $\delta(t)$ is a decreasing function. For a consumer who is indifferent between increasing present or future consumption when they are initially equal, $\delta(t) = 1$ for all t. For a consumer who likes to delay gratification, $\delta(t)$ is an increasing function.) When the lifetime utility function can be written as such a sum, it is said to be **additive**. Most research on intertemporal choice presumes additivity—albeit more for convenience than realism.

The combination of consistency and additivity has a remarkable implication for the form of the discount function: $\delta(t)$ must be an exponential function, d^t, where d is a positive constant, known as the **discount factor**, that is less than 1 for impatient consumers, equal to 1 for consumers who are indifferent between present and future consumption, and greater than 1 for consumers who prefer future to present consumption. Any nonexponential discount function can induce inconsistent choices. (A simple proof that additivity and consistency imply exponential discounting is given in the appendix to this chapter, Section 18.9.)

207

18.3   Hyperbolic Discounting and Inconsistent Preferences

Many experiments have produced evidence that is inconsistent with a constant discount factor. For example, subjects' median responses in one experiment indicated indifference between $15 now, $20 in one month, $50 in a year, or $100 in 10 years. Suppose, for simplicity that our instantaneous utility function $u(\ )$ is linear, so we do not have to concern ourselves with initial wealth. Letting d denote an annual discount factor, we can see that indifference between $15 now and $50 in 1 year implies that $15 = 50d$ and thus $d = 0.3$. In contrast, indifference between $15 now and $20 in 1 month implies that $15 = 20d^{1/12}$ and thus $d = 0.0317$, and indifference between $15 now and $100 in 10 years implies $15 = 100d^{10}$ and thus $d = 0.8272$. These and similar experimental results suggest that discount factors typically rise with the length of the interval (Frederick et al. 2002). This pattern contrasts with the traditional assumption of exponential discounting with a constant discount factor.

The experimental evidence suggests that discount functions usually are not exponential but roughly hyperbolic. A generalized hyperbolic form that approximately fits most experimental data is $\delta(t) = (1 + \alpha t)^{-\gamma/\alpha}$, where α and γ are positive constants (Ainslie and Haslam 1992; Loewenstein and Prelec 1992). Use of a discount function of this form can produce inconsistent choices. For example, let $\alpha = \gamma = 1$ so that $\delta(t) = (1 + t)^{-1}$. Given a linear instantaneous utility function and a choice between $1000 in 10 years and $1100 in 11 years, we would take the latter because $1000(1 + 10)^{-1} < 1100(1 + 11)^{-1}$. If we could reverse our choice after a lapse of 10 years, we would because $1000 > 1100(1 + 1)^{-1}$. This reversal conforms to the principle of diminishing sensitivity; people are more sensitive to a delay of 1 year when it increases waiting time from zero to 1 year than when it increases waiting time from 10 to 11 years.

EXERCISE 18.1

Consider an individual whose discount function is $(1 + t)^{-1}$, where t denotes years remaining before an expected gain. The individual is offered his choice of $1000 in 10 years or $1200 in 11 years. Having a linear utility function, he chooses the latter option because $1000(1 + 10)^{-1} < 1200(1 + 11)^{-1}$. Before the 10 years elapses, the individual regrets his choice. Just how much time elapses before he is indifferent between the two offers?

18.4   Other Anomalies

How much an individual discounts future outcomes may depend on the absolute magnitudes involved, whether they are gains or losses, whether a reward is to be delayed or expedited, and whether rewards are isolated or placed in an explicit sequence.

18.4.1 Absolute Magnitudes

Large absolute magnitudes are typically discounted less than small ones, a pattern called the **magnitude effect** (Frederick et al. 2002). For example, one experiment produced the following result: "Subjects who were on average indifferent between receiving $15 immediately and $60 in a year, were also indifferent between an immediate $250 and $350 in a year, as well as between $3000 now and $4000 in a year" (Loewenstein and Prelec

1992, p. 575). Note that the implied discount factors for delayed rewards (for an individual with a linear utility function) are wildly different in the three choices: 0.25, 0.71, and 0.75.

18.4.2 Gains and Losses

Gains are typically discounted more rapidly than losses, a pattern termed the **sign effect** (Frederick et al. 2002). For example, one experiment indicated the following: "Subjects . . . were, on average, indifferent between receiving \$10 immediately and receiving \$21 in one year, and indifferent between losing \$10 immediately and losing \$15 in one year" (Loewenstein and Prelec 1992, p. 575).

> **EXERCISE 18.2**
>
> Consider an individual whose discount function is $\delta(t) = (1+t)^{-\gamma}$. Calculate the values for γ when (a) the individual expresses indifference between receiving \$10 immediately and getting \$21 in 1 year, and (b) when the individual expresses indifference between losing \$10 immediately and losing \$15 in 1 year.

Whether people view differences as gains or losses depends on their reference point. Thus intertemporal choice can be affected by framing, as demonstrated by an experiment in which 85 students were randomly assigned to one of two groups, each answering one of two versions of a question about installment payments.

Version 1.   Suppose that you bought a TV on a special installment plan. The plan calls for two payments; one this week and one in six months. You have two options for paying: (circle the one you would choose)

  A. An initial payment of \$160 and a later payment of \$110.
  B. An initial payment of \$115 and a later payment of \$160.

Version 2.   Suppose that you bought a TV on a special installment plan. The plan calls for two payments of \$200; one this week and one in six months. Happily, however, the company has announced a sale which applies retroactively to your purchase. You have two options: (circle the one that you would choose)

  C. A rebate of \$40 on the initial payment and a rebate of \$90 on the later payment.
  D. A rebate of \$85 on the initial payment and a rebate of \$40 on the later payment.

(Loewenstein and Prelec 1992, p. 588; © 1992 by the President and Fellows of Harvard College and the Massachusetts Institute of Technology; used with permission of MIT Press Journals)

Apart from framing, option A is the same as C, and B is the same as D. Thus the invariance assumption implies that the proportion of individuals choosing A should, apart from sampling error, match that choosing C. Contrary to this assumption, the two proportions were significantly different, with 54% of the respondents to version 1 choosing A but only 33% of the respondents to version 2 choosing C. A plausible explanation is that alternatives are framed in version 1 as large losses but in version 2 as smaller gains.

18.4.3 Events Delayed and Expedited

Discount rates can depend on whether an event is delayed or expedited, a pattern called the **delay-speedup asymmetry** (Frederick et al. 2002). Many people discount the future more heavily when a reward is to be delayed than when it is to be expedited. In one study the following was reported: "The amount required to compensate for delaying receiving a (real) reward by a given interval, from t to $t + s$, was from two to four times greater than the amount subjects were willing to sacrifice to speed consumption up by the same interval, i.e., from $t + s$ to t" (Loewenstein and Prelec 1992, p. 578). For example, a subject who was promised \$10 in 1 week was indifferent between that and \$13 in 2 weeks, whereas a subject who was promised \$13 in 2 weeks was indifferent between that and \$12 in 1 week. The reward for waiting in the former case (\$3) is three times as great as in the second (\$1). "Because the two pairs of choices are actually different representations of the same underlying pair of options, the results constitute a classic framing effect, which is inconsistent with any normative theory" (Loewenstein and Prelec 1992, p. 578).

Losses, as well as rewards, may be discounted differently, depending on whether they are expedited or delayed. People typically demand more to expedite a loss than they are willing to pay to defer it (Shelley 1993). The reluctance of individuals to forgo a scheduled reward or incur a loss before expected may be viewed as a special case of loss aversion and the endowment effect.

18.4.4 Rewards in Isolation and in Sequence

Some people who seem impatient when rewards are isolated appear willing to defer gratification when rewards are placed in an explicit sequence. This is illustrated by an experiment in which 95 students were asked about their preferences for restaurants. They were instructed to respond to three questions, ignoring any preexisting plans or other scheduling concerns. The questions were as follows, with the number of respondents and the percentage breakdown indicated on the right:

1. *Which would you prefer if both were free?* $n = 95$
    A. Dinner at a fancy French restaurant   86%
    B. Dinner at a local Greek restaurant   14%

For those who prefer French:

2. *Which would you prefer?* $n = 82$
    C. Dinner at the French restaurant on Friday in 1 month   80%
    D. Dinner at the French restaurant on Friday in 2 months   20%

3. *Which would you prefer?* $n=82$
    E. Dinner at the French restaurant on Friday in 1 month and
        dinner at the Greek restaurant on Friday in 2 months   43%
    F. Dinner at the Greek restaurant on Friday in 1 month and
        dinner at the French restaurant on Friday in 2 months   57%

(Loewenstein and Prelec 1993, p. 93; copyright ©1993 by the American Psychological Association; reprinted with permission)

Note that question 2 posed an isolated choice and elicited impatient responses, whereas question 3 posed a choice between sequences and elicited more patient responses.[1]

---

[1] Apart from eliciting patience, choices among sequences have another curious property: Faced with such choices, many people seem to prefer to spread out rewards in a manner that can violate additivity. An experiment demonstrating this is reported in Loewenstein and Prelec (1993).

A preference for an increasing sequence of rewards can help explain an otherwise puzzling feature of the relationship between age and earnings: In many occupations and industries, typical earnings rise monotonically with age even though productivity peaks some years prior to retirement. A plausible explanation is that workers (1) prefer a monotonically rising consumption profile, (2) doubt that they have the self-control required to save enough to derive a monotonically increasing consumption path from a differently shaped earnings path, and (3) therefore prefer a monotonically increasing earnings profile. (Kahneman and Thaler 1991; Loewenstein and Sicherman 1991).

18.5 Policy Implications

A person with inconsistent intertemporal preferences experiences an inner conflict between a patient planner and an impulsive consumer, that is, between a far-sighted self and a myopic self. Such an individual, in a far-sighted moment, may try to restrict the actions he can take in a future myopic moment. A restriction of this kind is called a *commitment device*. A classic example is Ulysses, who had his ship's crew tie him to the mast so that he could not succumb to the Sirens' call. Modern examples include dieters who move to fat-farms, alcoholics who take antabuse, one-time smokers who avoid parties where social smoking is tempting, and problem gamblers who steer clear of casinos (Elster 1979).

Individuals with inconsistent time preferences may use **commitment devices** to prevent themselves from squandering savings in moments of weakness. For example, such people may increase their saving by having their pay checks directly deposited in their savings accounts, taking on big mortgages, or enrolling in a retirement program—such as a 401(k) retirement savings plan—that puts assets beyond easy reach.[2]

The availability of commitment devices can be affected by features of capital markets and retirement plans that can be influenced by government policy. The capital market changes discussed in the previous chapter may have undermined the efforts of people with inconsistent preferences to curb their spendthrift tendencies. Consider, for example, an individual who had taken on a large mortgage in an effort to force himself to accumulate some wealth in the form of home equity. Home equity loans now allow the myopic self to run up debts as fast as the far-sighted self accumulates equity. As a second example, consider an individual who put most of her wealth in illiquid long-term bonds to avoid the temptation to spend it. Credit cards, with borrowing limits based on financial assets, allow the myopic self to spend what the far-sighted self had salted away (Laibson 1997). Individuals with inconsistent preferences might be helped to save by tighter regulation of home equity loans and credit cards.

18.6 Summary

1. Intertemporal preferences are consistent if plans made at one moment are still attractive at all subsequent moments when steps must be taken to implement them. Preferences are inconsistent if the mere passage of time makes individuals regret or abandon their previously adopted plans.

---

[2] The "401(k) assets are partially protected from splurges, because withdrawals from the accounts can be freely made only if the account holder is over fifty-nine and a half years old. For younger consumers, withdrawals are only allowed in cases of financial hardship or when a worker separates from a firm, and even then generate a 10 percent penalty" (Laibson et al. 1998, p. 145, quoted with the permission of the Brookings Institution Press).

2. If a utility function is additive and preferences are consistent, then discounting must be exponential.

3. Experimental evidence indicates that, for many individuals in many circumstances, discounting is not exponential but hyperbolic. Hyperbolic discounting can result in inconsistent choices.

4. How much an individual discounts the future may depend on not only the length of delays but also the absolute magnitudes involved, whether the magnitudes are gains or losses, whether a reward is to be delayed or expedited, and whether rewards are presented in isolation or in sequence. Intertemporal choices may depend on how the alternatives are framed.

5. A person with inconsistent intertemporal preferences experiences an inner conflict between a patient planner and an impulsive consumer. Individuals with inconsistent time preferences may be able to save more if they have access to commitment devices. The availability of such devices might be increased by policies that restrict use of credit cards and home equity loans and promote retirement plans that penalize or prohibit early withdrawals.

18.7   Solutions to Exercises

18.1. Letting t^* denote years left to wait for \$1000 when the individual becomes indifferent between 1000 in t^* years and 1100 in $t^* + 1$ years, we can write

$$1000\frac{1}{1+t^*} = 1200\frac{1}{2+t^*}$$
$$(2+t^*)1000 = 1200(1+t^*)$$
$$2000 + 1000t^* = 1200 + 1200t^*$$
$$800 = 200t$$
$$t^* = 4.$$

The number of years elapsed before the individual becomes indifferent is $10 - 4 = 6$.

18.2. (a) When the individual is indifferent between receiving \$10 immediately and getting \$21 in one year, we can write

$$10 = 21(1+1)^{-\gamma}$$
$$2^\gamma = 2.1$$
$$\gamma = \log 2.1 / \log 2$$
$$\gamma = 1.07.$$

(b) When the individual is indifferent between losing \$10 immediately and losing \$15 in one year, we can write

$$-10 = -15(1+1)^{-\gamma}$$
$$2^\gamma = 1.5$$
$$\gamma = \log 1.5 / \log 2$$
$$\gamma = 0.585.$$

18.8 Problems

1. Tabulate and sketch the exponential discount function 0.9^t for values of t from 0 to 50 by increments of 10. Tabulate the hyperbolic discount function $(1+t)^{-1}$ for the same values of t and sketch the curve in the same diagram you used for the exponential curve. Compare the shapes of the curves.

2. Consider an individual whose discount function is $(1+t)^{-1}$, where t denotes years remaining before an expected gain. The individual is offered his choice of $1000 in 10 years or $1100 in 11 years. Having a linear utility function, he chooses the latter option because $1000(1+10)^{-1} < 1100(1+11)^{-1}$. Before the 10 years elapses, the individual regrets his choice. Just how much time elapses before he is indifferent between the two offers?

3. Consider an exponential discounter.
   a. If the individual expresses indifference between receiving $10 immediately and getting $21 in 1 year, what is his discount factor for gains?
   b. If the individual expresses indifference between losing $10 immediately and losing $15 in 1 year, what is his discount factor for losses?

18.9 Appendix: Additivity, Consistency, and Discounting

To prove that additive and consistent intertemporal preferences imply exponential discounting, consider a consumer who can choose between two consumption bundles (a, a') and (b, b'), where a and b are alternative quantities of consumption one period in the future and a' and b' are alternative levels of consumption two periods in the future. Suppose the consumer is indifferent between these bundles. If the consumer's utility function is additive, we can express this indifference by writing

$$u(a)\delta(1) + u(a')\delta(2) = u(b)\delta(1) + u(b')\delta(2). \tag{18.1}$$

Consistency requires that the consumer is still indifferent between the bundles after the lapse of one time period. Now the consumer's choice is between consuming a immediately and a' with a one-period delay or consuming b immediately and b' with a one-period delay. To express continued indifference, we write

$$u(a) + u(a')\delta(1) = u(b) + u(b')\delta(1). \tag{18.2}$$

Solving Equation 18.1 for $\delta(2)$, we get

$$\delta(2) = \delta(1)\frac{u(a) - u(b)}{u(b') - u(a')}. \tag{18.3}$$

Solving Equation 18.2 for $\delta(1)$, we get

$$\delta(1) = \frac{u(a) - u(b)}{u(b') - u(a')}. \tag{18.4}$$

Using Equation 18.4 to substitute $\delta(1)$ for the fraction on the right side of eqn 18.3, we find that $\delta(2) = \delta(1)^2$. Thus the discounting function is exponential.

19

▓▓▓ Economics of Risk

Risk and Probability

We face **risk** when our well-being depends on events whose occurrence we cannot predict with certainty. For example, we take a risk when we venture out in the morning not knowing for sure whether the weather will be fair or rainy. Similarly, we face risk when we buy a bond without knowing for sure what its value may be at various dates in the future when we may need to sell it. As an aid to measuring and managing risks, we use the concept of probability.

19.1.1 Development of Probability Concepts

The earliest rigorous discussions of probability were in the context of games of chance such as those played by flipping coins, rolling dice, or drawing cards. In the 1600s, mathematicians such as Christian Huygens (Hī´ genz; 1629–95) studied the possible outcomes of many games of chance. The rules of these games establish a number of outcomes that may be called **equally likely** in the sense that we have no reason to prefer betting on one outcome rather than another. Consider two examples: First, when a symmetrical coin is flipped, heads and tails are equally likely. Second, when a six-sided die formed from a homogeneous material is rolled, each of the six sides is equally likely to come up on top. We would be indifferent between betting on heads or tails when the coin is flipped or between 1, 2, 3, 4, 5, or 6 when the die is rolled.

A set of outcomes is called an **event**. In the case of rolling a six-sided die, for example, the set $\{1, 3, 5\}$ is the event that the outcome is an odd number. An event is said to occur when any of its constituent outcomes occurs. Thus we say an odd number is rolled when 1, 3, or 5 is rolled. For any two events A and B, the statement "A or B occurs" is true if and only if the outcome is in the union of A and B (denoted $A \cup B$). The statement "A and B occur" is true if and only if the outcome is in the intersection of A and B (denoted $A \cap B$). For example, if $A = \{1, 2\}$ and $B = \{2, 3\}$, saying "A or B occurs" is equivalent to saying "the outcome is 1, 2, or 3 " and claiming "A and B occur" is equivalent to claiming "the outcome is 2."

As a set, an event may be specified by either stating a membership condition or (if the set is finite) listing its members. Some events may be specified by two or more equivalent membership conditions. In our die-rolling example, the event $\{2, 4\}$ satisfies the condition that outcomes are positive powers of two as well as the condition that outcomes are even numbers less than six. The **extension** of a membership condition is the set it specifies. According to the **axiom of extensionality**, if two sets have the same members, they are equal. Because events are sets of outcomes, we can equate two events covering the same outcomes. In the die-rolling case, we can equate the event of getting a positive power of two and the event of getting an even number less than six.

Classical writers on probability such as Huygens defined the probability of an event as the number of equally likely outcomes in which the event occurs divided by the total number of equally likely cases. For example, the probability of rolling an odd number was said to be $3/6 = 1/2$. Similarly, the probability of rolling 5 or more was said to be $2/6 = 1/3$. As a final example, suppose we had an urn containing 100 marbles. If 25 were red and the rest green and if the marbles were thoroughly mixed, the probability of drawing a red marble would be $25/100 = 1/4$.

Later writers on probability tried to extend the concept to situations in which possible outcomes aren't easily broken down into a finite number of equally likely cases. For example, were we to toss a thumb tack instead of a coin or a die, we would have trouble identifying equally likely cases. The tack could land point up or point down. However the tack is not symmetric; its center of gravity may lie near its head, making it more likely than not to land point upward. As a second example, we might like to assess the probability of rain tomorrow. However, we wouldn't be able to identify equally likely outcomes. The various possible weather conditions—rain, snow, clouds, sun, and so on—are not equally likely. Various ways of extending the concept of probability to such cases have been proposed.

The approach that seems most fruitful to me is one pioneered by Thomas Bayes (1702–61) and Pierre Simon de Laplace (1749–1827) and now usually termed "Bayesian." In this approach, probability is interpreted as a personal degree of belief, conditioned on available information. You and I may differently assess the probability of rain tomorrow, particularly if we have different information. However, each of us can give numerical expression to our degree of belief in rain by comparing it to a standard such as the probability of drawing a red ball from an urn. Here is how the comparison works.[1] Suppose we were given our choice of winning \$10 if it rains tomorrow or \$10 if a red ball is drawn from an urn containing 100 balls. We can gamble on the weather or the urn but not on both. Since the prize is the same, we prefer to bet on the more likely event. Before we bet, we would like to know how many red balls are in the urn. If there are no red balls in the urn, we'd prefer to bet on rain. If all the balls are red, we'd prefer to bet on drawing a red ball. Generally, the more red balls, the more attractive is gambling on the urn. Thus there must be some particular number of red balls such that we would be indifferent between betting on rain or betting on red; call this number r.[2] If the urn contained r red balls, the probability of drawing a red ball would, by the classical definition, be $r/100$. Because we are indifferent between the two gambles and the prizes are the same, we should say that the probability of rain is also $r/100$. An economist who says there is a 0.3 chance of a strike at GM is saying he would be indifferent between winning \$10 if there is a strike and winning \$10 if a red marble is picked at random from an urn containing 30 red marbles and 70 marbles of a different color.

The probability an individual assigns to an event depends on the information available to her. To emphasize that dependence, we use the following notation: If E denotes an event and I denotes some information, then $p(E|I)$ denotes the probability of event E given information I. For example, E might be the event that it rains tomorrow and I might be information on the barometric pressure today. When the conditioning information does not need to be made explicit, we can use $p(E)$ as a shorthand for $p(E|I)$.

---

[1] The following account is based on Lindley (1985).

[2] More precisely expressed, there must be some number r such that we like betting on the weather at least as well as on the urn but strictly prefer betting on an urn containing $r + 1$ red marbles to betting on the weather.

19.1.2 Basic Laws of Probability

The assignment of probabilities to events is personal but not capricious. Logic constrains the manner in which probabilities may be assigned. There are three fundamental laws of probability. First, all probabilities lie between 0 and 1:

$$0 \le p(E) \le 1.$$

This law holds because we assess probabilities by using the standard of an urn containing balls some fraction of which are red. The fraction must be in the interval $[0, 1]$ and hence so must the probability of drawing a red ball from the urn. An impossible event has probability 0; a certain event has probability 1.[3]

Second, the probabilities of two exclusive events obey an addition law. Two events E_1 and E_2 are said to be **exclusive** if they cannot both occur. For example, winning a game and losing the same game are exclusive events. The **addition law** says that if E_1 and E_2 are exclusive, then the probability that E_1 or E_2 occurs is the sum of the probability of E_1 and the probability of E_2:

$$\text{if } E_1 \text{ and } E_2 \text{ are exclusive,}$$

$$\text{then } p(E_1 \text{ or } E_2) = p(E_1) + p(E_2).$$

This law, like the first, holds because we assess probabilities by using the standard of an urn containing balls of various colors. Let E_1 be the event that the ball we pick is entirely red and E_2 the event that the ball we pick is entirely green. These events are exclusive because one ball cannot simultaneously be both all red and all green. Let N, N_g, and N_r denote, respectively, the total number of balls in the urn, the number of green balls in the urn, and the number of red balls in the urn. The addition law is established by noting that $p(E_1 \text{ or } E_2) = \frac{N_r + N_g}{N} = \frac{N_r}{N} + \frac{N_g}{N} = P(E_1) + P(E_2)$.

An important consequence of the first two laws concerns an event E and its negation $\bar{E}$— that is, the event that E does not happen. By the first law, $p(E \text{ or } \bar{E}) = 1$. By the addition law, $p(E \text{ or } \bar{E}) = p(E) + p(\bar{E})$. By substitution, $p(E) + p(\bar{E}) = 1$. Hence, $p(E) = 1 - p(\bar{E})$.

Another notable implication of the first two laws concerns an event (set of outcomes) S partitioned into two exclusive subsets B and C such that $B \cup C = S$. Suppose, for example, we draw a sample of two balls in succession from an urn containing green and red balls. Consider the event S that our two-ball sample contains *at least* one red ball. Letting G and R represent a green ball and a red ball, we can see that $S = \{GR, RG, RR\}$. Now let B denote the event that our sample contains *exactly* one red ball, so $B = \{GR, RG\}$ and $C = \{RR\}$. By the axiom of extensionality, S is equal to $B \cup C$. In other words, saying "S occurs" is equivalent to saying "B or C occurs." Thus $P(S) = P(B \text{ or } C)$. By the addition law, $P(B \text{ or } C) = P(B) + P(C)$. Thus $P(S) = P(B) + P(C)$. By the first law of probability, $P(B)$ and $P(C)$ are non-negative. Hence $P(S) \ge P(B)$ and $P(S) \ge P(C)$. In words, *the probability of an event is at least as great as the probability of any of its subsets*. This result is sometimes called the **extension rule** (Tversky and Kahneman

---

[3] Surprisingly, some possible events have probability 0 and some uncertain events have probability 1. For example, consider a uniform probability distribution on the closed interval [3, 4]. A number chosen at random from this distribution could turn out to be π, but the probability of that happening is 0. Likewise, the number chosen is not certain to be strictly less than 4, but the probability of it being so is 1. If these facts make your head spin, don't worry; they won't be mentioned again in this text, and the vertigo can be cured by a course in measure theory.

2002). Applied to our example, the extension rule means that the probability of a two-ball sample containing one or more red balls is at least as great as the probability of it containing exactly one red ball and at least as great at the probability of it containing two red balls.

Third, probabilities obey a **multiplication law**:

$$p(E_1 \text{ and } E_2) = p(E_1)p(E_2|E_1).$$

The events in question are not necessarily exclusive. This law, like the other two, is entailed by our choice of an urn as a standard by which to assess probabilities. Let E_1 be the event that the ball we pick is at least partially red and E_2 the event that the ball we pick is at least partially green. The event "E_1 and E_2" is the event that the ball is part red and part green. Let N, N_g, N_r, and N_{gr} denote, respectively, the total number of balls in the urn, the number of balls that are at least part green, the number of balls that are at least part red, and the number of balls that are part green and part red. The multiplication law is established by noting that $p(E_1 \text{ and } E_2) = \frac{N_{gr}}{N} = \frac{N_r}{N} \frac{N_{gr}}{N_r} = p(E_1)p(E_2|E_1)$.

EXERCISE 19.1

Suppose the probability that Airbus, within the next 5 years, will introduce an aircraft larger than any now made is 0.4 and the probability that Boeing will introduce such an aircraft in that period if Airbus does is 0.7. What is the probability that both companies will introduce such aircraft in the next 5 years?

19.1.3 Coherency and the Dutch Book

If you assign probabilities in a manner consistent with the three basic laws of probability, your judgments are said to be **coherent**. Probability judgments that violate the three laws are **incoherent**.

Incoherent judgments can be expensive (Lindley 1985). For example, suppose that, disregarding the addition law, we said $p(E) = 0.4$ and $p(\bar{E}) = 0.7$. We would then believe it fair to pay $0.40 for a lottery ticket that would win $1.00 if event E occurred and $0.70 for a lottery ticket that would win $1.00 if $\bar{E}$ occurred. If we bought both tickets, we would spend $1.10. However, then we would win just $1.00 gross, regardless of whether E or $\bar{E}$ occurs. In short, we would lose $0.10 net for sure. A set of bets such as this, which entail a sure loss, is called a **Dutch book**. When we are forced to take risks, the only way to avoid falling victim to a Dutch book is to respect the laws of probability.[4]

Although the laws of probability are simple, their implications for complex problems are not always obvious. Consider, for example, an individual who gambles on horse races. Suppose the gambler says that the probabilities of Nimble Nag winning the Kentucky Derby, the Preakness Stakes, and the Belmont Stakes are 0.13, 0.28, and 0.38, while the probability of its winning all three races (the Triple Crown) is 0.01. The gambler is asked what is the chance of Nimble Nag winning exactly two of the three races. To avoid falling victim to a Dutch book, the gambler wants to give a coherent answer. As an aid to

---

[4] William Safire, a prominent conservative columnist, once offered odds against various Democratic politicians winning their party's presidential nomination in 2004 (*New York Times*, June 25, 2001). The implied probabilities sum to 1.68. Had Safire been prepared to back his words with wagers, he would have willingly accepted a Dutch book costing him 68% more than it returned.

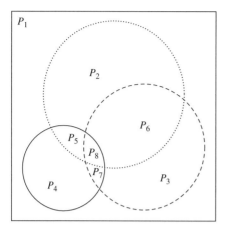

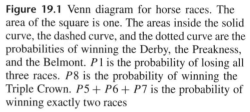

Figure 19.1 Venn diagram for horse races. The area of the square is one. The areas inside the solid curve, the dashed curve, and the dotted curve are the probabilities of winning the Derby, the Preakness, and the Belmont. $P1$ is the probability of losing all three races. $P8$ is the probability of winning the Triple Crown. $P5 + P6 + P7$ is the probability of winning exactly two races

establishing boundaries on coherent answers, the gambler might sketch a Venn diagram, such as Figure 19.1, where $P1, \ldots, P8$ represent the probabilities of eight exclusive and exhaustive events. In this notation, the probability of Nimble Nag winning just two races is $P5 + P6 + P7$.

Lower and upper bounds on the probability of Nimble Nag winning just two races can be established by minimizing and maximizing $P5 + P6 + P7$ subject to the following constraints:[5]

$$P1 + P2 + P3 + P4 + P5 + P6 + P7 = 0.99,$$

$$P4 + P5 + P7 = 0.12,$$

$$P3 + P6 + P7 = 0.27,$$

$$P2 + P5 + P6 = 0.37.$$

This is just a pair of linear programming problems.[6] If in MuPAD we type

```
linopt::minimize([P1+P2+P3+P4+P5+P6+P7=.99, P4+P5+P7=.12,
    P3+P6+P7=.27, P2+P5+P6=.37, P1>=0, P2>=0, P3>=0, P4>=0,
    P5>=0, P6>=0, P7>=0, P5+P6+P7]),
```

we get the lower bound, 0. If we type the MuPAD input again, replacing `minimize` with `maximize`, we get the upper bound, 0.38. Thus the gambler can maintain coherence by picking any number in the range $(0, 0.38)$ as an answer to the question about the probability of Nimble Nag winning just two races.

19.2 Expected Value

Most of the variables we'd like to predict have more than just two possible values. For example, if a test grade is recorded as an integer between 0 and 4, it has five possible values. A student trying to predict his score might draw up a table such as the following:

---

[5] The constraints could be expressed in an equivalent but more cumbersome form by adding $P8$ to the left side and 0.01 to the right side of each equation and appending an additional constraint, $P8 = 0.01$.

[6] Linear programming approaches to probability calculations are discussed by Lad (1996) and several works cited therein.

Grade	Probability
0	0.10
1	0.20
2	0.30
3	0.25
4	0.15

If he wanted to summarize the prediction in a single number, he could multiply the possible scores by the probabilities and add up the products, getting the "expected value" or "expectation" of his grade. In this case the expected value is $0.2 + 0.6 + 0.75 + 0.6 = 2.15$ (between a C and a $C+$). Notice that calculating an expected value is the same as calculating a mean except that the weights are subjective probabilities rather than frequencies. Don't confuse the expected value (2.15) with the modal, or most likely value (2).

Formally, the **expected value** or **expectation** of a discrete variable x that may assume values x_i with probabilities $p(x_i)$, where $i = 1, \ldots, n$, is

$$E(x) = \sum_{i=1}^{n} x_i p(x_i).$$

As another example, imagine a lottery that sells 1000 tickets. One ticket will win $1000; two tickets will win $500; four will win $250. The expected value of your winnings if you hold one ticket is $1000/1000 + 500(2/1000) + 250(4/1000) = \$3$. Again, don't confuse the expected value ($3) with the modal, or most likely value (0).

19.3 Attitudes Toward Risk

Individuals' attitudes toward risks are complex. Economists and psychologists are just beginning to understand these complexities. Some of their recent findings will be examined in the next chapter. For now let us just say that economists have traditionally assumed that each individual has one of three attitudes toward risk: risk-seeking, risk-neutral, or risk-averse. Risk-seekers like to gamble. Given a choice between $3 for sure or a ticket in the lottery we just discussed, a risk-seeker will take the ticket. More generally, risk-seekers will turn down a sure reward for a gamble with the same expected value. Risk-neutral individuals are indifferent among all options of equal expected value. A risk-neutral individual would be indifferent between $3 and a lottery ticket with a $3 expected value. Risk-averse individuals prefer a sure thing to a gamble with equal expected value. Thus a risk-averse individual will take $3 rather than a ticket in the lottery we have discussed. Economists have traditionally assumed that most individuals are risk-averse.

19.4 Insurance

Insurance is an important way of reducing risk. Insurance reduces risk by pooling the possible losses of individuals and firms into a larger population. This allows insurance companies to predict risk more accurately and then to price it with some statistical confidence that they will not be hit by an extraordinary number of claims at any one time. Insurance appeals to risk-averse individuals.

EXERCISE 19.2

An insurance company will pay $300 if a package is lost in shipping. The probability that the package will be lost is 0.01. What is the expected value of the insurance? If you were risk-neutral, would you pay $4 for the insurance?

Although individuals and firms can insure themselves against various risks, there are important risks that are not insurable. Two problems that limit the availability of insurance are moral hazard and adverse selection.

19.4.1 Moral Hazard

Having insurance against a misfortune reduces the insured person's incentives to avoid it. When a person is well insured against a calamity, there is a danger, from the insurer's standpoint, that the insured person will act in ways that increase the probability of the calamity and the resulting insurance claim. This danger is called moral hazard.

For example, if a landlord has a building fully insured against fire, he might be careless about maintaining its fire alarms. In a more extreme case, if a building is insured for more than its value, the owner has an incentive to burn it. Of course, there are also incentives not to burn it—arson is against the law. The question then becomes one of the relative strength of these differing incentives.

When moral hazard is a serious issue, insurance tends to be expensive or unattainable.

19.4.2 Adverse Selection

Adverse selection is the tendency for less desirable customers or suppliers of less desirable goods to be more eager to close a deal and thus willing to accept a price that others would reject. As the price rises, more desirable customers leave the market, and as the price falls, suppliers with superior goods leave the market. For example, a drop in the price of used cars drives owners of higher quality cars from the market, leaving only owners of "lemons" still willing to sell. In the context of insurance, the most important instance of adverse selection is the tendency for people facing greater risks to be more eager to buy insurance against those risks. If insurance companies raise premiums, their lower risk customers may cancel their policies.

Insurance companies try to classify individuals according to observable indicators of the risks they face. In some U.S. states, for example, auto insurance rates vary across zip codes. However, accurate classification is often very difficult; the risk indicators that insurance companies can observe tell only part of the story. Potential insurance buyers usually know more about their risks than do insurance companies, an instance of what economists call **asymmetric information**. For pioneering research on markets with asymmetric information, George A. Akerlof, A. Michael Spence, and Joseph E. Stiglitz (Figure 19.2) were awarded the Nobel Prize in Economics in 2001.

Poorly informed insurance companies can sometimes extract information from better informed potential clients by offering a variety of contracts, a process called **screening through self-selection**. A pioneering theoretical exploration of this process was provided by Rothschild and Stiglitz (1976). They show that some contracts that would be available if information were fully shared will cease to be available if buyers can withhold information from insurers. To illustrate their analysis, let us focus on disability insurance. Individuals earn an income Y_a as long as they are able-bodied. If and when they become disabled, they

Figure 19.2 George A. Akerlof, A. Michael Spence, and Joseph E.Stiglitz (The photograph of Akerlof is by Noah Berger and used with the permission of the University of California, Berkeley. The photographs of Spence and Stiglitz are used with the permission of Stanford University and Columbia University respectively.)

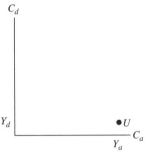

Figure 19.3 An uninsured individual has a higher income when able-bodied than when disabled

earn a reduced income Y_d. We can think of these incomes as coordinates of a point in a plane whose axes represent consumption when able (C_a) and disabled (C_d). In Figure 19.3 the point U represents the income prospects for an uninsured worker.

Rothschild and Stiglitz (1976; hereafter RS) suppose that insurance companies are risk-neutral, maximizing expected profits. They further assume that the insurance industry is competitive, so profits are driven to zero in equilibrium. Abstracting from administrative costs, they deduce that premiums should just cover compensation on average.

If all individuals have the same risk of being disabled, the mean or expected value of an insurance policy should be zero: $a(1 - p) - bp = 0$, where a is the premium paid by an able-bodied worker, b is the compensation to a disabled worker, and p is the probability of being disabled. This equation implies that the ratio of the compensation to the premium b/a should equal the odds against being disabled, $(1 - p)/p$. For example, if the probability of being disabled is $p = 1/4$, the odds ratio is 3 and we could buy \$3 worth of insurance for a \$1 premium, or for that matter, \$3000 worth of insurance for a \$1000 premium. Buying enough insurance would enable us to move from point U along a line with slope -3, as shown in Figure 19.4. This is called the **fair-odds line**.

Risk-averse individuals would choose full coverage—that is, they would buy enough insurance so that $Y_a - a = Y_d + b$. They would select the point where the fair-odds line intersects a ray drawn from the origin with slope 1, as shown in Figure 19.5.

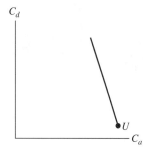

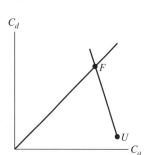

Figure 19.4 The absolute value of the slope of the fair-odds line is equal to the odds against being disabled

Figure 19.5 A risk-averse individual seeks full insurance coverage, trying to move from U to F

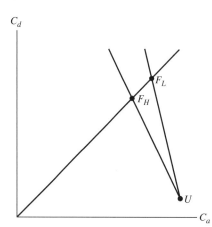

Figure 19.6 Insurance companies that can identify high-risk and low-risk individuals offer F_H to the former and F_L to the latter

Now suppose that there are two groups of insurance buyers who differ in just one respect—their chance of becoming disabled. Let the odds against disability be 4:1 in the low-risk group and 2:1 in the high-risk group. If the insurance companies can identify who belongs to which group, the analysis can proceed as before except that now we have two fair-odds lines, as shown in Figure 19.6. Each group selects full coverage. The high-risk group moves to F_H, and the low-risk group moves to F_L.

Now let us introduce asymmetrical information. Suppose that individuals know their risk status but insurance companies do not. If insurance companies persist in offering both kinds of policies, represented by the two fair-risk lines, all individuals would move to F_L, including the high-risk individuals. But insurance companies would go bankrupt if they allowed this. They can go on offering the contract F_H but they can no longer afford to offer

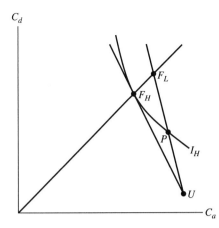

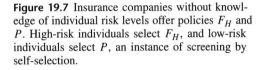

Figure 19.7 Insurance companies without knowledge of individual risk levels offer policies F_H and P. High-risk individuals select F_H, and low-risk individuals select P, an instance of screening by self-selection.

the contract F_L. They may try to offer some contract with fair odds for the low-risk group, but they will have to restrict it to be less attractive to the high-risk group than contract F_H.

To see what kind of restriction is needed, we draw an indifference curve for the high-risk group through F_H, as in Figure 19.7. A high-risk individual prefers any point on the indifference curve I_H to any point below it. In particular, a high-risk individual prefers F_H to P. In contrast, a low-risk individual, RS show, has steeper indifference curves. Low-risk individuals prefer limited coverage at fair odds such as P to any other policy on offer. Thus individuals' selection of policies sorts them by risk type.

The welfare implications of this analysis are disturbing. "The presence of the high-risk individuals" imposes a cost on the low-risk individuals. This cost is a dead-weight loss because "the high-risk individuals are no better off than they would be in isolation. If only the high-risk individuals would admit to their having high accident probabilities," the low-risk individuals would be able to get full coverage at no cost to others (RS, p. 638). This is an instance in which competitive equilibrium is not Pareto optimal.

19.5 Summary

1. We say two outcomes are equally likely when we have no reason to prefer betting on one rather than the other. An event is a set of outcomes. The probability of an event was conceived by Huygens as the number of equally likely outcomes in which the event occurs divided by the total number of equally likely outcomes.

2. Bayes and Laplace extended the concept of probability to situations in which equally likely cases cannot be identified, defining probability as a personal degree of belief. Coherent probability judgments conform to three basic laws: First, all probabilities lie in the interval [0,1]. Second, according to the addition law, if two events are exclusive, then the probability of one or the other occurring is the sum of their individual probabilities. Third, according to the multiplication law, the joint probability of two events is equal to the probability of one event times the probability of the second event conditional on the first.

3. The expected value or expectation of a discrete variable x that may assume values x_i with probabilities $p(x_i)$, where $i = 1, \ldots, n$, is

$$E(x) = \sum_{i=1}^{n} x_i p(x_i)$$

4. Individuals are called risk-adverse, risk-neutral, or risk-seeking, depending on whether—when given a choice between a fixed prize and an uncertain prize with the same expected value—they select the fixed prize, express indifference between the prizes, or select the uncertain prize.

5. Insurance appeals to risk-averse individuals. Moral hazard and adverse selection make some risks uninsurable. Insurance companies try to cope with adverse selection by classifying applicants by observable correlates of risk and by offering a variety of policies designed to achieve screening by self-selection.

19.6 Solutions to Exercises

19.1. The probability that both introduce aircraft larger than any now in operation is $.4 \times .7 = 0.28$.

19.2. If you were risk-neutral you would be willing to pay up to $\$300 \times 0.01 = 3.00$ to insure the package. However, you would not pay \$4.

19.7 Problems

1. An insurance company will pay \$100 if a package is lost in shipping. The probability that the package will be lost is 0.02. What is the expected value of the insurance? If you were risk-neutral, would you pay \$3 for the insurance?

2. Consider the following game: A fair coin is flipped until it comes up heads. You receive a prize equal to $\$2^n$, where n is the number of flips. What is the expected value of the prize? If you would not pay your life's savings for an opportunity to play the game, what is your attitude toward risk?

3. A bond with a zero coupon will be worth \$1000 at maturity unless the issuer goes bankrupt first. The chance of bankruptcy is 0.4. What is the expected value of the bond? If the bond matures in 2 years and the interest rate is 0.1, what is the present value (discounted expected value) of the bond? If you are willing to pay \$500 for the bond, what is your attitude toward risk?

4. Suppose that the probability that Dell will cut the prices of its computers in the next 3 months is 0.5 and the probability that Gateway will cut its prices in that period if Dell does is 0.8. What is the probability that both companies will cut their prices in the next 3 months?

5. Suppose that a firm has bid on three contracts. Its manager believes that the probabilities of winning the contracts are 0.34, 0.35, and 0.36. Sketch a Venn diagram showing all possible combinations of wins and losses. Suppose the manager asks you what his stated probabilities for the individual contracts imply about the probability of winning two or more contracts. Formulate a pair of linear programming problems whose solutions would provide lower and upper bounds on coherent answers to the manager's question. (Hint: You need to minimize and maximize a sum subject to four equality constraints.) If you have convenient access to linear programming software (like MuPAD), solve the problems you formulated.

20

▓▓▓ Behavior in the Face of Risk

Normative Theories

When trying to decide whether to buy a good or asset, we are often uncertain about the circumstances or state of the world in which it would be used or held. For example, when we are considering whether to buy a ticket to a football game, we may not know what the weather will be on the day of the game. If the weather is nice, attending the game will give us great pleasure. If the weather is cold and wet, attending the game wouldn't be nearly as much fun. As a second example, suppose we have a chance to buy a lottery ticket. At the time of purchase, we don't know whether or not it will be a winner. This example is particularly useful because almost any asset of uncertain future value can be thought of as a lottery ticket. These assets include stocks, bonds, real estate, and insurance policies. It is worthwhile analyzing lotteries carefully because they are representative of many uncertain situations.

What constitutes rational choice under uncertainty? This question has been pondered by generations of economists, mathematicians, and statisticians. Two theories that at different times received widespread support focus on expected value and expected utility. These are examined briefly in the following subsections.

20.1.1 Expected Value

Early probability theorists usually advocated accepting gambles with positive expected values and rejecting those with negative expected values. According to this strategy, known as the **principle of mathematical expectation**, we should, for example, accept a gamble in which we lose $1 with probability 0.9 and gain $10 with probability 0.1 but reject a gamble in which we lose $1 with probability 0.9 and gain $8 with probability 0.1. The best argument for this strategy is that if it were applied consistently in many small gambles, net winnings would very likely be positive.

The principle of mathematical expectation is less appealing when applied to a gamble that is large relative to the gambler's wealth. An extreme case was examined in Chapter 19, Problem 2, where we considered paying our life's savings to play a game with an infinite expected value. A pioneering analysis of this case was published in the 1730s by Daniel Bernoulli (1700–82; Figure 20.1) in a journal of the Saint Petersburg Academy of Sciences; the problem analyzed by Bernoulli is called the **Saint Petersburg paradox**. The fact that virtually everyone with substantial savings prefers to keep the savings rather than play the game suggested to Bernoulli and many subsequent commentators that (1) people are not interested in wealth per se but rather the utility it affords them and (2) for many people utility is an increasing but concave function of wealth. People may turn down a gamble

Figure 20.1 Daniel Bernoulli. (The image is from *Die Werke von Daniel Bernoulli*, band 1 [Birkhäuser Verlag, 1996].)

with a positive expected value because the gain in utility associated with a rise in wealth is less than the loss in utility associated with an equal fall in wealth.

20.1.2 Expected Utility

Bernoulli proposed that instead of maximizing the expected value of wealth, gamblers should aim to maximize their expected utility, which can be defined as follows: If a decision can result in n different levels of utility u_i, then the expected utility associated with the decision is $\sum_{i=1}^{n} p_i u_i$. This is a weighted average of utility levels, with the weights being probabilities.

In economic applications, we usually think of utility as depending directly on consumption. Indeed, we have previously written utility as a function of quantities of goods consumed, $u = U(q_1, \ldots, q_m)$. However, we have seen that rational consumers choose their consumption bundles according to their preferences and budget constraints. The budget constraint in turn depends on prices and how much money the consumer has to spend, that is, her wealth. Thus given preferences and prices, we can say that a consumer's wealth determines her choice of a consumption bundle and hence her utility. To formalize this notion that utility indirectly depends on wealth, we will write $u = U(w)$. According to the nonsatiation axiom, $U(w)$ is a monotonically increasing function. Substituting this indirect utility function into the expression for expected utility, we get $\sum_{i=1}^{n} p_i U(w_i)$.

If we wish to maximize expected utility we should take the following steps: First, we should list all possible outcomes for each alternative. The possible outcomes are summarized in terms of our wealth. For example, suppose I have an initial wealth $w_0 = \$9$ and consider betting \$5 on a horse that will pay \$7 if it wins. If I do not bet, the outcome is certain: My wealth will remain at its initial level, \$9. If I do bet, matters are slightly more complicated: My final wealth will be \$16 if my horse wins and \$4 if it loses, as shown in Table 20.1.

Second, we should evaluate the utility of each outcome, $U(w)$. If I do not bet, my utility level will be $U(9)$. If I do bet, my utility level will be $U(16)$ or $U(4)$. Figuring out the

Table 20.1 Wealth in four combinations of actions and states of the world

	Wins	Loses
Bet	$16	$4
Don't	$ 9	$9

form of our utility function can be a chore, but it is not impossible. A simple technique of eliciting a utility function or index is introduced in the next problem set. The shape of utility functions is important because, as shown in the appendix to this chapter, strictly concave utility functions induce risk-averse behavior, linear utility functions induce risk-neutral behavior, and strictly convex utility functions induce risk-seeking behavior. For purposes of illustration, let us suppose my utility function is $U = \sqrt{w}$. This is a concave function;[1] hence I am risk-averse. If I don't bet, my utility is $\sqrt{9} = 3$. If I do bet, my utility will be $\sqrt{16} = 4$ or $\sqrt{4} = 2$, depending on whether my horse wins or loses.

Third, we should evaluate the probability of each possible outcome. In doing so, we should make sure that our probabilities are coherent—that is, they obey the three basic laws of probabilities. If our probabilities are incoherent, you will recall, we can fall victim to a Dutch book. To continue with the horse-racing example, suppose I believe the odds against my horse's winning are 7 to 5. This means that the probability of victory is $\frac{5}{5+7} = \frac{5}{12}$. As a consequence of the first two laws of probability, the probability of loss is $1 - \frac{5}{12} = \frac{7}{12}$.

Finally, we should calculate expected utility for each alternative and choose the alternative that yields the highest expected utility. Which alternative is selected may depend on the shape of our utility function and our initial wealth. In the horse-racing example, my expected utility would be 3 if I didn't bet and $\frac{5}{12}(4) + \frac{7}{12}(2) = \frac{34}{12} = \frac{17}{6} = 2\frac{5}{6}$ if I did. Because my expected utility would be lower were I to bet, I decide not to bet.

The proposal to maximize expected utility is intuitively more appealing than the principle of mathematical expectation in cases like the Saint Petersburg paradox. However, Bernoulli provided no compelling argument that maximizing expected utility was a uniquely rational gambling strategy. Indeed, more than 2 centuries were to elapse before the rational basis for expected utility maximization was established.

A compelling argument for maximizing expected utility was finally established in 1944 by a mathematician, John von Neumann (Figure 20.2), and an economist, Oskar Morgenstern. They proposed eight axioms[2] to characterize rational choice under risk and demonstrated that the only strategy consistent with these axioms is that of expected utility maximization (von Neumann and Morgenstern 1944, pp. 26–29). While von Neumann and

---

[1] The assertion that $\sqrt{w}$ is concave is, by definition, equivalent to the assertion that $\sqrt{\lambda w_0 + (1-\lambda)w_1} > \lambda\sqrt{w_0} + (1-\lambda)\sqrt{w_1}$ whenever λ lies in the interval $(0, 1)$ and $w_0 \neq w_1$. Squaring both sides of the inequality and simplifying, we find it is equivalent to $\lambda(1-\lambda)(\sqrt{w_0} - \sqrt{w_1})^2 > 0$. The last inequality is obviously true, implying that $\sqrt{w}$ is indeed concave.

[2] Three of the axioms are easily stated. The completeness axiom asserts that an individual faced with two options prefers the first to the second, prefers the second to the first, or is indifferent between them. The transitivity axiom states that if an individual prefers option A to option B and option B to option C, the individual prefers option A to option C. The cancellation axiom asserts that in choosing between two actions we can ignore states of the world in which the two actions have the same consequences. The remaining axioms are a little more complicated but nonetheless normatively appealing in the view of most commentators.

Figure 20.2 John von Neumann (used with permission of Los Alamos National Laboratory)

Morgenstern focused on cases in which probability can be interpreted as a long-run fre-quency, a parallel analysis, with probability interpreted as a subjective degree of belief, was provided by Leonard J. Savage (1954). Although expected utility maximization is hard to fault as an ideal, using it to solve complex problems requires three forms of information that may be difficult to obtain. First, decision makers need to specify their utility functions. People may have difficulty specifying utility functions over ranges of wealth that they have not experienced. Second, the decision makers need to keep a running tally of their wealth, some components of which may be less than obvious. (What is the market value of your personal property or the present value of your future earnings?) Third, the decision makers need to make coherent assessments of the probabilities of the various states of the world. Even decision makers who are well versed in probability theory may find such assessment to be mentally taxing.

Textbooks in decision analysis, such as Clemen and Reilly (2001) and Pratt et al. (1995), suggest ways of obtaining or approximating the information required to maximize expected utility. However, the vast majority of decision makers are unacquainted with these texts and unlikely to follow their precepts exactly. Decision makers who do not consciously maximize expected utility might nonetheless act *as if* they did. Endowed with ideal preferences over lotteries, an individual could intuitively make optimal choices without the bother of consciously calculating and comparing expected utilities. Such an individual might recoil from suboptimal lotteries as spontaneously as from rotten meat. Whether people actually act as if maximizing expected utility is an empirical question.

Empirical assessments of the accuracy of expected utility theory have been accumulating since the early 1950s. These studies document many anomalies—that is, behavior inconsis-tent with the theory—a few of which we will examine later in this chapter. On balance, the evidence suggests that much of the time many people do *not* act as if maximizing expected utility (Schoemaker 1982; Camerer and Kunreuther 1989; Harless and Camerer 1994). In short, expected utility theory is normatively attractive but predictively weak.

▓ **EXERCISE 20.1**

Suppose your utility function is $1 - e^{-w/10000}$, where $e \approx 2.7183$ and w denotes wealth expressed in dollars. Your current wealth is $5000. You want to maximize your expected utility. Should you take a gamble in which you win $5000 with probability 0.6 and lose $4000 with probability 0.4?

20.2 Positive Theories

The predictive failures of expected utility theory have stimulated economists and psychologists to develop alternative theories that are designed to predict rather than prescribe choices under risk (Machina 1987, Starmer 2000).

One key to developing positive theories of judgment and choice is distinguishing between two systems or modes of mental activity. System 1, which roughly corresponds to what we ordinarily call "intuition," is fast, parallel, automatic, effortless, and emotionally charged. System 2, which resembles what we commonly call "reasoning," is slow, serial, controlled, effortful, and emotionally neutral (Kahneman 2003). Traditional economic theory says little about system 1, concentrating instead on how people behave when guided by system 2.

Another key to developing positive theories is recognition that system 1 is in constant operation, imperfectly monitored and inconsistently overridden by system 2. For example, system 1 generates impulses to eat appetizing foods and avoid nasty-smelling medicines. System 2 may or may not intervene with reminders to stick to our diets and comply with prescriptions. Even for questions that arouse no visceral impulses, system 1 may suggest an erroneous response, which may or may not be corrected by system 2. Consider, for example, the following problem:

A bat and a ball cost $1.10 in total. The bat costs $1 more than the ball. How much does the ball cost?[3]

The first response that springs to mind for most people is $.10, which becomes the default answer unless system 2 intervenes to correct the error (Kahneman 2003).

A leading example of a positive account of intuitive choice under risk is **prospect theory**. The founders of prospect theory, Kahneman and Tversky, distinguish two phases in the decision process: framing and choosing among framed alternatives. In the former phase, the decision maker constructs a representation of the acts, contingencies, and outcomes that are relevant to the decision. In the latter phase, the decision maker chooses one of the framed prospects. Framing was discussed in Chapter 12. In the remainder of the present chapter, we shall suppose that the decision makers have framed their alternatives and are ready to choose among them.

Prospect theory distinguishes two ways of choosing among prospects: detecting that one dominates another or comparing their values. Having discussed dominance in Chapter 12, we can move on to value comparisons.

As noted in Chapter 12, when people cannot spot a dominant alternative, they make choices by comparing values. Let $(x, p; y, q)$ denote a prospect that yields x with probability p and y with probability q and that preserves the status quo with probability $(1 - p - q)$. According to prospect theory, there are subjective values $v(\cdot)$, defined on gains and losses, and subjective decision weights $w(\cdot)$, defined on stated probabilities, such that people tend

---

[3] This quotation is from Kahneman (2003), who cites a personal communication from Shane Frederick.

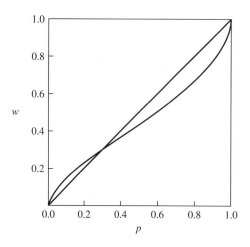

Figure 20.3 A weighting function compared to a 45° reference line

to choose the prospect with the highest overall value, $w(p)v(x) + w(q)v(y)$. The value function was described in Chapter 12; the weighting function is examined in the next subsection.

20.2.1 Weighting Probabilities

In expected utility theory, the utility of each possible outcome is weighted by its probability p. However, in prospect theory, the value of an uncertain outcome is multiplied by a decision weight $w(p)$, which is a monotonically increasing function of p but is not a probability. When w is plotted against p, most of the points lie close to a function of the form

$$w(p) = \frac{\delta p^{\gamma}}{\delta p^{\gamma} + (1-p)^{\gamma}}, \qquad (20.1)$$

where $\delta \approx .77$ and $\gamma \approx .69$, as illustrated in Figure 20.3 (Tversky and Fox 1995).

The weighting function has four important properties. First, impossible events are discarded, and certain events are given full weight—that is, $w(0) = 0$ and $w(1) = 1$. (Indeed, some people also discard events with very small positive probability and give full weight to events with probabilities slightly less than 1.)

Second, small probabilities that are not treated as impossibilities are overweighted, but high probabilities that are not treated as certainties are underweighted. For many people, $w(p) > p$ when $0 < p < 0.3$, but $w(p) < p$ when $0.3 < p < 1$.[4] The overweighting of small probabilities contributes to the popularity of bets on long shots and insurance against unlikely losses.

Third, for any given ratio of probabilities, the ratio of decision weights is closer to unity when the probabilities are low than when they are high, a phenomenon that Kahneman and Tversky (1979) call **subproportionality**. For example, $w(0.4)/w(0.8) < w(0.1)/w(0.2)$.

A historically important special case of subproportionality came to light in 1952 when a French economist, Maurice Allais, invited several prominent proponents of expected utility

---

[4] The underweighting of high probabilities is more pronounced than the overweighting of low probabilities. Thus if $p \neq 0$, $w(p) + w(1-p) < 1$, an inequality that Kahneman and Tversky (1979) call subcertainty.

Table 20.2 Prospects involved in Allais's paradox

	More Risky Prospects	Less Risky Prospects
High probability Pair	win 500 with probability 0.98	win 100 with probability 1
Low probability Pair	win 500 with probability 0.0098	win 100 with probability 0.01

theory to choose one prospect from both pairs shown in Table 20.2.[5] According to expected utility theory, a strongly risk-averse individual should choose the two prospects in the right (less risky) column, while other individuals should choose the two in the left (more risky column). No one acting on the basis of this theory would choose one prospect from the right column and another from the left column.[6] Nonetheless, several people who responded to Allais's invitation opted to win 100 with probability 1 but win 500 with probability 0.0098, a pattern now known as **Allais's paradox**. This paradox was one of the first indications of the predictive weakness of expected utility theory.

Prospect theory interprets Allais's paradox as follows: A preference for winning 100 with probability 1 over winning 500 with probability 0.98 indicates that $v(500)w(.98) < v(100)w(1)$ and thus $w(.98)/w(1) < v(100)/v(500)$. A preference for winning 500 with probability 0.0098 over winning 100 with probability 0.01 indicates that $v(500)w(.0098) > v(100)w(0.01)$ and thus $v(100)/v(500) < w(0.0098)/w(0.01)$. Hence by transitivity, $w(0.98)/w(1) < w(0.0098)/w(0.01)$, an instance of subproportionality.

Fourth, the slope of the weighting function $w(p)$ is greater near the end points of the [0, 1] probability interval than near the middle. A vivid illustration is provided by Russian roulette. Suppose you were handed a fully loaded six-shooter and asked to put it to your head and pull the trigger. By removing one bullet you would reduce the probability of immediate death from 1 to 5/6. This change, although numerically slight, creates some hope where there was none and thus feels important. Reducing the number of bullets from four to three or from three to two might not seem so exciting. However, removing the last bullet converts fear to security and hence feels like a momentous change (Prelec 2000).

The leveling out of the weighting function toward the middle of the probability interval can be viewed as another instance of the principle of diminishing sensitivity. The weighting function has two natural anchors: 0 and 1. Starting from either end, people are initially quite sensitive to small changes. Toward the center of the range, their sensitivity to further change is diminished.

---

[5] In Allais's original example, the winnings were expressed in millions of 1952 French francs. However, the units are unimportant in this context. The conclusions would be the same if the units were current dollars.

[6] To understand why expected utility theory counsels against choosing one prospect from both columns, think of the low probability prospects as two-stage lotteries. In the first stage, we have a 0.01 probability of progressing to the second stage (and a 0.99 probability of dropping out). In the second stage of the prospect in the lower left cell, we have a 0.98 probability of winning 500. In the second stage of the prospect in the lower right cell, we win 100 with probability 1. Both of these prospects involve a state of the world (an unlucky draw in the first stage) that occurs with probability 0.99 and eventuates in winning nothing. Because our choice between the two prospects makes no difference in this state of the world, we should—according to the cancellation axiom of expected utility theory—ignore it and focus on the other state of the world (a favorable draw in the first stage), where our choice makes a difference. The second-stage lotteries are precisely the prospects in the first row. Thus we should make both choices from the same column.

20.2.2 Attitudes Toward Risk

As we saw in Chapter 19, decisions and the individuals who make them are often classified as risk-averse, risk-neutral, or risk-seeking. Economists have traditionally assumed that an individual consistently exhibits one of these attitudes in all decisions, at least over certain ranges of wealth.

In contrast, prospect theory indicates that one individual may be risk-averse, risk-neutral, or risk-seeking depending on whether her choices involve gains or losses and whether the probabilities of gains or losses are large or small. Risk neutrality occurs where $v(x)w(p) = v(px)$. For estimated values of the parameters ($\alpha = \beta = .88, \delta = .77, \gamma = .69$), risk neutrality occurs when p is approximately 0.15. For lower probabilities, people tend to be risk-averse for losses but risk-seeking for gains. For greater probabilities, the pattern reverses: Here people tend to be risk-seeking for losses but risk-averse for gains. Thus it is not uncommon for an individual to buy insurance against a low probability loss, take a substantial chance by not paying a parking ticket, shun equities with large probabilities of capital gains, and buy a lottery ticket with a minute probability of winning.

> **EXERCISE 20.2**
>
> Consider an individual who behaves according to prospect theory. His value function is
>
> $$v(x) = \begin{cases} x^{.8} & \text{if } x \geq 0 \\ -3(-x)^{.8} & \text{if } x < 0 \end{cases}. \tag{20.2}$$
>
> His weighting function is
>
> $$w(p) = \frac{.8p^{.7}}{.8p^{.7} + (1-p)^{.7}}. \tag{20.3}$$
>
> Would he accept a gamble in which he won \$5000 with probability 0.6 and lost \$4000 with probability 0.4?

20.3 Judging Probabilities

In the course of decision making, questions often arise about the probabilities of various events. Answering these questions coherently while making good use of all relevant information can be a daunting task. Challenged to answer a difficult question, people commonly (and often unconsciously) substitute an answer to an easier question. Such substitution procedures are known in the psychological literature as **judgmental heuristics** (Kahneman and Frederick 2002). Use of judgmental heuristics often results in **biases**, that is, deviations of heuristic-based estimates from true values or estimates warranted by the laws of probability[7] (Gilovich and Griffin 2002).

---

[7] Economists use a heuristic when they respond to a question about the economy with answers about their models of the economy. We cannot avoid using models but should strive to identify their biases and replace inaccurate models with more realistic alternatives when that is possible without unduly increasing model complexity. The testing of expected utility theory and its replacement by prospect theory is a case in point.

Many econometricians have used another heuristic, rooted in frequentist (sampling theory) statistics. Asked about the probability distribution (given currently available data) of an unobserved quantity such as an elasticity or future income, they have responded with answers about the distribution of an estimator in imaginary repeated samples. This potentially misleading heuristic can, and increasingly is, avoided by using Bayesian rather than frequentist methods (Poirier 1995; Rossi et al. 2005.)

Three heuristics are often used in assessing probabilities. First, the **availability** heuristic is used when people estimate the probability or frequency of an event by the availability of such events in memory, that is, the ease with which such events are remembered. The availability heuristic works well when probability and ease of recall are highly correlated, as they often are because more frequent events tend to be easier to recall, other things being equal. However, ease of recall may be influenced not only by frequency but also by other factors, such as vividness, media attention, and ease of classification. Finding vivid, prominently reported, and easily categorized events easier to recall than undramatic, under-reported, and difficult to classify events users of the availability heuristic commonly overestimate the frequency of the former and underestimate that of the latter.

The role of vividness and media attention was documented by studies of judgments about the frequency of various lethal events in the United States. Subjects believed that deaths due to tornadoes were more common than those due to asthma (although the latter are twenty-one times more numerous) and that deaths due to floods were more common than those due to tuberculosis (although the latter are eighteen times more numerous). In general, "overestimated causes of death were dramatic and sensational, whereas underestimated causes tended to be unspectacular events, which claim one victim at a time and are common in nonfatal form" (Slovic et al. 1982 p. 467). A follow-up study of newspaper reporting of deaths found that "the biases in newspaper coverage and people's judgments were quite similar" (Slovic et al. 1982 p. 468). These biases may be even more pronounced in television news, long associated with the motto "If it bleeds, it leads."

Safety experts' analyses of complicated technologies such as nuclear power rarely reassure people who use the availability heuristic to assess the probability of accidents. As Paul Slovic notes, "the very act of telling somebody about a low-probability catastrophe and going through the fault tree to show why it's improbable may make the accident more imaginable and memorable, and thus seemingly more likely" [quoted by McKean (1985) p. 26].

The role of classification in availability is suggested by an experiment with word endings. In one phase of the experiment, students were given sixty seconds to list seven letter words with specified characteristics. They were able to list many more words ending in "ing" than having "n" as the next to the last letter, even though all words satisfying the former criterion also satisfy the latter. This result shows that words identified as ending in "ing" are more available (easily recalled) than those identified as having "n" as the penultimate letter (Tversky and Kahneman 2002). Perhaps that is because "ing" calls to mind a category (present participles) with many familiar examples, whereas a penultimate "n" does not identify any equally familiar category.

In another phase of the experiment subjects were asked how many seven letter words of a specified form they would expect in four pages of a novel. Some subjects were asked about words ending in "ing" and others about words with "n" as the penultimate letter. The median responses were 13.4 for words ending in "ing" and 4.7 for words with "n" in the penultimate position. Taken together, the results of the two phases of the experiment strongly suggest that the availability heuristic influenced the estimates of word frequency.

Because *ing* words are a subset of _n_ words, the frequency of the former cannot exceed that of the latter. Nonetheless, availability-based estimates of the former do exceed those of the latter. Estimates based on the availability heuristic evidently cannot be relied on to obey the extension rule (Tversky and Kahneman 2002).

A second heuristic for judging probabilities is **representativeness**. If an object has a characteristic that is representative of some class of objects, many people judge that the object probably belongs to that class. Their judgment may be guided by intuition or by faulty reasoning that confuses the probability of having a characteristic given membership in

Table 20.3 Health status and diagnostic test results

Test Result	Sick	Well	Total
Negative	2	72	74
Positive	8	18	26
Total	10	90	100

a class with the probability of membership given a characteristic. To see how this confusion can occur, suppose you go to a doctor and are tested for a rare disease suffered by 10% of the population. The doctor says that he regrets to tell you that you tested positive. You ask how accurate the test is. The doctor replies that the test is 80% accurate, in the sense that 80% of people with the disease test positive and 80% without the disease test negative. What is the probability that you have the disease? Many people would say that since you test positive and since testing positive is representative of people with the disease, you probably have the disease. What such a response overlooks is the base rate—that is, the proportion of the total population that has the disease, 10% in this case, and the implied probability that a randomly selected individual would test positive. To work out the correct answer, we can imagine a representative sample of 100 individuals, as in Table 20.3: 10% of the 100, that is 10, are sick; the other 90 are well. Of the 10 sick individuals, 80%, or 8, test positive and the other 2 test negative. Of the 90 well individuals, 80%, or 72, test negative and the other 18 positive. A total of 26 test positive. Of these only 8 are actually sick. Thus if you test positive, the probability that you are sick is not 4/5 but just $8/26 = 4/13$. People who believe that the probability is 4/5 are confusing the probability of testing positive if sick with the probability of being sick if testing positive.

The representativeness heuristic, like the availability heuristic, can lead to judgments that conflict with the extension rule. This was demonstrated by an experiment which began with subjects reading the following statement:

> Linda is 31 years old, single, outspoken and very bright. She majored in philosophy. As a student, she was deeply concerned with issues of discrimination and social justice, and also participated in anti-nuclear demonstrations. (Tversky and Kahneman 2002 p. 24)

Subjects were then presented with statements identifying eight classes of individuals including two of particular interest in the present context: bank tellers and the subset of bank tellers who are active in the feminist movement. Some subjects were asked to rank the eight classes based on how closely Linda "resembles" typical members of the classes (Tversky and Kahneman 2002, p. 24). As expected, a large majority deemed Linda's resemblance to a typical bank teller weaker than her resemblance to a typical bank teller active in the feminist movement. In other words, the subjects judged Linda less representative of bank tellers in general than of active feminist bank tellers. Another group of subjects were asked to rank the eight classes according to the probability that Linda is a member. A large majority responded that the probability of Linda being a bank teller was lower than the probability of her being an active feminist bank teller. Taken together, the two rankings suggest that the representativeness heuristic was used in judging probabilities. The subjects' probability judgments violate the extension rule because the probability of belonging to the set of bank tellers cannot be less than the probability of belonging to a subset of that set.

In some experiments with the representativeness heuristic, we may have to think twice about what conditional probability, if any, subjects confound with the conditional probability they are asked to assess. A good example is a 1980 experiment in which subjects were asked to rank the probabilities of various events in the final match of the 1981 Wimbledon men's singles tennis tournament, supposing the match involves Bjorn Borg and an unnamed opponent. The subjects, violating the extension rule, judged Borg less likely to lose the first set than to lose the first set but win the match. What conditional probability could the subjects have assessed? "It makes no sense to assess the conditional probability that Borg will reach the finals given the outcome of the final match" (Tversky and Kahneman 2002). It would make more sense to assess the probability that if a player loses the first set (or loses the first set but wins the match) the player in question is Borg rather than his opponent. A subject who believed Borg better than his likely opponents could have sensibly assigned a lower value to the probability that the first set is lost by Borg than to the probability that if a player loses the first set but wins the match the player is Borg. Another possibility, of course, is that subjects judged intuitively without any reasoning about conditional probabilities.

The third heuristic used in assessing probabilities is **affect**. As its name suggests, the affect heuristic operates mainly through intuition (system 1) rather than reasoning (system 2). Asked to make choices that logically require probability assessments, users of the affect heuristic substitute assessments of how they feel about their chances. Feelings about chances sometimes seem to be influenced more by how many ways an event can occur or how easily numerous occurrences can be imagined than by how probable it is. Two experiments serve to illustrate this somewhat bizarre phenomenon. In an experiment involving drawing jelly beans from bowls, subjects were told that anyone who drew a red bean would win a prize. Offered a choice between two bowls, "subjects often elected to draw from a bowl containing a greater absolute number, but a smaller proportion, of red beans (e.g. 7 in 100) than from a bowl with fewer red beans but a better probability of winning (e.g. 1 in 10)" (Slovic et al. 2002, 413). In an experiment with health risk assessment, subjects "rated a disease that kills 1,296 people out of every 10,000 as more dangerous than one that kills 24.14% of the population" (Slovic et al. 2002, 414).

People sometimes assess a probability or other quantity using a heuristic known to be biased and then adjust their assessment to reduce the bias. This two-step procedure is called **anchoring and adjustment**. The preliminary assessment is the anchor and the subsequent revision is the adjustment.[8] Usually the adjustments people make are insufficient to eliminate the bias (Epley and Gilovich 2001).

20.4 Summary

1. An early normative approach to decision making under risk advocated maximizing the expected value of wealth. This strategy is less appealing when applied to large gambles than to small ones.
2. Bernoulli proposed maximizing expected utility rather than the expected value of wealth. To calculate the expected utility of a decision, we should list all possible outcomes of the decision, evaluate our utility for each outcome, evaluate the probability of

---

[8] Anchoring and adjustment was originally regarded as heuristic on a par with availability and representativeness. However, further consideration has led to the view that anchoring and adjustment does not involve substitution of one answer or attribute for another, the essential feature of heuristics as now defined (Kahneman and Frederick 2002).

each outcome, multiply together the utilities and probabilities, and add up the products. We should calculate the expected utility of each possible decision and then adopt the decision that yields the greatest expected utility.

3. Von Neumann, Morgenstern, and Savage showed that expected utility maximization is the only strategy consistent with certain axioms of rational behavior. However, obtaining and processing all the information needed for maximizing expected utility can be difficult. Recent empirical studies suggest that expected utility theory makes poor predictions.

4. Positive theories of judgment and choice distinguish two mental systems: intuition (system 1) and reasoning (system 2). Prospect theory is the leading positive theory of intuitive choice under risk. Its founders, Kahneman and Tversky, report evidence that the overall value of a prospect depends in part on a weighting function, that is, a nonlinear increasing function of probabilities.

5. When people assess probabilities, they often employ three judgmental heuristics: availability, representativeness, and affect. These heuristics may give biased estimates. Final assessments are sometimes reached through anchoring and adjustment. When a preliminary assessment is anchored to an erroneous value, the subsequent adjustment often reduces but seldom eliminates the bias.

20.5   Solutions to Exercises

20.1. If you reject the gamble, your utility is $1 - e^{-0.5} = 1 - 0.6065 = 0.3935$. If you accept the gamble, your expected utility is $0.6(1 - e^{-1}) + 0.4(1 - e^{-0.1}) = 0.6(0.6321) + 0.4(0.0952) = 0.4173$. To maximize expected utility, you accept the gamble.

20.2. The value of the gamble is evaluated as

$$5000^{0.8} \frac{0.8(0.6^{0.7})}{0.8(0.6^{0.7}) + 0.4^{0.7}} - 3(4000^{0.8}) \frac{0.8(0.4^{0.7})}{0.8(0.4^{0.7}) + 0.6^{0.7}} =$$

$$910.28 \frac{0.55949}{0.55949 + 0.52655} - 3(761.46) \frac{0.42124}{0.42124 + 0.69936} =$$

$$910.28(0.51517) - 2284.38(0.37591) =$$

$$-389.77.$$

Thus the individual rejects the gamble.

20.6   Problems

1. Imagine that you are employed as a consultant to an entrepreneur. You have just finished explaining the importance of maximizing expected utility when he exclaims, "But I don't know my utility function!" You assure him that all he needs is a utility *index*, of which there are infinitely many. (If $U(w)$ is a utility index, so is $a + bU(w)$ for any a and any $b > 0$.) To help him construct a utility index, you ask him to imagine the worst and the best that could happen to his business in the forseeable future. He replies, "My wealth could fall to zero or rise to $100 million." You therefore suggest scaling a utility index U so that $U(0) = 0$ and $U(100 \text{ million}) = 1$. You ask him to imagine a gamble that would raise his wealth to $100 million with probability p and lower it to 0 with probability $1 - p$. You ask him what value of p would make him indifferent

between the gamble and a wealth of $25 million for sure. He replies, 0.40. You ask him what value of p would make him indifferent between the gamble and a wealth of $50 million for sure. He answers, 0.70. Finally, you ask him what value of p would make him indifferent between the gamble and a wealth of $75 million for sure. He replies, 0.90. Sketch his utility index. Is he risk-averse, risk-neutral, or risk-seeking?

2. Dopey is unable to spell "expected utility," let alone maximize it. Cognitively challenged as an ox, he behaves according to prospect theory. Letting x denote gains (+) and losses (−), we can write his value function as

$$v(x) = \begin{cases} x^{.5} & \text{if } x \geq 0 \\ -2(-x)^{.5} & \text{if } x < 0 \end{cases}.$$

His weighting function is given in the following table:

Probability	0	.01	.30	.40	.50	.60	.70	.99	1.0
Weight	0	.16	.31	.35	.40	.46	.53	.80	1.0

  a. Dopey can choose either a sure gain of 4 ($x = 4$) or a gamble in which he wins 9 with probability 0.5 and 0 with probability 0.5. Which does he pick? In this case, is Dopey risk-averse, risk-neutral, or risk-seeking?

  b. Dopey has to choose either a sure loss of 4 ($x = -4$) or a gamble in which he loses 9 with probability 0.5 and 0 with probability 0.5. Which does he pick? In this case, is Dopey risk-averse, risk-neutral, or risk-seeking?

  c. Dopey can choose either a sure gain of 16 or a gamble in which he wins 900 with probability 0.01 and 0 with probability 0.99. Which does he pick? Is he risk-averse, risk-neutral, or risk-seeking in this case?

  d. Dopey can choose either a sure loss of 16 or a gamble in which he loses 900 with probability 0.01 and 0 with probability 0.99. Which does he pick? Is he risk-averse, risk-neutral, or risk-seeking in this case?

3. Dopey can choose either a gamble in which he wins 4 with probability 0.6 and 0 with probability 0.4 or a gamble in which he wins 9 with probability 0.3 and 0 with probability 0.7.

  a. Recalling the value and weight functions specified in (2), determine which gamble Dopey chooses.

  b. Demonstrate that Dopey's combination of choices in (2a) and (3a) is inconsistent with maximization of expected utility.

4. Consider a town in which 80% of the taxis are blue and 20% are green.[9] One night a taxi hits a pedestrian and speeds off. A witness says that the taxi was green. The pedestrian sues the Green Cab Co. The court orders a test of the witness's nighttime color perception. The test reveals that the witness correctly identifies 70% of blue color samples and 90% of green color samples.

  a. What is the probability, conditional on all the evidence, that the hit-and-run taxi was green?

  b. If a juror were to employ the representativeness heuristic to estimate the probability that the cab is green, what would his estimate be?

20.7   Appendix: Shapes of Utility Functions and Attitudes Toward Risk

An individual's attitude toward risk is intimately related to the shape of his or her utility function. Supposing utility to be an increasing function of wealth, we may distinguish concave, convex, and linear utility functions. Let w denote wealth and u denote utility.

$u(w)$ is **linear** if $u(\lambda w_0 + (1 - \lambda)w_1) = \lambda u(w_0) + (1 - \lambda)u(w_1)$ for all $0 \leq \lambda \leq 1$ and all w_0 and w_1.

$u(w)$ is **concave** if $u(\lambda w_0 + (1 - \lambda)w_1) \geq \lambda u(w_0) + (1 - \lambda)u(w_1)$ for all $0 \leq \lambda \leq 1$ and all w_0, and w_1. $u(w)$ is **strictly concave** if $u(\lambda w_0 + (1 - \lambda)w_1) > \lambda u(w_0) + (1 - \lambda)u(w_1)$ for all $0 < \lambda < 1$ and all w_0 and w_1.

$u(w)$ is **convex** if $u(\lambda w_0 + (1 - \lambda)w_1) \leq \lambda u(w_0) + (1 - \lambda)u(w_1)$ for all $0 \leq \lambda \leq 1$ and all w_0, and w_1. $u(w)$ is **strictly convex** if $u(\lambda w_0 + (1 - \lambda)w_1) < \lambda u(w_0) + (1 - \lambda)u(w_1)$ for all $0 < \lambda < 1$ and all w_0 and w_1.

For example, when $w \geq 0$, the function w^a is linear if $a = 1$, strictly concave if $0 < a < 1$, and strictly convex if $a > 1$.

Consider a risky prospect that would make an individual's wealth equal w_0 with probability $0 < \lambda < 1$ and equal w_1 and with probability $(1 - \lambda)$. The expected value of this prospect is $E(w) = \lambda w_0 + (1 - \lambda)w_1$, and the expected utility of an individual facing this prospect is $E(u(w)) = \lambda u(w_0) + (1 - \lambda)u(w_1)$. For an individual with a linear utility function, $u(E(w)) = E(u(w))$. Hence such an individual is indifferent between certain and uncertain prospects of equal expected value.

For an individual with a strictly concave utility function, $u(E(w)) > E(u(w))$, as shown Figure 20.4. Hence such an individual prefers a certain prospect to a risky prospect with the same expected value.

For an individual with a strictly convex utility function, $u(E(w)) < E(u(w))$, as shown in Figure 20.5. Hence such an individual prefers a risky prospect to a certain prospect with the same expected value.

In short, individuals with linear utility functions are risk-neutral, those with strictly concave utility functions are risk-averse, and those with strictly convex utility functions are risk-seeking.

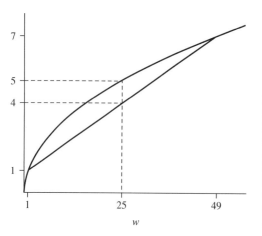

Figure 20.4 For an individual facing risk and having a strictly concave utility function, the utility of expected wealth $u(E(w))$ exceeds the expected utility of wealth $E(u(w))$. In this example, the individual can have a wealth w equal to 1 or 49 with equal probability. Thus his expected wealth is 25. His utility function is $u = \sqrt{w}$. Thus his utility u can be 1 or 7 with equal probability. His utility of expected wealth is $\sqrt{25} = 5$, but his expected utility is $(1 + 7)/2 = 4$

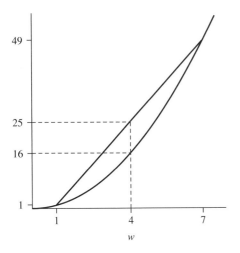

Figure 20.5 For an individual facing risk and having a strictly convex utility function, the utility of expected wealth $u(E(w))$ is less than the expected utility of wealth $E(u(w))$. In this example, the individual can have a wealth w equal to 1 or 7 with equal probability. Thus her expected wealth is 4. Her utility function is $u = w^2$. Thus her utility u can be 1 or 49 with equal probability. Her utility of expected wealth is $4^2 = 16$ but her expected utility is $(1 + 49)/2 = 25$.

These ideas can be made more concrete by considering the **constant relative risk aversion (CRRA) utility function**, which involves a single parameter (ρ) and is defined as follows:

$$u(w, \rho) = \begin{cases} \frac{w^{1-\rho}-1}{1-\rho} & \text{if } \rho \neq 1 \\ \ln w & \text{if } \rho = 1 \end{cases}$$

Although this function has two branches, no discontinuity occurs at $\rho = 1$. If you know L'Hospital's rule you can use it to verify that

$$\lim_{\rho \to 1} \frac{w^{1-\rho} - 1}{1 - \rho} = \ln w.$$

The marginal utility of wealth is $w^{-\rho}$ and the elasticity of this marginal utility with respect to wealth is $-\rho$. The elasticity's absolute value ρ is called the **coefficient of relative risk aversion**.

Some special cases of the CRRA utility function are of interest. If $\rho = 0$, the utility function simplifies to $w - 1$. Because that fuqnction is linear, it induces risk-neutrality. If $\rho < 0$, the utility function is convex and behavior is risk-seeking. If $\rho > 0$, the utility function is concave and behavior is risk-averse. The larger ρ, the greater the risk aversion.

As ρ tends to infinity, the decision maker becomes concerned solely with the worst case scenario, that is, the state of the world in which w is lowest. This can be proved as follows: Consider an individual who maximizes expected utility $Eu = \sum p_i u(w_i)$, where p_i is the probability of having wealth w_i. The summation is across all states of the world i having positive probability. Thus $p_i > 0$ and $\sum p_i = 1$. Suppose the individual has a CRRA utility function with $\rho > 1$. In this case,

$$Eu = \sum p_i \frac{w^{1-\rho} - 1}{1 - \rho} = \frac{1}{1 - \rho} \left[\left(\sum p_i w_i^{1-\rho} \right) - 1 \right]$$

Maximizing Eu is equivalent to maximizing any increasing function of Eu. In particular, it is equivalent to maximizing $M = \left(\sum p_i w_i^{1-\rho} \right)^{\frac{1}{1-\rho}}$. Let $\underline{w}$ denote the smallest wealth having positive probability—that is, the smallest value of w_i. Using this notation, we can rewrite the last equation as

$$M = \underline{w}\left[\sum p_i \left(\frac{w_i}{\underline{w}}\right)^{1-\rho}\right]^{\frac{1}{1-\rho}} = \underline{w}\left[\sum p_i \left(\frac{\underline{w}}{w_i}\right)^{\rho-1}\right]^{\frac{1}{1-\rho}}.$$

Let $\underline{i}$ be the value of i for which $w_i = \underline{w}$. Obviously $p_{\underline{i}}(\underline{w}/w_{\underline{i}})^{\rho-1} = p_{\underline{i}}$. For all other values of i, $w_i > \underline{w}$ and thus $0 < p_i(\underline{w}/w_i)^{\rho-1} < p_i$. Hence $p_{\underline{i}} < \sum p_i(\underline{w}/w_i)^{\rho-1} < \sum p_i = 1$. Raising terms to the (negative) power $1/(1 - \rho)$ reverses the direction of the inequalities, giving us

$$p_{\underline{i}}^{\frac{1}{1-\rho}} > \left[\sum p_i \left(\frac{\underline{w}}{w_i}\right)^{\rho-1}\right]^{\frac{1}{1-\rho}} > 1^{\frac{1}{1-\rho}} = 1.$$

As $\rho \to \infty$, the exponent $\frac{1}{1-\rho} \to 0$ and the upper bound $p_{\underline{i}}^{1/(1-\rho)} \to 1$. Thus the term in square brackets approaches 1 and the maximand M approaches $\underline{w}$.

In other words, maximizing expected utility leads an individual with a CRRA utility function and infinite risk aversion to choose the action that maximizes minimum wealth. This course of action is said to satisfy the "maximin" criterion. Thus we see that acting according to the maximin criterion is a special case of maximizing expected utility.[10]

---

[10] These ideas have a long lineage. Seminal works include Arrow et al. (1961) and Arrow (1973). A textbook exposition and related exercises are provided by Mas-Colell et al. (1995).

21

Game Theory and Modern Models of Oligopoly

Origins and Goals of Game Theory

As noted in Chapter 1, early efforts to extend economic reasoning from problems of farm management to those of markets and public policy encountered a fundamental difficulty: while a farm manager need not worry about what crops or livestock might think of his conduct, a business person or public official must recognize that other people may adjust their behavior to their expectations about her actions. Although this problem was already acknowledged by Ibn Khaldun in the fourteenth century, developing analytical tools for handling it proved difficult. Even after learning mathematical techniques for constrained optimization, economists had trouble modeling human interaction.

The nature of the trouble was expressed by two pioneers of game theory, John von Neumann and Oskar Morgenstern, as follows:

> If two or more persons exchange goods with each other, then the result for each one will depend in general not merely upon his own actions but on those of others as well. Thus each participant attempts to maximize a function . . . of which he does not control all variables. This is certainly no maximum problem, but a peculiar and disconcerting mixture of several conflicting maximum problems . . . . Every participant can determine the variables which describe his own actions but not those of the others. Nevertheless those "alien" variables cannot, from his point of view, be described by statistical assumptions. This is because the others are guided, just as he himself, by rational principles. (von Neumann and Morgenstern 1944, p. 11)

Special cases of such interaction had been considered by Cournot, Bertrand, and Stackelberg in connection with oligopolies. However, a general theory of strategic interaction was still wanting. Aiming to lay the foundations for that general theory, von Neumann and Morgenstern focused on the *interaction of individuals who are rational (in the sense of maximizing expected utility) and recognize each other as rational*. This focus remains characteristic of mainstream game theory.

Basic Concepts

In the language of game theory, decision makers are called **players**. Each player chooses a **strategy**—a complete plan or decision rule specifying what the player will do in any circumstance that might arise in the game. A combination of strategies, one for each player, is called a **profile**. To make matters simple, we shall confine ourselves initially to games with two players, each with two possible strategies.

Economists distinguish **cooperative games,** in which players can make binding agreements, and **noncooperative games,** in which they cannot. The latter, often regarded as more fundamental, are the focus of this chapter.

We will first examine games in which the players simultaneously choose strategies and then games in which they move sequentially. The distinction between simultaneous and sequential choice is not necessarily based on time literally interpreted. Choices are **simultaneous** in the economic sense if each player makes his choice without knowing what choice the other player is making. Choices are **sequential** in our sense if the symmetry is broken, so that one player learns her opponent's strategy before making her own choice.

21.3   Simultaneous Choice

The incentives facing two players who choose strategies simultaneously can be conveniently represented in a payoff matrix. Along the top, we list the strategies open to one player; along the left edge, we list the strategies open to the other player. In the cells formed by intersecting rows and columns, we record the payoffs to the players. By convention, a payoff to the player listed at the top of the matrix is shown in the upper right corner of its cell, and a payoff to the player listed on the left is shown in the lower left corner of its cell. Payoffs to individuals can generally be interpreted as utility levels. In the special case of an individual with a linear utility function (i.e., a risk-neutral player), the payoffs can also be interpreted as values of the utility function's argument, for example, wealth. Payoffs to firms can usually be interpreted as profits. In all cases, larger payoffs are preferred. Games thus represented in terms of profiles (combinations of strategies) and the resulting outcomes are said to be in **normal form** or **strategic form**.

Consider, for example, a duopoly in which each firm has two strategies: cooperate (C) and defect (D). To be concrete, C might mean abide by a cartel agreement about pricing and D might mean selling at a price below that set by the cartel. The payoffs associated with each pair of strategies can be arranged in a matrix. For example, if Firm 1 cooperates but Firm 2 defects, Firm 1 gets 0 and Firm 2 gets 3, as shown in the lower left cell of the matrix below.

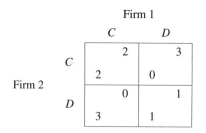

As the matrix is structured, this game is an example of the **prisoners' dilemma**, so called because in early illustrations the players were prisoners suspected of being partners in crime. Suppose the game is played only once. Whatever strategy Firm 1 adopts, Firm 2 is better off defecting. Similarly, whatever Firm 2 does, Firm 1 is better off defecting. In cases like this we say that defecting is the **dominant strategy** for each firm. In general, a dominant strategy for a player is a strategy that produces the best results for that player regardless of the strategy chosen by his opponent. Of course not all games have dominant strategies for each player.

In the prisoners' dilemma, when both players adopt their dominant strategies, they end up in the lower right corner, obtaining smaller payoffs than if both had cooperated. Neither player is motivated to change strategy given her opponent's strategy. This is an example of a **Nash equilibrium**, which is defined as "a profile of strategies such that each player's strategy is an optimal response to the other players' strategies" (Fundenberg and Tirole 1991, p.11). In a Nash equilibrium, no player has an incentive to change strategy, given the strategies of the other players. This equilibrium is named for John F. Nash, Jr., who shared the 1994 Nobel Prize in Economics with two other game theorists—John C. Harsanyi and Reinhard Selten—and who is the central figure in the book and film titled *A Beautiful Mind*.

The prisoners' dilemma has a unique Nash equilibrium, in which both players defect. However, other games may have more than one Nash equilibrium or none at all. As an informal example of a game with two Nash equilibria, consider a duopoly in the automobile industry of a country with prohibitive tariffs on auto imports. Both firms could profitably produce either a large car or a small car—provided its rival does not produce a car in the same size category. Neither duopolist wants to make the same kind of car as its rival. Thus there are two Nash equilibria: one in which the first duopolist produces the big car and the second duopolist produces the small car, and another equilibrium in which the two duopolists reverse roles.

As an example of a game with no Nash equilibrium, consider two software companies, one of which produces a copy-protected spreadsheet; the other produces a lock-pick program that facilitates illegal copying of the spreadsheet.[1] Suppose there are two ways to copy-protect the spreadsheet (A and B) and, correspondingly, two ways of overriding the copy protection (A' and B'). The payoff matrix for these two firms might be as follows:

Spreadsheet Co.

		A		B	
			0		1
Lockpick Co.	A'	1		0	
			1		0
	B'	0		1	

As this payoff matrix is structured, Spreadsheet Co. makes a profit whenever it adopts a copy-protection method for which Lockpick Co. offers no override. But Lockpick Co. makes a profit in precisely the opposite case. If we are in the northwest or southeast quadrants, Spreadsheet Co. has an incentive to change strategy. If we are in the northeast or southwest quadrants, Lockpick Co. has an incentive to change strategy. Thus there is no Nash solution to this game as long as players' strategies are limited to those examined so far.

---

[1] More precisely stated, this game has no Nash equilibrium in "pure strategies." The meaning of this qualification will be explained in Section 21.4.

EXERCISE 21.1

Suppose that Christie's and Sotheby's are considering offering guarantees that the paintings they sell are not forgeries. The payoff matrix below shows the profits for each firm under the four possible profiles.

		Christie's	
		Guarantee	No guarantee
Sotheby's	Guarantee	1 / 1	0 / 3
	No guarantee	3 / 0	2 / 2

(a) Do the auction houses have dominant strategies? (b) Is there a Nash equilibrium? (c) Is this game a prisoners' dilemma?

21.4 Pure and Mixed Strategies

The strategies considered so far have been deterministic in the sense that they involve no randomization. They are called **pure strategies** and are contrasted to a **mixed strategy**, which is a lottery over pure strategies. An example of a mixed strategy in the prisoners' dilemma is flipping a coin and then cooperating if the coin lands heads up and defecting if the coin lands tails up. More generally, in this game a mixed strategy is any strategy that involves cooperating with probability p and defecting with probability $1 - p$, where $0 < p < 1$.

Introducing mixed strategies does not affect the outcome of the prisoners' dilemma. To see why, note that if player 2 cooperates with probability p and defects with probability $1 - p$, the expected payoff to player 1 is $2p + 0(1 - p) = 2p$ if he cooperates and $3p + 1(1 - p) = 2p + 1$ if he defects. Similarly, if player 1 cooperates with probability q and defects with probability $1 - q$, the expected payoff to player 2 is $2q$ if she cooperates and $2q + 1$ if she defects. Thus defecting is still a dominant strategy for both players, and the sole Nash equilibrium involves defection by both players.

In contrast, introducing mixed strategies can change the outcome of the game between Spreadsheet and Lockpick. If Spreadsheet chooses A with probability p and B with probability $1 - p$, the expected payoff to Lockpick is p if it chooses A' and $1 - p$ if it chooses B'. If $p = 0.5$, Lockpick is indifferent among A', B', and any mixed strategy that involves choosing A' with some probability q and B' with probability $1 - q$. Similarly, if Lockpick adopts a mixed strategy with $q = 0.5$, Spreadsheet is indifferent among A, B, and any of its mixed strategies. Thus if Spreadsheet adopts the mixed strategy with $p = 0.5$ and Lockpick adopts the mixed strategy with $q = 0.5$, then neither company has any incentive to change strategy. In other words the profile with $p = q = 0.5$ is a Nash equilibrium.

Although the literature on the Nash equilibrium in mixed strategies is predominantly theoretical, a few empirical studies indicate that this equilibrium predicts behavior well in some simple games between highly experienced and strongly motivated players. One such study examined penalty kicks in professional soccer games. In this phase of a game, a player for one team attempts to kick the ball into the goal while the goalkeeper for the

Table 21.1 Frequencies (%) of actions in penalty kicks

	Kick to kicker's natural side	Jump to kicker's natural side
Equilibrium	61.46	58.01
Observed	60.02	57.69

other team tries to block the ball. Simplifying the game a bit, we could say that each player has two pure strategies: The kicker may aim the ball to the goalkeeper's left or right and the goalkeeper may jump left or right. Because the ball takes only 0.3 seconds on average to reach the goal, the goalkeeper may have to jump as soon as the ball is kicked and before its direction is evident. In this case the players act simultaneously—that is, each player acts without prior knowledge of the other's action. Kickers find it easier to kick to their "natural" side (the goalkeeper's right for right-footed kickers and the goalkeeper's left for left-footed kickers). However, if they always kicked to their natural side, the goalkeeper would block that side. Kickers have to adopt mixed strategies to keep goalkeepers uncertain. Similarly, goalkeepers must use mixed strategies to keep kickers in the dark. In a Nash equilibrium, a kicker's success rate (expected payoff) is the same whether he kicks left or right, and a goalkeeper's success rate is the same whether he jumps left or right. The Nash equilibrium mixed strategies have been compared to professional players' actual behavior by Palacios-Huerta (2003) at both the individual and aggregate levels. The aggregate level results are shown in Table 21.1. The correspondence of equilibrium and observed frequencies is remarkably close.

EXERCISE 21.2

Consider a game with the following payoff matrix. Find a Nash equilibrium in mixed strategies.

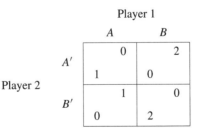

21.5 Repeated Games

We have been discussing games that are played only once. Games that are played repeatedly give players opportunities to reward or punish their partners. Thus repeated play may alter the incentives and outcome of games. A player in a repeated two-person game could adopt a **tit-for-tat** strategy, under which he cooperates in the first round of the game and thereafter mimics his opponent's choice in the previous round. Computer simulations of repeated prisoner's dilemma games suggest that players who adopt the tit-for-tat strategy get larger cumulative payoffs than do players using other strategies, provided the following two conditions are met. First, players must know what each other did in previous rounds of the game. Second, players must expect to continue interacting with each other indefinitely, creating continuing opportunities for retaliation (Axelrod 1984). Note that the second condition requires that there be no known point at which play terminates. If players knew that the game would be played exactly 100 times, then they would have an incentive to defect on the last play. Expecting his partner to defect on the one-hundredth play, each player would have an incentive to defect on the ninety-ninth play, and so on. Reasoning in this manner, the players would see no incentive to cooperate in any play of the game. Under these two conditions, a tit-for-tat strategy is successful because it (a) never starts conflicts, (b) always immediately punishes defection, and (c) always immediately rewards cooperation. The success of tit-for-tat in the conditions just described makes it an attractive strategy for duopolists provided that substantial barriers to entry keep other firms out of their market. Behavior consistent with tit-for-tat strategies has been observed in experiments with duopoly markets (Feinberg and Husted 1999) and in observational studies of airfares on routes served by two airlines (Varian 1999).

Tit-for-tat may become impractical if there are more than two firms in the industry or if there are no barriers to entry by new firms. When there are several firms and one defects, the cooperators cannot punish it by cutting their prices without hurting each other as well. Some other, more targeted response must be devised. Perhaps the cooperators could punish the defector by negative advertising, locating outlets next to the defector, or hiring away the defector's prize employees.

Oligopolists have to worry about potential entrants, as well as incumbents. If entry appears very likely, incumbents may see little gain in colluding with each other. The effect of potential entrants in undermining collusion among oligopolists is particularly important in markets in which entry entails no irrevocable investments, that is, no sunk costs. Whatever other costs are incurred by entry can be recouped by exit. For example, outlays on real estate can normally be recovered by reselling it. Markets that can be entered without incurring sunk costs are said to be **contestable**. Such a market provides an opportunity for profitable **hit-and-run entry**, a process in which a firm enters the market without incurring sunk costs, undercuts the incumbents' prices, earns profits until the incumbents lower their prices, and then exits. Proponents of the idea of contestable markets argue that the threat of potential entry can force oligopolists to behave much like perfect competitors. Thus, they say, there is no necessary correspondence between the number of firms currently in a market and the deviation of prices from perfectly competitive levels (Baumol et al. 1988). Two factors limit the empirical relevance of the theory of contestable markets. First, entry into almost any market entails some (perhaps small) sunk costs. Initial outlays for market surveys and advertising, for example, are generally unrecoverable. Second, even small sunk costs may deter entry, particularly if the incumbents appear prepared to cut prices swiftly (Shy 1995).

21.6 Sequential Choice

So far we have discussed games in which players simultaneously choose strategies. Now we turn to sequential games. Take, for example, two firms called OldGold (OG) and Jolly Roger (JR). The former has a profitable patented product on the market, and the latter has a choice between strategies: produce a pirated clone or a differentiated product. If JR introduces a clone, OG has a choice of two other strategies: File suit for damages due to copyright infringement or do nothing. We can depict the possible combinations of strategies and

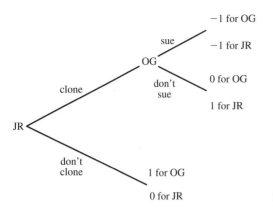

Figure 21.1 A game with sequential choice

the associated payoffs in a tree diagram like Figure 21.1. A game shown in this fashion, emphasizing who knows and can do what and when, is said to be in **extensive form**.

To discover what each player will do, we start from the twigs of the game tree on the right and work back to the left. As this tree is constructed, if OG's product is cloned, it is better off not suing, perhaps because suits are expensive and their outcome uncertain. Knowing that OG will not sue, JR decides to clone OG's product.

Dissatisfied with the game's outcome, OG could try to change it by adopting a commitment device. For example, OG could post a bond worth 2 units, which it would forfeit if it failed to sue a company that infringed on its patents. Posting the bond would reduce the payoff to not suing to -2. That would make suing attractive. Knowing that OG would sue, JR would not clone OG's product.

21.7 Normative and Positive Interpretations

As initially developed by von Neumann and Morgenstern (1944), game theory was concerned with how rational people (expect utility maximizers) interact with other people they know to be rational. The originators did not hazard a guess about what proportion of the population might meet their standard of rationality. In the early 1950s, Nash and other game theorists tried some experiments to test the predictive value of game theory but found the results discouraging. Those who continued to develop mathematical game theory in the 1960s and 1970s seem to have been more interested in its internal logic than its predictive power or practical use. Indeed, Selten reportedly asserted that "game theory is for proving theorems, not for playing games" (quoted in Goeree and Holt 1999, p. 10564).

One reason that game theorists took little interest in experimental work was a sense that behavior contrary to expected utility theory in general and game theory in particular was largely a matter of random errors. If deviations from game theoretic predictions were mainly random and hence unpredictable, alternative theories would be unlikely to be more accurate. This view was shaken by Kahneman and Tversky's (1979) demonstration that many deviations from expected utility theory are predictable by prospect theory. Starting in the 1980s, economists returned to experimental work on strategic behavior, hoping to develop a theory that was predictively more accurate than the traditional game theory, which focused on expected utility maximizers.

21.8   Behavioral Game Theory

The wave of experimental work on strategic behavior that began in the 1980s has contributed to a new perspective, dubbed "behavioral game theory," that—in the words of one of its pioneers—"is explicitly intended to predict behavior of people" (Camerer 2003, p. 465).

To illustrate behavioral game theorists' approach to strategic interaction, let's reconsider the prisoners' dilemma game. Recall that traditional game theory predicts that if players know the game will be played only once (or any fixed number of times), each will defect rather than cooperate. However, in experiments with single plays of this game, players cooperate approximately half the time (Camerer 2003, p. 46). This unexpected cooperation could occur because some people are either altruistic or bad at strategic thinking. To determine whether one or both of these explanations is correct, behavioral game theorists have devised further experiments.

To test for altruism, behavioral game theorists have devised **dictator games**, in which the experimenters give one player (the dictator) a sum of money that she can divide in any way she chooses between herself and the other player. Traditional theory, based on the assumption that players are self-interested rather than altruistic, predicts that the dictator will keep all the money, giving none to the other player. However, in numerous experiments, the mean share given to the second player has ranged from 10 to 52% (Camerer 2003, pp. 57–58). This outcome cannot easily be explained by errors in strategic thinking because the dictator does not have to think about the second player's response; indeed, the second player has no opportunity to respond. Thus the dictator games afford strong evidence of altruism.

To assess abilities in strategic reasoning, behavioral game theorists have used **beauty contest games**, in which people have to think about what others are thinking. (The game gets its name from a feature once carried by some British newspapers: Readers were invited to pick the most beautiful of several photos, beauty being determined by majority vote. In effect, contestants were guessing which photo other contestants would identify as most beautiful.) In this game a large number of players pick a number in the range [0, 100], and the game is won by the player whose guess is closest to 70% of the average guess. Traditional game theory predicts that everyone will choose zero because "all players want to choose 70 percent of the average" and "if they all choose the same number it must be zero," that being the only solution to the equation $x = 0.7x$ (Camerer 2003, p. 16). However, experimental subjects rarely choose zero. More common are answers around 35. This outcome suggests that subjects are reasoning as follows: "If others guess at random, the average will be 50; 70% of 50 is 35." A player who reasons in this manner supposes (often falsely) that he is smarter than the others. This outcome suggests less strategic reasoning ability than had been assumed by traditional game theorists.

These and other experimental results indicate that many people are somewhat altruistic but only boundedly rational. Behavioral game theorists are endeavoring to provide a coherent account of how such people interact.

21.9   Summary

1. Game theory, as originally developed by von Neumann and Morgenstern, focuses on the strategic interaction of rational individuals who know each other to be rational. Rationality is interpreted as maximizing expected utility.

2. Game theorists have investigated a variety of strategic interactions, including cooperative and noncooperative games, simultaneous and sequential choice, single and repeated games, and pure and mixed strategies. Many of their concepts have been applied to modern theories of oligopolies.

3. In response to the predictive shortcomings of traditional game theory, economists have conducted a large number of experiments whose results are synthesized in behavioral game theory. This theory asserts that many people are more altruistic but less rational than had been assumed by traditional game theorists.

21.10 Solutions to Exercises

21.1. (a) Yes, providing a guarantee is a dominant strategy for both firms. (b) Yes, the upper left cell, where both firms provide guarantees is a Nash equilibrium. (c) Yes, the game is a prisoners' dilemma because the payoff in equilibrium is less than in the lower right cell for both firms.

21.2. If player 1 chooses A with probability p and B with probability $1 - p$, the expected payoff for player 2 is p if he chooses A' and $2(1 - p)$ if he chooses B'. Player 2 is indifferent among A', B', and mixed strategies when $p = 2(1 - p)$, that is, when $p = 2/3$. Similarly, if player 2 chooses A' with probability q and B' with probability $(1 - q)$, the expected payoff for player 1 is $1 - q$ if she chooses A and $2q$ if she chooses B. She is indifferent among A, B, and mixed strategies when $1 - q = 2q$, that is, when $q = 1/3$. Thus the Nash equilibrium is a pair of mixed strategies with $p = 2/3$ and $q = 1/3$.

21.11 Problems

1. The market for commercial aircraft is divided between Airbus and Boeing. Suppose that the two companies are considering whether to equip their newest model with ejection seats and parachutes for all passengers. The payoff matrix below shows the profits for each firm under the four possible profiles.

		Airbus	
		Equip	Don't
Boeing	Equip	500 / 500	750 / 400
	Don't	300 / 600	600 / 200

a. Does Airbus have a dominant strategy? Does Boeing?

b. Is there a Nash equilibrium? Is it unique?

2. Consider the two firms discussed in Section 21.6. Suppose that if JR produces a differentiated product, OG can respond by either buying JR or not buying it. The two firms are in a game whose extensive form is represented in the tree diagram in Figure 21.2.

a. What would JR and OG do?

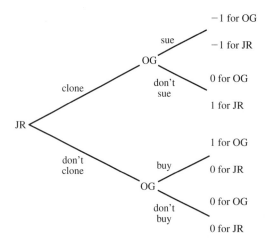

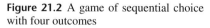

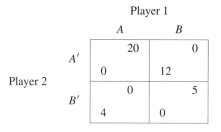

Figure 21.2 A game of sequential choice with four outcomes

b. Suppose OG had posted a bond worth 2 units, which it would forfeit if it failed to sue a company that infringed on its patents, thus reducing its payoff from not suing to −2. What would OG and JR do in this case?

3. Consider a game with the payoff matrix shown below.

Player 1

		A	B
		20	0
A′			
		0	12
		0	5
B′			
		4	0

Player 2

a. Does the game have a Nash equilibrium in pure strategies?
b. What is the Nash equilibrium in mixed strategies?

22

▓▓▓ Time, Risk, and Investment

Net Present Value and Options

In Chapter 16 we noted that the present value of a sequence of future revenues, $FV_0, \ldots,$ FV_T, could be calculated as

$$PV = FV_0 + \frac{FV_1}{(1+r)} + \cdots + \frac{FV_T}{(1+r)^T} = \sum_{t=0}^{T} \frac{FV_t}{(1+r)^t}.$$

We did not restrict the signs of the terms in the sequence of revenues. Negative terms represent outlays, as in Problem 3, Chapter 16. When economists wish to stress the fact that the sequence may include negative terms, they call the sum of discounted items the **net present value** (*NPV*).

Until recently, most economists advised (risk-neutral) business people to undertake any investment project with a positive expected *NPV*.[1] However, as Avinash Dixit and Robert Pindyck (1994, 1995) argue, this advise is not always appropriate. The trouble with the conventional *NPV* criterion is that it considers only two alternatives: either we immediately begin a project and carry it to completion or we never undertake it. In many cases we should also consider two other alternatives. First, we might immediately begin the project but leave open the possibility of aborting it later if it turns out to be unprofitable. Second, we might delay a decision about the project until we have more information. By reserving the right to abort a project or by delaying a decision to undertake a project, we preserve opportunities that may be valuable at a later date. Such opportunities, without obligations, are called **options**. Investments that create options may be worth starting even if they do not have a positive expected *NPV*. Investments that exercise or kill an option should sometimes be postponed and perhaps ultimately rejected even if they initially have a positive expected *NPV*. To illustrate these points, let us consider two examples.

---

[1] Expected values and present values are both linear combinations. Thus a project's expected present value is the same as its present expected value. In other words, we will get the same result regardless of whether we first calculate the present value and then its expectation or first calculate the expectations of future values and then their present value. Because the probabilities at various dates can differ, it will often be simpler to first take expectations (at each date) and then discount them.

251

22.2   Examples

22.2.1 Creating an Option

Consider a computer consulting firm that has been offered $264,000 to write some software, to be paid with a 1-year delay. The interest rate used to discount future receipts is, let us assume, 0.1. Although the price is certain, the cost of programming is uncertain, depending on whether the problem turns out to be easy or hard. For simplicity, let us say that there is a 50% chance that the software can be finished for $100,000 and a 50% chance that after spending $100,000 the firm will discover that the problem is so hard that to solve it would require spending another $300,000. The mean or expected cost is thus $250,000. (The costs, whatever they are, will all be incurred this year, so we will not discount them.) The expected *NPV* of starting the project and carrying it to completion is

$$NPV = -250,000 + \frac{264,000}{1.1} = -250,000 + 240,000 = -10,000.$$

Thus the conventional *NPV* criterion suggests that the firm should refuse the job. The trouble with this conventional reasoning is that it overlooks the possibility of spending $100,000 to get the option of developing the software and then exercising the option only if it is profitable. After spending the first $100,000, the firm will either have completed the software or know that another $300,000 would be required to finish it. In the former case, it will sell the software; in the latter, it will abandon it unfinished. The two cases are equally likely. Thus Dixit and Pindyck would say that the correct present value for starting the project is

$$NPV = -100,000 + 0.5\left(\frac{264,000}{1.1}\right) = -100,000 + 0.5(240,000) = 20,000.$$

Thus the firm should begin the project and see whether it is worth finishing.

22.2.2 Killing an Option

Now consider a construction company that can build a house for $99,000. If it starts now, the house will be ready for occupancy in 1 year. If it delays a year, the house will be ready for occupancy in 2 years. The only uncertainty is whether the state department of transportation (DOT) will widen the road in front of the house. Widening the road would increase traffic, making the area less attractive for residential use. The department will announce its decision in 1 year. If DOT decides to leave the road alone, the house can be sold for $121,000. If it decides to widen the road, the house's market value will fall to $99,000. The two decisions are equally likely in the opinion of the manager of the construction company. Thus the mean or expected value of the house is $110,000. Again, we will assume that the interest rate is 0.1. Construction costs are incurred a year before the house is sold. If asked whether the firm should build the house now, an economist who knew only the conventional *NPV* criterion would say yes, calculating that

$$NPV = -\$99,000 + \frac{110,000}{1.1} = 1,000.$$

However, this analysis overlooks the possibility that the firm might do even better by waiting a year before deciding whether to build. By waiting a year, the firm can resolve the uncertainty about the selling price of the house. If the price is $99,000 the firm would not bother to build it; hence its costs and expenses would both be zero. If the price is $121,000, the firm will build. Thus the net present value when the firm waits is

$$NPV = \frac{1}{2}\left(0 + \left(-\frac{99,000}{1.1} + \frac{121,000}{1.21}\right)\right)$$

$$= \frac{1}{2}(0 - 90,000 + 100,000)$$

$$= 5,000.$$

Thus the firm is better off waiting a year to resolve the uncertainty about the selling price of the house. It doesn't pay to prematurely exercise or kill the option to build the house.

EXERCISE 22.1

An electrical engineering student who happens to be into body piercing has come up with an idea for a miniature two-piece cell phone. The speaker and the microphone would be worn as an earring and a tongue stud. The student believes that if he competed and patented the design, he could sell it to a manufacturer for $121,000. The only unsolved problem is how to keep saliva from shorting out the microphone. The student believes that if he invests $20,000 in the project now, he has a 40% chance of completing the project in 1 year at no additional expense. However, there is also a 60% chance that an additional expenditure of $220,000 at the beginning of the second year will be needed to complete the project at the end of the second year. Suppose the interest rate is 10%. (a) What is the *NPV* of immediately undertaking a commitment to complete the project? (b) What is the *NPV* of investing the $20,000 needed to start the project, while keeping open the options of completing or canceling the project?

EXERCISE 22.2

The student in the previous exercise has another idea for a miniature two-piece cell phone. The microphone would be worn as a nose ring, avoiding the saliva problem. The student believes that if he invests $66,000 in the project now, he could certainly complete the project in 1 year at no additional expense. The only uncertainty is what a manufacturer would be willing to pay for the patent. The manufacturer is worried that most potential customers for wearable cell phones would object to the nose ring because it interferes with snorting cocaine. Market research will resolve this question in 1 year. The manufacturer will offer to pay $121,000 or $60,500 for the patent, depending on whether the market is large or small. The student believes that the market will be large with probability 0.3 and small with probability 0.7. The interest rate is 10%. (a) What is the *NPV* of starting the project immediately? (b) What is the *NPV* of waiting a year for the market research to be completed before deciding whether to undertake the project?

22.3   Irreversible Investments

The consequences of starting and then aborting a project differ from those of never undertaking it in two respects. First, as we have seen, by starting a project, we often learn something about cost or demand conditions. Second, some investment is **irreversible** in the sense that the assets it creates cannot be sold for enough to recover the investment expenditure. Investments are apt to be irreversible in two common cases.

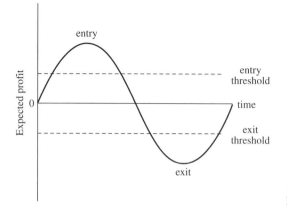

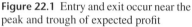

Figure 22.1 Entry and exit occur near the peak and trough of expected profit

The first case arises when the assets are **firm-specific**, in the sense that they are of less use to other firms than to the firm that made the investment. Most marketing and advertising investments are firm-specific. For example, goodwill or brand loyalty that Coca-Cola creates through its advertising cannot be sold to Pepsi or any other firm.

The second case occurs when the sellers of used assets are better informed than potential buyers about the quality of the assets.[2]

> Buyers in markets for used machines, unable to evaluate the quality of an item, will offer a price that corresponds to the average quality in the market. Sellers, who know the quality of the item they are selling, will be reluctant to sell an above-average item. This will lower the market average quality, and therefore the market price. This 'lemons' problem . . . plagues many such markets. (Dixit and Pindyck 1994, p. 8)

For example, late model, used computers, cars, and trucks sell at prices far below their prices when new.

22.4 Implications

The example in Subsection 22.2.2 shows that a positive net present value isn't always enough to induce investment. This point is equivalent to saying that a small positive expected rate of profit isn't always sufficient to induce immediate investment or market entry. Waiting is sometimes more prudent. Similarly, small expected losses aren't always enough to induce firms to immediately exit a market. The expected rate of profit would have to rise above a positive threshold to induce entry and fall below a negative expected threshold to induce exit. If the expected rate of profit lies between these thresholds, we will not observe any firms entering or exiting (see Figure 22.1).

Economists used to interpret positive profits and no entry as evidence of monopoly power and barriers to entry. But in light of Dixit and Pindyck's (1994, 1995) work, we should now understand that even in competitive industries with free entry, there may be periods in which incumbents enjoy positive profits without inducing entry. These periods of positive profit alternate with periods of negative profit, yielding zero average profits. Before undertaking antitrust action against an industry with positive profits and zero entry, the government may be justified in waiting a few years to see if conditions change.

---

[2] This, like the insurance markets analyzed in a previous chapter, is an example of *asymmetric information*.

The same principles that apply to investment in plant and equipment apply to any activity that involves sunk costs. Two important examples are employment decisions and marketing decisions. There are substantial costs to hiring and laying off workers. Small positive profits won't induce firms to hire more, and small losses will not induce them to layoff workers. Thus in the recovery from a recession, profits can became positive long before firms resume hiring.

Exporters incur major costs when they first enter a new national market. Small changes in the rate of profit on exporting are not enough to induce exporters to enter or abandon national markets.

> From 1980 to 1984, the dollar rose sharply against other currencies. The cost advantage of foreign firms in US markets became very substantial, and ultimately led to a large rise in US imports. Then the dollar fell sharply, and by 1987 was back to its 1980 level. However, the import penetration . . . hardly decreased at all. It took a larger fall in the dollar to achieve any significant reduction in imports. (Dixit and Pindyck, 1994, p. 17)

22.5 Summary

1. The net present value of a project is the sum of its receipts discounted for the passage of time, with outlays being counted like negative receipts. The traditional advice of economists is to undertake projects with positive NPV. However, we should usually also consider opportunities to delay or abort a project.
2. An option to invest gives us the right but not the obligation to buy an asset.
3. When we can delay starting a project, we may gain information about whether the project is worth completing. When we can start a project without committing ourselves to finishing it, we may gain further information. To be weighed against these benefits are the possibilities that delay may give a competitor a chance to take market share from us and that funds used in starting a project may be irrecoverable.
4. When the expected rate of profit is within a small range around zero, firms may decide to wait rather than enter or exit. This range of profit rates that induces neither entry nor exit has important implications for antitrust policy, labor markets, and international trade.

22.6 Solutions to Exercises

22.1. (a) The NPV of immediately undertaking a commitment to finish the project, expressed in thousands of dollars, is $-20 + 0.4(121/1.1) + 0.6(-220/1.1 + 121/1.21)$ $= -20 + 44 - 60 = -36$. (b) The NPV of starting the project while reserving the option of completing or canceling it, expressed in thousands of dollars, is $-20 + .4(121/1.1) = 24$.

22.2. (a) The NPV of undertaking the project immediately, expressed in thousands of dollars, is $-66 + 0.3(121/1.1) + 0.7(60.5/1.1) = -66 + 33 + 38.5 = 5.5$. (b) The NPV of waiting a year is $0.3(-66/1.1 + 121/1.21) = 0.3(-60 + 100) = 12$.

22.7 Problems: Economists in Deep Water

1. Consider a marine salvage company that has located a sunken ship known to contain treasure that could be sold for $12.1 million if it were brought to the surface. The time

and cost required to recover the treasure are uncertain. If the firm invests $2 million now, there is a 50% chance that it will recover the treasure in 1 year at no additional cost. However, there is also a 50% chance that the firm will find that an additional expenditure of $22 million at the beginning of the second year will be needed to salvage the treasure at the end of the second year. Suppose that the interest rate is 10%.

  a. What is the expected *NPV* of immediately undertaking a commitment to raise the sunken treasure?

  b. What is the expected *NPV* of immediately investing the $2 million needed to start the project while keeping open the options of completing or canceling the project?

2. Now suppose the salvage company has located another sunken ship that also contains treasure that could be sold for $12.1 million if it were brought to the surface. In this case, the firm is certain that if it invests $6.6 million now, it can recover the treasure in 1 year at no additional cost. The uncertainty in this case relates to ownership of the treasure. A government agency is currently considering whether treasure found at this location belongs wholly to the finder or must be shared with a previous owner. In the latter case, the finder would be allowed to recover its direct costs ($6.6 million) but would have to turn over the remaining proceeds from the sale of the treasure to the previous owner. A ruling on this issue is expected in 1 year. The salvage company's manager believes the probability of a favorable ruling is 0.3. The rate of interest is 10%.

  a. What is the expected *NPV* of immediately undertaking the recovery of the treasure?

  b. What is the expected *NPV* of waiting until the ownership issue is settled in 1 year before deciding whether to undertake the project?

23

█████ Technological Change

23.1 Key Concepts

Technology, as the word is used by social scientists, means a body of knowledge relevant to producing goods and services. Alteration in this body of knowledge is called **technological change**. Although knowledge can be lost, as when the library of Alexandria burned, knowledge more usually accumulates over time. Thus technological progress is often used as a synonym for technological change.

Technological change can occur in several ways. In earlier times, discoveries by workers, entrepreneurs, and amateur inventors played a big role. In recent times, technological change has become more organized. Nowadays, numerous scientists work to extend the frontiers of basic knowledge, and many engineers and technologists seek applications of science to production (see Figure 23.1).

23.2 Basic Research

Basic research generates scientific ideas, which may have diverse applications. The scientific ideas generated by basic research are **nonrivalrous**—that is, you can use them without interfering with my using them. Furthermore, scientific ideas, once published, are often virtually **nonexcludable**—that is, their utilization cannot be restricted to paying customers because scientific ideas, unlike particular inventions, cannot be patented.[1] Products that are nonrivalrous and nonexcludable are called **public goods**. Scientific ideas, along with national defense and clean air, are important examples.

Public goods are not produced in sufficient volume by the private sector.[2] Hence the private sector's meager production of public goods needs to be supplemented with government-funded public goods. This argument is as valid for scientific ideas as for any other public good. Governments in most large, wealthy countries pay for basic research programs. Examples of government-funded basic research in the United States include the projects financed by the National Science Foundation (NSF) and the National Institutes of Health (NIH).

---

[1] The boundary between ideas and inventions is contentious. Disputes over what can and cannot be patented are resolved by courts. In recent years U.S. courts have upheld patents on gene sequences and other scientific discoveries that many people had previously assumed could not be patented. This development alarms observers who note that patents on such basic discoveries could impose heavy costs on society in terms of monopoly power, restriction of related research, and transaction costs including licensing and litigation (Jackson 2003; Nelson 2003).

[2] The standard of sufficiency here is a volume such that marginal social benefit equals marginal social cost.

Figure 23.1 Process generating technological change

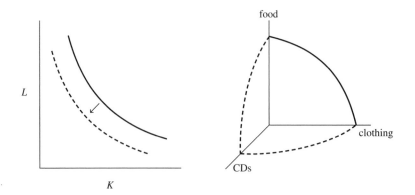

Figure 23.2 Development of less costly processes shifts isoquants toward the origin, whereas development of a new product adds a dimension to the production possibilities frontier

23.3 Development

The second stage in the process of generating technological change adapts scientific ideas to practical tasks. Two kinds of applications can be distinguished: invention of new processes for producing old products and invention of new products. The first can be represented by an inward shift in isoquants. The second can be represented by adding a new dimension to a production possibility frontier. (See Figure 23.2.)

The fruits of development work may be either used by the developer or sold to another party. The distinction between new processes and new products roughly corresponds to the distinction between development for internal use and development for sale. Many new processes are developed for the developer's own use. The assembly line method of manufacture developed by Henry Ford is a classic example. A new process could, in principle, be developed mainly for sale, but this is comparatively rare, probably because of the difficulty in monitoring and enforcing licensing agreements. New products are, of course, very frequently developed for sale. Less commonly, new products are created for internal use, for example, a new machine tool for use by its maker. The motivation and organization of development work depend on whether development is aimed at creating something for sale or internal use.

23.3.1 Development of Products for Sale

Development work aimed at creating a salable product is motivated by the expectation of establishing and profiting from intellectual property rights through use of copyright or patent law.

Copyrights and patents are granted by governments to provide incentives to creative and inventive activity. However, they have the unfortunate side effect of creating monopolistic distortions, including impediments to diffusion of new ideas. By varying the length and breadth of copyrights and patents, governments can alter the strength of incentives and the severity of distortions. Short copyrights and patents create weak incentives to creative and inventive activity but correspondingly transient monopolistic distortions; long copyrights and patents create stronger incentives but more lasting inefficiencies. Similarly, a narrow copyright or patent, which protects a specific product or process, creates weaker incentives and distortions than a broad one, which protects an entire class of products or processes.

The U.S. Constitution gives Congress the power "to promote the progress of science and useful arts, by securing for limited times to authors and inventors the exclusive right to their respective writings and discoveries." Congress initially limited the duration of copyrights to 28 years and patents to 14. These limits have gradually been extended. Under a 1998 law, a copyright granted to a corporation lasts 95 years, and a copyright granted to an individual expires 70 years after the individual's death. Under current law and treaties, patents last 20 years. Determining optimal patent length for various objectives and circumstances is a matter of considerable subtlety.[3]

23.3.2 Development for Internal Use

Development work aimed at producing a process or product for internal use can thrive without copyright or patent protection. Indeed, many developers argue that copyrights and patents tend be a impediment to such progress.

Although machine tools and scientific instruments have long exemplified development for internal use, computer software affords the most notable recent examples.

Many software developers decline either to seek copyrights or to exercise copyrights' restrictive powers. These developers prefer a license granting to anyone the right to use, modify, and redistribute the software in any manner that does not restrict others' rights to do the same. To facilitate tinkering by others, these developers offer (human readable) source code, not just cryptic binary files. They describe their creations as **free** or **open source** software.[4]

Free and open source software has a large share of the user base in some sectors. Approximately a third of servers run GNU/Linux, a free operating system with some resemblance to Unix. Most live content on the World Wide Web depends on Perl, an open source programming language. Most mathematicians and many scientists produce their papers and books by using TeX, a free typesetting program. The most used e-mail transport software is Sendmail, an open source program. Two-thirds of all web servers use Apache, another open source program.

The success of free and open source software surprises people who are accustomed to thinking that private property rights are essential to motivate production of reliable goods. What motivates the developers of free and open source software? In most cases they expect

---

[3] Horowitz and Lai (1996) present a model in which the patent length that maximizes consumer welfare is shorter than the length that maximizes the rate of innovation. Gilbert and Shapiro (1990) identify conditions under which optimal patent length is infinite. However, Iwaisako and Futagami (2003) develop a model in which the optimal patent life is finite.

[4] The distinction between free and open source software is of secondary importance here but nonetheless interesting. Free software is covered by a general public license (GPL) that applies not only to the original software but also to any enhancements added subsequently by other programmers. Computer code covered by a GPL is said to be under "copyleft." It is "free" in the sense that it may be freely used, modified, and redistributed. This status does not preclude distributors from selling it. The GPL was introduced by the Free Software Foundation and applied to its GNU (GNU's Not Unix) software. In contrast to free software, "open source" software is covered by a license that permits anyone to add new features that may or may not be similarly licensed. This license—promoted by the Open Source Initiative—may make it more appealing to commercial users (Lerner and Tirole 2002).

some mix of the following benefits. First, the code they develop usually addresses some pressing problem of their own.[5] Second, by making the source code available to others with similar needs, the developers get free help in identifying and fixing bugs. Third, they hope that grateful users will reciprocate by contributing more free and open source software, some of which will make their jobs easier. Fourth, developers often enjoy discussing code with widely scattered peers, a process greatly facilitated by e-mail. Fifth, making their clever code public enhances their professional reputation, which may provide an ego boost and eventuate in job offers.[6]

Apart from the personal preferences of software developers, their employers sometimes have additional reasons for releasing their creations as free or open source software. First, an employer may view an external community of users as a guarantee that maintenance and updates can be sustained even if the originators leave the firm. Second, a firm may hope that schools will adopt its free or open source software and thus provide free training for a future cohort of workers. Third, by submitting its code to public scrutiny, a firm secures for it a credibility analogous to that achieved by scientific publications in refereed journals. (Software for critical applications is seldom trusted unless the source code is open to scrutiny.) Fourth, a firm may hope that opening the source code will create a group of interested users who will be willing to buy auxiliary items such as programming manuals or consulting services. Fifth, a firm trying to challenge an entrenched monopoly may find open source software to be its best bet. The challenger's open source code will attract sophisticated users. The incumbent cannot match the challenger's offer without opening its own code, which would destroy its monopoly.[7] Sixth, free and open source code software makes for good public relations, at least for a firm that sells to academics and hackers (Hippel 2005; Lerner and Tirole 2002; Raymond 1999).

23.3.3 Models of Development

How do firms determine how much to invest in developing new products and processes? Economists have tackled this question using two approaches. One approach extends standard models of profit maximizing firms such as those in chapters 5, 14, and 15. In the extended models, a firm's salable output depends on its technological knowledge as well as its capital and labor inputs. The firm has an R&D department that produces new knowledge. The flow of new knowledge is a (known) function of inputs (such as engineers and lab equipment) employed in the R&D department. Increasing knowledge can raise the firm's future output and profits. The firm chooses inputs for its R&D and production departments so as to maximizes the present value of its future profits. Models featuring such firms are simple enough to allow analytical derivation of some interesting general equilibrium results.

---

[5] Donald Knuth developed TEX to typeset his own books on computer programming. Former Unix programmers developed GNU software when AT&T tried to impose copyright restrictions on Unix. Seven programmers launched the Apache project to integrate their patches to Unix-based web server software. Larry Wall created Perl to help him perform repetitive tasks as a systems administrator. Eric Allman created Sendmail to coordinate computer networks that he administered.

[6] Employers in the computer business recognize the public relations value of recruiting well-known creators of free and open source software and giving them enough free time to continue overseeing their creations. Thus Transmeta, a microprocessor maker, hired Linus Torvalds (creator of the Linux kernel); and O'Reilly, a publisher of computer books, hired Brian Behlendorf (an Apache pioneer) and Larry Wall (Perl's creator).

[7] Sun Microsystems has challenged Microsoft Office's near monopoly by providing OpenOffice as open source software. OpenOffice can be downloaded free, and an enhanced version called StarOffice can be purchased for about one-sixth the cost of Microsoft Office.

Analyzing one such model, Peretto (1999) shows that firms will not undertake R&D expenditure (a fixed cost) until the population (market size) exceeds a critical threshold. Even when this condition is met, the equilibrium level of R&D expenditure may not generate the output growth rate that maximizes social welfare.

The other approach focuses on firms which lack precise information about the function mapping R&D inputs into new knowledge. (Such information is arguably unobtainable; knowledge created by an R&D project wouldn't be new if it were predictable before the project was undertaken Arrow (1971).) A firm's manager may try to assess a probability distribution for new knowledge obtainable from an R&D project. However, coherent probability assessment is itself a costly process with an uncertain payoff. Faced with such deep uncertainties, a manager may be unable to identify a well-defined maximization problem. Although unable to determine a technology or R&D plan that maximizes the present value of profits, a firm can always search for new techniques that increase profits. A firm that discovers and adopts an unusually profitable technique can, by reinvesting its profits, grow faster than less profitable rivals. Firms that fall badly behind the technological frontier are apt to go bankrupt. Differential growth rates and bankruptcy constitute an evolutionary mechanism that selects in favor of profitable technological mutations. Which mutations are profitable in a particular environment depends on input prices and indirectly on input supplies.[8] Some evolutionary models are too complicated be fully analyzed with pencil and paper. Interesting results can nonetheless be obtained by supplementing analysis with computer simulation. For example, Bottazzi et al. (2001) use a combination of analysis and simulation to show that easy entry is conducive to rapid productivity growth.

23.4 Neutral and Biased Technological Change

23.4.1 Classification

Technological progress in producing existing goods can, as we saw in Section 23.3, be represented by an inward shift of an isoquant. If the shift preserves the slope of the isoquant at the initial factor proportions and output level, as illustrated in Figure 23.3, the technological progress is **neutral**.[9] Neutral technological progress preserves the cost-minimizing factor proportions at the original relative factor prices and output level.

If technological change alters the slope of the isoquant at the original factor proportions and output level, the change is said to be **biased**. If the isoquant becomes flatter at the original factor proportions and output, the technological change is biased in favor of saving the factor on the horizontal axis, as shown in the left panel of Figure 23.4. If the isoquant becomes steeper at the original factor proportions and output level, the technological progress is biased toward saving the factor on the vertical axis, as shown in the right panel. For example, if the technological progress raises the marginal product of capital relative to the marginal product of labor, making the isoquant steeper when capital is on the horizontal axis and labor is on the vertical, then the progress is labor saving, as in the right panel. If factor prices are unchanged, labor-saving technological progress induces cost-minimizing

---

[8] Evolutionary models of technological search and selection in industries composed of profit-seeking firms are developed in Nelson and Winter (1982). Some of these models are adapted to industries composed of labor-managed firms in Burkett (1986).

[9] Technological progress can be classified in various ways. Here we use a taxonomy introduced by John Hicks and Joan Robinson and surveyed by Blaug (1963).

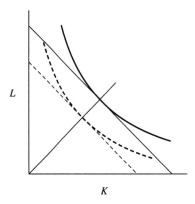

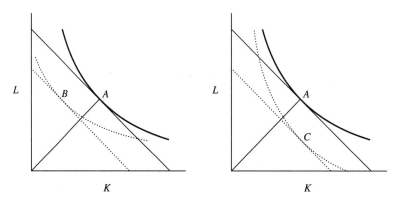

Figure 23.3 Technological progress is illustrated here by a shift in an isoquant for a given level of output from its initial position (solid curve) to a new position (dashed curve). The progress is neutral because the slope of the isoquant is preserved along the ray that indicates the initial factor proportions.

Figure 23.4 The left panel illustrates capital-saving technological change. In this case, as an isoquant for a given level of output shifts from its original position (solid curve) to its new position (dotted curve), it becomes flatter at the original factor proportions, indicated by the ray from the origin. The cost-minimizing input combination, given the original relative factor prices, shifts from point A to point B. The right panel illustrates labor-saving technological change. In this case, as the isoquant shifts inward, it becomes steeper at the original factor proportions. The cost-minimizing input combination shifts from point A to point C.

or profit-maximizing entrepreneurs to substitute capital for labor, whereas capital-saving technological progress has the opposite effect.

23.4.2 Determinants of Bias

The bias in technological progress alters from time to time, at least partly in response to changing factor prices. Any event that raises the cost of one factor relative to others strengthens the incentive to pursue technological progress biased in favor of saving that factor. For example, the bubonic plague sharply reduced the labor force in medieval Europe, raising the cost of labor relative to other factors and providing a strong incentive to pursue labor-saving technology.

Another example is afforded by the experience of early European settlers in North America. Here they found themselves in an environment with lower ratios of labor to land and capital to land than those found in the Old World. Faced with high costs for labor and capital relative to that of land, they had an incentive to pursue labor- and capital-saving as opposed to land-saving technological progress.

23.4.3 Skilled and Unskilled Labor

In the nineteenth century, English cities became magnates for unskilled workers from rural Britain and Ireland. The influx of unskilled workers drove up the relative wages of skilled workers, creating an incentive to seek skilled labor–saving technological progress. This search led to the use of interchangeable parts and the displacement of artisans' workshops by factories.

Following World War II, college enrollment rates in the United States rose. When the baby boomers entered the labor market, they greatly increased the supply of college-educated labor. Predictably, the return to college education (the differential between the earnings of college graduates and others) fell in the 1970s. The decline in the cost of college-educated labor created incentives to seek technological progress biased toward using more college graduates relative to other workers. These incentives probably contributed to the development of computer-based technologies. As these technologies matured, demand for college graduates rose, pushing the return to college education back up in the 1980s and 1990s (Acemoglu 2002).

23.5   Positive Externalities and Public Policy

Product and process development, unlike basic research, is not a pure public good. However, it does involve **positive externalities**—benefits that accrue to individuals other than those who bear the cost of creating them. Consider, for example, the development of transistors. This occurred at AT&T, which captured *some* of the benefits of transistors by building them into better and cheaper telephone equipment. However, many of the benefits went to other companies or consumers, thanks to transistor-based products like radios and televisions. Because no single firm can expect to capture all of the benefits of its R&D expenditures, private-sector R&D expenditures tend to be too small, in the sense that the marginal social benefit exceeds the marginal social cost.

The positive externalities create a case for public subsidies to R&D work through, for example, corporate tax credits. In the United States in recent years, the federal government has offered a tax credit for increases in R&D expenditures. Under this provision of the tax code, a firm that increases its R&D expenditures above its average expenditures during the previous 3 years can subtract 20 percent of the increase from its taxes. The government in effect pays a fifth of the increased expenditures (Viscusi et al., 2000).

In another attempt to deal with the positive externalities, the federal government has recently tried to facilitate the formation of cooperative R&D ventures at the industry level. These ventures are particularly useful where the R&D benefits that are external to firms are nonetheless internal to the industry. In such cases, firms in the industry have an incentive to jointly finance R&D efforts that no one firm would undertake alone. The formation of such joint ventures in the United States was blocked for years by antitrust laws. The legal obstacles were reduced by the National Cooperative Research Act of 1984, later amended and renamed as the National Cooperative Research and Production Act of 1993. Registered joint ventures (JRVs) are partially protected under the act from private antitrust suits.[10] Participation in JRVs was further encouraged by awards granted by the Advanced Technology Program (ATP) established in 1991 by the U.S. Department of Commerce. The

---

[10] Registered joint ventures can limit their liability under antitrust law to actual rather than the usual treble damages.

number of newly registerd JRVs peaked in 1995.[11] Prominent examples of JRVs include Bell Communications Research, the Electric Power Research Institute, Sematech (electronics), and the SNP Consortium (pharmaceuticals).[12]

By some measures, the productivity of development work has been declining in the United States and western Europe. In the late 1950s "one million 1982-dollars of company-funded research produced over three patents. By the late 1980s, however, the same R&D funds produced about one patent" (Kortum 1993, p. 450). Similar trends have been noted in France, Germany, and the United Kingdom (Evenson 1993). Economists do not yet have a complete explanation for the declining ratio of patents to R&D expenditure. However, part of the decline appears to be due to the expanding size of markets, connected with increasing international trade. The idea is that "the expansion of markets has raised the value of patents and that competition in the research sector has resulted in greater R&D expenditures per patent" (Kortum 1993, p. 450). In other words, the amount that firms are willing to pay for a patent has grown with the size of the market in which it can be used. This idea is supported by an analysis of data for U.S. manufacturing firms, 1980–93, which found that "differences across firms in research productivity are negatively and significantly related to differences in the level of sales" (Lanjouw and Schankerman 2004, p. 461).

23.6   Technological Change and Market Structure

To the extent that technological progress is generated mainly by the R&D expenditures of for-profit firms, we may expect it to be particularly rapid in sectors with high market concentration, that is, industries that are structured as monopolies or oligopolies. Numerous reasons can be given for this association, two of which we will examine here. First, a firm that introduces a new product or cost-cutting process may secure a temporary monopoly based on exclusive control of vital information. The monopoly lasts as long as the patents or trade secrets on which it is based. A familiar example of a temporary monopoly based on product innovation is Rollerblade, which enjoyed a monopoly on in-line skates until its patent expired in 1985. Several other examples can be found in the pharmaceutical industry, as we shall see later. New processes, as well as new products, may create temporary monopoly power because a firm that is the first to introduce a cost-saving technique may cut the product's price, enlarging its market share. In an extreme case, the innovating firm may cut the price below the minimum average cost of its competitors, driving them out of business and securing a monopoly for itself. For example, Walmart has secured a near monopoly in some small communities by cutting prices below the costs of traditional retailers.

A second link between technological change and imperfect competition is provided by the fact that a firm's R&D expenditure is a fixed cost (FC) in the sense that it does not depend on the volume of products sold. As we saw in Chapter 14, high fixed costs give an advantage to large firms and thus are conducive to high market concentration.

Before concluding that monopoly or oligopoly inevitably accompany technological progress, we should consider that technological progress need not be generated exclusively within for-profit firms. Much technological progress can be generated by government agencies and private not-for-profit groups and then made freely available to the public.

---

[11] The subsequent decline in joint venture filings may be related to the decline in ATP funding Link et al. 2002.

[12] The initials SNP stand for single nucleotide polymorphisms, which are DNA sequence variations among individuals. The SNP Consortium discovered over a million such variations during its active existence, 1999–2002.

An important example is the long tradition of agricultural research carried out by the U.S. Department of Agriculture and land-grant colleges (both established under legislation adopted in 1862) and state agricultural experiment stations (with federal research funding under the 1887 Hatch Act). This research has generated many ideas about how to control erosion, raise soil fertility, keep livestock healthy, and raise crop yields. These ideas have been transferred to farmers through the Cooperative Extension Service, established by the 1914 Smith-Lever Act (Huffman and Evenson 1993). Because all farmers have had access to the ideas, none could gain monopoly power. In this way farming has remained highly competitive while achieving dramatic productivity growth. In the United States from 1948 to 1996, agricultural output grew at an average annual rate of 1.80% while input use *fell* at an average annual rate of 0.09%, resulting in productivity growth at an average annual rate of 1.89%. In contrast, productivity over the same period in nonfarm business grew at an average annual rate of just 1.10% (Newton and Yee 2003). Because farming remains competitive, its productivity gains result in falling prices for agricultural products rather than monopoly profits for farmers. Public funding of agricultural research has thus benefited mainly consumers of agricultural products.

EXERCISE 23.1

Consider a nondiscriminating monopoly whose demand function is $P = 100 - 2Q$. Suppose the firm has no fixed cost and that its average and marginal costs are both constant (and hence equal to each other). (a) If average and marginal costs are 60, what is the firm's profit? (b) If the firm acquired a new technology that reduced its average and marginal costs to 20, what would the firm's profit be? (c) If the firm were to be in business for a single period, what is the most it should be willing to pay for the new technology?

EXERCISE 23.2

Using the information in the previous exercise, calculate Marshallian consumer surplus when the marginal cost is 60 and again when it is 20. How much benefit do consumers derive from the new technology?

23.7 Technological Change in the Pharmaceutical Industry: A Case Study

Technological progress became a conspicuous feature of the pharmaceutical industry in the mid-1930s when the first important anti-infective drugs were introduced. In recent years the industry has been "consistently at the top of American industries in terms of R&D spending per dollar of sales" (Viscusi et al. 2000, p. 847). From 1977 to 1997, R&D spending as a percentage of revenue in the U.S. pharmaceutical industry rose from 11.1 to 21.2% (Henderson 1999).

In Section 23.1 we noted that in recent times technological progress has been a two-stage process, with basic research feeding a stock of scientific principles that is drawn upon by development work, eventuating in productive know-how. This two-stage process is well illustrated by pharmaceuticals (see Figure 23.5). In the United States, basic research on pharmaceuticals is funded principally by the NIH. Responding to lobbying by highly motivated constituencies, it tends to favor research proposals that aim at finding cures for

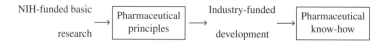

Figure 23.5 Process that generates technological change in the drug industry

life-threatening diseases, including some, like leukemia, that are comparatively rare. Development research is funded mainly by pharmaceutical companies. Responding to commercial considerations, they tend to concentrate research on conditions that are prevalent enough to ensure a mass market. These conditions include some, such as baldness, heartburn, and impotence, that are hardly life-threatening.

Although the priorities of the NIH and the drug companies are different, NIH-funded basic research often has applications to conditions of interest to drug companies. A 1% increase in NIH-funded basic research in a particular therapeutic category has been estimated to produce within 7 years approximately a 0.7% "increase in industry R&D expenditures in that category" and a 1.5% increase in other categories (Ward and Dranove 1995, pp. 83–84). Similarly, "a 1995 study by the Massachusetts Institute of Technology found that, of the 14 drugs the [pharmaceutical] industry identified as the most medically significant in the preceding 25 years, 11 had their roots in studies paid for by the government" (*New York Times*, April 23, 2000, p. 8). A 1997 study of the "most significant scientific research papers cited in medicine patents . . . found that half of the cited studies were paid for with United States public funds" (p. 8).

The pace of technological change is driven by pursuit of profits based in part on patents. United States' law gives an inventor the exclusive right to produce a patented product for 20 years. However, as we will see in Section 25.3.2, the effective length of drug patents was substantially reduced, starting in the early 1960s, by regulations that required lengthy testing of drugs prior to approval. This shortened patent life was probably responsible in part for a sharp drop during the 1960s in the rate at which drug companies introduced new drugs in the U.S. market.[13]

The 1984 Drug Price Competition and Patent Restoration Act authorizes extending drug patents by a period equal to the sum of the FDA's review time and one-half the company's clinical testing time, subject to two limits. First, the maximum extension is 5 years. Second, the effective patent life is not to exceed 14 years (Viscusi et al. 2000).

From the standpoint of the producers of brand name drugs, the 1984 act was a mixed blessing. Although it extended the effective life of their patents, it also facilitated entry by competing generic drugs following the expiration of patents. Prior to the 1984 act, potential entrants had sometimes been deterred by the cost of FDA-mandated tests. The act lowered this barrier to entry by allowing the would-be producer of a generic drug to gain approval by merely demonstrating the "bioequivalency" of the generic drug and the already approved brand name. (One would-be producer of a generic drug tried to satisfy the bioequivalency test by grinding up a sample of the brand-name drug and re-forming it in the generic's pill press.)

Viscusi et al. (2000) incline toward the view that the 1984 act "has, on balance, reduced the incentives to R&D" (p. 858). If this is true, it appears regrettable because by some measures, drugs are a comparatively cost-effective form of medical care. One recent econometric study concludes that "a $1 increase in pharmaceutical expenditure is associated with a $3.65

---

[13] From 1960 to 1969 the number of new drugs introduced in the United States fell from 50 to 9 (Santerre and Neun 1996).

reduction in hospital care expenditure" (Lichtenberg 1996, p. 27). (However, this study was funded by Pfizer; perhaps we should take its conclusion with a grain of generic sodium chloride.)

Even if drugs are often more cost-effective than hospitalization, current patterns of drug use may be far from optimal, in part because many prescribers and patients remain ill informed about the risks of drug use. Information generated by pharmaceutical R&D often reaches prescribers and patients primarily through the marketing efforts of the drug producers. Marketing efforts understandably do not stress the possible ill effects of drug use. Although the effects of a drug on a patient are observable (albeit only retrospectively) by the patient and his or her physician, the external effects (effects on others) are apt to go unnoticed. In particular, patients and their physicians are unlikely to directly observe the tendency of antimicrobial drugs to select in favor of drug-resistant microbes. This negative externality is likely to be overlooked when patients and doctors get their information mainly from drug marketers. This problem is one reason why some experts on the health care system now call for creating new public programs to transfer unbiased information about drugs to prescribers (Avorn 2004). Several states have begun to create such programs, which are sometimes known as "academic detailing" in reference to the commercial "detailers" drug companies send to visit physicians. If widely implemented, academic detailing could facilitate rapid diffusion and appropriate use of technology in health care, as the Cooperative Extension Service did in farming.

23.8 Summary

1. Technological change means alteration in the stock of knowledge relevant to producing goods and services. Under modern conditions, technological change is produced by basic research, aimed at advancing the scientific frontier, and applied research, aimed at creating new products and processes.
2. Basic research yields scientific ideas that are neither rivalrous nor easily excludable. Hence basic research creates a public good and needs government support.
3. Development of new products for sale is usually motivated by an expectation of using copyright or patent law to create intellectual property rights. Copyrights and patents have been lengthened in the United States but their optimal duration remains controversial.
4. Development of processes and products for internal use can proceed without the benefit of copyrights and patents. Indeed, developers often find advantages in making their creations freely available. An interesting example is provided by free and open source software.
5. A firm's R&D department generates technological knowledge as an intermediate input for its production department. If the firm knows the function mapping R&D inputs into new knowledge, it can choose the quantity of inputs for each department so as to maximize the present value of profits. If not, the firm may simply search for new techniques that increase profits without necessarily maximizing them. The market selects in favor of firms that discover and adopt particularly profitable techniques. Search and selection are key ingredients of evolutionary models of technological change.
6. Technological progress affecting productive processes can be neutral or biased toward saving a particular factor or subset of factors. The direction of bias changes from time to time, partially in response to changes in factor prices. Changes in the relative supplies of skilled and unskilled workers have more than once altered relative earnings enough to affect the direction of technological progress.

7. Private development efforts often create positive externalities. Recognizing these positive externalities, the U.S. federal government has tried to stimulate private sector R&D by offering tax credits and legal protection for firms that come together to form cooperative research ventures. The amount firms are willing to spend on R&D per patent has increased in recent decades, in part because of the growing size of their markets.

8. To the extent that R&D is mainly carried on by for-profit firms, sectors experiencing rapid technological progress tend to have highly concentrated markets. However, R&D can also be carried out by government agencies and private not-for-profit groups. When the resulting ideas are made freely available, rapid productivity growth can occur in highly competitive sectors such as agriculture.

9. In the pharmaceutical industry, basic research is funded principally by the National Institutes of Health and focuses on cures for life-threatening diseases. Development, funded mainly by pharmaceutical companies, focuses on alleviating conditions that are prevalent enough to ensure a mass market. The rate of introduction of new drugs fell in the 1960s, probably in part because the 1962 Kefauver-Harris Drug Amendments extended testing and shortened effective patent life. The 1984 Drug Price Competition and Patent Restoration Act extended the life of patents but also facilitated the entry of generics following the expiration of patents, thus having mixed effects on incentives to develop new drugs. Concerned that the flow of pharmaceutical information from researchers to prescribers and patients is distorted by drug marketers, some experts call for increased use of academic detailing.

23.9 Solutions to Exercises

23.1. (a) Marginal revenue is $MR = 100 - 4Q$. Equating marginal revenue to marginal cost, we find that the profit-maximizing quantity is 10 and the corresponding price is 80. Thus profits are $(80 - 60)10 = 200$. (b) Profit would be 800. (c) The most the firm should pay to get the new technology is the difference between the profit levels with the new and old technology, namely, 600.

23.2. Marshallian consumer surplus is the area under the demand curve and above the price line. When the marginal cost is 60, the Marshallian consumer surplus is $(100 - 80)10/2 = 100$. When the marginal cost is 20, the surplus is $(100 - 60)20/2 = 400$. The new technology thus raises the surplus by 300.

23.10 Problems

1. Consider a nondiscriminating monopoly whose total and marginal cost functions are $TC = Q^3 - 30Q^2 + 1201Q$ and $MC = 3Q^2 - 60Q + 1201$ and whose demand and marginal revenue functions are $P = 1501 - 30Q$ and $MR = 1501 - 60Q$.
   a. Find the profit-maximizing values of Q and P and then the firm's profit and the Marshallian consumer surplus.
   b. Suppose the firm could invest in a new technology that would shift its cost functions down so that the firm could make a profit of 16,000 per period. Assuming that the firm will be in business for just one period, determine the most the firm should be willing to spend on the new technology.
   c. Suppose that if the new technology is adopted, the new equilibrium quantity and price would be $Q = 20$ and $P = 901$. Calculate the Marshallian consumer surplus when the firm uses this technology. Recalling the Marshallian consumer surplus with the old

technology (in part a), determine the most the public should be willing to subsidize the new technology.

2. Suppose that by developing and patenting a new product, you could create a (nondiscriminating) monopoly whose cost functions are the same as in Problem 1.

  a. Recalling the firm's profit in 1(a) and assuming the firm will be in business for a single period, determine the most you would consent to pay to develop and patent the new product.

  b. Now suppose that demand and marginal revenue functions in part a are replaced by $P = 2401 - 30Q$ and $MR = 2401 - 60Q$. Determine the new profit-maximizing values of Q and P and then calculate the firm's profit. Assuming that the firm will be in business for a single period, determine how much you would be willing to pay to develop and market the new product.

  c. Explain any difference between what you would be willing to pay under the conditions of parts a and b.

24

▓▓▓ Assets, Investment and Financial Markets

Assets types

An **asset** is a durable item providing its owner with a flow of benefits. The item may be a physical entity such as a cow or a legal title such as a bond. The benefits, often called "returns," may be physical—e.g. milk—or monetary—e.g., interest payments. Depending on whether the benefits are physical or monetary, the asset is called "real" or "financial."[1] In this chapter we will focus more on financial assets than real ones.

A financial asset owned by one agent (individual or organization) represents a liability (debt or obligation) for another agent. For example a bond is an asset to its owner but a liability for its issuer. Among financial assets we usually distinguish three types: fixed-income securities, equity, and derivative securities.

Fixed-income securities pay a prespecified stream of income. For example, a bond usually pays its owner a fixed amount of interest each year. Although bonds are the most important example, annuities and preferred stock could also be considered fixed-income securities.

Equities, or common stocks, are titles to partial ownership of a corporation. A corporation pays part of its profits to stockholders in the form of dividends. It uses the rest to acquire more assets, boosting its market value.

Derivative securities—derivatives for short—are assets whose value derives from that of some other asset. Derivatives include futures contracts and options. A **futures contract** is "an agreement to buy or sell a fixed quantity of a particular commodity, currency, or security for delivery at a fixed date in the future at a fixed price" (Butler and Isaacs 1993, p. 121). An **option** is a

> right to buy or sell a fixed quantity of a commodity, currency, security, etc., at a particular date at a particular price (the exercise or striking price). . . . The purchaser of an option [unlike a party to a futures contract] is not obliged to buy or sell at the exercise price and will only do so if it is profitable. . . . An option to buy is known as a call option and is usually purchased in the expectation of a rising price; an option to sell is called a put option and is bought in the expectation of a falling price. (p. 206)

---

[1] This distinction is clear in most modern economies, where monetary benefits take the form of paper money. However, the distinction is blurred in economies that use gold or other precious substances as money.

24.2 Rate of Return

Although the return on assets can take many different forms, they may all be grouped into two categories: income and capital gains. Income includes interest, dividends, and rent. An individual's **capital gains** on an asset are the difference between the price at which she sells it (P_1) and the price she paid for it (P_0); that is, capital gains $= P_1 - P_0$.

Once we know the income Y, beginning value P_0, and ending value P_1 associated with an asset, we can easily calculate its rate of return r:

$$r = \frac{P_1 - P_0 + Y}{P_0}.$$

In calculating the rate of return we should be careful to measure capital gains and income net of any taxes and expenses. Taxes may be levied on both capital gains and income, although not necessarily at the same rate. The maximum U.S. federal tax rates on capital gains are (as of 2004) generally lower thatn those on income.[2]

Most forms of asset income are taxable at the same rate as other incomes. The marginal rates for U.S. federal taxes in 2004 were 10%, 15%, 25%, 28%, 33%, or 35%, depending on the taxpayer's income and marital status. However, interest income on state and local government bonds is not taxed by the federal government[3] and is also generally exempt from state and local taxes if the recipient resides in the jurisdiction that issued the bonds.

The favorable tax treatment of capital gains and interest from state and local bonds is more important to high-income individuals who are in the 35% tax bracket than to the rest of us. People in high tax brackets usually bid up the price of state and local bonds to the point that these assets are not attractive to people in lower tax brackets.

The sale price of an asset should be calculated net of sales costs when we figure the rate of return. Some assets, such as shares of stock in U.S. companies, can be sold cheaply. Others, such as a house, can be expensive to sell. A real estate broker is apt to claim about 4 to 6% of the sales price. Assets that can be turned into cash quickly and cheaply are said to be **liquid**; others are said to be illiquid.

EXERCISE 24.1

Suppose you buy a stock for $100, get $7 in dividends, and sell the stock after a year for $99. What is your rate of return on the stock?

24.3 Investors and Financial Markets

Acquisition of assets is termed **investment**. An agent may invest (make investments) by either creating assets—e.g., raising cattle—or obtaining them from other agents by purchase, gift, inheritance, or some less reputable means such as cattle rustling.[4] The

---

[2] The maximum capital gains tax rates for 2004 ranged from 5 to 28%, depending on the type of gains and the taxpayer's income tax bracket.

[3] It is exempt because of an 1819 ruling by the Supreme Court that the federal, state, and local governments do not have the power to tax each other (Hirt and Block, 1993).

[4] The economy as a whole can of course acquire assets only by producing them because there are no outside agents from whom they could be obtained.

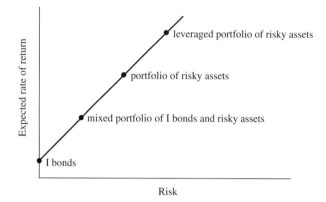

Figure 24.1 Spectrum of portfolios

investments on which we focus in this chapter involve purchase of financial assets. Agents who invest are naturally termed "investors."

24.3.1 Rational Investors and Efficient Markets

An investor's collection of assets and liabilities is called her **portfolio**. A rational individual chooses her portfolio to maximize her expected utility. Economists have usually assumed that most expected utility maximizers are risk-averse.

Investors can avoid some risk by **diversifying** their portfolios—that is, by investing in a variety of assets. Portfolio diversification is just a financial application of the old saying, "Don't put all your eggs in one basket." The traditional way of getting a diversified portfolio—buying stocks and bonds from a wide variety of industries and countries—is only feasible for the wealthy. A modern alternative, which is practical for small, as well as large, investors, is to buy shares in a broadly based **index fund**—a passively managed fund that mimics the behavior of a market average such as the Standard and Poors 500 or the Wilshire 5000. Even a well-diversified portfolio of stocks and bonds has some risks. The values of shares in index funds fluctuate, although not as wildly as the values of shares in many individual companies.

Rational risk-averse investors will hold a risky portfolio only if it has an expected rate of return above that of a nearly risk-free asset such as inflation-indexed savings bonds (I bonds). If these investors dominate the financial markets, we should expect there to be a positive relationship between risk and return: The higher a portfolio's expected rate of return, the higher its risk. Neoclassical economists, assuming that most investors are rational (perhaps because irrational investors supposedly soon lose their investments and drop out of the market), conclude that once portfolios are diversified, lower risks entail lower average returns.

A spectrum of portfolios ordered by increasing risk[5] and expected rates of return is sometimes portrayed as a positively sloped line in the space of risk and expected rates of return, as in Figure 24.1.

Neoclassical economists believe that an investor should concentrate on picking a point on the tradeoff line that best suits his degree of risk aversion. A highly risk-averse investor

---

[5] In this context, risk is usually measured as the standard deviation of the rate of return.

will stay near the vertical axis, assembling a portfolio that contains mostly I bonds. A less risk-averse investor will pick a point higher up the line, holding a portfolio that contains mostly risky assets such as stocks. A very venturesome investor might choose a leveraged portfolio of risky assets—that is, borrow money to buy risky assets, betting that the return on the risky assets would more than cover interest payments on the debt.

Neoclassical economists, assuming that investors are rational, believe that financial markets do a good job of pricing assets. An asset will have a high price if investors rationally expect it to yield a large income or a high future value with near certainty. An asset will have a low price if investors rationally expect it to yield a low or very uncertain income or future value. In short, markets do an efficient job of pricing assets. If financial markets are efficient, there is little hope of beating the markets by buying low and selling high.

EXERCISE 24.2

Suppose you have your choice of placing your wealth in portfolio A or B. Neither portfolio will yield any income, but both may yield capital gains or losses. After 1 year, portfolio A will be worth $1000 with probability 0.5 and $4000 with probability 0.5; portfolio B will be worth $2000 with probability 0.5 and $3000 with probability 0.5. Your utility function is $u = 1 - 0.5^{(w/1000)}$, where w is the value of your portfolio at the end of the year. To maximize expected utility, which portfolio should you choose?

24.3.2 Noise Traders and Excess Volatility

In opposition to this neoclassical view, some economists argue that the prices of assets are pushed up and down by the actions of less than fully rational investors. Experiments surveyed in Chapter 20 indicate that many people have trouble accurately applying the multiplication law of probabilities. Recall that this law states that for any two events A and B, $P(A \text{ and } B) = P(A)P(B|A) = P(B)P(A|B)$. An important consequence of this multiplication law is that

$$P(B|A) = \frac{P(A|B)P(B)}{P(A)}.$$

This result is called **Bayes's theorem**, after Thomas Bayes (1702–61), who first noted it. People who have trouble with the multiplication law generally have trouble with Bayes's theorem as well and often look for shortcuts. One widely but foolishly used shortcut, the representativeness heuristic, asserts that $P(B|A) = P(A|B)$. That's false unless the so-called base rates are equal ($P(B) = P(A)$). One example of the inappropriate use of the representativeness heuristic is the case, discussed in Chapter 20, of confusing the probability of having a disease (conditional on testing positive for it) with the probability of testing positive for it (conditional on having it). Another example is the case, analyzed in the problems in Chapter 20, of confusing the probability that a cab was blue, given that it looked blue, with the probability that it looked blue, given that it was blue.

Let us consider how an investor who uses the representativeness heuristic might assess the probabilities that a firm will go bankrupt or survive over the next year. Suppose 10% of all firms go bankrupt in a typical year. Suppose further that 80% of firms that go bankrupt in a typical year lost money in the quarter preceding that year, whereas 70% of the surviving firms were profitable in that quarter. This information is recorded in Table 24.1.

Suppose we own stock in a company and learn that it lost money last quarter. What is the probability that it will go bankrupt in the coming year? $P(\text{bankruptcy} \mid \text{lost money}) = 8/35$.

Table 24.1 Firms cross classified by past and future characteristics

Firms that last quarter	Firms that will		
	go bankrupt	survive	total
lost money	8	27	35
made money	2	63	65
total	10	90	100

Investors using the representativeness heuristic estimate this probability as P(lost money | bankruptcy) $= 8/10$. Panicked by this large estimate, these dopey investors rush to sell their stock in the company, driving down its price. When the firm survives, the panic subsides and the price of the stock rises again.

Investors who rely on the representativeness heuristic are part of a larger class of **noise traders**, who base investment decisions in part on irrational factors. The idea that stock prices sometimes are temporarily depressed by the irrational panics of noise traders and at other times boosted by their irrational optimism is called the **excess volatility hypothesis**. This hypothesis is supported by some recent statistical research. One study found that stocks that had below average rates of return for a few years tended to have above average rates of return in subsequent years. You could make more money by buying stocks with low recent rates of return than by buying other stocks (De Bondt and Thaler, 1989). People who try to buy up stocks whose prices are temporarily depressed are called **value investors** or **contrarians**. Some of them are quite successful, for example, Warren Buffet. Their success suggests that the typical investor is not so rational as neoclassical economists have maintained.

It is conceivable that a few fully rational investors could make financial markets efficient (and themselves fabulously rich) by buying what noise traders want to sell and selling what they want to buy. Indeed, precisely this possibility is often cited by defenders of the efficient market hypothesis. However, dealing in markets influenced by noise traders is risky. (If we sell an overvalued stock to a fool, we cannot be sure that he won't make a tidy profit by reselling it to a greater fool. If we buy an undervalued stock from a panicked noise trader, we cannot be sure that delayed reactions by even slower witted traders won't drive the price down further.) If the rational investors are risk-averse, they may opt to limit their exposure to such risky markets. As a result, their contrarian intervention may be too small to stabilize prices at a level that could be justified by fundamentals such as dividend prospects. In short, a few risk-averse rational investors are not necessarily sufficient to make financial markets fully efficient (Shleifer and Summers 1990).

24.4   Loss Aversion, Myopia, and Portfolio Selection

The average annual rate of return on equity is about 7% whereas that on bonds is less than 1%.[6] Faced with such rates, why are investors willing to devote large portions of their portfolios to bonds? This question is known as the **equity premium puzzle**.

Noting that bonds are less risky than equity, and assuming that investors maximize expected utility, an economist's first guess might be that investors must be sufficiently risk-

---

[6] The figures refer to real (inflation adjusted) rates of return on U.S. stocks and short-term bonds since 1926.

averse that bonds look attractive despite their low average rate of return. Before accepting this conjecture, we should ask what degree of risk aversion is entailed. Considering the relative risks involved, financial economists believe that the risk aversion would have to be extreme: An expected utility maximizer who is risk-averse enough to be indifferent between bonds paying about 1% and equity paying 7% would also be indifferent between $51,209 for sure and a gamble with a 50-50 chance of getting either $50,000 or $100,000. It's hard to believe that many investors are that risk-averse (Benartzi and Thaler 1995).

Finding risk aversion inadequate to explain the equity premium puzzle, economists have recently turned to loss aversion as a possible alternative explanation.[7] As explained in Chapter 12, a loss-averse individual is concerned with gains and losses relative to some reference point and feels losses more acutely than equal gains. The most obvious reference point is current wealth. Thus the argument of a loss-averse investor's value function can plausibly be assumed to be the rate of return on her portfolio.

The implications of loss aversion for portfolio selection depend on how often investors evaluate their portfolios. To see why frequency matters, consider an individual whose value function is the following:

$$v(x) = \begin{cases} x & \text{if } x \geq 0 \\ 2.5x & \text{if } x < 0 \end{cases}. \tag{24.1}$$

For simplicity, assume that the individual's weighting function for probabilities is the trivial $w(p) = p$. Suppose the individual is offered, once a year, a bet giving him a 50-50 chance of winning $200 or losing $100. If he evaluates the bets one year at a time, he would reject the bets because $0.5(200) + 0.5(2.5)(-100) < 0$. If he evaluates the bets 2 years at a time, he would see that the probability distribution of his gains and losses after two bets is (-200, 0.25; 100, 0.50; 400, 0.25). He would accept a sequence of two bets because $0.25(2.5)(-200) + 0.5(100) + 0.25(400) > 0$. Thus **myopia**—defined in the present context as a tendency to evaluate prospects exclusively over short periods—can induce loss-averse individuals to turn down bets that would appear attractive if evaluated over longer periods.

The longer the evaluation period, the more highly a loss-averse investor values equity relative to bonds. For evaluation periods of 6 months or less, bonds appear more attractive. For periods of 18 months or more equity appears more attractive. For an evaluation period of 1 year, equity and bonds appear about equally attractive.[8] Investors, of course, evaluate their portfolios at various intervals. However, if a single representative evaluation period had to be chosen, a plausible argument could be made for supposing it to be 1 year.

> Individual investors file taxes annually, receive their most comprehensive reports from their brokers, mutual funds, and retirement accounts once a year, and institutional investors also take the annual reports most seriously. As a possible evaluation period, one year is at least highly plausible. (Benartzi and Thaler 1995, p. 83)

A loss-averse investor who annually evaluates alternative portfolios of bonds and equities would find that putting 45 to 70% of his wealth in bonds particularly attractive. Many portfolios, both individual and institutional, fall in this range (Benartzi and Thaler 1995).

---

[7] Although loss-aversion's role in explaining the equity premium puzzle is the focus of this section, we should note that loss aversion may also have explanatory value in connection with other financial phenomena. For example, loss aversion may help explain "the disposition effect, the tendency of investors to hold losing investments too long and sell winning investments to soon" (Odean 2000 [1998], p. 371).

[8] These comparisons are based on a value function such as that described in the chapter on prospect theory, with $\alpha = \beta = 0.88$ and $\lambda = 2.25$, estimates based on analysis of controlled experiments (Tversky and Kahneman 1992).

If these portfolios reflect their owners' loss aversion and myopia, then they should have no normative appeal to maximizers of expected utility and far-sighted loss-averse investors. These investors may be glad for the opportunity to buy underpriced equities.

24.5 Summary

1. An asset is a durable item providing a flow of benefits to its owner. Financial assets include fixed income securities, equities, and derivatives. Acquisition of assets is termed investment.
2. The rate of return on an asset is the sum of income and capital gains, divided by the purchase price.
3. If all investors were risk-averse maximizers of expected utility, there would be a strict tradeoff between risk and expected rate of return. Asset markets would be efficient in the sense that asset prices would reflect all available information. Neoclassical economists believe that asset markets closely approximate this ideal.
4. If not all investors are expected utility maximizers, there may be opportunities for more rational investors to beat the market. In particular, if many investors use the representativeness heuristic, they may overreact to news, giving contrarians a chance to profit at their expense. However, if the rational investors are risk-averse, they may limit their market exposure to a scale that is insufficient to sustain market efficiency.
5. The equity premium puzzle is the problem of explaining why investors are willing to hold bonds as large parts of their portfolios when the rate of return on equity is about seven times higher than that on bonds. One plausible explanation is that many investors are both loss-averse and myopic.

24.6 Solutions to Exercises

24.1. The rate of return on the stock is

$$r = \frac{99 - 100 + 7}{100} = 0.06.$$

24.2. The expected utility of portfolio A is $0.5(1 - 0.5) + 0.5(1 - 0.5^4) = 23/32$. The expected utility of portfolio B is $0.5(1 - 0.5^2) + 0.5(1 - 0.5^3) = 26/32$. As an expected utility maximizer, you would choose portfolio B.

24.7 Problems

1. Suppose you buy a stock for $100, get $5 in dividends, and sell the stock after a year for $105. What is your rate of return on the stock?
2. Suppose you have your choice of placing your wealth in portfolio A or B. Neither portfolio will yield any income, but both may yield capital gains or losses. After 1 year, portfolio A will be worth $81 with probability 0.5 and $144 with probability 0.5; portfolio B will be worth $100 with probability 0.6 and $121 with probability 0.4. Your utility function is $u = \sqrt{w}$, where w is the value of your portfolio at the end of the year. To maximize expected utility, which portfolio should you choose?
3. Dopey subscribes to an investment newsletter that terms a firm a "star" if its profits amount to more than 25% of its book value. In a typical year only 10% of firms are

stars. The newsletter has been moderately accurate in predicting stars: Of firms that became stars, 60% were so predicted by the newsletter; of firms that failed to become stars, 10% were predicted to be stars. The newsletter has just predicted that Dreck Inc. will become a star.

a. What is the probability that Dreck Inc. becomes a star, given all the information in the problem?

b. If Dopey uses the representativeness heuristic, what is his estimate of that probability?

c. If many investors are like Dopey, what might happen to the price of Dreck stock?

25

▨ Government's Roles in the Economy

Functions of Government

25.1.1 Areas of Consensus

Although markets (rather than central planning) are the predominant resource allocation mechanism in most countries, they could hardly function without government support. Almost all economists would agree that governments in market economies should perform the following functions:

1. Provide a legal framework hospitable to markets. This framework includes clearly defined property rights and enforceable contracts.
2. Redistribute income or wealth as needed to prevent social unrest.
3. Provide public goods, that is, goods that are nonexcludable and nonrivalrous. Examples include national defense, city streets, public sanitation, and basic scientific research.
4. Create a context enabling markets to work efficiently despite externalities, that is, costs and benefits accruing to individuals other than those who caused them.
5. Curb monopolistic distortions by antitrust action or price regulation.
6. Provide a stable currency by operating a central bank.

25.1.2 Areas of Controversy

The functions enumerated in the last subsection can be performed in various ways. In some cases, the best choice is controversial. Two notable examples are choices with regard to redistribution and externalities.

Redistribution

From a normative perspective, expected utility theory provides an attractive framework within which alternative distributions of income or wealth can be assessed. Imagine that you had to choose a distribution of wealth without knowing anything about your location in the distribution. You might turn out to be the poorest individual, the richest, or anyone in between. Without any information about your position in the distribution, you might reasonably assess your probability of being any one individual as $1/n$, where n is the population. Suppose the utility of individual i is $u(w_i)$, where w_i is the individual's wealth. Your wealth could with equal probability be w_1, w_2, . . . , or w_n. As a rational and self-interested person, you would choose the distribution that maximizes

$$\frac{1}{n} \sum_{i=1}^{n} u(w_i).$$

Since n is given, your choice also maximizes the sum of all individual utilities. This is the essence of the **utilitarian** approach to questions of distributive justice. This approach, sometimes traced back to David Hume (1711–76), has in recent years been rigorously developed by Harsanyi, one of the trio of Nobel Prize–winning game theorists introduced in Chapter 21.

The utilitarian framework can accommodate any utility function and thus be used to defend a wide range of distributions of wealth. Risk-averse utilitarians favor a relatively egalitarian distribution.[1] Risk-neutral utilitarians favor the distribution that maximizes total wealth. (Note that total wealth may vary from one distribution to another, in part because inequality may provide incentives to work and save.) Risk-seeking utilitarians (a rare breed) should favor a relatively inegalitarian distribution.[2]

As a step toward constructing a utilitarian ranking of wealth distributions, one might conceivably survey a population in hopes of discovering a representative utility function. However, such a survey would very likely merely provide additional evidence that few people maximize expected utility.

From a positive perspective, prospect theory provides important insights into what forms of redistribution are popularly perceived as fair or just. According to this theory, most people are (a) concerned with gains and losses rather than levels of wealth and (b) loss-averse. Thus they are more upset by losing accustomed wealth or income than by forfeiting opportunities to gain additional wealth or income (Kahneman et al. 1991). Economic discontent and social unrest tend to become explosive when many people suffer falling standards of living rather than when standards of living are abysmal but stable (Moore 1978). A government wishing to avert social unrest would be well advised to provide a safety net to groups in danger of suffering losses while limiting its active redistribution to gains in income and wealth.

Correcting Externalities

The normative literature includes proposals to deal with externalities by (1) creating property rights in goods affected by externalities or (2) a system of subsidies to producers of positive externalities (benefits to other parties), such as those associated with vaccination against contagious diseases, and taxes on producers of negative externalities (costs to other parties), such as those associated with pollution.

The first approach is associated with Ronald H. Coase, winner of the 1992 Nobel Prize in Economics. Coase (1959, 1960) argues that if the parties creating negative externalities and those damaged can negotiate at negligible cost, the parties will arrive at an efficient solution regardless of who is legally responsible for the damages. The legal responsibility for damages may affect wealth distribution but will not otherwise affect the solution.

To illustrate his contention, Coase considers the case of a doctor's office situated next to a confectioner or candy maker. Noise and vibrations from the confectioner's equipment disturbs the doctor while he works. Suppose the right to make noise is worth $50,000 to the confectioner and quiet is worth $70,000 to the doctor. If the confectioner can be held liable for costs imposed on the doctor, he will see that it is cheaper to stop making noise ($50,000) than to compensate the doctor ($70,000) and thus will decide to stop making

[1] As shown in the appendix to Chapter 20, an extremely risk-averse individual may be concerned only with the worst-case scenario, in which he ends up as the poorest individual in society. Maximizing his expected utility requires choosing the distribution that affords the greatest wealth to the poorest individual. This is the "maximin" criterion of justice, derived by John Rawls through another line of reasoning.

[2] For a more detailed survey of normative theories of distribution, see Jehle and Reny (1998).

noise. If the confectioner cannot be held liable, the doctor will see that it is cheaper to pay the confectioner $50,000 to stop making noise than to suffer $70,000 in damages due to noise. In both cases, the confectioner stops making noise. The only difference between the two cases is that the cost of adjustment falls on the confectioner in the first case and on the doctor in the second. An important implication of this reasoning is that the government merely needs to clearly indicate whether the doctor has a right to quiet or the confectioner a right to make noise. The parties can be left to negotiate whether the party with legal rights sells these rights to the other or not. The government need not estimate the damages and impose corresponding fines on the party creating them.

If many people are involved in creating negative externalities or suffering their consequences, negotiations over compensation can be prohibitively costly. In such cases, an alternative approach is suggested by the work of A. C. Pigou. Government representatives can survey the parties adversely affected to determine the extent of the aggregate damages and then impose corresponding fines on the parties creating the externalities. If the cost of stopping the activities that create negative externalities is less than the fines, the perpetrators will desist. Otherwise, they will continue to produce the negative externality, paying fines from which the victims can be compensated. In principle, the government could elicit the needed information about damages by asking affected parties either (1) what they would be willing to pay to stop the damage or (2) what they would be willing to accept in return for putting up with the damage. Apart from small income effects, the answers should be the same provided that indifference curves are smooth, as economists have traditionally assumed.

From a positive perspective, the approaches of Coase (1959, 1960) and Pigou (1932) are both open to question with respect to their assumption that the value of a right (such as freedom from noise or pollution) to an individual is independent of whether the individual currently poses it. In other words, both approaches posit that, apart from small income effects, willingness to pay and willingness to accept are equal. In still other words, they assume that indifference curves are smooth. These assumptions are in conflict with extensive evidence that most people are loss-averse.[3] Loss aversion can contribute to dramatic differences between stated willingness to accept and willingness to pay in responses to questions about externalities. For example, over 70% of respondents in a phone survey would not accept a hazardous waste facility "within 100 miles of their homes, even if they were paid up to $5000 per year for the next 20 years. Yet, only 40% of the respondents said they would pay an extra $100 in annual taxes over 20 years" to remove such a facility (Camerer and Kunreuther 1989, p. 574).

25.2   Taxes and Regulation

The services of government do not come cheaply. Citizens who want quality government services have to be prepared to pay taxes and endure regulations that may impose other costs. However, these taxes and regulations should not be any more burdensome than necessary. The study of how to design minimally burdensome taxes and regulations is an important specialty within economics. A few examples of how economists assess the burdens imposed by taxes and regulations are provided in the remainder of this chapter.

---

[3] The relevant literature, apart from the studies cited in earlier chapters, includes Kahneman et al. (1990, 1999).

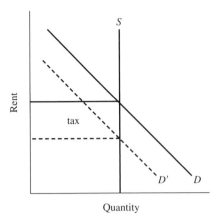

Figure 25.1 Effects of a tax on land rent

25.2.1 Taxes

Incidence

Supply and demand analysis is useful in understanding how taxes affect prices and quantities and how the burden of taxes is divided among individuals. The distribution of the tax burden is often called the **tax incidence**. Economists have studied the incidence of a wide variety of taxes including those on income, capital gains, property, imports, and sales. Taxes on rent, wages, and sales—being among the easiest to analyze—are the focus of this section.

Adam Smith, in his *Wealth of Nations* (published in 1776), discussed taxes on rent and wages. He argued that because the quantity of land supplied is not sensitive to price, the burden of a tax on rent is borne entirely by landlords.[4] Taxes on rent reduce the landlord's aftertax income regardless of whether they are collected from the landlord or the tenant. In the first case, the landlord's pretax income is unaffected but he has to pay tax. In the second, he has to cut the rent he charges, and the tenant uses the savings to pay the tax (see Figure 25.1.) This illustrates an important distinction, that between the legal and economic incidence of a tax. The legal incidence indicates from whom the tax is collected. The economic incidence indicates who bears the burden of a tax.

Smith contrasted the vertical supply curve for land to the supply curve for labor, which he believed to be horizontal. He supposed that practically any quantity of labor could be hired at a subsistence wage and inferred that the burden of a tax on wages would be borne by employers.[5]

Today, Smith's analysis of taxes on rent would still be endorsed by many economists. However, his views concerning taxes on wages now seem antiquated. It no longer seems realistic to assume that the supply curve for labor is horizontal at a subsistence wage. If we must make an extreme assumption to simplify the analysis, it might be more realistic today

---

[4] In restating Smith's point, modern economists often use the concept of elasticity, which was covered in Chapters 5 and 9. Because the supply curve in Smith's example is vertical, the percentage change in quantity along it is zero no matter how large the corresponding percentage change in price. Thus the price elasticity of supply in Smith's example is zero.

[5] Along a horizontal supply curve, the percentage change in price is zero no matter how great is the corresponding percentage change in quantity. In this case, the price elasticity of supply has zero in the denominator and is thus, strictly speaking, undefined. Loosely speaking, supply in this case is said to be "perfectly elastic."

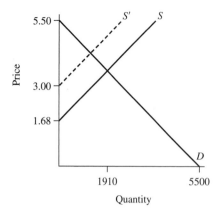

Figure 25.2 Effects of a tax on cigarettes

to suppose that the supply of labor is vertical. In that case a tax on wages is borne entirely by workers.

Smith's examples are limiting cases, useful for clarifying the principles of tax incidence but rarely met in practice. Most real world examples involve positively sloped supply curves. Consider the case of an excise tax on cigarettes. Suppose that before the tax is introduced, the cigarette market in a particular community has the following characteristics. The demand equation is $P = \$5.50 - 0.001Q^d$ where Q^d is demand expressed in packs per day. The supply equation in this community is $P = \$1.68 + 0.001Q^s$, where Q^s is supply, also expressed in packs per day. In equilibrium $Q^d = Q^s$. Let's denote this common value as Q^* and write $5.50 - 0.001Q^* = 1.68 + 0.001Q^*$. It follows that $Q^* = 1910$ and $P^* = \$3.59$. Now let's introduce a tax of \$1.32 per pack, collected from the seller. Letting P_g and P_n denote the gross and net prices (i.e., the prices including and excluding the tax), we note that $P_g = P_n + 1.32$. There are two equivalent ways of analyzing the effects of this tax. We may think of it as either shifting the supply curve up by \$1.32 or shifting the demand curve down by \$1.32. Let's first think of the tax as shifting the supply curve, as in Figure 25.2.

Our old supply curve represented the pretax costs of the seller. After the tax is imposed, the seller will have to collect \$1.32 on each pack sold and hand it over to the government. Hence, the posttax supply curve is shifted up by \$1.32 and can be written as $P_g = \$3.00 + 0.001Q^s$. The demand curve is, of course, $P_g = \$5.50 - 0.001Q^d$. The new equilibrium is given by $5.50 - 0.001Q^* = 3.00 + 0.001Q^*$; hence $Q^* = 1250$. The new price paid by the buyer, inclusive of the tax, is $P_g^* = \$4.25$. The new price received by the seller, net of the tax, is $P_n^* = 4.25 - 1.32 = 2.93$. In this case the buyer and seller each bear \$0.66 of the \$1.32 tax burden. The burden is split equally because the slopes of the demand and supply curves are of equal absolute value.[6]

Equivalently, we could think of the tax as shifting downward the demand curve perceived by the seller. Our old pretax demand curve represented how much the buyers were prepared to pay for any given quantity of cigarettes. It makes no difference to the buyer whether his money goes to the producer or the government. If the government is going to take \$1.32 a pack, the buyers reduce what they are prepared to give to the producer by an equal amount. Thus the demand curve, net of taxes, perceived by the seller shifts down by \$1.32. We can write the new demand curve as $P_n = \$4.18 - 0.001Q^d$. The supply curve is, of course, $P_n = \$1.68 + 0.001Q_2^*$. The new equilibrium quantity is given by

---

[6] In other words, demand and supply are equally elastic at the equilibrium point.

$4.18 - 0.001Q^* = 1.68 + 0.001Q^*$. That implies that $Q^* = 1250$. Note that the quantity is precisely the same as that calculated when we shifted the supply curve. The equilibrium price net of tax is $P_n^* = 2.93$. The price, including tax, is $P_g = \$4.25$, just as when we shifted the supply curve.

In this instance, although the entire tax is collected from the seller, the burden of the tax is divided equally between sellers and buyers. If the entire tax had been collected from buyers, the result would have been the same. Note that, as in Adam Smith's examples, the legal incidence of the tax does not suffice to determine the economic incidence.

In this particular case, the buyer and seller happen to share the burden equally. This is not true in all or even most cases. The general formula for the share of the tax borne by the buyer is

$$t_b = \frac{P_g^* - P^*}{T},$$

where T is the tax, P^* is the equilibrium price before imposition of the tax, and P_g^* is the new equilibrium price inclusive of the tax. The share of the seller is, of course, $1 - t_b$. Generally speaking, the buyer's share of the tax burden is an increasing function of the absolute value of the slope of the demand curve and a decreasing function of the slope of the supply curve. This proposition is easily confirmed for the case of linear supply and demand curves, as shown in Exercise 25.2.1.

EXERCISE 25.1

Let the demand equation be $P = a_0 - a_1 Q^d$, and let the supply curve be $P = b_0 + b_1 Q^s$, where $a_0, a_1, b_0,$ and b_1 are positive parameters. Express the buyer's share t_b of an excise tax as a function of a_1 and b_1.

EXERCISE 25.2

Consider a community in which demand for beer is $q = 100 - 10p$ and supply is $q = 10p$, where q is quantity (six packs per day) and p is price (dollars per six-pack). (a) What are the equilibrium price and quantity? (b) Suppose that a 50% sales tax is imposed on beer. What are the net and gross prices of beer after the tax is imposed? What share of the tax does the buyer bear?

The preceding exercises are examples of partial equilibrium analysis of tax incidence, in contrast to the general equilibrium analysis of corporate income taxes outlined in Chapter 8.

Welfare Effects of Taxes

We have seen that sales taxes typically reduce the price received by the seller and increase the price paid by buyer, imposing a burden on both parties. From society's standpoint, these burdens are partially offset by the government's gain of tax revenue. To quantify the burdens and gains and assess their relative magnitudes, we can again resort to partial equilibrium analysis. Consider a market where the equilibrium quantity and price, before tax, are Q_0 and P_0, as shown in Figure 25.3. The consumer surplus is the area under the demand curve and above the price P_0. Analogously, the gain to a producer from selling a unit is the excess of the price received over the minimum price the producer would have accepted, as shown by

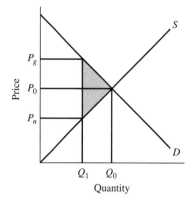

Figure 25.3 Welfare effects of a sales tax

the supply curve. The aggregate gain to producers from participating in the market, termed **producer surplus**, is represented by the area below the price P_0 and above the supply curve.

When a tax is imposed, the gross price rises to P_g and the net price falls to P_n. The tax revenue per unit sold is $t = P_g - P_n$. The quantity sold drops to Q_1. The change in the quantity sold is $\Delta Q = Q_1 - Q_0$. The burden on buyers is the loss of consumer surplus, represented by the chisel shaped area above P_0, below P_g and left of the demand curve. The loss of producer surplus is represented by the chisel-shaped area below P_0, above P_n and left of the supply curve. The government's gain in tax revenue is represented by the rectangle below P_g, above P_n and left of Q_1. The excess of the loss of consumer and producer surplus over the gain in tax revenue is thus the area of the shaded region bounded by the demand curve, the supply curve, and the vertical line at Q_1. This net loss is termed the tax's **deadweight loss** or **excess burden**. The width of the shaded region is the loss of output $Q_0 - Q_1$. The height of the shaded region grows from right to left as the demand and supply curves diverge. Moving left from (Q_0, P_0) we find that the first unit lost due to taxes would have cost nearly as much to produce as it was worth to buyers. Its loss is thus of negligible importance to society. The net loss per unit increases as the tax goes up. The height of the shaded region measured at its left edge is the net value to society of the last unit lost due to taxes. It thus represents the marginal cost to society of increasing the tax rate.

The excess burden of a tax depends on the tax rate t and the steepness of the demand and supply curves. With t constant, the steeper the curves, the smaller the excess burden. If either curve is vertical, the excess burden is eliminated. For example, if the supply curve for land is vertical, taxing land creates no excess burden. At the other extreme, taxing an item for which both demand and supply curves are nearly horizontal creates a large excess burden. Indeed, a tax greater than the distance between the vertical intercepts of the demand and supply curves would drive the quantity sold to zero.

EXERCISE 25.3

Consider a market in which the demand and supply curves are linear. The demand curve is $P = a_0 - a_1 Q$ and the supply curve is $P = b_0 + b_1 Q$, where all four parameters are non-negative. Suppose a tax t is collected on each unit sold.

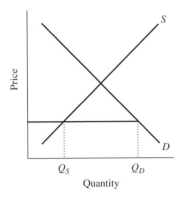

Quantity

Price

Q_S Q_D

Figure 25.4 Effect of a price ceiling set below the equilibrium price

a. Express the excess burden in terms of t, a_1, and a_2.
b. Express tax revenue in terms of t, a_0, a_1, b_0, and b_1.
c. Using your results from parts (a) and (b), express the ratio of the excess burden to the tax revenue in terms of t, a_0, and b_0.
d. Now consider a second market with linear demand and supply curves with vertical intercepts α_0 and β_0. Let τ denote the tax rate in this market. The government aims to collect a specified total tax revenue from the two markets while minimizing the total excess burden. To achieve this aim, it equates the two markets' ratios of excess burden to tax revenue. Express the resulting ratio of tax rates τ/t in terms of a_0, b_0, α_0, and β_0.

25.2.2 Price Ceilings and Floors

Governments sometimes try to alter prices for the benefit of buyers or sellers. Frequently these interventions have harmful side effects. Usually economists can devise better ways to help needy people, ways that do not cripple the market mechanism.

Intending to help buyers, governments may establish price ceilings. If these are set low enough to have any effect, they create excess demand in competitive markets, as in Figure 25.4. Buyers are frustrated because they cannot buy as much as they want at the controlled price. Goods are allocated inefficiently because some people who value the good highly are prevented from buying it from other people who value it less.[7]

In the United States the most important examples of price ceilings are rent-control laws, which exist in a number of cities. I saw one such law in operation while a student in Berkeley, California. Berkeley's rent-control law held rents below market-clearing levels. It no doubt initially benefited people who were renters when the law was adopted. But over time landlords let their properties deteriorate, resulting in many inefficiencies. For example, a friend of mine lived in a rent-controlled apartment that used to have central heating. When the furnace broke down, the landlord refused to repair it. Thereafter the tenants had to use electric space heaters, which are notoriously expensive to operate. The tenants would have been better off paying the landlord to keep the furnace in working order.

---

[7] These remarks apply to price ceilings imposed on one or few products in an otherwise largely unregulated market economy. A different analysis would be required to deal with comprehensive price ceilings used together with income policies to control inflation. Such measures have been adopted in war time by some market economies and routinely in centrally planned economies. The extent of excess demand resulting from these measures is a controversial topic (Kornai 1980; Portes and Winter 1980; Burkett 1988).

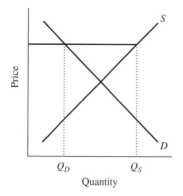

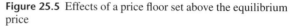

Figure 25.5 Effects of a price floor set above the equilibrium price

But that would have amounted to an illegal rent increase. As for renters who moved to the area since the adoption of rent control, they seldom shared in its intended benefits. To obtain a rent-controlled apartment, you generally have to pay an exorbitant finder's fee. Were it feasible to ditch the rent-control law and adopt an income transfer program instead, almost all economists would applaud the change.

A price floor or support is a governmental program designed to hold a product's price above its equilibrium level for the benefit of sellers. Price supports create excess supply, as shown in Figure 25.5. Depending on what is done about the excess supply, we can distinguish two kinds of price supports.

First, the government may let the frustrated sellers fend for themselves. An example of this kind of price support program is provided by minimum wage laws. In competitive markets, these laws—when they establish a minimum above the equilibrium level—create excess supply but leave the unemployed to fend for themselves. The laws result in an inefficient allocation of time: Because employment is below equilibrium, the value of leisure to workers is, at the margin, less than the value of labor to employers.[8]

Second, the government may absorb the excess supply, buying whatever the private sector doesn't. An example of this kind of program is provided by the agricultural price supports practiced on occasion in the United States and in the European Union. These programs also entail inefficiency: Because output is above equilibrium, the cost of production at the margin exceeds the value of food to consumers. A government that runs such programs has a problem disposing of the agricultural surplus. The quantities given to soup kitchens and other charities serving the poor seldom exhaust the surplus. The remainder cannot be sold on the domestic market for fear of undercutting the support price. The government usually ends up destroying the surplus, storing it indefinitely (which may amount to destroying it), or selling it abroad at a loss. Destroying food is clearly wasteful. Long-term storage is costly even if the food doesn't rot. Sale of the food abroad at subsidized prices often creates trade frictions.

Most economists feel that price supports are an inefficient way of helping their intended beneficiaries. If we want to help unskilled workers in competitive markets, it would usually be more efficient to send them to school or simply give them transfer payments than to impose a minimum wage that results in unemployment. Similarly, if we want to help low-income farmers, it would usually be more efficient to assist them in finding nonagricultural

---

[8] Recall, however, from Chapters 14 and 15 that a minimum wage in a monopsony, a monopsonistically competitive industry, or an oligopsony can raise employment, as well as wages.

employment or simply give them transfer payments rather than to impose price supports that create excess supply.

▨ **EXERCISE 25.4**

Consider a community in which the demand for milk is $q = 80 - 10p$ and the supply is $q = 10p$, where q is quantity (gallons/day) and p is price (dollars/gallon). If the government sets the minimum price of milk at $5/gallon, how much is excess supply? If the government buys the excess supply at $5/gallon, how much does the price support program cost per day?

25.3 Government Regulation of Pharmaceuticals: A Case Study

25.3.1 Health Information as a Public Good

Information has some characteristics of a public good although the medium that conveys the information may not. In particular, information is usually nonrivalrous and nonexcludable. Consider information about the efficacy and safety of drugs. Because this information is nonrivalrous, it would be wasteful for every potential consumer to do her own testing. It's more efficient for a single agency do the testing once and make the information available to everyone. But because the information is nonexcludable, it would be hard for a business to make a profit just testing and rating drugs. In most cases a business can make a profit by distributing information about drugs only if in so doing it promotes the sale of one of its products, most obviously a drug it manufactures.

A century ago, information about drugs was compiled and distributed mainly by their producers. Drug producers who wanted to stay in business for a long time had to be concerned about their credibility and reputation. This concern may have induced such manufacturers to be truthful. However, there were other drug producers who planned on making a quick profit and then getting out of the business. Without government restraint, they had strong incentives to exaggerate the benefits of their products. Indeed snake oil salesmen and patent medicine sellers generally became notorious for their exaggerations. Against this background, it made sense to many turn-of-the-century progressives for the government to review claims about drugs and prosecute drug sellers who made false claims. That sentiment was the basis for the first important drug legislation in the United States.

25.3.2 Evolution of U.S. Drug Regulations

Pure Food and Drug Act of 1906

The Food and Drug Act of 1906 prohibited fraudulent claims about the strength and purity of drugs in interstate commerce. If the FDA could prove a drug's labeling "false and fraudulent," it could prohibit its sale (FDA 1995, p. 27). Unfortunately, the law

> was generally ineffective . . . because initially only a very small staff of chemists was available for enforcement and, more significantly, because a series of court decisions put the burden on the government to demonstrate fraud in prosecuting producers making unproven claims for their products. (Grabowski and Vernon 1983, p. 2)

Considering that the probability of successful prosecution was not great, drug producers continued to affix misleading labels to their products. For example, the Massengill Company applied the label "Elixir Sulfanilamide" (sul-fa-nĭl'-a-mĭd) to what was in fact a solution of sulfanilamide in dietheylene glycol. This label was misleading because an elixir is technically an ethyl alcohol solution, not a dietheylene glycol solution. The risks (and pleasures) of alcohol were familiar but those of dietheylene glycol were unknown at the time. The latter turned out to be poisonous; in 1937 it killed 107 people, mostly children.

For many economists, who assume that consumers are rational and well informed, the appropriate response to this tragedy would have been to give the FDA the power to keep drugs off the market until their makers proved them to be accurately labeled. However, we may wonder whether accurate labeling would have been sufficient to avert this tragedy. Suppose the label had read "sulfanilamide solution" or more specifically "solution of sulfanilamide in dietheylene glycol." Would drug purchasers have been savvy enough to shun this untested product? Could parents have been trusted to keep it out of the reach of children? Lawmakers at the time apparently had misgivings about these issues; in any event, they went well beyond strengthening the requirement for accurate labeling.

Food, Drug, and Cosmetic Act of 1938

The Food, Drug, and Cosmetic Act of 1938

> required firms to submit a new drug application (NDA) to the FDA before introducing any new pharmaceutical into interstate commerce. The application had to enumerate the uses of the drug and demonstrate that it was safe under the recommended conditions. The application was automatically approved in sixty days unless the secretary of agriculture (under whose jurisdiction the FDA rested at the time) determined that it did not contain sufficient tests of drug safety. (Grabowski and Vernon 1983, p. 2)

The requirement that drugs be "safe" proved very difficult to interpret. No drug is absolutely safe for absolutely everyone. You could choke to death on an aspirin. More seriously, many drugs might have severe side effects in people who have unusual allergies or take other medicines. Unfortunately, the 1938 law said nothing about what level of risk is acceptable. Thirteen years were to pass before lawmakers attempted to clarify the meaning of safety.

Durham-Humphrey Amendment of 1951

Noting that some drugs that are unsafe for self-medication may be used more safely under a doctor's supervision, the Durham-Humphrey amendment established the distinction between prescription drugs and over-the-counter (OTC) drugs. Useful as this distinction was, the FDA was still left to grapple with the difficult problem of determining what level of risk might be termed safe.

Kefauver-Harris Drug Amendments of 1962

In the early 1960s in western Europe, women who had taken the sedative thalidomide gave birth to thousands of malformed babies. The United States was spared this tragedy because the drug never got FDA approval. Nonetheless, Congress reacted by tightening drug laws. The Kefauver-Harris amendments had three principal provisions:

1. The amendments "repealed the automatic approval of an NDA within 60 days . . . . The FDA now had to take affirmative action on an NDA for the drug to enter the marketplace" (Grabowski and Vernon 1983, p. 4).
2. They "required firms to provide substantial evidence of a new drug's efficacy," as well as its safety (Grabowski and Vernon 1983, p. 3).

The FDA has interpreted this to mean that firms should demonstrate that a drug's benefits outweigh its risks (Farley, 1995). Consider a simple example in which a patient either gets well or dies, with no messy intermediate possibilities like varying degrees of morbidity or disability. Suppose the patient is at risk of dying from either the illness or the medicines. On the basis of controlled experiments, we might construct a table like the following:

	Probability of death from disease	Probability of death from medicine
Control group	P_1	P_2
Treated group	P_3	P_4

If $P_1 + P_2 > P_3 + P_4$, we might say that the risk under the new treatment is less than under the old (control) regime—in other words, for the new treatment, the benefits exceed the risks. In this case, the new drug should be approved. When the adverse outcomes under control and treatment conditions are different—say, paralysis and blindness—they must somehow be expressed in comparable terms such as loss of utility.

3. The amendments set up a two-stage process for demonstrating safety and efficacy. First, the firm must test the drug on animals. If the firm believes these preliminary tests are promising, it may file a so-called investigational new drug (IND) application. If the FDA approves the IND, then the firm may proceed to testing the drug on human volunteers. The experimental design favored by the FDA involves a double blind: Neither the physicians nor the patients should know which group of patients is receiving the experimental treatment and which is getting the control treatment. If the firm believes that the results are encouraging, it may submit them to the FDA in the form of a NDA. When and if the NDA is approved, the firm may market the drug.

The Kefauver-Harris amendments substantially increased the time and money firms had to expend to obtain permission to market a new drug. We can think of the amendments as raising the quality standard for drugs. Increased quality standards generally cause both supply and demand curves to shift up. Price predictably rises. What happens to the quantity is less certain. In the case of drugs for rare diseases, it turned out that the upward shift in the supply curve was often more than in the demand curve. In some cases, the two curves no longer intersected in the positive quadrant. In other words, firms no longer found it profitable to bring these drugs for rare illnesses to market. These abandoned drugs are called **orphans**. It's hard for economists to justify safety regulations that make potentially useful drugs unavailable. "When the disease is quite rare, the number of patients who might be harmed by the side effects of the drug is also quite small, hence presumably reducing society's concerns about harmful side effects" (Phelps 1992, p. 458).

EXERCISE 25.5

Consider a group of patients whose life expectancy under current medical treatment is 5 years. Suppose the FDA is reviewing an application to market a new drug. Experiments indicate that 70% of patients treated with the new drug can expect to live 10 years but 30% die immediately because of to an unpredictable allergic reaction. Would a risk-neutral individual say that the benefits of this drug outweigh the risks?

Orphan Drug Act of 1983

"To foster orphan product development, this law [Orphan Drug Act of 1983] allows drug companies to take tax deductions for about three-quarters of the cost of their clinical studies. Firms also are given exclusive marketing rights for seven years for any orphan products that are approved" (FDA 1995, p. 27). The former provision in effect subsidizes treatment of rare diseases. Perhaps it can be rationalized as part of the government-provided safety net for unlucky citizens. The latter provision is important for older drugs on which patents may have expired.

The problem of patent expirations has extended beyond drugs for rare illnesses. Under U.S. law, a patent holder or her licensees had the exclusive right to produce the patented product for 17 years.[9] However, under the 1962 amendments, "a drug company could not begin testing the drug until after the patent was filed, so that the 'effective' patent life was shortened by the time necessary to obtain FDA marketing approval. This approval took so long that the effective patent life was shortened" to about 8 years (Phelps 1992, p. 460). That reduced the present value of anticipated revenue. For example, suppose the firm anticipated revenues of $3 million a year during the life of the patent and $1 million a year thereafter, for a total of 30 years. If the discount rate is 0.1, then the present value with a 17-year patent is

$$\sum_{t=1}^{17} \frac{3}{1.1^t} + \sum_{t=18}^{30} \frac{1}{1.1^t} = 25.5.$$

If the effective patent life is shortened to 8 years, the present value of anticipated revenue is just

$$\sum_{t=1}^{8} \frac{3}{1.1^t} + \sum_{t=9}^{30} \frac{1}{1.1^t} = 20.1.$$

If the cost of developing and manufacturing the drug were estimated at, say, $22 million, the drug would be worth marketing with a 17-year patent but not with an 8-year patent.

Drug Price Competition and Patent Term Restoration Act of 1984

The Drug Price Competition and Patent Term Restoration Act of 1984, also known as the Hatch-Waxman Act, allows an extension of patents by up to 5 years to make up for time lost in testing. Although this law restores the profitability of marketing drugs with long testing periods, it leaves untouched another problem with prolonged testing, namely, that people can die while waiting for a drug to be tested and approved. This has been a particularly prominent concern among people who are HIV positive.

Prescription Drug User Fee Act of 1992

To speed up the drug approval process, the FDA needed a bigger staff. Enlarging the staff in the face of federal budget deficits was tricky. The solution provided by the Prescription Drug User Fee Act of 1992 was to finance an expansion of the FDA staff by making drug

---

[9] Although patents lasted 17 years during the period under discussion, they now last 20 years, under the terms of the 1995 World Trade Organization treaty (Schweitzer 1997).

manufacturers "pay user fees for certain new drug applications and supplements, an annual establishment fee, and annual product fees" (FDA 1995, p. 27).[10] With the help of its expanded staff, the FDA succeeded in 1992–97 in cutting by about 40% the time that firms must wait to get their new drug applications reviewed.

Accelerated review of new drug applications has not been an unmixed blessing. It carries the risk that more unsafe drugs may be approved. Indeed, statistical analysis indicates that accelerated review is associated with more adverse drug reactions that end in hospitalization or death (Olson 2002).

Damage done by mistaken approval of unsafe drugs might be limited if such errors were quickly rectified. However, public confidence in the FDA's ability to promptly correct its errors was shaken by the case of Vioxx, a painkiller suspected to have damaged the hearts of 100,000 American users between its approval in 1999 and its withdrawal from the market in 2004 (*The Economist*, November 25, 2004). The root of the problem appears to be that the 1992 act and ensuing budget cuts made the FDA increasingly dependent for financing on the drug companies it is supposed to regulate (Harris 2004). Under these conditions, according to a senior FDA scientist, the agency began treating drug makers as its clients, leaving the public "virtually defenseless"(Graham 2004, p. 4).

▓ EXERCISE 25.6

Consider a pharmaceutical company that tries to market its products in both the United States and the European Union. It is uncertain whether a new drug will be approved by the FDA and its European counterparts. The firm believes that the probability of approval is 0.7 in the United States and 0.8 in Europe. The present value of revenue from the drug would be $9 million if it were to be approved in the United States alone, $8 million if approved in Europe alone, $20 million if approved in both markets, and zero if approved in neither market. What is the *expected* present value of revenue from the drug?

25.4 Summary

1. Governments have important economic functions even where markets constitute the basic resource allocation mechanism. How best to perform some such functions—e.g., redistirbuting income and correcting externalities—remains controversial.
2. To carry out their functions, governments have to levy taxes and impose regulations. Economists try to measure the burdens that various forms of taxation and regulation impose, with the hope of devising taxes and regulations that are no more burdensome than necessary.
3. Supply and demand analysis illuminates the economic incidence of taxes. Regardless of whether a sales tax is collected from the seller or the buyer, the burden is divided among buyers and sellers in a manner determined by the slopes of the demand and supply curves. Generally, the buyers' share of the tax burden is an increasing function of the absolute value of the slope of the demand curve and a decreasing function of the slope of the supply curve. The burden of sales taxes on consumers is often measured in terms of loss of consumer surplus.

---

[10] That act expired on September 30, 1997, but was amended and extended through September 30, 2007, by the FDA Modernization Act of 1997 and the PDUF Amendments of 2002.

4. Government programs are usually more efficient if they work through the market rather than against it. Price ceilings and floors usually create excess demand or supply and frustrate sellers or buyers. Simple income transfers usually constitute a more efficient way to help the poor.

5. The case of pharmaceutical regulation illustrates ideas about public goods and policy making under uncertainty.

25.5 Solutions to Exercises

25.1. Before the tax is imposed the equilibrium is given by $a_0 - a_1Q^* = b_0 + b_1Q^*$ or $Q^* = \frac{a_0-b_0}{a_1+b_1}$. Substituting this value for Q^* into the demand equation, we find that $P^* = a_0 - a_1\left(\frac{a_0-b_0}{a_1+b_1}\right)$. Now suppose there is a tax T on each unit sold. If we think of the tax as shifting the supply curve, we can write the demand curve as $P_g = a_0 - a_1Q^d$ and the supply curve as $P_g = b_0 + b_1Q^s + T$. The new equilibrium is given by $a_0 - a_1Q^* = b_0 + b_1Q^* + T$. It follows that the new equilibrium price, inclusive of tax, is $P^*_g = a_0 - a_1\left(\frac{a_0-b_0-T}{a_1+b_1}\right)$. Now we find that $t_b = \frac{P^*_g-P^*}{T} = \frac{a_1}{a_1+b_1}$.

25.2. (a) Equating the quantities demanded and supplied, we find that the price is $\frac{100}{10+10} = 5$. Substituting 5 for p in either the demand curve or the supply curve, we find that the quantity is 50.

(b) If p is the net price, the gross price is $1.5p$. Suppliers care about the former, buyers about the latter. Thus the equilibrium condition is $10p = 100 - 10(1.5p)$. This condition implies that the net price is 4 and hence that the gross price is $4(1.5) = 6$. Substituting 4 for the net price in either the demand or supply curve, we find that quantity is 40. The buyers' share of the tax is $(6 - 5)/2 = 1/2$.

25.3. (a) Because the demand and supply curves are linear, the region representing excess burden is a triangle, the area of which is $-.5t\Delta Q$. The demand curve implies that the tax raises the price paid by the buyer by $P_g - P_0 = -a_1\Delta Q$. The supply curve implies that the tax lowers the price received by the seller by $P_0 - P_n = -b_1\Delta Q$. Adding these equations, we see that the tax per unit is $t = P_g - P_n = -(a_1+b_1)\Delta Q$, which implies that $\Delta Q = -t/(a_1 + b_1)$. Thus the excess burden is $.5t^2/(a_1 + b_1)$.

(b) Tax revenue is tQ_1. To find an expression for Q_1 in terms of the parameters and t, we note that $t = P_g - P_n = a_0 - b_0 - (a_1 + b_1)Q_1$, which implies that $Q_1 = (a_0 - b_0 - t)/(a_1 + b_1)$. Thus tax revenue is $t(a_0 - b_0 - t)/(a_1 + b_1)$.

(c) The ratio of excess burden to tax revenue is $.5t/(a_0 - b_0 - t)$.

(d) Equating the ratios of excess burden to tax revenue, we get $.5t/(a_0 - b_0 - t) = .5\tau/(\alpha_0 - \beta_0 - \tau)$, which implies $\tau/t = (\alpha_0 - \beta_0)/(a_0 - b_0)$. In words, the ratio of tax rates equals the ratio of differences between vertical intercepts of demand and supply curves.

25.4. Excess supply is $10(5) - [80 - 10(5)] = 20$. The program costs the government $20(5) = \$100$ per day.

25.5. A risk-neutral individual would compare the expected values of remaining years of life under the two treatments. The expected value under the existing treatment is 5 years, whereas that under the new treatment is $0.7(10) = 7$. A risk-neutral individual would thus agree that the benefits of the new treatment outweigh the risks.

25.6. The expected present value is $(0.7)(1 - 0.8)9 + (1 - 0.7)(0.8)8 + (0.7)(0.8)20 = 1.26 + 1.92 + 11.2 = 14.38$.

25.6 Problems

1. Demand for gasoline at Podunk Petrol Plaza is $q = 1000 - 400p$, where q is quantity (gallons/day) and p is price ($/gallon). Supply is $q = 600p$.

   a. What are the equilibrium price and quantity?

   b. Calculate the Marshallian consumer surplus.

   c. A 50% sales tax is imposed on gasoline. What are the net and gross prices after the tax is imposed? What share of the tax falls on the buyers?

   d. What is the Marshallian consumer surplus after the tax is imposed?

2. Suppose that in France the demand for snails is $p = 40 - 0.01q$, where p is price (euros/kilogram) and q is quantity (kilograms per day). Supply is $p = .01q$.

   a. What are the equilibrium price and quantity?

   b. Calculate the Marshallian consumer surplus.

   c. Suppose the government sets the price of snails at 30 euros/kg. How much excess supply will result? If the government buys up the excess supply at 30 euros/kg, how much will it spend?

   d. Calculate the Marshallian consumer surplus after the government sets the price at 30 euros/kg.

3. Since 1962, pharmaceutical companies seeking FDA approval for a new drug have been required by law to show that it is "safe" and "effective." The FDA has interpreted this requirement to mean that the drug's benefits should outweigh its risks. Consider a disease whose only cost is time lost from work. At present, let us suppose, everyone who gets the disease misses 10 days of work. A new drug would reduce the loss to 5 days with probability 0.9. Unfortunately, an unpredictable allergic reaction to the drug could cause a patient to lose a total of 30 days' work with probability 0.1. What is the expected loss of work days for a person treated with the new drug? If you were risk-neutral, would you say that the benefits of the new drug outweigh its risks?

4. Since 1992, drawing on user fees, the FDA has increased its staff and expedited its drug approval process. From the standpoint of a drug producer, the user fee is a cost but quicker approval is a benefit. Suppose that quicker review extends the effective life of a drug patent from 8 to 12 years. A firm expects to make $3 million a year while the drug is under patent but only $1 million a year after the patent expires. The firm expects to sell the drug for a total of 20 years. Suppose the interest rate is 10 percent. How much would the present value of the drug be increased by extending its effective patent from 8 to 12 years? What is the largest user fee that the firm would be willing to pay to get the quicker review?

25.7 Appendix: Experiment with Social Choice of Income Distributions

25.7.1 Background (to be read before the experiment)

This experiment relates to ideas about social choice of income distribution, as covered in Subsection 25.1.2. The experiment has three stages. In the first stage, we vote on an initial income distribution and then draw lots to determine where individuals fall in the chosen distribution. Individuals will retain these positions throughout the remainder of the experiment. In the second stage, we vote on income redistribution. In the third stage, individuals begin to use their income to influence political decisions. In this stage—time permitting—we will have several rounds. In each round individuals divide their income

Table 25.1 Income distributions

Dist'n	Income level y_i for quintile $i =$					$\sum_{i=1}^{5} y_i^n$ for $n =$				
	1	2	3	4	5	1	$\frac{3}{4}$	$\frac{1}{2}$	$\frac{1}{4}$	Min.
A	4	5	6	7	11	33	20.35	12.65	7.92	4
B	3	6	7	8	12	36	21.62	13.12	8.05	3
C	2	4	8	10	14	38	22.13	13.15	8.00	2
D	1	3	5	12	19	40	22.17	12.80	7.76	1
E	0	2	4	11	24	41	21.39	11.63	6.64	0

between consumption and political donations. Proposals to change the income distribution win if supported by more than half of all political donations. You earn extra-credit points based on your income minus your political donations.[11]

In all stages we will be choosing among five income distributions, shown in Table 25.1. In order of increasing inequality, the distributions are A, B, C, D, and E. The population (class) will be divided into five income groups of equal size. In order of increasing income, these groups are quintiles 1, 2, 3, 4, and 5.

25.7.2 Stage 1

You should rank the distributions based on your own attitude toward risk. You may wish to consult the last five columns of the table. A risk-neutral individual, wanting to maximize the sum of incomes, can find useful information in the column labeled $n = 1$. This column indicates that total income increases as we move down the list of distributions from A to E. Thus risk-neutral and risk-seeking individuals will prefer distribution E. Individuals who are risk-averse to various degrees will find useful information in the last four columns. For utility functions of the form $u = y^n$, concavity and risk aversion increase as n decreases. For $n = \frac{3}{4}, \frac{1}{2}$, and $\frac{1}{4}$, expected utility is maximized by distributions D, C, and B, respectively. An extremely risk-averse individual, wanting to maximize the income of the poorest quintile, will find the relevant information in the last column, which reminds us that as we move down the list of distributions, income in the poorest quintile falls. Thus an extremely risk-averse individual will prefer distribution A.

We will vote on distributions in a pairwise fashion. That is, we will vote on A vs. B then C vs. the winner of the first match, . . . , and then E vs. the winner of the previous match. To check for transitivity, we can also vote on previously rejected distributions vs. the winner of the last match. Once a distribution is chosen, we will draw lots to determine who falls in each of the five income groups.

Record the selected distribution here: ———. After lots have been drawn as directed by your instructor, record your quintile here: ———. Given the distribution and quintile you have just recorded, use Table 25.1 to look up your income for Stage 1 and record it on the first line of Table 25.2. On this line, consumption equals income because donations are zero. However, on the next four lines, consumption will equal income less donations.

---

[11] Potential income minus donations is at most $24 \times (2 + r)$, where r is the number of rounds in the third stage. Extra-credit points will be in the interval [0, 10], calculated as $10(\text{income} - \text{donations})/[24 \times (2 + r)]$.

Table 25.2 Income and expenditure record.

	Income	Donations	Consumption
Stage 1		0	
Stage 2			
Stage 3 Round 1			
Stage 3 Round 2			
Stage 3 Round 3		0	
Total consumption in all stages			

25.7.3 Stage 2

Now that all individuals know the quintiles to which they belong, we will vote on changing from the distribution selected in Stage 1 to one of the other four. Again, the voting will be pairwise. Table 25.1 indicates that rational and self-interested members of quintiles 1, 2, 3, 4, and 5 will prefer distributions A, B, C, D, and E, respectively. Can you predict which distribution will be selected?

Record the distribution selected in Stage 2 here: ————. Given this distribution and your (unchanged) quintile, find your income in Table 25.1 and record it on the second line of Table 25.2. Now decide how much if any of your current (Stage 2) income you want set aside for political donations in Stage 3. (Your donations will certainly reduce your current consumption, but they may substantially raise your future income and consumption.) Record your donation in the middle column of the second line in Table 25.2. Now subtract the donation from the income to get consumption, and record that in the last column, second line.

25.7.4 Stage 3

In each round of this stage, individuals decide how to allocate funds set aside (in the previous stage or round) for political action guided by their ranking of distributions. For example, individuals in quintile 4 may want to contribute to political action that would support change consistent with the ranking $A \prec B \prec C \prec E \prec D$. Instead of counting votes, as we did in the first two stages, we will now count donations. A proposal to replace one distribution with another will be adopted whenever the total donations supporting the proposal exceed those opposing it. Suppose, for example, that in Stage 2 we adopted distribution C. A proposal to change from C to D would pass in Stage 3 if the donations that support changing to D exceed those that favor retaining C.

Within any one round, you make a single donation (which could be zero), which determines your political influence on all decisions taken during the round.

To facilitate counting the donations on either side of each vote, your instructor will probably distribute forms on which you can record your donations and preferences. You can indicate your preference order by using the symbol $\prec$.

In the last round there is no reason to set aside income for future political action. Thus income received in the last round should be fully consumed.

Record the distributions selected by the class in Stage 3 on the following lines:

Round 1 ———
Round 2 ———
Round 3 ———

Add up your consumption in the last column of Table 25.2. If you want extra-credit points, remember to give your instructor a record of your consumption.

25.7.5 Analysis of Experiment

Did the result in Stage 1 confirm the argument (associated with John Rawls) that people who do not know their position in an income distribution would all favor the distribution that maximizes the income of the poorest individual? If not, why do you think some people favored another distribution?

Suppose all the voters had transitive preferences. Could the voting procedure in Stage 1 nonetheless produce cycles in which, for example, A is replaced by B, B by C, C by D, D by E, and E by A? Can you think of a condition on individual preferences that would rule out such cycles?

In Stage 2, which quintile got its preferred distribution? Why couldn't another quintile win a vote to change the distribution to suit itself?

Did the political actions in Stage 3 make the distribution more or less egalitarian than those adopted in Stages 1 and 2? Why? Did the distribution adopted in Round 1 persist in Rounds 2 and 3? Why or why not?

Glossary

Terms in *slanted font* are defined elsewhere in this glossary. Entries ending with a sideways wink and grin—;)—may be taken with a grain of salt.

acceptance rule: In *prospect theory*, the proposition that decision makers are prone to accept any reasonable formulation of a choice problem rather than generating alternative representations. Acceptance explains why different formulations of the same problem often yield different preferences.

addition law: The proposition in probability theory that if events E_1 and E_2 are *exclusive*, then the probability that E_1 or E_2 occurs is the sum of the probability that E_1 occurs and the probability that E_2 occurs.

additive intertemporal utility function: An intertemporal *utility* function that can be written as a sum of discounted instantaneous utilities, $U = u(c_0) + u(c_1)\delta(1) + u(c_2) \delta(2) + \cdots$, where $u(c_t)$ is the instantaneous utility function evaluated at c_t and $\delta(t)$ is the *discount function* evaluated at t.

Allais's paradox: Violations of the *cancellation axiom*, first reported by Maurice Allais in 1953.

anchoring and adjustment: In *prospect theory*, a rule of thumb people (rashly) use to estimate probabilities. Using this rule of thumb, people first choose a preliminary estimate—an anchor—and then adjust it in accordance with whatever additional information they have that appears relevant. This procedure often leads to biased estimates, for two reasons. First, the initial anchor may be poorly chosen, and second, even when it is reasonable, people adjust too little from it.

auctioneer: "The man who proclaims with a hammer that he has picked a pocket with his tongue" (Bierce 1911, p. 29) ;)

autarky: The absence of international trade.

availability heuristic: In *prospect theory*, a rule of thumb people (rashly) use for assessing frequencies. Users of this heuristic estimate the frequency of an event, or class of events, by the ease with which they can summon examples from memory.

Bayes's theorem: A proposition in probability theory, stating that for any two events A and B,

$$P(B|A) = \frac{P(A|B)P(B)}{P(A)},$$

where $P(\cdot)$ is a marginal probability and $P(\cdot|\cdot)$ is the conditional probability of the first argument given the second. This result is named for Thomas Bayes (1702–61), who first noted it.

budget constraint: A consumer's budget constraint is the set (or the equation that defines this set) of *consumption bundles* that cost just as much as the consumer has to spend.

cancellation axiom: An assumption of expected utility theory, according to which circumstances or states of the world that yield the same outcome for each choice cancel out of a decision problem. For example, suppose we have to choose a plan for a party. Plan 1 involves going boating if the weather is good and having an indoor buffet if the weather is bad. Plan 2 involves playing volleyball if the weather is good and having an indoor buffet if the weather is bad. If the weather is bad, both plans call for an indoor buffet. Hence under the cancellation axiom, our choice between plans should depend solely on what they entail if the weather is good, that is, solely on whether we prefer boating or volleyball. Formally speaking, the cancellation axiom asserts that if we prefer outcome A to B, then we should prefer a lottery that yields A with probability p and C with probability $1 - p$ to a lottery that yields B with probability p and C with probability $1 - p$, for any C and any $p > 0$.

capital: Assets created by *investment* and usable in production. **Physical** capital consists of equipment and structures. **Human** capital consists of knowledge and skills.

capital gains: Increases in wealth due to increases in asset prices.

certainty effect: An instance of *Allais's paradox* that involves choice of a certain prize over an alternative offering only uncertain prospects.

circular reference: *Reference, circular* ;)

coherent: Probability judgments are coherent if they are consistent with the *addition* and *multiplication* laws of probability and the rule that all probabilities are numbers between 0 and 1. A person who bets on the basis of probability judgments that are not coherent can fall victim to a *Dutch book*.

commitment devices: Arrangements people make to prevent themselves from squandering savings in moments of weakness, for example, investment in 401(k) retirement saving plans.

comparative advantage: A production unit has a comparative advantage in a good if it can produce the good at lower opportunity cost than other units.

compensating differentials: Wage differences offsetting nonpecuniary characteristics of jobs.

complements: A pair of goods such that an increase in the price of one tends to reduce demand for the other.

completeness assumption: The assumption that consumers can rank all *consumption bundles*.

compound lottery: A lottery with two or more stages, whose outcomes are themselves lotteries except in the final stage—for example, a two-stage lottery in whose first stage you can win either a ticket in lottery A or a ticket in lottery B, with lottery A yielding either \$10 or nothing and lottery B yielding either \$20 or \$5.

composite good: A basket or collection of goods whose prices are constant or changing proportionately to each other. If the prices are constant, the composite good can be conveniently measured in units costing \$1.

consistent intertemporal preferences: See *preferences*.

constant cost industries: Industries whose long-run average cost curves are horizontal.

consumer surplus: Consumers' gains from their purchases. The most commonly used such measure is one devised by Alfred Marshall, who regarded buyers' gains from a transaction as the difference between the most they would have been willing to pay and what they actually paid. Referring to a diagram with quantity on the horizontal axis and price on the vertical axis, we can calculate Marshallian consumer surplus as the area beneath the demand curve and above the price line.

consumption bundle: An ordered set of quantities of consumer goods, for example, (4 apples, 6 bananas, 1 canteen,..., 2 zippers).

contestable market: A market in which entry and exit are virtually costless.

contract curve: The segment of the *Pareto set* lying between specified indifference curves for two consumers.

contrarian: An investor who tries to profit by buying when *noise traders* are selling and selling when they are buying.

corner solution: An ordered set of quantities, including at least one zero, that solves an optimization problem. It is contrasted to an *interior solution*.

corporation: "An ingenious device for obtaining individual profit without individual responsibility" (Bierce 1911, p. 57) ;)

cost: The cost of producing something is the value of the cheapest bundle of inputs from which it can be made under specified conditions. The inputs in question include the entrepreneur's time, as well as inputs purchased from others. The conditions to be specified include the production function, the input prices, and which inputs are variable. Fixed costs are associated with *fixed inputs*. **Variable** costs are associated with *variable inputs*. The **total** cost of a specified quantity of output includes both fixed and variable costs. **Average** cost is total cost divided by output. The **marginal** cost of additional output is the change in total cost divided by the associated change in output.

credentials competition: Competition for academic degrees as signals of intelligence, perseverance, or other personal characteristics valued by employers.

decision weight: In *prospect theory*, the importance a decision maker attaches to a probability.

decreasing cost industry: An industry with a negatively sloped long-run average cost curve.

demand curve: A curve showing how the quantity of a good demanded depends on the price of the good, with other variables that could affect the quantity demanded held constant. Loosely speaking, an equation or table providing the same information.

derivative security: An asset whose value derives from that of some other asset. Derivatives include *futures contracts* and *options*.

dictator game: A game in which one player freely divides money between herself and another player.

discount function: A function of the time separating a decision from its consequences that assigns a weight to those consequences in an intertemporal *utility* function. For example, an **exponential** discount function is e^{-rt}, where r is a discount rate and t is the time separating decision from consequence.

dividends: A share of corporate profits paid to stockholders.

dominance axiom: An assumption of expected utility theory, according to which a rational individual offered a choice among lotteries chooses the *dominant lottery* if one exists.

dominant lottery: One lottery is said to dominate another if for each possible outcome the probability of doing that well or better is at least as high in the first lottery as in the second and strictly greater for at least one outcome.

dominant strategy: In game theory, a dominant strategy for a player is a strategy that produces the best results for that player regardless of the strategy chosen by his opponent.

duopoly: An market structure with just two sellers.

Dutch book: A set of bets that entail a sure loss. A Dutch book can be made against anyone who bets on that basis of probability judgments that are not *coherent*.

econometrics: A field of economics devoted to applying mathematical and statistical methods to answer economic questions.

economies of scale: Reductions in average *cost* associated with increases in output.

Edgeworth production box: A rectangular figure with two inputs measured along the axes, in opposite directions, for two industries, usually with *isoquants* for the two industries shown in the interior.

elasticity: A percentage change in one variable divided by a percentage change in another variable supposed to cause the change in the first variable. For example, the price elasticity of demand (or supply) is the percentage change in the quantity demanded (or supplied) divided by the percentage change in the price.

endogenous: Economic theorists say a variable is endogenous in a model if its values are determined within the model. These variables are contrasted to exogenous variables, whose values are taken as given. (A somewhat different usage of the terms prevails in *econometrics*.)

endowment effect: A tendency for people who have been given a good to value it more highly than do those who lack the good.

equilibrium: A state of affairs that can persist because individuals have no incentives to change their behavior.

equilibrium price: A price that persists until demand or supply shifts. Often this is a *market-clearing price*.

equities: Common stocks. Titles to partial ownership of a *corporation*, held in expectation of dividends and/or capital gains.

equity premium puzzle: A question about why some investors are willing to devote large portions of their portfolios to bonds despite the fact that the average annual rate of return on equity has been several times greater than that on bonds.

equivalence axiom: An assumption of expected utility theory, according to which a *compound lottery* is just as attractive as the simple lottery that would result from multiplication of probabilities in a sequence leading to a prize.

excess volatility hypothesis: A claim that stock prices sometimes are temporarily depressed by the irrational panics of *noise traders* and at other times boosted by their irrational optimism.

excludable: A good or service is excludable if people who have not paid for it can be excluded from enjoying it. Ship cabins are excludable; lighthouse services are not.

exclusive events: Events of which one at most can occur.

expectation: In statistics, the expectation of a random variable is its *mean* or *expected value*. In informal economics, an expectation is a forecast or prediction. The two meanings coincide in economic analysis based on the *rational expectations hypothesis*.

expected utility: If a decision can result in n different levels of *utility* u_i, then the expected utility associated with the decision is $\sum_{i=1}^{n} p_i u_i$. This is a weighted average of utility levels, with the weights being probabilities.

expected value: *Mean.*

extensive form: A representation of a game by a tree diagram or similar means, emphasizing the sequence in which players gain information and take actions.

externality: A cost or benefit of an action, borne by someone other than the individual who undertook the action, and transmitted directly rather than through price changes. Costs of this kind are **negative** externalities; benefits of this kind are **positive** externalities.

fixed-income security: A financial asset that pays a prespecified stream of income. For example, a bond usually pays its owner a fixed amount of interest each year. Bonds are the most important example of fixed-income securities, but annuities and preferred stock could also be considered to be fixed-income securities.

futures contract: an agreement to buy or sell a fixed quantity of a particular asset for delivery at a fixed future date at a fixed price.

general equilibrium analysis: Analysis of a set of interacting markets.

Giffen good: An *inferior good* with a positively sloped *demand curve.*

income effect: A change in the quantity demanded due to changes in real income or utility, with relative prices held constant.

increasing-cost industry: An industry with a positively sloped long-run average cost curve.

index fund: A passively managed fund that mimics the behavior of a market average like the Standard and Poors 500 or the Wilshire 5000.

indifference curve: A set of *consumption bundles* among which a consumer is indifferent.

indifference map: A set of *indifference curves* for a single individual or a group of individuals with identical preferences.

industrial revelation: "The discovery (made by all the rich men in England at once) that women and children could work for 25 hours a day in factories without many of them dying or becoming excessively deformed. This . . . completely changed the faces of the North of England" (Sellar and Yeatman 1931, pp. 92–93) ;)

inferior good: A good for which demand falls as per capita income rises.

input: Something used in production. Some inputs are used up in the production process, for example, fuels and materials such as cement and steel. Other inputs are durable, such as, land, workers, buildings, and equipment. An input is **variable** or **fixed** depending on whether the quantity of it used in production can or cannot be changed within a specified period.

interest rate: A price for the use of money for a period of time.

interior solution: An ordered set of positive quantities that solves an optimization problem, such as choosing the minimum-cost bundle of inputs to produce a specified output or choosing the utility-maximizing bundle of goods subject to a budget constraint. It is contrasted to a *corner solution.*

investment: An allocation of resources to acquire an asset in hopes of increasing wealth. **Real** investments are purchases or creation of real assets like land, buildings, equipment, livestock, gold, or wheat. **Financial** investments are purchases of financial assets—paper claims to some of the income generated by use of real assets.

irrelevant alternative: An option that is inferior to others and hence should be rejected. *Rational agents* do not allow the presence of an irrelevant alternative to influence their choice among the remaining alternatives.

isoquant: A set of input combinations that all yield the same output. For example, if the inputs are K and L, the isoquant corresponding to a particular level of output $\bar{Q}$ is $\{(K, L) : Q(K, L) = \bar{Q}\}$. A collection of isoquants based on the same production function is called an **isoquant map**.

labor: "One of the processes by which A acquires property for B" (Bierce 1911, p. 182) ;)

law of supply and demand: The claim that market prices tend to move toward their *equilibrium* levels.

learning by doing: Productivity gains in production of a good, attributed to cumulative experience in producing it, rather than to separate research and development.

long run: A period sufficient to alter the amounts of all *inputs*.

loss aversion: A disinclination to accept a small loss of any good without large compensation in terms of other goods. A tendency to take losses more seriously than gains of equal size.

marginal product of capital: The ratio of the increase in output to the increase in capital input when other inputs are held constant. In mathematical terms, this is the first partial derivative of output with respect to capital.

marginal product of labor: The ratio of the increase in output to the increase in labor input when other inputs are held constant. In mathematical terms, this is the first partial derivative of output with respect to labor.

marginal rate of substitution: In consumer theory, the quantity of a good a consumer is just willing to exchange for a unit of another good. In the two-dimensional case, the marginal rate of substitution of the good on the horizontal axis for the good on the vertical axis at any point is the absolute value of the slope of the *indifference curve* passing through the point. In production theory, the rate at which one input can be exchanged for another without altering total output. The absolute value of the slope of an *isoquant* at a specified point in input space.

marginal rate of transformation: The amount by which output of one good must be reduced in order to increase output of another good by one unit. In other words, the absolute value of the slope of a *production possibilities curve*.

market-clearing price: A price at which the quantities demanded and supplied are equal.

Marshallian money: *Composite good.*

mean: The mean of a discrete random variable that takes values x_1, x_2, ..., x_n with probabilities p_1, p_2, ..., p_n is $p_1 x_1 + p_2 x_2 + \cdots + p_n x_n$.

mixed strategy: A lottery over *pure strategies*.

monopolistic competition: A market structure defined by two characteristics: (1) the existence of numerous firms each producing a product that is a close, but imperfect, *substitute* for the products of other firms and (2) free entry and exit of firms.

monopoly: An industry in which there is a single seller of a good with no close substitute. A **natural** monopoly is an industry in which *economies of scale* enable a large firm to undersell any smaller firm.

mpk: *Marginal product of capital.*

mpl: *Marginal product of labor.*

mr: *Marginal revenue.*

mrs: *Marginal rate of substitution.*

mrt: *Marginal rate of transformation.*

myopia: In finance, a tendency to evaluate prospects exclusively over short periods.

multiplication law: The proposition in probability theory that, for any two events E_1 and E_2, the joint probability of E_1 and E_2 equals the marginal probability of one event times the conditional probability of the other given the first. Symbolically expressed, $p(E_1 \text{ and } E_2) = p(E_1) p(E_2 | E_1)$.

Nash equilibrium: A combination of strategies such that no player has an incentive to change strategy given the strategies of the other players.

noise trader: A person whose decisions to buy and sell assets are based in part on irrational factors.

nonsatiation assumption: In consumer theory, the assumption that other things being equal, consumers prefer more of any good to less of it.

normal form: A representation of a game in terms of combinations of the players' strategies and the resulting outcomes.

normal good: A good for which demand increases with per capita income.

oligopoly: A market structure in which there are only a few important sellers. These few sellers take one another's actions into account when making price and output decisions.

opportunity cost: The opportunity cost of a choice is the value of the best alternative choice.

opportunity set: A consumer's opportunity set consists of all the *consumption bundles* that cost no more than the consumer can spend.

option: An opportunity to take a certain action without an obligation to do so. In finance, an option is a type of *derivative security* that gives its owner the right to buy or sell an asset at a stipulated price and time.

orphan drug: A pharmaceutical product that is not offered for sale, usually because costs of testing, production, and marketing are expected to exceed revenue.

Pareto efficient allocation: *Pareto optimal allocation.*

Pareto optimal allocation: An allocation such that each individual is as well satisfied as possible given others' levels of satisfaction.

Pareto set: The set of Pareto optimal allocations.

partial equilibrium analysis: Analysis of one market at time, ignoring possible interactions among markets.

pecuniary diseconomy: An increase in the prices of an industry's inputs due to an increase in this industry's demand for these inputs.

pecuniary economy: A decrease in the prices of an industry's input due to an increase in this industry's demand for these inputs.

portfolio: An investor's collection of assets and liabilities.

ppc: *Production possibilities curve.*

ppf: *Production possibilities frontier.*

preference: A binary relation among *consumption bundles*, presumed to explain choice between feasible alternatives. A consumer who chooses bundle A over another feasible bundle B is said to have revealed a preference for A over B, often written as $A \succ B$. A **preference ordering** is a ranking of *consumption bundles* in order of preference or *utility*. **Intertemporal preferences** are tastes regarding streams of consumption over time. Intertemporal preferences are said to be **consistent** if plans made at one moment are still attractive at all subsequent moments when steps must be taken to implement them.

price: "Value, plus a reasonable sum for the wear and tear of conscience in demanding it" (Bierce 1911, pp. 266–7) ;)

principle of diminishing sensitivity: A psychological regularity according to which the impact of a change diminishes with the distance from the reference point.

prisoners' dilemma: A game with two strategies (cooperate or defect) for each of two players, each player having incentives to defect but both being better off if both cooperate.

production possibilities curve: A curve showing how much of one good can be produced as a function of how much of another good is produced.

production possibilities frontier: *Production possibilities curve.*

profit: Total revenue minus total cost.

prospect theory: A positive theory of choice under risk, first proposed by Daniel Kahneman and Amos Tversky.

public good: A good that is neither *excludable* nor *rivalrous*, for example, radio broadcasts.

pure strategy: A *strategy* involving no randomization.

rational agents: Individuals or organizations that choose means appropriate to their objectives.

rational expectations hypothesis: The hypothesis that economic decision makers form expectations (forecasts) with regard to uncertain variables as skilled econometricians or statisticians do—by calculating *expected values*, using the relevant models and data.

reaction function: An equation showing how one agent responds to another. For example, in Cournot's theory of duopoly, a reaction function shows how one firm's output depends on the other firm's output.

reference, circular: *Circular reference* ;)

representativeness heuristic: In *prospect theory*, a rule of thumb people (rashly) use to assess probabilities. Users of this heuristic act as if an object probably belongs to a particular class if the object has characteristics shared by most members of that class. In so doing, they overlook the possibility that some members of a larger class may have the same characteristics.

revenue: Income. **Total revenue** from sales of a good is calculated by multiplying price by quantity. **Marginal revenue** is the slope of a tangent to the total revenue curve. In mathematical terms it is the first derivative of total revenue with respect to quantity.

riches: "The reward of toil and virtue"—J. P. Morgan. "The savings of many in the hands of one"—Eugene Debs (cited by Bierce 1911, p. 294) ;)

risk: The possibility of various events with different effects on an individual's well-being. Some writers reserve this term for cases in which the probability (interpreted as frequency) of each event is known, using "uncertainty" in other cases. In this text, however, there is no need to distinguish risk from uncertainty because individuals are assumed to be able to assess their probability (interpreted as a degree of belief) for any event.

rivalrous: A good or service is rivalrous if one individual's enjoyment of it diminishes the amount of it that can be enjoyed by others. Food is rivalrous; radio broadcasts are not.

scale: A unidimensional measure of aggregate inputs, when inputs are used in fixed proportions. For example, a farm with two workers, 20 cows, and 200 acres has twice the scale of a farm with one worker, 10 cows, and 100 acres. **Returns to scale** are **decreasing**, **constant**, or **increasing** depending on whether multiplying all input quantities by a factor greater than one causes output to rise by a smaller, equal, or greater factor. For example, if the production function is $F(K, L)$ and $c > 1$, the returns to scale at (K_0, L_0) are decreasing if $F(cK_0, cL_0) < cF(K_0, L_0)$, constant if $F(cK_0, cL_0) = cF(K_0, L_0)$, and increasing if $F(cK_0, cL_0) > cF(K_0, L_0)$.

segregation rule: In *prospect theory*, the proposition that people frame decision problems by focusing on the acts, outcomes, and contingencies that appear most directly relevant to the choice under consideration while ignoring the wider context. A prime example of segregation of outcomes is the nearly universal practice of thinking about choice problems in terms of gains and losses, rather than in terms of final wealth. In this representation, the part of the outcome that depends on the choice is isolated from preexisting wealth.

self-interested individuals: People whose main objective is their own welfare.

short run: A period during which the quantity of at least one of the inputs is fixed.

status quo bias: A tendency to retain rather than exchange the goods initially in one's possession.

Stolper-Samuelson theorem: The proposition that in a competitive general equilibrium model with two goods, two factors, and two countries, if an import tariff raises the relative price of the imported good, the price of the factor used intensively in its production will rise relative to both commodity prices, and the price of the other factor will fall relative to both commodity prices.

strategic form: *normal form*

strategy: In game theory, a complete plan or decision rule specifying what a player will do in any circumstance that might arise in a game.

subproportionality: In *prospect theory*, the proposition that for any given ratio of probabilities, the ratio of *decision weights* is closer to unity when the probabilities are low than when they are high. For example, $w(0.4)/w(0.8) < w(0.1)/w(0.2)$, where $w(p)$ is the decision weight associated with probability p.

substitutes: A pair of goods such that an increase in the price of one tends to increase demand for the other.

substitution effect: A change in the quantity demanded due to a change in relative prices with real income or utility held constant.

sunk costs: Costs that are beyond recovery at the moment a decision is made.

supply curve: A curve showing how the quantity of a good supplied depends on the price of the good, other variables that might affect the quantity supplied being held constant. Loosely speaking, an equation or table showing the same information.

tariff: "A scale of taxes on imports, designed to protect the domestic producer against the greed of his consumer" (Bierce 1911, p. 339) ;)

tastes: *Preferences.*

tax incidence: The distribution of a tax burden among individuals or groups such as buyers and sellers.

technically efficient allocation: An allocation of inputs such that no reallocation could increase output of one good without reducing output of some other good.

technology: A body of knowledge relevant to producing goods and services.

tit-for-tat: A strategy in which a player cooperates in his or her first interaction with the other player and subsequently does what the other player did in the previous interaction.

tr: *Total revenue.*

transitivity assumption: In consumer theory, the assumption that consumer preferences are transitive. This involves three propositions: (1) if a consumer prefers A to B and B to C, then he or she prefers A to C; (2) if a consumer is indifferent between A and B and indifferent between B and C, then the consumer is indifferent between A and C; and (3) if a consumer prefers A to B and is indifferent between B and C, then the consumer prefers A to C.

utility: Originally, a measure of well-being or satisfaction. In more recent economic theory, any function whose maximization explains or rationalizes individual behavior.

value added: The value of output net of the value of inputs used up in its production. Value added is attributed to the services of durable inputs such as labor, land, structures, and equipment.

value investors: People who try to buy up stocks whose prices are temporarily depressed.

References

Abel, J. R. 2000. The Performance of the State Telecommunications Industry under Price-cap Regulation: An Assessment of the Empirical Evidence. Working Paper 00-14, National Regulatory Research Institute, Colubus, Ohio.

Acemoglu, Daron. 2002. Technical Change, Inequality, and the Labor Market. *Journal of Economic Literature* 40(1): 7–72.

Ai, Chunrong, and David E. M. Sappington. 2002. The Impact of State Incentive Regulation on the U.S. Telecommunications Industry. *Journal of Regulatory Economics* 22(2): 133–60.

Ainslie, George, and Nick Haslam. 1992. Hyperbolic Discounting. In Loewenstein and Elster (1992), pp. 57–92.

Akerlof, George A., and Janet L. Yellen, editors. 1986. *Efficiency Wage Models of the Labor Market*. Cambridge University Press, Cambridge.

Anderson, James L. 1985. Market Interactions Between Aquaculture and the Common-property Commercial Fishery. *Marine Resource Economics* 2(1): 1–24.

——— editor. 2003. *The International Seafood Trade*. CRC Press, Boca Raton, Fla.

Anderson, Lee G. 1986. *The Economics of Fisheries Management*. Johns Hopkins University Press, Baltimore, second edition.

Arrow, Kenneth. 1971. Economic Welfare and the Allocation of Resources for Invention. In Rosenberg (1971), pp. 164–81. First published in 1962.

Arrow, Kenneth J. 1973. Some Ordinalist-Utilitarian Notes on Rawls's Theory of Justice. *Journal of Philosophy* 70(10): 245–63.

Arrow, Kenneth J., Hollis B. Chenery, Bagicha S Minhas, and Robert M. Solow. 1961. Capital-Labor Substitution and Economic Efficiency. *Review of Economics and Statistics* 43(3): 225–50.

Arrow, Kenneth J., Enrico Colombatto, Mark Perlman, and Christian Schmidt. 1996. *The Rational Foundations of Economic Behaviour*. Macmillan, Houndmills, Blasingstoke, Hampshire.

Averch, Harvey, and Leland L. Johnson. 1962. Behavior of the Firm under Regulatory Constraint. *American Economic Review* 52(5): 1052–69.

Avorn, Jerry. 2004. *Powerful Medicine: The Benefits, Risks, and Costs of Prescription Drugs*. Knopf, New York.

Bain, Joe S. 1956. *Barriers to New Competition: Their Character and Consequences in Manufacturing Industries*. Harvard University Press, Cambridge, Mass.

Baldry, J. C. 1980. *General Equilibrium Analysis: An Introduction to the Two-sector Model*. Wiley, New York.

Baltagi, Badi H., editor. 2001. *A Companion to Theoretical Econometrics*. Blackwell, Oxford.

Banerjee, Aniruddha. 2003. Does Incentive Regulation 'Cause' Degradation of Retail Telephone Service Quality? *Information Economics and Policy* 15(2): 243–69.

Bar-Hillel, Maya. 1980. The Base-Rate Fallacy in Probability Judgments. *Acta Psychologica* 44(3): 211–33.

Bateman, Ian, Alistair Munro, Bruce Rhodes, Chris Starmer, and Robert Sugden. 1997. A Test of the Theory of Reference-Dependent Preferences. *Quarterly Journal of Economics* 112(2): 479–506.

Bateman, Ian J., Daniel Kahneman, Alistair Munro, Chris Starmer, and Robert Sugden. 2003. Is There Loss Aversion in Buying? An Adversarial Collaboration. Working Paper EDM 03-07, Centre for Social and Economic Research on the Global Environment, Norwich, England.

Baumol, William J. 1967. *Business Behavior, Value and Growth*. Harcourt, Brace & World, New York, revised edition.

Baumol, William J., John C. Panzar, and Robert D. Willig. 1988. *Contestable Markets and the Theory of Industry Structure*. Harcourt Brace Jovanovich, San Diego, second edition.

Becker, Gordon M., Morris H. DeGroot, and Jacob Marschak. 1964. Measuring Utility by a Single-Response Sequential Method. *Behavioral Science* 9: 226–32.

Becsi, Zsolt. 2000. The Shifty Laffer Curve. *Federal Reserve Bank of Atlanta Economic Review* 85(3): 52–64.

Benartzi, Shlomo, and Richard H. Thaler. 1995. Myopic Loss Aversion and the Equity Premium Puzzle. *Quarterly Journal of Economics* 110: 73–92.

Beneke, Raymond R., and Ronald Winterboer. 1973. *Linear Programming Applications to Agriculture*. Iowa State University Press, Ames.

Bergstrand, Jeffrey H. 1989. The Generalized Gravity Equation, Monopolistic Competition, and the Factor-Proportions Theory in International Trade. *Review of Economics and Statistics* 71(1): 143–53.

Bergstrom, Theodore C., and John H. Miller. 1997. *Experiments with Economic Principles*. McGraw-Hill, New York.

Berndt, Ernst R. 1991. *The Practice of Econometrics: Classic and Contemporary*. Addison-Wesley, Reading, Mass.

Bernoulli, Daniel. 1954 [1738]. Exposition of a New Theory on the Measurement of Risk. *Econometrica* 11: 23–36. A translation by Louise Sommer of Specimen theoriae novae de mensura sortis.

Bhaskar, V., Alan Manning, and Ted To. 2002. Oligopsony and Monopsonistic Competition in Labor Markets. *Journal of Economic Perspectives* 16(2): 155–74.

Bhide, Sashanka, F. Epplin, Earl O. Heady, B. E. Melton, and M. P. Hoffman. 1984. Silage-Concentrate Substitution in Beef Production. In Heady and Bhide (1984), pp. 206–33.

Bierce, Ambrose. 1911. *Collected Works*, vol. 7, *The Devil's Dictionary*. Neale, N.Y.

Binkley, Clark S. 1993. Long-run Timber Supply: Price Elasticity, Inventory Elasticity, and the Use of Capital in Timber Production. *Natural Resource Modeling* 7(2): 163–81.

Binmore, Ken. 1992. *Fun and Games*. Heath, Lexington, Mass.

Bivand, Roger, and Stefan Szymanski. 2000. Modelling the Spatial Impact of the Introduction of Compulsory Competitive Tendering. *Regional Science and Urban Economics* 30(2): 203–19.

Blackley, Dixie M. 1999. The Long-run Elasticity of New Housing Supply in the United States: Empirical Evidence for 1950 to 1994. *Journal of Real Estate Finance and Economics* 18(1): 25–42.

Blanchard, Olivier Jean, and Nobuhiro Kiyotaki. 1987. Monopolistic Competition and the Effects of Aggregate Demand. *American Economic Review* 77(4): 647–66.

Blaug, Mark. 1963. A Survey of the Theory of Process-Innovations. *Economics* 30(117): 13–32. Reprinted in Nathan Rosenberg, editor. 1971. *The Economics of Technological Change*. Baltimore, Penguin, pp. 86–113.

———. 1996. *Economic Theory in Retrospect*. Cambridge University Press, Cambridge, fifth edition.

Boggess, William G., K. D. Olson, and Earl O. Heady. 1984. Gain Isoquants and Production Functions for Swine. In Heady and Bhide (1984), pp. 267–303.

Bottazzi, Giulio, Giovanni Dosi, and Gaia Rocchetti. 2001. Modes of Knowledge Accumulation, Entry Regimes and Patterns of Industrial Evolution. *Industrial and Corporate Change* 10(3): 609–38.

Bowles, Samuel. 1998. Endogenous Preferences: The Cultural Consequences of Markets and Other Economic Institutions. *Journal of Economic Literature* 36: 75–111.

———. 2004. *Microeconomics: Behavior, Institutions, and Evolution*. Princeton University Press, Princeton, N.J.

Brandenburger, Adam, and Ben Polak. 1996. When Managers Cover Their Posteriors: Making the Decisions the Market Wants to See. *RAND Journal of Economics* 27(3): 523–54.

Brent, Robert J. 1996. *Applied Cost-Benefit Analysis*. Edward Elgar, Brookfield, Vt.

Bresson, Georges, Joyce Dargay, Jean-Loup Madre, and Alain Pirotte. 2004. Economic and Structural Determinants of the Demand for Public Transportation: An Analysis on a Panel of French Urban Areas. *Transportation Research, Part A: Policy and Practice* 38(4): 269–85.

Burkett, John P. 1986. Search, Selection, and Shortage in an Industry Composed of Labor-Managed Firms. *Journal of Comparative Economics* 10(1): 26–40.

———. 1988. Slack, Shortage, and Discouraged Consumers in Eastern Europe: Estimates Based on Smoothing by Aggregation. *Review of Economic Studies* .

———. 1989. Trends in the Share of Skilled Occupations in Total Employment. *International Journal of Manpower* 10(1): 10–15.

———. 2000. Cones of Diversification in a Model of Comparative Advantage. *Journal of International Trade and Economic Development* 9(2): 193–211.

Butler, Brian, and Alan Isaacs, editors. 1993. *A Dictionary of Finance*. Oxford University Press, Oxford.

Camerer, Colin F. 2003. *Behavioral Game Theory: Experiments in Strategic Interaction*. Roundtable Series in Behavioral Economics. Princeton University Press, Princeton, N.J.

Camerer, Colin F., and Howard Kunreuther. 1989. Decision Processes for Low Probability Events: Policy Implications. *Journal of Policy Analysis and Management* 8(4): 565–92.

Camerer, Colin F., and George Loewenstein. 2004. Behavioral Economics: Past, Present, Future. In Camerer et al. (2004), pp. 3–51.

Camerer, Colin F., George Loewenstein, and Matthew Rabin, editors. 2004. *Advances in Behavioral Economics*. Russell Sage Foundation and Princeton University Press, New York and Princeton.

Canner, Glenn B., Thomas A. Durkin, and Charles A. Luckett. 1998. Recent Developments in Home Equity Lending. *Federal Reserve Bulletin* 84(4): 241–51.

Castle, Emery N. 1989. Is Farming a Constant Cost Industry? *American Journal of Agricultural Economics* 71(3): 574–82.

Chamberlin, Edward H. 1936. *The Theory of Monopolistic Competition: A Re-orientation of the Theory of Value*. Harvard University Press, Cambridge, Mass., second edition.

Chamberlin, Edward H. 1948. An Experimental Imperfect Market. *Journal of Political Economy* 56: 95–108.

Charnes, Abraham, William W. Cooper, Arie Y. Lewin, and Lawrence M. Seiford, editors. 1994. *Data Envelopment Analysis: Theory, Methodology, and Application*. Kluwer Academic, Dordrecht.

Clapham, J. H. 1922. Of Empty Economic Boxes. *Economic Journal* 32: 305–14.

Clemen, Robert T., and Terence Reilly. 2001. *Making Hard Decisions*. Duxbury, Pacific Grove, second edition.

Coase, Ronald. 1959. The Federal Communications Commission. *Journal of Law and Economics* 2(1): 1–40.

———. 1960. The Problem of Social Cost. *Journal of Law and Economics* 3(1): 1–44.

Cobb, Charles W., and Paul H. Douglas. 1928. A Theory of Production. *American Economic Review* 18(supplement): 139–65.

Copes, Parzival. 1970. The Backward-bending Supply Curve of the Fishing Industry. *Scottish Journal of Political Economy* 17: 69–77.

Cournot, Antoine Augustin. 1927 [1838]. *Researches into the Mathematical Principles of the Theory of Wealth*. Macmillan, New York. Translated by Nathaniel T. Bacon from *Recherches sur les principes mathématiques de la théorie des richesses*.

Cremer, Jacques, and Djavad Salehi-Isfahani. 1989. The Rise and Fall of Oil Prices: A Competitive View. *Annales d'Économie et de Statistique* (15-16): 427–54.

Cubitt, Robin P., Chris Starmer, and Robert Sugden. 2001. Discovered Preferences and the Experimental Evidence of Violations of Expected Utility Theory. *Journal of Economic Methodology* 8(3): 385–414.

Culyer, A. J., and J. P. Newhouse, editors. 2000. *Handbook of Health Economics*, vol. 1B. Elsevier, Amsterdam.

Currie, Janet, Mehdi Farsi, and W. Bentley MacLeod. 2002. Cut to the Bone? Hospital Takeovers and Nurse Employment Contracts. www.irs.princeton.edu/ashenfelter/currie.pdf.

Davis, Douglas D., and Charles A. Holt. 1993. *Experimental Economics*. Princeton University Press, Princeton, N.J.

Davis, George C., and Michael K. Wohlgenant. 1993. Demand Elasticities from a Discrete Choice Model: The Natural Christmas Tree Market. *American Journal of Agricultural Economics* 75(3): 730–38.

Deaton, Angus, and John Muellbauer. 1980. *Economics and Consumer Behavior*. Cambridge University Press, Cambridge.

De Bondt, Werner F. M., and Richard H. Thaler. 1989. A Mean-Reverting Walk Down Wall Street. *Journal of Economic Perspectives* 3(1): 189–202.

Dempsey, B. W., editor. 1960. *The Frontier Wage*. Loyola University Press, Chicago.

Demsetz, Harold. 1968. Why Regulate Utilities? *Journal of Law and Economics* 11: 55–65.

Dixit, Avinash K., and Robert S. Pindyck. 1994. *Investment under Uncertainty*. Princeton University Press, Princeton, N.J.

———. 1995. The Options Approach to Capital Investment. *Harvard Business Review*, pp. 105–11.

Dorfman, Robert, Paul A. Samuelson, and Robert M. Solow. 1987 [1958]. *Linear Programming and Economic Analysis*. Dover, New York.

Drake, Leigh M., and Mark J. Holmes. 1997. Adverse Selection and the Market for Building Society Mortgage Finance. *Manchester School of Economic and Social Studies* 65(1): 58–70.

Dunn, L. F. 1996. Loss Aversion and Adaptation in the Labor Market: Empirical Indifference Functions and Labor Supply. *Review of Economics and Statistics* 78(3): 441–50.

Dupuit, Jules. 1962 [1849]. On Tolls and Transport Charges. *International Economic Papers* (11): 7–31.

Economic Report of the President. 2005. U.S. Government Printing Office, Washington, D.C.

Ekelund, Robert B., Jr., and Robert F. Hébert. 1999. *Secret Origins of Modern Microeconomics: Dupuit and the Engineers*. University of Chicago, Chicago.

Elmendorf, Douglas W. 1996. The Effect of Interest-rate Changes on Household Saving and Consumption: a Survey. Board of Governors of the Federal Reserve System, Finance and Economics Discussion Series: 96-27, http://www.federalreserve.gov/pubs/feds/1996/199627/199627pap.pdf.

El Moghazy, Yehia E. 1992a. Optimizing Cotton Blend Costs with Respect to Quality Using HVI Fiber Properties and Linear Programming, Part I: Fundamentals and Advanced Techniques of Linear Programming. *Textile Research Journal* 62(1): 1–8.

———. 1992b. Optimizing Cotton Blend Costs with Respect to Quality Using HVI Fiber Properties and Linear Programming, Part II: Combined Effects of Fiber Properties and Variability Constraints. *Textile Research Journal* 62(2): 108–14.

Elster, Jon. 1979. *Ulysses and the Sirens*. Cambridge University Press, Cambridge.

Epley, Nicholas, and Thomas Gilovich. 2001. Putting Adjustment Back in the Anchoring and Adjustment Heuristic. *Psychological Science* 12: 391–96. Reprinted in Gilovich et al. 2002, pp. 139–49.

Evenson, R. E. 1993. Patents, R&D, and Invention Pontential: International Evidence. *American Economic Review* 83(2): 463–68.

Farley, Dixie. 1995. Benefits vs. Risks: How FDA Approves New Drugs. In *From Test Tube to Patient: New Drug Development in the United States* (1995).

Farrell, M. J. 1957. The Measurement of Productive Efficiency. *Journal of the Royal Statistical Society, Series A* 120(III): 253–90.

Feinberg, Robert M., and Thomas A. Husted. 1999. Estimating Reaction Functions in Experimental Duopoly Markets. *International Journal of the Economics of Business* 6(1): 57–63.

Ferguson, C. E. 1969. *Microeconomic Theory*. Richard D. Irwin, Homewood, Ill., revised edition.

Fishbein, Martin, editor. 1980. *Progress in Social Psychology*, vol. 1. Lawrence Erlbaum, Hillsdale, New Jersey.

Food and Drug Administration (FDA). 1995. Evolution of U.S. Drug Law. In *From Test Tube to Patient: New Drug Development in the United States* (1995).

Frank, Mark W. 2003. An Empirical Analysis of Electricity Regulation on Technical Change in Texas. *Review of Industrial Organization* 22(4): 313–31.

Frank, Richard G., and David S. Salkever. 1995. *Generic Entry and Pricing of Pharmaceuticals*. National Bureau of Economic Research, Cambridge. Working Paper 5306.

Frank, Robert H. 1994. *Microeconomics and Behavior*. McGraw-Hill, New York, second edition.

———. 2003. *Microeconomics and Behavior*. McGraw-Hill Irwin, New York, fifth edition.

Frederick, Shane, George Loewenstein, and Ted O'Donoghue. 2002. Time Discounting and Time Preference: A Critical Review. *Journal of Economic Literature* 40(2): 351–401.

Friedman, Daniel, and Shayam Sunder. 1994. *Experimental Methods: A Primer for Economists*. Cambridge University Press, Cambridge.

Friedman, Milton. 1953. *Essays in Positive Economics*. University of Chicago Press, Chicago.

From Test Tube to Patient: New Drug Development in the United States. 1995. Food and Drug Administration, Washington, D.C.

Fundenberg, Drew, and Jean Tirole. 1991. *Game Theory*. MIT Press, Cambridge, Massachusetts.

Gass, Saul I. 1970. *An Illustrated Guide to Linear Programming*. Dover, New York.

Genesove, David, and Christopher Mayer. 2001. Loss Aversion and Seller Behavior: Evidence from the Housing Market. *Quarterly Journal of Economics* 116(4): 1233–60.

Gerhard, Jürgen, W. Oevel, Frank Postel, and S. Wehmeier. 2000. *MuPAD Tutorial, English Edition, A Version and Platform Independent Introduction*. Springer-Verlag, New York.

Gescheider, George A. 1997. *Psychophysics: The Fundamentals*. Lawrence Erlbaum Associates, Mahwah, New Jersey, third edition.

Gilbert, Richard, and Carl Shapiro. 1990. Optimal Patent Length and Breadth. *RAND Journal of Economics* 21(1): 106–12.

Gillispie, Charles Coulston, editor. 1959. *A Diderot Pictorial Encyclopedia of Trades and Industry*. Dover Publications, New York.

Gilovich, Thomas, and Dale Griffin. 2002. Introduction—Heuristics and Biases: Then and Now. In Gilovich et al. (2002), pp. 1–18.

Gilovich, Thomas, Dale Griffin, and Daniel Kahneman, editors. 2002. *Heuristics and Biases*. Cambridge University Press, Cambridge.

Goeree, Jacob K., and Charles A. Holt. 1999. Stochastic Game Theory: For Playing Games, Not Just for Doing Theory. *Proceedings of the National Academy of Sciences* 96: 10564–67.

Gilovich, Thomas, Dale Griffin, and Daniel Kahneman, editors. 2002. *Heuristics and Biases*. Cambridge University Press, Cambridge.

Gómez-Lobo, Andrés, and Stefan Szymanski. 2001. A Law of Large Numbers: Bidding and Compulsory Competitive Tendering for Refuse Collection Contracts. *Review of Industrial Organization* 18(1): 105–13.

Grabowski, Henry G., and John M. Vernon. 1983. *Regulations of Pharmaceuticals: Balancing the Benefits and Risks*. American Enterprise Institute for Public Policy Research, Washington, D.C.

Graham, David J. 2004. Testimony before the U.S. Senate Finance Committee. http://finance.senate .gov/hearings/testimony/2004test/111804dgtest.pdf.

Gross, David B., and Nicholas S. Souleles. 2002. Do Liquidity Constraints and Interest Rates Matter for Consumer Behavior? Evidence from Credit Card Data. *Quarterly Journal of Economics* 117(1): 149–85.

Harbaugh, William T., Kate Krause, and Lise Vesterlund. 2001. Are Adults Better Behaved Than Children? Age, Experience, and the Endowment Effect. *Economics Letters* 70(2): 175–81.

Harberger, Arnold C. 1959. The Corporation Income Tax: An Empirical Appraisal. In *Tax Revision Compendium*, House Committee on Ways and Means, 86th Congress, First Session, pp. 231–40. U.S. Goverment, Washington, D.C.

———. 1962. The Incidence of the Corporate Income Tax. *Journal of Political Economy* 70: 215–40.

Harless, David W., and Colin F. Camerer. 1994. The Predictive Utility of Generalized Expected Utility Theories. *Econometrica* 62(6): 1251–1289.

Harris, Gardiner. 2004. At F.D.A., Strong Drug Ties and Less Monitoring. *New York Times*, December 6, section A, p. 1.

Hausman, Jerry A. 1981. Exact Consumer's Surplus and Deadweight Loss. *American Economic Review* 71(4): 662–76.

Hausman, William J., and John L. Neufeld. 2002. The Market for Capital and the Origins of State Regulation of Electric Utilities in the United States. *Journal of Economic History* 62(4): 1050–73.

Heady, Earl O., and Sashanka Bhide, editors. 1984. *Livestock Response Functions*. Iowa State University Press, Ames.

Heady, Earl O., Joseph F. Guinan, and S. L. Balloun. 1980. *Egg Production Functions*. Iowa State University, Ames, Research Bulletin 589.

Heimlich, Ralph, editor. 2003. *Agricultural Resources and Environmental Indicators*. No. AH722 in Agriculture Handbooks. Economic Research Service, U.S. Department of Agriculture, http:/ /www.ers.usda.gov/publications/arei/ah722.

Henderson, James. 1999. *Health Economics and Policy*. South-Western College Publishing, Cincinnati.

Hicks, J. R., and R. G. D. Allen. 1934. A Reconsideration of the Theory of Value. *Economica* 1, new series(1 and 2): 52–97 and 196–219.

Hippel, Eric von. 2005. *Democratizing Innovation*. MIT Press, Cambridge, Massachusetts.

Hirt, Geoffrey A., and Stanley B. Block. 1993. *Fundamentals of Investment Management*. Irwin, Homewood, Ill.

Hoeffler, Steve, and Dan Ariely. 1999. Constructing Stable Preferences: A Look into Dimensions of Experience and Their Impact on Preference Stability. *Journal of Consumer Psychology* 8(2): 113–39.

Horowitz, Andrew W., and Edwin L.-C. Lai. 1996. Patent Length and the Rate of Innovation. *International Economic Review* 37(4): 785–801.

Hotelling, Harold. 1929. Stability in Competition. *Economic Journal* 39(153): 41–57.

Huber, Joel, John Payne, and Christopher Puto. 1982. Adding Asymmetrically Dominated Alternatives: Violations of Regularity and the Similarity Hypothesis. *Journal of Consumer Research* 9: 90–98.

Huffman, Wallace E., and Robert E. Evenson. 1993. *Science for Agriculture: A Long-term Perspective*. Iowa State University Press, Ames.

Humphrey, Thomas M. 1997. Algebraic Production Functions and Their Uses Before Cobb-Douglas. *Federal Reserve Bank of Richmond Economic Quarterly* 83(1): 51–83.

Huntington, E. V. 1938. A Paradox in the Scoring of Competing Teams. *Science* 88(2282): 287–88.

Intriligator, Michael D., Ronald G. Bodkin, and Cheng Hsiao. 1996. *Econometric Models, Techniques, and Applicatioins*. Prentice Hall, Upper Saddle River, N.J., second edition.

Iwaisako, Tatsuro, and Koichi Futagami. 2003. Patent Policy in an Endogenous Growth Model. *Journal of Economics (Zeitschrift fur Nationalokonomie)* 78(3): 239–58.

Jackson, Brian A. 2003. Innovation and Intellectual Property: The Case of Genomic Patenting. *Journal of Policy Analysis and Management* 22(1): 5–25.

Jehle, Geoffrey A., and Philip J. Reny. 1998. *Advanced Microeconomic Theory*. Addison-Wesley, Reading, Mass.

Johnson, Harry G. 1971. *The Two-sector Model of General Equilibrium*. Aldine, Chicago.

Jones, Ronald W. 1961. Comparative Advantage and the Theory of Tariffs: A Multi-country, Multi-commodity Model. *Review of Economic Studies* 28(3): 161–75.

Kafker, Frank A., and Serena L. Kafker. 1988. *The Encyclopedists as Individuals: A Biographical Dictionary of the Authors of the Encyclopédie*. No. 257 in *Studies on Voltaire and the Eighteenth Century*. The Voltaire Foundation at the Taylor Institution, Oxford.

Kahneman, Daniel. 2003. Maps of Bounded Rationality: Psychology for Behavioral Economics. *American Economic Review* 93(5): 1449–75.

Kahneman, Daniel, and Shane Frederick. 2002. Representativeness Revisited: Attribute Substitution in Intuitive Judgment. In Gilovich et al. (2002).

Kahneman, Daniel, Jack L. Knetsch, and Richard Thaler. 1986. Fairness as a Constraint on Profit Seeking: Entitlements in the Market. *American Economic Review* 76(4): 728–41.

———. 1990. Experimental Tests of the Endowment Effect and the Coase Theorem. *Journal of Political Economy* 98(6): 1325–48.

———. 1991. Anomalies: The Endowment Effect, Loss Aversion, and Status Quo Bias. *Journal of Economic Perspectives* 5(1): 193–206.

Kahneman, Daniel, Ilana Ritov, and David Schkade. 1999. Economic Preferences or Attitude Expressions? An Analysis of Dollar Responses to Public Issues. *Journal of Risk and Uncertainty* 19(1–3): 203–35. Reprinted in Kahneman and Tversky (2000).

Kahneman, Daniel, and Richard Thaler. 1991. Economic Analysis and the Psychology of Utility: Applications to Compensation Policy. *American Economic Review* 81(2): 341–46.

Kahneman, Daniel, and Amos Tversky. 1979. Prospect Theory: An Analysis of Decision under Risk. *Econometrica* 47(2): 263–91.

Kahneman, Daniel, and Amos Tversky. 1984. Choices, Values, and Frames. *American Psychologist* 39(4): 341–50.

———, editors. 2000. *Choices, Values, and Frames*. Cambridge University Press, Cambridge.

Kahneman, Daniel, Peter P. Wakker, and Rakesh Sarin. 1997. Back to Bentham? Explorations of Experienced Utility. *Quarterly Journal of Economics* 112(2): 375–405.

Katz, Michael L. 1983. Non-Uniform Pricing, Output and Welfare under Monopoly. *Review of Economic Studies* 50(1): 37–56.

Keynes, John Neville. 1955. *The Scope and Method of Political Economy*. Kelley & Millman, New York, fourth edition.

Kimes, Sheryl, and Jochen Wirtz. 2003. Has Revenue Management Become Acceptable? *Journal of Service Research* 6(2): 125–35.

Knetsch, Jack. 1989. The Endowment Effect and Evidence of Nonreversible Indifference Curves. *American Economic Review* 79(5): 1277–84.

Kolpin, Van. 2001. Regulation and Cost Inefficiency. *Review of Industrial Organization* 18(2): 175–82.

Koop, Gary, and Mark F. J. Steel. 2001. Bayesian Analysis of Stochastic Frontier Models. In Baltagi (2001), pp. 520–37.

Kornai, János. 1980. *Economics of Shortage*. North-Holland, Amsterdam.

Kortum, Samuel. 1993. Equilibrium R&D and Patent-R&D Ratio: U.S. Evidence. *American Economic Review* 83(2): 450–57.

Krueger, Alan B., and Mikael Lindahl. 2001. Education for Growth: Why and For Whom? *Journal of Economic Literature* 39(4): 1101–36.

Kumbhakar, Subal C., and C. A. Knox Lovell. 2000. *Stochastic Frontier Analysis*. Cambridge University Press, Cambridge.

Kurz, Heinz D., and Neri Salvadori. 1995. *Theory of Production: A Long-period Analysis*. Cambridge University Press, Cambridge.

Lad, Frank. 1996. *Operational Subjective Statistical Methods*. Wiley, New York.

Laibson, David. 1997. Golden Eggs and Hyperbolic Discounting. *Quarterly Journal of Economics* 112(2): 443–77.

Laibson, David, Andrea Repetto, and Jeremy Tobacman. 1998. Self-control and Saving for Retirement. *Brookings Papers on Economic Activity* (1): 91–196.

Lanjouw, Jean O., and Mark Schankerman. 2004. Patent Quality and Research Productivity: Measuring Innovations with Multiple Indicators. *Economic Journal* 114(495): 441–65.

Leamer, Edward E. 1984. *Sources of International Comparative Advantage: Theory and Evidence*. MIT Press, Cambridge, Mass.

———. 1997. Questions, Theory, and Data. In Medema and Samuels (1997).

Leibenstein, Harvey. 1950. Bandwagaon, Veblen, and Snob Effects in the Theory of Consumers' Demand. *Quarterly Journal of Economics* 64(2): 183–207.

Lerner, Abba P. 1934. The Concept of Monopoly and the Measurement of Monopoly Power. *Review of Economic Studies* 1: 157–75.

———. 1944. *The Economics of Control: Principles of Welfare Economics*. Macmillan, New York.

———. 1953. *Essays in Economic Analysis*. Macmillan, London.

Lerner, Josh, and Jean Tirole. 2002. Some Simple Economics of Open Source. *Journal of Industrial Economics* 50(2): 197–234.

Liberman, Marvin B. 1987. Excess Capacity as a Barrier to Entry: An Empirical Appraisal. *Journal of Industrial Economics* 35(4): 607–27.

Lichtenberg, Frank R. 1996. *The Effect of Pharmaceutical Utilization and Innovation on Hospitalization and Mortality*. National Bureau of Economic Research, Cambridge.

Lindley, D. V. 1985. *Making Decisions*. Wiley, New York.

Link, Albert N., David Paton, and Donald S. Siegel. 2002. An Analysis of Policy Initiatives to Promote Strategic Research Partnerships. *Research Policy* 31(8-9): 1459–66.

List, John A. 2003. Does Market Experience Eliminate Market Anomalies? *Quarterly Journal of Economics* 118(1): 41–71.

———. 2004. Neoclassical Theory versus Prospect Theory: Evidence from the Marketplace. *Econometrica* 72(2): 615–25.

Loewenstein, George, and Jon Elster, editors. 1992. *Choice over Time*. Russell Sage Foundation, New York.

Loewenstein, George, and Dražen Prelec. 1992. Anomalies in Intertemporal Choice: Evidence and an Interpretation. *Quarterly Journal of Economics*, pp. 573–97.

———. 1993. Preferences for Sequences of Outcomes. *Psychological Review* 100(1): 91–108.

Loewenstein, George, and Nachum Sicherman. 1991. Do Workers Prefer Increasing Wage Profiles? *Journal of Labor Economics* 9(1): 67–84.

Luce, R. Duncan. 1959. *Individual Choice Behavior*. Wiley, New York.

Luce, R. Duncan, and Howard Raiffa. 1989 [1957]. *Games and Decisions*. Dover, New York.

Machina, Mark J. 1987. Choice under Uncertainty: Problems Solved and Unsolved. *Journal of Economic Perspectives* 1(1): 121–54.

Manning, Alan. 2003. *Monopsony in Motion: Imperfect Competition in Labor Markets*. Princeton University Press, Princeton, N.J.

Marx, Karl. 1965 [1867]. *Capital*, vol. 1. Progress Publishers, Moscow.

Mas-Colell, Andreu, Michael D. Whinston, and Jerry R. Green. 1995. *Microeconomic Theory*. Oxford University Press, Oxford.

McAfee, R. Preston, Hugo M. Mialon, and Michael A. Williams. 2004. What Is a Barrier to Entry? *American Economic Review* 94(2): 461–65.

McKean, Kevin. 1985. Decisions, Decisions. *Discover*, pp. 22–31.

Mckenzie, David. 2002. Are Tortillas a Giffen Good in Mexico. *Economics Bulletin* 15(1): 1–7.

Meade, James E. 1952. *A Geometry of International Trade*. Allen and Unwin, London.

Medema, Steven G., and Warren J. Samuels, editors. 1997. *Foundations of Research in Economics: How Do Economists Do Economics?* Edward Elgar, Brookfield, Vt.

Mincer, Jacob. 1974. *Schooling, Earning, and Experience*. Columbia University Press, New York.

Moore, Barrington. 1978. *Injustice: The Social Bases of Obedience and Revolt*. M. E. Sharpe, White Plains, N.Y.

Murphy, Kevin, and Finis Welch. 1989. Wage Premiums for College Graduates: Recent Growth and Possible Explanations. *Educational Researcher* 18(4): 17–26.

National Science Foundation (NSF). 1999. *U.S. Corporate R&D*, vol. 1. Department of Commerce, Washington, D.C.

———. 2003. National Patterns of R&D Resources: 2002 Data Update. Http://www.nsf.gov/sbe/srs /nsf03313/start.htm.

Nelson, Richard R. 2003. The Market Economy and the Scientific Commons. *Research Policy* 33(3): 455–71.

Nelson, Richard R., and Sidney G. Winter. 1982. *An Evolutionary Theory of Economic Change*. Harvard University Press, Cambridge, Mass.

Newton, Doris, and Jet Yee. 2003. Agricultural Productivity. In Heimlich (2003), chap. 5.1.

Nicholson, Walter. 1995. *Microeconomic Theory*. Dryden, New York.

Niehans, Jürg. 1990. *A History of Economic Theory*. Johns Hopkins University Press, Baltimore.

Odean, Terrance. 2000 [1998]. Are Investors Reluctant to Realize Their Losses? In *Choices, Values, and Frames*, edited by Daniel Kahneman and Amos Tversky, pp. 371–92. Cambridge University Press, Cambridge.

Odlyzko, Andrew. 2003. Privacy, Economics, and Price Discrimination on the Internet. Working paper, University of Minnesota, Minneapolis. Downloaded from www.dtc.umn.edu/~odlyzko /doc/privacy.economics.pdf.

Ohlin, Bertil. 1935. *Interregional and International Trade*. Harvard University Press, Cambridge, Mass.

Olmstead, Alan L., and Paul Rhode. 1985. Rationing without Government: The West Coast Gas Famine of 1920. *American Economic Review* 75(5): 1044–55.

Olson, Mary K. 2002. Pharmaceutical Policy Change and the Safety of New Drugs. *Journal of Law and Economics* 45(2): 615–42.

Palacios-Huerta, Ignacio. 2003. Professionals Play Minimax. *Review of Economic Studies* 70(2): 395–415.

Payne, John W., James R. Bettman, and David A. Schkade. 1999. Measuring Constructed Preferences: Towards a Building Code. *Journal of Risk and Uncertainty* 19(1-3): 243–70.

Pecorino, Paul. 2002. Should the US Allow Prescription Drug Reimports from Canada? *Journal of Health Economics* 21(4): 699–708.

Peretto, Pietro F. 1999. Firm Size, Rivalry and the Extent of the Market in Endogenous Technological Change. *European Economic Review* 43(9): 1747–73.

Pescatrice, Donn R. 2004. The Real 'Laugher' Curve. *Journal of Economic and Social Policy* 8(2): 2–6.

Petersen, E., G. Muldoon, and B. Johnston. 2004. Economic Modelling of the Live Reef Fish Trade in Asia-Pacific. Paper contributed to the Forty-eighth Annual Conference of the Australian Agricultural and Resource Economics Society, Melbourne.

Petry, Nancy M., and Warren K. Bickel. 1998. Polydrug Abuse in Heroin Addicts: A Behavioral Economic Analysis. *Addiction* 93(3): 321–35.

Phelps, Charles E. 1992. *Health Economics*. HarperCollins, New York.

Pigou, A. C. 1932. *The Economics of Welfare*. Macmillan, London, fourth edition.

Pinch, Philip L., and Alan Patterson. 2000. Public Sector Restructuring and Regional Development: The Impact of Compulsory Competitive Tendering in the UK. *Regional Studies* 34(3): 265–75.

Plott, Charles R. 1996. Rational Individual Behavior in Markets and Social Choice Processes: The Discovered Preference Hypothesis. In Arrow et al. (1996).

Plott, Charles R., and Kathryn Zeiler. 2005. The Willingness to Pay-Willingness to Accept Gap, the "Endowment Effect," Subject Misconceptions, and Experimental Procedures for Eliciting Valuations. *American Economic Review* 95(3): 530–45.

Poirier, Dale J. 1995. *Intermediate Statistics and Econometrics*. MIT Press, Cambridge, Massachusetts.

Portes, Richard, and David Winter. 1980. Disequilibrium Estimates for Consumption Goods Markets in Centrally Planned Economies. *Review of Economic Studies* 47(1): 137–59.

Pratt, John W., Howard Raiffa, and Robert Schlaifer. 1995. *Introduction to Statistical Decision Theory*. MIT Press, Cambridge, Mass.

Pratt, John W., David A. Wise, and Richard Zeckhauser. 1979. Price Differences in Almost Competitive Markets. *Quarterly Journal of Economics* 93(2): 189–211.

Prelec, Dražen. 2000. Compound Invariant Weighting Fucntions in Prospect Theory. In Kahneman and Tversky (2000), chap. 5, pp. 67–92.

Resende, Marcelo. 2000. Regulatory Regimes and Efficiency in US Local Telephony. *Oxford Economic Papers* 52(3): 447–70.

Rosenberg, Nathan, editor. 1971. *The Economics of Technological Change*. Penguin, Harmondsworth, Middlesex.

Quattrone, George Q., and Amos Tversky. 2000 [1988]. Contrasting Rational and Psychological Analyses of Political Choice. In Kahneman and Tversky (2000), pp. 451–72. Originally published in the *American Political Science Review*, pp. 719–36.

Ray, Paramesh. 1973. Independence of Irrelevant Alternatives. *Econometrica* 41(5): 987–91.

Ray, Subhash C. 2004. *Data Envelopment Analysis: Theory and Techniques for Economics and Operations Research*. Cambridge University Press, Cambridge.

Raymond, Eric S. 1999. The Magic Cauldron. http://www.tuxedo.org/ esr/writings/magic-cauldron/.

Ricardo, David. 1963 [1817]. *Principles of Political Economy and Taxation*. Richard D. Irwin, Homewood, Ill.

Robinson, Joan. 1965 [1933]. *The Economics of Imperfect Competition*. St. Martin's, New York.

Ross, Stephen A. 2005. *Neoclassical Finanace*. Princeton University Press, Princeton, N.J.

Rossi, Peter, Greg Allenby, and Rob McCulloch. 2005. *Bayesian Statistics and Marketing*. Wiley, New York.

Rothschild, Michael, and Joseph Stiglitz. 1976. Competitive Insurance Markets: An Essay on the Economics of Imperfect Information. *Quarterly Journal of Economics* 95: 629–49.

Royal Swedish Academy of Sciences. 2002. Foundations of Behavioral and Experimental Economics: Daniel Kahneman and Vernon Smith. http://nobelprize.org/economics/laureates/2002/adv.html.

Rubenstein, Ariel. 1998. *Modeling Bounded Rationality*. MIT Press, Cambridge, Mass.

Samuelson, Paul A. 1948. International Trade and the Equalization of Factor Prices. *Economic Journal* 58(2): 181–97.

Samuelson, William, and Richard Zeckhauser. 1988. Status Quo Bias in Decision Making. *Journal of Risk and Uncertainty* 1(1): 7–59.

Santerre, Rexford E., and Stephen P. Neun. 1996. *Health Economics: Theories, Insights, and Industry Studies*. Irwin, Chicago, first edition.

Santerre, Rexford E., and Stephen P. Neun. 2004. *Health Economics: Theories, Insights, and Industry Studies*. South-Western, Mason, Ohio, third edition.

SAS Institute. 1999. *SAS/OR User's Guide: Mathematical Programming,* version 8. SAS Institute, Cary, N.C.

Savage, Leonard J. 1954. *The Foundations of Statistics*. Wiley, New York.

Scarf, Herbert E., and John B. Shoven. 1984. *Applied General Equilibrium Analysis*. Cambridge University Press, Cambridge.

Scherer, F. M. 2000. The Pharmaceutical Industry. In Culyer and Newhouse (2000).

———. 2001. An Early Application of the Average Total Cost Concept. *Journal of Economic Literature* 39(3): 897–901.

Schmalensee, Richard, and Robert D. Willig, editors. 1989. *Handbook of Industrial Organization*, vol. 1. North-Holland, Amsterdam.

Schmidt-Hebbel, Klaus, Steven B. Webb, and Giancarlo Corsetti. 1992. Household Saving in Developing Countries: First Cross Country Evidence. *World Bank Economic Review* 6(3): 529–47.

Schoemaker, Paul. 1982. The Expected Utility Model: Its Variants, Purposes, Evidence, and Limitations. *Journal of Economic Literature* 20: 529–63.

Schweitzer, Stuart O. 1997. *Pharmaceutical Economics and Policy*. Oxford University Press, New York.

Sellar, Walter Carruthers, and Robert Julian Yeatman. 1931. *1066 and All That*. E. P. Dutton, New York.

Sen, Amartya. 1993. Internal Consistency of Choice. *Econometrica* 61(3): 495–521.

Senbongi, Shuichi, and Joseph E. Harrington, Jr. 1995. Managerial Reputation and the Competitiveness of an Industry. *International Journal of Industrial Organization* 13(1): 95–110.

Sharif, Mohammed. 2003. *Working Behavior of the World's Poor*. Ashgate Publishing Company, Burlington, Vt.

Shelley, Marjorie K. 1993. Outcome Signs, Question Frames and Discount Rates. *Management Science* 39(7): 806–15.

Shleifer, Andrei, and Lawrence H. Summers. 1990. The Noise Trader Approach to Finance. *Journal of Economic Perspectives* 4(2): 19–34.

Shoven, John B., and John Whalley. 1992. *Applying General Equilibrium*. Cambridge University Press, Cambridge.

Shumway, Tyler. 1997. Explaining Returns with Loss Aversion. University of Michigan working paper.

Shy, Oz. 1995. *Industrial Organization: Theory and Applications*. MIT Press, Cambridge, Mass.

Silva-Risso, Jorge M., and Randolph E. Bucklin. 2004. Capturing the Effects of Coupon Promotions in Scanner Panel Choice Models. *Journal of Product & Brand Management* 13(6): 442–52.

Simon, Herbert A. 1976. *Administrative Behavior: A Study of Decision-Making Processes in Administrative Organization*. Free Press, third edition.

Simonson, Itamar. 1989. Choice Based on Reasons: The Case of Attraction and Compromise Effects. *Journal of Consumer Research* 16: 158–74.

Simonson, Itamar, and Amos Tversky. 1992. Choice in Context: Tradeoff Contrast and Extremeness Aversion. *Journal of Marketing Research* 29: 281–95.

Slovic, Paul. 1991. The Construction of Preference. *American Psychologist* 50(5): 364–71. Reprinted in Kahneman and Tversky (2000).

Slovic, Paul, Melissa Finucane, Ellen Peters, and Donald G. MacGregor. 2002. The Affect Heuristic. In Gilovich et al. (2002).

Slovic, Paul, Baruch Fischhoff, and Sarah Lichtenstein. 1982. Facts Versus Fears: Understanding Perceived Risk. In *Judgment Under Uncertainty: Heuristics and Biases*, edited by Daniel Kahneman, Paul Slovic, and Amos Tversky, chap. 33, pp. 463–89. Cambridge University Press, Cambridge.

Smith, Adam. 1985 [1776]. *An Inquiry into the Nature and Causes of the Wealth of Nations*. Modern Library, New York.

Smith, Vernon L. 1991. *Papers in Experimental Economics*. Cambridge University Press, Cambridge.

Snyder, Thomas D., and Charlene M. Hoffman. 2003. Digest of Education Statistics, 2002. Published online by the National Center for Education Statistics.

Staiger, Douglas, Joanne Spetz, and Ciaran Phibbs. 1999. Is There Monopsony in the Labor Market? Evidence from a Natural Experiment. National Bureau of Economic Research Working Paper No. 7258.

Stango, Victor. 1999. The Tax Reform Act of 1986 and the Composition of Consumer Debt. *National Tax Journal* 52(4): 717–39.

Starmer, Chris. 2000. Developments in Nonexpected-Utility Theory: The Hunt for a Descriptive Theory of Choice under Risk. *Journal of Economic Literature* 38(2): 332–82.

Stigler, George J. 1945. The Cost of Subsistence. *Journal of Farm Economics* 27(2): 303–14.

———. 1968. *The Organization of Industry*. Irwin, Homewood, Ill.

Stigler, Stephen M. 1980. Stigler's Law of Eponymy. *Transactions of the New York Academy of Sciences*, Series II (39): 147–57.

Stiglitz, Joseph E. 1997. *Principles of Microeconomics*. W. W. Norton, New York.

Strauss, Leo, editor. 1970. *Xenophon's Socratic Discourse*. Cornell University Press, Ithaca, N.Y.

Sugden, Robert. 2004. The Opportunity Criterion: Consumer Sovereignty without the Assumption of Coherent Preferences. *American Economic Review* 94(4): 1014–33.

Sullivan, Daniel. 1989. Monopsony Power in the Market for Nurses. *Journal of Law & Economics* 32(2): S135–78.

Thaler, Richard H. 1980. Toward a Positive Theory of Consumer Choice. *Journal of Economic Behavior and Organization* 1: 39–60. Reprinted in Kahneman and Tversky (2000), pp. 269–87.

———. 1999. Mental Accounting Matters. *Journal of Behavioral Decision Making* 12(3): 183–206. Reprinted in Kahneman and Tversky (2000), pp. 241–87.

Theocharis, Reghinos D. 1983. *Early Developments in Mathematical Economics*. Porcupine Press, Philadelphia.

Thünen, Johann Heinrich von. 1960 (1850). Der isolierte Staat in Beziehung auf Landwirtschaft und Nationalökonomies, Zweiter Teil. In Dempsey (1960).

Trigeorgis, Lenos. 1995. *Real Options: Managerial Flexibility and Strategy in Resource Allocation*. MIT Press, Cambridge, Mass.

Tversky, Amos, and Craig R. Fox. 1995. Weighing Risk and Uncertainty. *Psychological Review* 102(2): 269–83. Reprinted in Kahneman and Tversky (2000), pp. 93–142.

Tversky, Amos, and Daniel Kahneman. 1980. Causal Schemas in Judgments Under Uncertainty. In Fishbein (1980), chap. 2, pp. 49–72.

Tversky, Amos, and Daniel Kahneman. 1981. The Framing of Decisions and the Psychology of Choice. *Science* 211: 453–58.

———. 1991. Loss Aversion in Riskless Choice: A Reference-Dependent Model. *Quarterly Journal of Economics* 106(4): 1039–61.

———. 1992. Advances in Prospect Theory: Cumulative Representation of Uncertainty. *Journal of Risk and Uncertainty* 5: 297–323.

———. 2002. Extensional versus Intuitive Reasoning: The Conjunction Fallacy in Probability Judgment. In Gilovich et al. (2002). First published in 1984.

Tversky, Amos, and Itamar Simonson. 1993. Context-dependent Preferences. *Management Science* 39(10): 1179–1189.

U.S. Department of Education, Office of Policy Planning & Innovation, Office of Postsecondary Education. 2002. *Federal Student Loan Programs Data Book, Fiscal Years 1997–2000*. U.S. Department of Education, Washington, D.C.

Varian, Hal R. 1992. *Microeconomic Analysis*. W. W. Norton, New York, third edition.

Varian, Hal R. 1989. Price Discrimination. In Schmalensee and Willig (1989), pp. 597–654.

Vartia, Yrjö O. 1983. Efficient Methods of Measuring Welfare Change and Compensated Income in Terms of Ordinary Demand Functions. *Econometrica* 51(1): 79–98.

Viscusi, W. Kip, John M. Vernon, and Jr. Joseph E. Harrington. 2000. *Economics and Regulation and Antitrust*. MIT Press, Cambridge, third edition.

von Neumann, John, and Oskar Morgenstern. 1944. *Theory of Games and Economic Behavior*. Wiley, New York.

von Weizsäcker, Carl Christian. 1980. *Barriers to Entry: A Theoretical Treatment*. Springer-Verlag, New York.

Ward, Michael R., and David Dranove. 1995. The Vertical Chain of Research and Development. *Economic Inquiry* 33: 70–87.

Williamson, Oliver E. 1976. Franchise Bidding for Natural Monopolies—In General and with Respect to CATV. *Bell Journal of Economics* 7(1): 73–104.

Willig, Robert D. 1976. Consumer's Surplus Without Apology. *American Economic Review* 66(4): 589–97.

Wilson, Robert B. 1993. *Nonlinear Pricing*. Oxford University Press, New York.

Xenophon. 1970. Oikonomikos. In Strauss (1970). Written circa 370 B.C. Translated by Carnes Lord.

Yule, George Udny. 1899. An Investigation into the Causes of Changes in Pauperism in England. *Journal of the Royal Statistical Society* 62: 249–95.

Zellner, Arnold, and Hang Ryu. 1998. Alternative Functional Forms for Production, Cost and Returns to Scale Functions. *Journal of Applied Econometrics* 13: 101–27.

Index